POWER AND THE PROFESSIONS
IN BRITAIN 1700–1850

Near the Church-yard, grim Death's Purveyors see,
With Emblems fit a close connected three!
One shows a Phial, and the other two
Look their Assent, as if they'd say 'twill die; —

THE
CONSPIRATORS.

The Sexton pleas'd, stands ready to attend,
Points to the Grave, and eyes his greatest Friend;
Th'ill boding Raven seems to croak aloud,
Swallow the Dose, and that bespeaks your Shroud

Printed for Carington Bowles, at his Map & Print Warehouse, N°69 in S'Pauls Church Yard, London . Published as the Act directs

The Conspirators – anonymous print (c. 1760). A parson, lawyer and doctor meet
by moonlight in the churchyard – with sexton and raven in attendance – to
calculate the professional gains to be made from human mortality.
Published by permission of the British Museum, Department of Prints and
Drawings

POWER AND THE PROFESSIONS IN BRITAIN 1700–1850

Penelope J. Corfield

London and New York

First published 1995
by Routledge
11 New Fetter Lane, London EC4P 4EE

Simultaneously published in the USA and Canada
by Routledge
29 West 35th Street, New York, NY 10001

Typeset in Palatino by
Ponting–Green Publishing Services, Chesham, Bucks
Printed and bound in Great Britain by
Biddles Ltd, Guildford and King's Lynn

British Library Cataloguing in Publication Data
A catalogue record for this book is available from
the British Library

Library of Congress Cataloguing in Publication Data
A catalogue record for this book has been requested

ISBN 0–415–09756–8

CONTENTS

FIGURES

TABLES

TABLES

PREFACE

If goodwill alone were enough, it would be relatively easy, though not totally plain sailing, to write books. But the process requires a large amount of undivided time and concentration that is difficult to find, in this age of intensive teaching and burgeoning academic administration. As a result, two periods of study leave, which were devoted to the development of the arguments presented here, have proved invaluable. The Institute for Advanced Study in Princeton provided stimulating company and time for cogitation in the Autumn Semester 1987; and thanks go especially to Inga Clendinnen, Lawrence Duggan, John Elliott, Josep Fradera, Charles McClelland, James Van Horn Melton, Peter Paret, Maurice Slavin and Lawrence Stone for many good discussions. In addition, the British Nuffield Foundation generously awarded a Social Science Fellowship, tenable in London, for the academic year 1989–90. That conferred a true lifeline, without which the whole project would have stalled.

There are other practical and intellectual debts that it is also a pleasure to acknowledge. Colleagues in the History Department at Royal Holloway furnish a supportive and stimulating work environment; and students kindly humour my predilection for debating the definition of historical terms. In addition, many friends have provided references and arguments, including Peter Clark, Joy Dixon, Eric Evans, Tony Henderson, Tim Hitchcock, Geoffrey Holmes, Julian Hoppit, Ludmilla Jordanova, Serena Kelly, Charles Medawar, Simon Renton, John Styles, John Turner, Amanda Vickery and Tim Wales. In addition, Arthur Burns, Margaret Pelling and David Sugarman have criticised individual chapters; and Simon Renton provided advice on eighteenth-century legislative procedures.

Research seminars at Lancaster and Stockholm Universities have also responded to early versions of this material with stimulating discussions. In practical terms, the Leverhulme Trust generously awarded funding to facilitate the computerisation of data relating to the professions and Tim Hitchcock supplied timely technical aid. Similarly, the research fund of Royal Holloway helped to initiate the creation of an 'Attornies' database, with the expert assistance of Matthew Woollard. Throughout, the Royal

Holloway Computer Centre has been a mainstay of support, with thanks especially to Phil Taylor and to Cathy Harbor, and to Claire Steward at the University of London Computer Centre for help with the optical character reader.

In addition, a host of specialist libraries and institutions – many of them generated by the professions in their prime – have kindly answered queries and made resources available. Special mention should be made of John Symons of the Wellcome Institute Library for his knowledgeable advice and friendly interest. And the hard-worked staff at the British Library get my heartfelt thanks for delivering thousands of books and answering queries with good humour and patience.

Illustrations have been made available from the following sources, whose assistance is acknowledged with thanks: the British Library; the British Museum (Department of Prints and Drawings); the Harry Price Library, Senate House, University of London; Princeton University's Firestone Library (Prints Department); the Law Society; and the Wellcome Institute Library (London).

Making a case study of power, this study sets out to analyse the textual, statistical, and visual material that relates to the 'public face' and social prestige of the professions in Britain between 1700 and 1850. As part of that, it also considers the varieties of consumer response, which characteristically ran the gamut from sincere admiration to deep suspicion. George Bernard Shaw was not the first to fear that the friendly mask of the specialist services concealed a large amount of occupational self-interest. His 1906 dictum that the professions 'are all conspiracies against the laity' was a vigorous warning to the public not to be too gullible. That concern had a long history behind it. As a result, the contested power of the professions has attracted much probing research and analysis, which is being produced at an ever increasing rate. The discussion here acknowledges inspiration from the fertility and scope of these continuing debates.

Lastly, three special debts of gratitude call for special record: with thanks to Jack Fisher, the meta-critic who first suggested this topic for enquiry; to Barry Supple and Michael Thompson, who have given staunch backing and encouragement to the project throughout its gestation; and, indubitably, to Tony Belton.

Penelope J. Corfield
London: 1994

1

POWER

Nam et ipsa scientia potestas est – knowledge itself is power.

(Francis Bacon, 1598)

Power is protean and takes many forms. It is forceful, renewable and divisible – although in practice not infinitely so. It is also notoriously difficult to apportion or quantify. There are often many different sources of power within any given community; and outer manifestations do not always coincide with real command. Contests may produce immediate winners and losers. But even then, if success has been brought at too high a price, the long-term impact may differ from the short-term result. Furthermore, in an expanding universe, there is no 'fixed cake' or restricted quota of power. As a result, it cannot be tallied by strict rules of accounting. An increase in power for one person or group does not automatically mean that all others lose by an absolutely equal amount, although that does not prevent established power-brokers from generally fearing such an outcome. Equally, however, authority can decline as well as rise. Some power – above all, monopoly power – is genuinely diminished by the advent of successful rivals.

Indeed, even the definition of such a strong but abstract concept is not simple. The connotations of power in its human application are, however, undeniably robust. Its synonyms indicate authority, control, dominion, puissance, predominance, command, hegemony. It converges with ideas of might and force. At the same time, it is similar but not identical to vaguer notions of influence, which can also confer power. And it overlaps with prestige, which often adorns authority. Yet here the match is not absolute. There have been *éminences grises* with covert supremacy but only little public fame – just as there have been gilded figureheads with social glory but no real executive authority.

At its core, therefore, power in human affairs refers to the capacity of one individual, group, institution or cultural agency to exert dominance over others.[1] It may be wielded through force and/or persuasion. It may be exercised overtly or covertly. And it may be sustained by conscious will

1

or by deep-rooted predispositions within society or by the two in conjunction. Consequently, it gains in force when strong power-brokers work within strong systems of power. But it does not not invariably triumph. Power, which is augmented if it is used skilfully, may also be weakened, if it is not. Above all, it may be challenged by open or covert opposition. One clear signal of power in action is therefore the successful coercion and defeat of an enemy force. At the same time, however, contests for dominance are not always as starkly identified as a pitched battle between two rivals. Contests may be much more diffuse and their outcome not instantly apparent.

All this makes power, and indeed powerlessness, into fascinating topics of enquiry, with a truly global scope. This study has selected a specific focus in order to consider some general issues. It is a case history of the power of the professions in Britain, during the years from approximately 1700 to 1850 when the economy was gradually industrialising and society liberalising. The focus is deliberately upon a history of change, and upon a contentious social group with specialist knowhow. After all, the professions were credited with mysterious powers not upon the basis of any special political, military or economic resources but by virtue of their command of professional knowledge. Yet such an approach does not assume that there were no other forms of authority in eighteenth-century Britain. On the contrary, it is because the professions were challengers not supreme wielders of power that their role attracts attention.

When investigating the sources of terrestrial command, it quickly becomes apparent that there is no single and universally accepted answer. That is indicated by the many definitions of power that have been canvassed over time.[2] It seems more plausible to assume, instead, that power can take many forms, often simultaneously – rather as physicists argue that light can have at the same time the properties of both waves and particles.

The quest for definitions certainly lends itself to striking dicta. Thus, military leaders know the sentiment (though of course the technology has varied) which asserts that 'political power grows out of the barrel of a gun'. These words came from Mao Zedong, but Oliver Cromwell and Hermann Goering, for example, both made very similar observations.[3] By contrast, Edward Bulwer Lytton in 1839 had countered classically on behalf of all opinion-formers with the rival claim that 'the pen is mightier than the sword'.[4] That highlighted the debate between the brutal power of force and the more insidious but often compelling power of ideas.

Others instead note that people have to eat before they can either fight or write. The famous dictum, attributed to Napoleon, held that 'an army marches on its stomach'. His comment was at once jovial and deeply serious. It emphasised the importance of economic resources as the substratum of power. Versions of this were often stated. 'Money masters all things', ran an anonymous English verse in 1696[5] – and money was able to buy not only weapons but also propaganda. 'All property is *power*', noted Archdeacon William Paley in 1785.[6] This drew upon the ideas of political theorists such as James Harrington and John Locke. They stressed the importance of property as the basis of governmental authority. Meanwhile, Karl Marx gave a radical turn to the analysis by identifying the deep-rooted dynamic of changing economic infrastructures as the key to changing political systems.

Yet armed force, ideas and property hardly exhaust the list. Political rulers are positively expected to wield and to represent power; and religious teachers to lead their flocks. In addition, in many walks of life, senior figures often control advancement within their hierarchies of command. Thus Archdeacon Paley again noted that: 'Patronage universally is power'.[7] Assumptions about gender roles also coloured views about authority. Traditional patriarchy defined men as the stronger sex and therefore powerful. Some, however, argued that women had their own attributes. Female beauty has 'strange power', mused John Milton's Samson Agonistes.[8] 'And the hand that rocks the cradle/ Is the hand that rules the world', suggested William Wallace in the later nineteenth century.[9] But others rejected both the stark and the gilded versions of domestic hierarchy. Men's apparent superiority was based upon 'unnatural violence and lawless usurpation', snorted an anonymous lady in 1739, identified only as 'Sophia' or 'Wisdom'.[10] Instead, power should be shared by all rational beings.

Many impersonal forces, beyond the scope of individual will-power, were also cited. Disease and death have been said to triumph over all, including sceptres and crowns; yet faith, memory and love may outlast even death. Others have pointed to the continuing power of tradition, custom, culture, the past, law, ideology, religion. To that list can be added the force of music, art, science, technology. Recently, the role of words and language in mediating or even forming human thought has been much debated. And there are many variants on the power of ideas and access to ideas. 'Soap and education are not as sudden as a massacre, but they are more deadly in the long run', wrote Mark Twain playfully although not entirely flippantly.[11]

Famously, too, in a dictum that has found many later echoes, the scientist and politician Francis Bacon asserted roundly in 1598 that: 'Knowledge itself is power.'[12] He was writing of divine omniscience, but the proposition was eminently capable of secular adaptation. Thus Bacon's one-time secretary, the political philosopher Thomas Hobbes, decided that all people coveted power – since 'riches, knowledge, and honour [reputation] are but several sorts of power.'[13] As that indicates, the linkages could be interpreted in different ways. Knowledge could be viewed as a source

3

of individual and social empowerment. That gave it a liberal and humanist meaning.

Alternatively, knowledge could be construed not so much as an intellectual system in its own right but instead as a form of power, that could moreover be used as a cloak for power-broking purposes. That has been much explored in the twentieth century. For example, the novelists Zamyatin, Huxley and Orwell wrote about the totalitarian possibilities of state-operated 'thought control'.[14] And the political theorist Antonio Gramsci reshaped Marx's stress upon economic infrastructures to propound an alternative theorisation of ruling-class power based upon a pervasive ideological and cultural 'hegemony'.[15]

Such approaches entailed a distinctly unreverential view of knowledge systems. No Whig concept of 'progress' or triumphalist 'march of ideas' here. The most extreme version was propounded in the pugnacious philosophy of Friedrich Nietzsche in the later nineteenth century. For him, all human beliefs did not spring from abstract reasoning or from a spiritually sanctioned sense of good or evil but instead derived from a fundamental human 'will-to-power', elsewhere defined as the will-of-life itself.[16] This formulation has influenced a number of later thinkers. Above all, the French cultural theorist Michel Foucault has extended the analysis. His own much quoted central statement in *Surveiller et punir* (1975) explained that within the power/knowledge equation the former constituted the latter:

> We should admit rather that power produces knowledge (and not simply by encouraging it because it serves power or by applying it because it is useful); that power and knowledge directly imply one another; that there is no power relation without the correlative constitution of a field of knowledge, nor any knowledge that does not presuppose and constitute at the same time power relations.[17]

Foucault's statement was not intended as a manifesto for the rule of the *savant*– or professor–king. On the contrary. His formulation explicitly gave primacy to power relations in the generation of ideas. Thus he stressed that knowledge systems were shaped by external factors rather than by their own internal logic or intellectual progression or fundamental truth. In that assumption, there was some common ground between Foucault and Antonio Gramsci. For both, absolute knowledge was dethroned from its pedestal. 'Philosophy in general does not in fact exist', agreed Gramsci.[18] Choice was always possible, although dissidents had to work hard to combat the ideological hegemony of the ruling elite. By contrast, Foucault was not interested in the concept of class struggle, whether defined in economic or ideological terms. It was the intellectual and institutional construction of sets of ruling ideas rather than the social origins of authority that intrigued him. As a result, his fertile and controversial writings focused upon the ways in which power relations were inscribed in knowledge systems – making strong claims about the nature both of power and of knowledge.

These issues for debate are relevant to the history of Britain's emergent professions in a number of ways. Not only did these 'experts' excercise power by virtue of their specialist knowledge but the extent and nature of their power were changing. Furthermore, they did not exercise supreme authority. They were subject to hostility and satire. And they faced other mighty contenders for power.

One obvious problem relates to the methods of adjudication when discussing general concepts such as these. There is no simple test to identify power in either its systemic or its active agencies. Past declarations about the location of authority are helpful as a starting point. As power – unless otherwise disturbed – runs easily in established grooves, it is very relevant to know where it officially reposed. But contemporary descriptions often concentrated upon the outward and 'reputational' forms of authority. That could obscure not only the manoeuvres behind the scenes but also the cultural frameworks in which power was operated.

Another perspective is afforded by varying the focus to look at 'events' as well as 'reputations'. Such a tactic does not mean that there is an absolute gulf between deeds and words, since not only are deeds often (but not always) recorded in words but in Wittgenstein's pithy phrase 'words are also deeds'.[19] Still less does an examination of 'events' imply that ideas are mere illusions that do not correspond to a gritty 'reality'. Instead, people's views about the location of power were just as authentically part of the past as were people's actions. It simply means that a change of focus can throw additional light upon a multi-faceted problem. Thus a close study of power in action can look behind the formalities. It can identify the lobbyists who pressurised governments, the bankers who funded industry, the arms dealers who primed military machines, the press barons who influenced the news, the secret-service chiefs who ran covert policies. Equally, a study of conflicts can be revealing. The limitations of authority are highlighted when authority is challenged, while a failed attempt at opposition may conversely demonstrate the ultimate resources of power.

'Events', however, also need their context. Long-term patterns of ideas, language use, cultural traditions and economic conditions, for example, need to be analysed over time, rather than simply in moments of time. That applies above all to gradual changes in the distribution of power, which are not necessarily displayed by immediate 'events'. New forces may be quietly accommodated without crisis or overt conflict. Therefore, the historian's retrospective analysis is challenged to weld together a constation of authority in its long-term context as well as in its allocation, its exercise and its response to opposition.

Eighteenth-century observers certainly knew the concept of power. Samuel Johnson's *Dictionary* (1755) was one of many that was ready to define it. He noted thirteen close synonyms, including 'command, authority, dominion, influence' and specifically 'government; [the] right of governing'.[20] Also listed was divine power. That was assumed to pervade the universe. Most people – other than a few overt atheists – located the ultimate source of power in God the Almighty, the Everlasting and Omnipotent. At the same time, fallen men and women lived under many different forms of government. Traditional Christian teaching endorsed the Pauline affirmation that 'There is no power but of God; the powers that be are ordained of God.'[21] Legal authority was to be honoured and Caesar's taxes paid. But the Christian churches accepted variety in the actual forms of secular power.

After the claims of the deity, then, matters were complex. Some have always dreamed that power could be so completely shared between equals that it would in effect come to be abolished. Yet the worldly-wise Edmund Burke thought otherwise. 'A certain *quantum* of power must always exist in the community, in some hands, and under some appellation', he warned the French revolutionaries.[22] In the case of France, the overthrow of the *ancien régime* in 1789 necessitated a radical rethinking, even though the implementation of change proved to be vastly complex and in some cases self-defeating. In Britain, by contrast, there was in the course of the eighteenth century no dazzling single moment of opportunity when everything seemed ripe for revision. Reformers – especially young ones – were exhilarated by the early events of the French Revolution. 'Bliss was it in that dawn to be alive', remembered Wordsworth.[23] However, for many their radical optimism, if not their faith in reform, was clouded within a few years.

In Britain, things moved apparently more slowly. Without a power vacuum, there was no overt power struggle. At the apex of society, the monarchy retained its constitutional status. In Westminster, ministers of the crown ran the king's government. In the counties, the squire presided on the bench. In the corporate towns, the mayor paraded in his chain of office. In the household, the patriarch was the head of the domestic unit, with legal powers to chastise his wife and children (provided that the beating was not so severe that it qualified as an assault).[24] These continuing generalities, however, did not preclude a substantial diversification in the sources of social power.

Pluralism of legal authorities was encouraged also by the constitutional complexity of the accumulating British 'empire'. There were different political systems in England and Scotland even after parliamentary Union in 1707. Ireland also remained a separate fiefdom until formal Union in 1800.[25] And the growing number of overseas colonies were administered under a miscellany of constitutional arrangements. At the same time, the

English rulers were simultaneously electors (and after 1815 kings) of Hanover in Germany between 1714 and 1837.[26] As a result, the monarch did not exercise centralised authority within a unitary empire, despite his elevated titular status. It remained true that, for the most determined traditionalists, kingship was still hedged with divinity. In general, however, the Hanoverians were accepted rather than adored. Though their power was held to be consecrated by God, they themselves were not God-like. 'The English do not consider their King to be so very much above them that they dare not salute him, as in France', suggested a Swiss visitor in 1719.[27]

Kowtowing fulsomely to grandees was considered to be 'foreign' behaviour. An anonymous lawyer recorded complacently in 1735 that, whereas in many places the word *king* conveyed the '*Idea* of an *absolute despotick* national *Bully*', in Britain it had a much milder meaning. It signified 'only a certain Ruler placed over a People to provide for their *Security*, promote their *Interests*, and defend their *Liberties*, and who ceases to be a *King* when he ceases to take care of his *Country*'.[28] This did not smack of enthusiasm. Similarly, in 1765–9 the celebrated jurist, William Blackstone, summed up the conventional wisdom in terms almost as devoid of awe. The British monarchy had a role in the process of legislation but could not act without the constitutional authority of Parliament. Kings generally took the throne by succession, not by election. But the crown was potentially revocable. Indeed, there had been two interregnums in the seventeenth century – for eleven years between 1649 and 1660, and for a few weeks in 1688–9, after the *de facto* abdication of James II. Ultimately, therefore, royal authority depended upon political acceptance rather than upon the unsullied operation of a 'divine right'. Even the cautious Blackstone stigmatised such a doctrine as 'thoroughly slavish and dreadful'.[29]

If power was not absolutely concentrated in the hands of kings, where else was it to be found? Between 1700 and 1850, the number of influential interest groups within society diversified. Overall, it was an era of expansionism. Great Britain (as it was known after 1707) developed impetuously from a second-ranking European state into a major imperial and commercial power by 1815 with an innovating industrial base. The 1800 Act of Union referred proudly to the 'British Empire' as an established entity.[30] Half a century after that, it was the predominant world power and the 'workshop of the world'. It was true that its emergence did not go unchallenged by other countries, above all by France. It was also true that new rivals for supremacy emerged in the course of the nineteenth century. Thus, while Queen Victoria was empowered by Parliament in 1876 to assume the high-flying title of 'Empress of India',[31] the designation did not last for even a century among her descendants. The later precipitous disappearance of the empire in the mid-twentieth century did not detract, however, from the excitements of the long process of expansion.

Changes in Britain's domestic economy matched the process of acquisition overseas. Historians notoriously disagree about the extent and chronology of innovation.[32] Nonetheless, in the long term there was a cumulative process of commercial and naval expansion, accelerating population growth, mushrooming towns, extensive industrial development, a streamlining of agricultural production and the multiplication of a new range of service industries, including the professions. There was also a comparable change in the terminology of social description. In the early eighteenth century, the traditional hierarchic language of 'ranks', 'degrees' and 'orders' was already being juxtaposed with a new vocabulary of 'sorts'. By the 1770s, the yet-more-modern concept of economic 'class' had joined the repertoire. Within a few decades, it began to oust all the older terminology. The compromise 'sorts' quickly disappeared.[33]

'Class' simplified things to some degree, since it contained fewer of the minute distinctions that were inherent in the old hierarchy. Instead, simple antagonisms were often vividly expressed in the midst of social conflicts. On the other hand, in calmer times, 'class' usage was very eclectic and variegated. There was no consensus about the number or identity of the significant groupings. Nor were the class boundaries clearly defined. As a result, the social classes within British society were not homogeneous blocs but drew upon a tessellation of rival interest groups. It was within this pluralist context that the emergent professions jostled for power.

Land, wealth and titles already constituted three overlapping but competing claims to social authority. All three had cachet. Undoubtedly, the ownership of large tracts of freehold land retained immense prestige throughout this period. Britain's *terra firma* was revered for its permanence. Hence the owners of such a coveted asset generally enjoyed a reflected status, especially if they sprang from an ancient family and visited their estates frequently. Absentees, on the other hand, were less glorified, however grand their lineage. That was notoriously the case in Ireland. There the English absentee landowners were often hated by their bitter tenantry. In general, however, large landownership was well esteemed and its allure was often augmented by wealth, since land, if commercially managed with improved farming practices, was generally profitable. In the process, old estate customs were turned into new legal contracts.[34] The change was seen dramatically in the Scottish Highlands. After the final defeat of the Jacobites by the British state in 1745–6, dispossessions and ruthless commercial development followed. 'The admission of money into the Highlands will soon put an end to the feudal modes of life, by making those men landlords who were not chiefs', wrote Dr Johnson in 1777, musing sadly that 'there was in the [old] patriarchal authority something venerable and pleasing.'[35]

Political decisions also upheld the attractions of landownership. It was defined as 'having a stake in the country'. Thus in the local government

SUPPORTING CHURCH AND STATE

Figure 1.1 The old order changes – radical print (1832). The king, church and judiciary rule on high, surrounded by trumpeting cherubs – while below a don and an army general fail to prop up the rotting system – and the radical lawyer Henry Brougham rushes in wielding a new broom.
Robert Seymour, 'Supporting Church and State' (1832). Published by permission of the British Museum, Department of Prints and Drawings

9

of the shires, the all-commanding Justices of the Peace were regularly selected from the ranks of landowning society. And access to the House of Commons – the forum of national politics – was similarly constricted. In 1710, a Tory Parliament had passed a special Property Qualifications Act for England and Wales (but excluding the Scottish and University seats). This law was designed to preserve the 'landed interest'. It required that upon election each county MP had to have an income of at least £600 p.a. – and each borough MP at least £300 p.a. – derived from land that was either freehold or copyhold for life. Only the oldest sons of peers and the sons of county MPs were exempt, since they were heirs apparent to *bona fide* legislators.[36] Moreover, despite its contentious origin, the Act was not repealed by later Whig governments. It remained on the statute book for well over a century, until a general income qualification was substituted in 1838.[37]

Nonetheless, the legislation did not succeed in excluding other 'interests'. Wealthy men with political ambitions undertook a minimum investment in land. Impecunious men sought the assistance of wealthy patrons to do likewise.[38] Yet others acquired a fictitious rental income simply for the election – a practice that continued discreetly despite new curbs introduced in 1760. Thus, in the early nineteenth century, certain bankers and lawyers were said to specialise in providing paper qualifications for eager clients.[39] The poor remained excluded. Determined candidates, however, without land but with sufficient wealth, patronage and/or lack of scruple were not deterred from standing for election. Hence, a modern historian's survey of the 5,034 MPs in the Commons between 1734 and 1832 has found that over 50 per cent of them had a commercial, manufacturing or professional interest, as well as the nominally requisite landed income.[40]

Wealth in particular was fast becoming a rival source of prestige. Its attraction lay not in its permanence, but in its capital mass, its flexibility, its purchasing capacity and, when spent lavishly, its conspicuous glitter. Traditional landowners by inheritance often resented the advent of conspicuous 'new' money in the hands of 'mushroom men'. Those attitudes undoubtedly indicated ambivalence about the status of mere money in some circles. But such resentments were unable to halt the trend that they deplored. Rather, they indicated the extent to which riches were generally admired. 'In this country one is esteemed for one's wealth more than for anything else', wrote the sober Swiss Protestant César de Saussure after his visit to England in 1722, adding: 'It is true that riches are accounted happiness everywhere, but more particularly here.'[41] In 1772, Boswell and Johnson discussed the relative status of ancient family *vis à vis* wealth. Boswell, himself the son of a Scottish laird, ventured the view that 'riches seem to gain most respect', while Dr Johnson, who lived by his pen and state pension, argued that riches got 'external attention' but not the hearty deference that went to ancient family. Later, in 1778, however, Johnson took a somewhat different view, acknowledging that 'gold and silver destroy feudal subordination'.[42]

Of course, the ownership of wealth and land often overlapped. Some of the country's major landowners were very rich. Thus 310 of them in 1760 enjoyed large annual incomes of over £4,000; among these a magnificent ten had incomes of over £20,000.[43] On the other hand, the match between wealth and land was not total.[44] Not all landowners were very rich; and far from all rich people were landowners. For example, a historian has surveyed the fourteen men whose probated wealth made them millionaires at their deaths between 1809 and 1859. Their ranks did include four landowners, headed by the famous 'Leviathan of wealth', otherwise the first Duke of Sutherland.[45] The remaining ten, however, featured five merchant bankers, three manufacturers, one builder (Thomas Cubitt) and one 'Bengal civil servant', though it is unlikely that his wealth had been gleaned from his official salary.[46] These figures are indicative only, as they referred to personal estates – and took no account of goods disposed of before death or fixed property. Nor are the occupational categories mutually exclusive, as many landowners (including the Duke of Sutherland) had investments in mining and transport, just as bankers and industrialists put money into land.

An unmistakeable plurality of interests therefore underpinned Britain's social leadership. They were forming what Robert Southey identified in 1807 as a new intermingled 'aristocracy of wealth'.[47] Another old term that was also being increasingly pressed into use from the 1830s onwards was 'plutocracy', or the rule of the rich.[48]

Titles, meanwhile, offered another overlapping source of social prestige. Noble families held the highest of ranks. Their value was also enhanced by their scarcity. In England and Wales there were no more than 173 peers in 1700; 267 in 1800; and 399 in 1850.[49] Each had special legal immunities and a seat in the House of Lords – excluding the much smaller number of hereditary peeresses, who held titles in their own right but were not summoned to legislate.[50] Moreover, a nobleman was traditionally expected to have sufficient financial (and preferably landed) resources to sustain his rank. New titles were often conferred upon well-qualified candidates. But, if a relatively poor man inherited or was promoted as a reward for service, then government pensions could be provided to uphold the dignity.[51] Thus the new creations, who replenished the traditional titled families, were quickly assimilated.

However, this variegated peerage did not have a monopoly of wealth or status. Of the fourteen millionaires who died between 1809 and 1859, for example, only three were members of the Lords. The remaining eleven included three titled commoners (one was the grandson of a duke known by courtesy as 'Honourable') and eight who were gentlemen known by no more than the appellation of 'Mr'.[52] Successive governments indeed tried to retain the exclusivity of the peerage, in order to preserve its status and also to avoid enlarging the Upper House too much *vis à vis* the fixed size of the Commons. One solution, before the political Union in 1800, was to grant Irish titles which did not then entail a seat in the British House of Lords. For example, Robert Clive 'of India' received this qualified accolade: in 1762 his reward for victory at Plassey (1757) was to become Lord Clive, but as Baron Clive of Plassey in the Irish peerage. Many other Englishmen with just as little connection with Ireland were similarly honoured. The number of Irish peers almost doubled from 88 in 1700 to 169 by 1800.[53] By contrast, however, there was an absolute decline in separate Scottish titles in the half-century after the Anglo-Scottish Union in 1707. As a result, the total British peerage declined slightly from 396 in 1700 to 375 in 1750, before then rising rapidly again to 504 in 1800.[54]

Noble families did not, however, form a separate caste. The brothers, younger sons, and cousins of peers were all commoners in law, unless they held another title in their own right. If elected to Parliament – as they were in some numbers[55] – these individuals sat in the Lower House. The social elite therefore spread beyond those strictly in possession of noble titles and with a seat in the House of Lords. After the peerage the highest ranks were allocated to the knights of the shires and especially the baronets (who were hereditary knights). They were given the prefix of 'Sir' and their wives were styled as 'Ladies'. But all of these remained non-noble. Moreover, the supply of these lesser titles in the eighteenth century was even more constricted. As a result, the total number of knights and baronets in the whole of Great Britain and Ireland fell steeply from 1150 in 1700 to 721 in 1750, before rising significantly again but not overwhelmingly to 859 in 1800.[56]

Since official titles were not commensurate with demand, there was instead a rapid growth in the numbers claiming to be 'gentlemen'. That was also a position of social prestige. The 'gentleman' was deemed to be part of the 'quality', to use the expressive eighteenth-century phrase. He was described as 'Mr'. and his spouse was a lady, although not formally a 'Lady'. In fiction, he was admirably represented by Austen's untitled but much admired Mr Knightley of Donwell Abbey – or later by Trollope's Mr Thorne of Ullathorne. However, the position was completely informal. It was not granted by official decree, but was awarded by a subtle mixture of individual assertion and social acceptance.[57]

Complaints then followed that the net of gentility was becoming spread too widely. 'We are a Nation of Gentry', declaimed a commentator in 1755. 'We have no such thing as Common People among us: between Vanity and Gin the whole Species is utterly destroyed.'[58] That was, of course, journalistic hyperbole, not evidence under oath. It was not remotely true. But it made it evident that the grandees were not viewed as distant, awesome figures, separated from the masses by an unbridgeable gulf.

Instead, the number of gentlemen ran into thousands. They were still a small minority of the total population, but they bridged the gap between the elite and the middle class, just as they bridged the divide between town and country. Indeed, from at least the sixteenth century onwards, there were many non-landed gentleman, including the respectable professions.

Britain's oligarchy was neither static nor homogeneous. Landowner-ship, wealth and titles contested for power and status. As a guide to occupations in 1747 nicely observed, 'in so great a trading Country as *England*' there was 'a Complication of monied, landed, and commercial Interests'.[59] It meant too that there were many ways of joining the oligarchy. That gave hope to the 'pseudo-gentlemen', as the aspirants who did not quite succeed were dubbed scornfully in 1824 by the self-styled 'Chevalier' Lawrence.[60] At the same time, accession to high status was not available to all. It required a combination of inheritance, capital assets, patronage, luck and (in certain circumstances) also ability and application.

Access to specialist knowledge was clearly not the prime requisite for social power. The prestige of land, wealth and titles did not depend upon a stock of technical knowhow. Instead, the plutocracy stressed an ethos of exclusivity of property rights based upon an admixture of inheritance, title and wealth. Its beliefs did not amount, however, to a unified dogma but remained heterogeneous and eclectic. In particular, landed men continued to snipe at new 'monied men'. The Foucaultian equation of power/ knowledge was thus already complicated. And in the same period, it was further challenged by new power-brokers whose stature did depend upon the control of key areas of specialist information. Here entered the gentlemanly – and sometimes not-so-gentlemanly – professions, armed with knowledge.

NOTES

1 Often quoted is Weber on power as 'the possibility of imposing one's will upon the behaviour of other persons': see M. Rheinstein (ed.), *Max Weber on Law in Economy and Society* (Harvard University Press, Cambridge, Mass., 1954), p. 323. But that restricts the concept too much to the intentional and understates the power of impersonal forces. See too discussions in B. Barnes, *The Nature of Power* (Polity Press, Cambridge, 1988), pp. 1–20, 55–67; R. Martin, *The Sociology of Power* (Routledge, London, 1977), pp. 35–49; P. Morriss, *Power: a philosophical analysis* (Manchester University Press, Manchester, 1989), pp. 8–35; and D.H. Wrong, *Power: its forms, bases and uses* (Blackwell, Oxford, 1979), pp. 1–20.

2 E.g. M. Mann, *The Sources of Social Power*, vol. 1: *A history of power from the beginning to A.D. 1760* (Cambridge University Press, Cambridge, 1986), p. 2, summarises four sources of power, viz: ideological, economic, military and political; while A. Giddens, *A Contemporary Critique of Historical Materialism*, vol. 1: *Power, property and the state* (Macmillan, London, 1981), p. 47, offers four categories as: symbolic orders/modes of discourse; political institutions; economic institutions; and law/modes of sanction.

3 Mao Zedong, *Quotations from Chairman Mao Tse-tung* (Foreign Languages Press, Peking, 1966), p. 61. Compare Hermann Goering in 1936 speech cited by W. Frischauer, *Goering* (Odhams, London, 1951), p. 134: 'Would you rather have butter or guns? . . . Preparedness [i.e. guns] makes us powerful. Butter merely makes us fat'; and Oliver Cromwell facing opposition in 1653 cited by C. Hill, *God's Englishman: Oliver Cromwell and the English Revolution* (Weidenfeld, London, 1970), p. 154: 'What if I should disarm the nine and put a sword in the tenth man's hands? Would that not do the business?'

4 E.G.E. Lytton Bulwer (later Bulwer Lytton), *Richelieu: or, the conspiracy* (London, 1839), II, ii.

5 Ballad by Anon., *Pecuniae Obediunt Omnia: or, money masters all things* (York, 1696; London, 1698).

6 W. Paley, *The Principles of Moral and Political Philosophy* (London, 1785), p. 604.

7 Ibid., p. 469.

8 J. Milton, *Samson Agonistes* (London, 1674), l. 1003.

9 W.R. Wallace in John O'London (ed.), *Treasure Trove: being good things lost and found* (London, 1925), pp. 62–3.

10 'Sophia, Or, a Lady or Person of Quality', *Woman Not Inferior to Man: or, a short and modest vindication of the natural right of the FAIR-SEX to a perfect equality of power, dignity, and esteem, with the men* (London, 1739), p. 10.

11 S.L. Clemens, *Mark Twain's Sketches* (London, 1903), p. 219.

12 F. Bacon, 'Of Heresies', *Essays: religious meditations* (London, 1598), p. 27.

13 From T. Hobbes, *Leviathan*, ed. J. Plamenatz (Collins, Glasgow, 1983), p. 104: bk 1, ch. 8.

14 See variously Y. Zamyatin, *We* (New York, 1924), A. Huxley, *Brave New World: a novel* (London, 1932) and G. Orwell [E.A. Blair], *Nineteen Eighty-Four: a novel* (London, 1949).

15 Gramsci's *Prison Notebooks* (written 1929–35; publ. in Italy, 1948–51; in Engl. transl. 1971) had a great influence upon modern cultural studies, especially in the 1970s and 1980s.

16 F. Nietzsche, *Beyond Good and Evil* (1886), in *A Nietzsche Reader*, ed. R.J. Hollingdale (Penguin, Harmondsworth, 1987 edn), pp. 229, 230.

17 M. Foucault, *Discipline and Punish: the birth of the prison*, transl. A. Sheridan (Penguin, Harmondsworth, 1982 edn), p. 27. See also M. Foucault, *Power/ Knowledge: selected interviews and other writings, 1972–77*, ed. C. Gordon (Harvester, Brighton, 1980), p. 133, for Foucault's 1977 reformulation: '"Truth" is linked in a circular relation with systems of power which produce and sustain it, and to effects of power which it induces and which extend it.' See also the contrasting assessments in B. Smart, *Michel Foucault* (Routledge, London, 1985), esp. pp. 42–4, 64–6, 73–80; and J. Baudrillard, *Oublier Foucault* (Galilée, Paris, 1977), pp. 9–88.

18 A. Gramsci, 'The study of philosophy and of historical materialism', in his *The Modern Prince: and other writings* (International Publishers, New York, 1957), p. 61.

19 See L. Wittgenstein, *Philosophical Investigations*, transl. G.E.M. Anscombe (Blackwell, Oxford, 1989), pp. 5, 146.

20 S. Johnson, *A Dictionary of the English Language* (2 vols, London, 1755), vol. 2, *sub*: 'Power'.

21 *The Holy Bible*: St Paul, Epistle to the Romans, 13: 1. Cf. also Christ's injunction in Matthew, 22: 21: 'Render therefore unto Caesar the things which are Caesar's; and unto God the things that are God's.'

22 E. Burke, *Reflections on the Revolution in France* (1790), ed. C.C. O'Brien (Penguin, Harmondsworth, 1979 edn), p. 248.

23 W. Wordsworth, 'The Prelude', in *The Prelude, 1799, 1805, 1850: authoritative texts, context and reception . . .*, ed. J. Wordsworth, M.H. Abrams and S. Gill (Norton, New York, 1977), p. 396.

24 W. Blackstone, *Commentaries on the Laws of England* (Oxford, 1765–9), vol. 1, pp. 342–3. See also M. Hunt, 'Wife-beating, domesticity and women's independence in eighteenth-century London', *Gender and History*, 4 (1992), 10–33; and M.E. Doggett, *Marriage, Wife-beating and the Law in Victorian England: 'sub virga viri'* (Weidenfeld, London, 1992), pp. 6–15, 15–33.

25 See H. Kearney, *The British Isles: a history of four nations* (Cambridge University Press, Cambridge, 1989), pp. 128–30, 143–8.

26 There is scope for more research into the full implications of the Anglo-Hanoverian connection, but for a summary see H. Holborn, *A History of Modern Germany, 1648–1840* (Princeton University Press, Princeton, 1982 edn), pp. 98–9, 103–4, 295–7, 441.

27 Mme van Muyden (ed.), *A Foreign View of England in the Reigns of George I and George II: the letters of Monsieur César de Saussure to his family* (Murray, London, 1902), pp. 40–1.

28 'Crito' of Lincoln's Inn in Stonecastle's *The Universal Spectator: or weekly journal* (London, 1735–6), 4 Jan. 1735.

29 For Blackstone on monarchy, see his *Commentaries*, vol. 1, pp. 185–6, 188, 211. The monarchy did, however, retain many absolute prerogatives (usually wielded by ministers of the crown), which Blackstone listed (vol. 1, pp. 230–70), while reiterating (vol. 1, p. 243) his own opposition to absolute rule.

30 Preamble to the Act of Union between Great Britain and Ireland, 39 & 40 Geo. III, cap. 67 (1800). See also general survey in C.A. Bayley, *Imperial Meridian: the British Empire and the world, 1780–1830* (Longman, London, 1989), esp. Map 1, pp. 276–7.

31 39 & 40 Vict., cap. 10 (1876).

32 This study endorses the stress upon change, as in e.g. essays by J. Mokyr and D.S. Landes, in *The British Industrial Revolution: an economic perspective*, ed. J. Mokyr (Westview Press, Boulder, Colorado, 1993), pp. 1–170; or P. Langford, *A Polite and Commercial People: England, 1727–83* (Clarendon, Oxford, 1989), pp. 62–79, 391–459. But for an alternative emphasis upon traditionalism before 1832, see J.C.D. Clark, *English Society, 1688–1832: ideology, social structure and political practice during the ancien regime* (Cambridge University Press, Cambridge, 1985), esp. pp. 64–93, and for an economist's downward revision of growth rates, see N. Crafts, *British Economic Growth during the Industrial Revolution* (Clarendon, Oxford, 1985), esp. pp. 1–69.

33 See K. Wrightson, 'Estates, degrees and sorts: changing perceptions of society in Tudor and Stuart England', and P.J. Corfield, 'Class by name and number in eighteenth-century Britain', both in *Language, History and Class*, ed. P.J. Corfield (Blackwell, Oxford, 1991), pp. 30–52, and 101–30.

34 G.E. Mingay, *English Landed Society in the Eighteenth Century* (Routledge, London, 1963), pp. 167–77, argues that improved estate management often preceded innovative farming methods as a means of pushing up rentals. A picture of general efficiency is confirmed also by J.V. Beckett, 'Landownership and estate management', in *The Agrarian History of England and Wales*, vol. 6: *1750–1850*, ed. G.E. Mingay (Cambridge University Press, Cambridge, 1989), pp. 590–640.

35 Johnson to Boswell, 22 July 1777, *The Letters of Samuel Johnson*, ed. R.W. Chapman (Clarendon, Oxford, 1952), vol. 2, p. 528. For the onslaught on runrig (shared peasant tenancies), see M. Gray, *The Highland Economy, 1750–1850* (Oliver & Boyd, Edinburgh, 1957), pp. 11–31, 66–86; also T.M. Devine, 'Some

responses to agrarian "improvement": the highland and lowland clearances in Scotland', in *Scottish Society, 1500–1800*, ed. R.A. Houston and I.D. Whyte (Cambridge University Press, Cambridge, 1989), pp. 148–68.

36 9 Anne, cap. 5 (1710/11). In 1696 and 1702/3, similar bills had been passed by the House of Commons but blocked by the Lords.

37 1 & 2 Vict., cap. 48 (1838).

38 E.g. Philip Yorke, later Earl of Hardwicke and (1737–56) Lord Chancellor of England, was given a rent-charge from the estate of a wealthy patron to qualify as MP in 1719: G. Harris, *The Life of Lord Chancellor Hardwicke* (London, 1847), vol. 1, pp. 91–2. Others similarly assisted included Wilkes, Burke, Fox and Sheridan.

39 33 Geo. II, cap. 20 (1760) required MPs to swear their qualification before the House and to list their property. But evasion continued, as reformers noted when the qualification was amended in 1838 and abolished in 1858: see E. and A. Porritt, *The Unreformed House of Commons: parliamentary representation before 1832* (Cambridge University Press, Cambridge, 1903), vol. 1, pp. 170–81.

40 See G.P. Jupp, *Members of Parliament, 1734–1832* (Yale University Press, New Haven, 1955; repr. 1972), pp. 54–73. R. Sedgwick (ed.), *The House of Commons, 1715–54*, vol. 1 (History of Parliament Trust, London, 1970), p. 3, agrees that 'only about one half' of the Commons comprised landowners without other business or professional interests and (pp. 139–53) lists MPs with non-landed affiliations.

41 Mme van Muyden (ed.), *Foreign View of England*, p. 208.

42 R.W. Chapman (ed.), *Boswell: life of Johnson* (Oxford University Press, Oxford, 1976), pp. 464–5, 924.

43 Beckett, 'Landownership', pp. 618–19.

44 Instead there was movement between the two. Numerous businessmen invested in land, not always with success: see e.g. C. Shrimpton, *The Landed Society and the Farming Community of Essex in the Late Eighteenth and Early Nineteenth Centuries* (Arno, New York, 1977), pp. 93–153; while conversely many landowners invested in industry or sent their younger sons into business: see J.V. Beckett, *The Aristocracy in England, 1660–1914* (Blackwell, Oxford, 1986), esp. pp. 287–320; and D. Spring, 'English landowners and nineteenth-century industrialism', in *Land and Industry: the landed estate and the Industrial Revolution*, ed. J.T. Ward and R.G. Wilson (David & Charles, Newton Abbot, 1971), pp. 16–62.

45 George Granville Leveson-Gower (1758–1833) gained vast estates by inheritance and marriage, invested well and was awarded a dukedom: E. Richards, *The Leviathan of Wealth: the Sutherland estate in the Industrial Revolution* (Routledge, London, 1973).

46 W.D. Rubinstein, 'British millionaires, 1809–1949', *Bulletin of the Institute of Historical Research*, 47 (1974), pp. 204, 206–7.

47 R. Southey, *Letters from England*, ed. J. Simmons (Cresset Press, London, 1951), p. 171.

48 *Oxford English Dictionary* (subsequently *O.E.D.*), *sub*: 'plutocracy' and 'plutocrat', records an early use in 1652, but modern examples date from the 1830s.

49 J. Cannon, *Aristocratic Century: the peerage of eighteenth-century England* (Cambridge University Press, Cambridge, 1984), pp. 12–13, 15: figures for 1700 and 1800 exclude (a) royal princes, (b) Jacobite creations and (c) doubtful cases. For 1850, see Beckett, *The Aristocracy*, p. 487.

50 Between 1700 and 1800 there were 49 peeresses in their own right: Cannon, *Aristocratic Century*, p. 11.

51 See Beckett, *The Aristocracy*, pp. 44–6; and M.W. Cahill, 'Peerage creations and

the changing character of the British nobility, 1750–1830', *English Historical Review*, 96 (1981), pp. 273–6.

52 Rubinstein, 'British millionaires', pp. 206–7.

53 For this policy, see J. Brooke's introduction to L. Namier and J. Brooke (eds), *The House of Commons, 1754–90*, vol. 1: *Introductory survey, constituencies, appendices* (History of Parliament Trust, London, 1964), p. 101; and for origins and numbers, see Cannon, *Aristocratic Century*, pp. 16, 30–2. See also Cahill, 'Peerage creations', pp. 261–6.

54 From figures in Cannon, *Aristocratic Century*, pp. 27–8, 32.

55 For the estimate that c.20 per cent of MPs in the late eighteenth-century Commons were either Irish peers or the sons of British peers, see Namier and Brooke (eds), *House of Commons*, vol. 1, p. 99.

56 Cannon, *Aristocratic Century*, p. 32.

57 See P.J. Corfield, 'The rivals: landed and other gentlemen in eighteenth-century England', in *Land and Society in Britain, 1700–1914*, ed. N.B. Harte and R.E. Quinault (Manchester University Press, Manchester, forthcoming 1996).

58 *The World* (1755), quoted in Corfield, 'Class by name and number', p. 109.

59 Anon., *A General Description of all the Trades* (London, 1747), p. xxviii.

60 J. Lawrence, *On the Nobility of the British Gentry: or, the political ranks and dignities of the British Empire compared with those on the continent* (London, 1824), p. 24.

2

MYSTERY

> My father was an eminent Button-maker, in Birmingham, but I had
> a soul above buttons . . . I panted for a liberal profession.[1]

Numerous 'authority figures' were admired not for an inherited property
or an apprenticed trade but for their control of intangible expertise. The
fictional button-maker's son, who trod the London stage in 1795, was
expressing a common response to the 'liberal' or free professions. Their
special knowledge conferred its own power, since it was simultaneously
in great demand and in relatively restricted supply. Indeed, all forceful
individuals with mastery of a coveted expertise could wield a certain
authority on their own terrain. One case may be cited, not from the
professions but from Hanoverian sporting life. The thrills of fox-hunting
at a fast gallop were so successfully orchestrated by Hugo Meynell, Master
of the Quorn between 1753 and 1800, that the sport was jocularly dubbed
the 'Meynellian Science'.[2] In fact, his predominance was attributable partly
to the snob appeal of the Quorn, the fashionable Leicestershire hunt. But
Meynell's influence was additionally based upon his skills as a breeder of
hounds and as a tactician on the field – all aided by his exceptional
longevity in the post of Master.

Professional men also constituted increasingly pervasive figures of
authority, although they hunted over a more variegated terrain and held
a much greater variety of positions. A consultation with an expert offered
access to reservoirs of specialist knowledge. Even more, it held out the
prospect that such information could be applied in promoting the welfare
of others, whether that was defined in spiritual, mental, transactional or
bodily terms. Parsons, lawyers, doctors, were models of these professional
specialists. There was no limit to the potential demand for their custom.
As a result, their sphere of influence fell not only within the household,
but also within the locality, within the national arena, and, as it expanded,
within the empire.

Throughout this period, the professions themselves were not rigidly
defined or uniformly organised. On the contrary, the interest lies precisely

in the gradual clarification of their numbers, authority, knowledge, associations and training. That can be traced in their own evolution towards professionalisation. It was evident, too, in the marked social reactions that such moves generated.

While the professions consolidated their powers, so consumer fears were heightened that these potent authority figures were all leagued together in a conscious conspiracy against the public. In practice, those anxieties were exaggerated. There was no pan-professional body, then or now. On the contrary, there were frequent contests between the professions; and every specific profession had its own internal divisions. However, the public apprehension was simultaneously a tribute to the potential power of specialist knowledge. That was especially so when the professions became involved in issues of great personal moment, such as the arrival of the lawyer, the doctor and the parson at the deathbed scene.

Historically, there was not much semantic distinction between a 'profession' and any other 'occupation'. Both terms were commonly used to describe an individual's main source of employment.[3] Hence a reference to the 'professions and trades' in the eighteenth century could mean simply: all occupations.[4] Of these, one at least was notorious. Female prostitution had not yet received Kipling's famous, if unresearched, accolade (1888) as 'the most ancient profession in the world'; but *The Times* in 1786 explicitly referred to women of the streets as belonging to a 'profession', in the sense of an occupation or way of making a living.[5] At the same time, the term could also be used to refer to spiritual as well as bodily allegiance. A profession signalled a public affirmation, as in a 'profession' or 'confession' of faith. Hence in 1653, for example, one Sarah Barnwell, a Puritan convert, was perturbed by a preacher's reference to 'the sad *condition* of some (even *Professors*) that were in *Hell howling*'.[6] Here she was concerned about the eternal torments faced not by senior academics but by those who professed a mere outward faith in Christianity. The common thread was the concept of a visible adherence or a particular calling.

With time, however, this term also acquired a more precise application, which has – in modern times – become its predominant meaning. It came to refer to the skilled service occupations, that entailed a professional training in specialist knowledge to be applied in the service of others. The other usages did not disappear.[7] But gradually, the 'professions' ceased to be 'all occupations'. They became instead a sector of employment, contrasted not only with the industrial 'crafts' and commercial 'trades', but also with the often casualised unskilled services, which lacked the connotations of specialist knowledge, linked with long training and professional dedication.

Interestingly, the modern specialist meaning was not noted in Bailey's pioneering English dictionary of 1721.[8] That defined a profession as either an occupation or a public declaration. By the mid-eighteenth century, however, a new emphasis was gradually incorporated. Dr Johnson's 1755 *Dictionary* included a quotation about the 'learned professions' as an example of the occupational definition. By 1773, the fourth edition of his tome added: 'The term *profession* is particularly used of divinity, physick and law.'[9] Later authorities then began to follow suit. The 'professions' were acknowledged as a special sort of occupation; and to have a serious 'profession' began to mean much more than simply to have an occupation.[10] Instead, it became viewed as a vocation.

Knowledge was one of the prime attributes for this dedicated way of life. Great intelligence was not obligatory, and excessive 'cleverness' could become suspect. Nonetheless, some mental ability was required, since each profession was built around access to a specialist corpus of professional knowledge. Learned tomes stocked the cumulative wisdom of the experts. Thus a ballad of c. 1785, entitled *The Three Professions in Tribulation*,[11] envisaged a physician, a lawyer and a divine preparing for a festive trip by casting aside their canonical books:

> Over joy'd with the journey, they said to themselves
> Let Coke, Shaw, and Sherlock, now sleep on the Shelves:
> Farewell to Concordance, dull Statutes, and Mead;
> While we feast abroad, let the pale student read . . .
> Derry down, etc.

Perhaps the unknown balladeer had struggled with some of these weighty works. Certainly, the references were precise. Thus the fictional lawyer left behind Sir Edward Coke's *Institutes of the Laws of England* (1628–44) and the massive *Statutes of the Realm*. The cleric abandoned Dr Sherlock's *Practical Discourse concerning Death* (1689), which ran into 37 editions by 1776 with translations also in French (1696) and Welsh (1691), plus Downame's *Brief Concordance . . . to the Bible* (1726). And the physician deserted Peter Shaw's *New Practice of Physic* (1726) and Richard Mead's handbooks on poisons and infections. These works of scholarly learning buttressed professional authority, while at the same time they impressed the wider public.

Exclusive access to knowledge was indeed a potential source of power. It turned the professions into a 'mystery' not only in the medieval sense of a cohesive occupational group but also in the alternative sense of sharing a secret, known to the few. Special knowledge does not, of course, invariably command respect. If the subject is considered trivial, the command of relevant information is culturally unimportant. But that was not the case for the professions. Their knowledge and its application were in great demand. As a result, their 'mysteries' were powerful. And their own shared access to esoteric knowledge also cemented group solidarity among those in the know.[12]

'Mystery' was further sustained by an appropriate demeanour and clothing. The professions were expected to match public expectations of their role. For instance, a parson had to look and live the part. That point was stressed in 1779 by the Revd Vicesimus Knox. He wrote from experience since he was not only the son of the clergyman headmaster of Tonbridge School but subsequently succeeded his father in the same post. 'In vain will [a parson] preach, in vain will he set a good example, if his appearance and mode of living contradict the received opinions of congruity, and produce contempt', Knox confided.[13] Each profession established by custom its own identifiable garb. That elevated their style above the vagaries of passing fashions and individual whim, while it reinforced a collective image of continuity and trustworthiness.

Technical terminology enhanced the 'mystery' too. All the professions were and remain formidable progenitors of arcane language, often spilling over into incomprehensible jargon.[14] This developed partly from the requirements of their subject specialisms and partly to retain exclusivity. Many lay people were impressed. But jargon could prompt resentment as well. Hence in 1722 Steele's fictional merchant beldame voiced the complaint:

> 'Tis a wonderful thing, Sir, that Men of Professions do not study to talk the Substance of what they have to say, in the Language of the rest of the World.

To which in reply came a cynical argument for shrouding learning in mystery: 'The Vulgar [i.e: the masses] would have no respect for Truth or Knowledge, if they were exposed to naked View.'[15] In practice, the professions did not conspire quite so brazenly to conceal simple information, since a lot of their knowledge was based upon technical detail. Their command of specialist jargon did, however, enable and even encourage them to keep their information to themselves, despite the complaints of critics. In this way, the prestige of the professions was enhanced by an august self-presentation and by use of specialist terms. The desired image was one of calm wisdom and mastery of tongues, even if bungling individuals in practice sometimes dented the illusion.

Consumer reactions were crucially relevant. After all, the professions did not command their own battalions to enforce obedience. Instead, they relied upon public belief. Organised and applied knowledge was inoperative unless there were sufficient numbers of interested and receptive 'clients' (whether institutional or individual) to make use of professional expertise. Moreover, supply and effective demand were closely interlinked. One encouraged the other and *vice versa*. The authoritative image of the professions helped to encourage demand, while public custom and adherence could sustain professional authority or conversely public scepticism and rejection could undermine it. Knowledge was powerful,

Figure 2.1 The Triple Plea (c.1760). The power of black-garbed professional men, with their learned tomes, was a source of concern. Here they are majestic and stately – but they are compared (in the pictures behind them) with harpies and with wolves in sheep's clothing. The open text declares: 'Behold these three, too oft by Fate design'd/ To poison, plunder and delude Mankind.' Published by permission of the British Museum, Department of Prints and Drawings

when it was esteemed, but that did not follow automatically in all circumstances.

The long-term growth of the professions therefore depended upon favourable cultural dynamics as well as upon economic opportunity. Their history around the world has not followed an inevitable progression. Modern debates stress that these complex occupations are also complex to define.[16] The very concept of the professions has different nuances of meaning in different linguistic traditions.[17] Thus it was not surprising that the development of the knowledge-based service industries has occurred in diverse ways over time and place. After all, the professions have a long history. They cannot be interpreted as mere epiphenomena of modern economic growth or of a classic 'Industrial Revolution', which has anyway proved to be an oversimplified model of industrial change.[18] Case histories of the professions around the world have indicated that they exist and have existed in economies at very different levels of development.[19]

Nonetheless, the process of professionalisation was not simply random either. These occupations constitute the elite employments of the tertiary (service) sector. That describes all work not subsumed under primary (agriculture and mining) or secondary (manufacturing) production. Consequently, the emergence and growth of the professions can be viewed as part of the extension of tertiary activities.[20] Those in turn were crucially correlated with the expansion of commerce and distribution, which also occupied a sizeable part of the service sector, and with the growth of towns, which harboured the non-agricultural workforce. It meant that urbanised and trading societies characteristically tended to have large tertiary sectors, including among them the professions. In highly developed modern economies, services may easily employ more than a third of the workforce.[21] At the same time, the state of demand as well as the supply of labour was crucial. The professions did not just depend upon an available pool of skilled service workers. They required an effective demand for their particular forms of expertise.

Here came further complications. When the professions were funded chiefly by consumers paying for their services, then their presence or otherwise was related to consumer wants and rationed by consumer purchasing power. That meant that cultural priorities and expectations came into play. The lay public was not, however, the only employer and patron of the skilled services. The state (in the guise of both central and local governments) and civic institutions – such as the churches – have also played an important role. Hence there were other factors and requirements involved. It all meant that the size and role of the professions were not simply by-products of a given level of economic growth. Instead, their existence and numbers were simultaneously influenced by historically variable patterns of demand, which in turn entailed both economic and non-economic considerations.

23

One clear implication for the professions was the need for some form of regulation. In that way, standards could be imposed and consumer confidence maintained. Consequently, a major turning point in the long history of the professions proved to be the advent of systematic professional regulation and organisation. That began gradually in eighteenth-century Britain, and is now an expected component of modern professionalism. Yet, historically, regulation came in many guises. In the British-American tradition, it was the new professional associations that themselves pioneered self-regulation. However, that was not the only way in which performances were monitored. Institutions that made professional appointments – such as the churches – expected certain standards from their appointees, even if supervision was not always efficient. And, above all, in many countries of continental Europe, it was the government that took the initiative. In eighteenth-century Prussia, for example, the nascent professions were tested and licensed by the Hohenzollern state.[22] It meant that minimum standards could then be expected across the whole community. Moreover, the state itself gave backing to professional claims to authority.

All this indicates clearly enough that the growth of the professions did not take a uniform path through history. There was an intricate interplay between supply and demand, both being affected by more than purely economic factors. Thus the emergence of these skilled service-sector occupations cannot be explained solely in terms of the ambitions of the professions themselves – whether those be interpreted in terms of a hunger for power, for money or for social status. Despite that, Sarfatti Larson has suggested, in the light of her study of the post-1800 growth of professional organisations in Britain and the USA, that there was an undeclared but unstoppable professionalisation 'project'. The process constituted 'an attempt to translate one order of scarce resources – special knowledge and skills – into another – social and economic rewards'.[23] Her critique of professional motivation certainly chimes with a long, long tradition of scepticism about professional behaviour. A humorist in 1624, for example, teasingly described the modern physician as one whose most successful cure was the transformation of his own purse from lean sickliness into lusty wellbeing.[24] The professions, however, had a more complex motivation than such criticisms implied. And furthermore, they were unable to exercise their skills and knowledge without a social and cultural climate of acceptance.

In eighteenth-century Britain, the professions grew in numbers and, more importantly, in organisation and prestige. As that happened, the existing power structure began to respond to the emergence of new authority figures whose power and prestige were derived not from birth or title – nor from their money (which was often precarious) – but primarily from their occupation. It marked the onset of a major cultural shift of long-term importance. Moreover, it was a change that was not centrally planned or directed by the state, although successive governments did from time to time intervene to influence the process of change. Of course, professional occupations were not invented in this period.[25] And they have subsequently become much more numerous and their ethos more and more important.[26] But already, by the early eighteenth century, a professional occupation was a mark of status. Thus in 1711 the writer Joseph Addison (himself from a clerical family) warned sagely of the dangers of over-supply. Ambitious parents, who impelled their children into the 'learned' professions with more zeal than prudence, risked glutting the markets and leaving the novices without an adequate income.[27]

Many satirical references to 'swarms' of lawyers and 'plagues' of doctors added to that impression. In practice, the real numbers were certainly more modest than such sweeping claims implied. No official figures, however, were ever collected to show the size of the professions or any other occupational groups, before the mid-nineteenth-century censuses. The estimates that have survived were all unofficial and imperfect. Nonetheless, an examination of the available figures provide some indications of the scale and pattern of change.

Such an exercise, of course, highlights the problems involved in defining which occupations counted as professions. At one point, sociologists spent much time on that pursuit. They drew up lists of the attributes that distinguished the real professions[28] from the emergent or semi-professions, sometimes also ungraciously described as the pseudo-professions.[29] But that approach ran into problems, when applied too rigidly. Definitions were often unconsciously modelled upon one national tradition or upon one occupation to the exclusion of too many others. The role of the military profession, in particular, is left too much in analytical limbo, if the characteristics are centred too closely upon the 'learned' professions in the marketplace. Armies around the world have never been renowned for their interest in book learning. Yet it still makes historical sense to speak of a process of professionalisation within the armed forces – as *ad hoc* levies and feudal armies, with officers appointed by virtue of social or familial status, have been replaced over time by regular standing armies, with trained officer cadres, appointed, in theory at least, on merit.

Taking a broad definition, therefore, the professions may be taken as all skilled tertiary-sector occupations that are organised around a formal corpus of specialist knowledge with both a theoretical and a practical bearing, and very often a significant admixture of the two – as in the case of surgery, for example. In addition, there is often a distinctive ethos. That focuses upon 'service' (rather than production or distribution), indicating not that professionals are individually more altruistic or sweet-natured than others but simply that their occupations are centred upon the provision of expertise. Other correlates include: a high social prestige; a formalised process of training and qualification; and some degree of regulation or control of entry into the business – at its greatest extent leading to outright monopoly. The more successful any given profession, the more likely it was and is to enjoy those last attributes.

Eighteenth-century Britain saw the professionals striving for improved self-definition and organisation. There was, however, for most of this period no clear boundary to their terrain. Respectable practitioners competed with 'irregular' rivals, who were denounced as 'quacks'. But that accusation was made so freely that it became a matter of subjective judgement rather than systematic definition.[30] As a result, a professional was anyone who had public acceptance as such. Another problem that complicated the statistical tally was existence of part-timers. For example, Norwich's commercial Directory of 1783 listed Peter Finch Esquire simultaneously as an attorney and a beer-brewer, while it named John Hardy as an attorney and wine- and brandy-merchant, both men evidently ready to fortify legal wisdom with alcohol.[31] Another case was that of George Winter, who not only farmed near Bristol and published a manual on husbandry but also practised as a physician at specified hours on three days a week. He treated the local poor *gratis* and attracted so many patients that his residence 'frequently appeared more like a hospital than a private dwelling-house', as he reported cheerfully.[32] Examples of occupational pluralism such as these were not uncommon. On the other hand, the trend towards specialisation became increasingly marked as the work of the professions expanded.

Leading their ranks throughout this period were the powerful trinity of lawyers, clergymen and doctors. They were known as the 'learned professions' or in Addison's phrase (1711) as the 'three great professions'.[33] In the seventeenth century, the most rapidly growing of these were the lawyers. They flourished with the expansion of litigation and with the rising prestige of the common law, especially once the prerogative courts of the Stuarts had been abolished. The attorney ranked lower than the august barrister, yet even the occupation of an attorney 'is an Employment worthy of a Scholar and a Gentleman, their Time being wholly taken up in officiating in that learned and laudable Profession', as a handbook explained in 1747.[34] All in all there were perhaps 10,000 adult householders in England and Wales who were 'Persons in the Law', estimated the statistician Gregory King. He matched that with a similar total of 10,000 clerics (2,000 eminent, 8,000 lesser), including both Anglicans and Nonconformists. Another 16,000 household heads were 'Persons in the Sciences and Liberal Arts'. Assuming that the doctors numbered perhaps half of those or 8,000 persons, the respectable core of the three learned professions then numbered at a minimum some 28,000 heads of household.[35] And these, of course, were no more than cautious estimates.

On the other hand, the figures were compiled by a knowledgeable observer, who was aware of the uncertainties of social statistics. Gregory King, who was born in 1648, had a checkered early career as an engraver and map-maker. But from 1677 onwards he was appointed to a series of Heraldic posts at the College of Arms, for which body he went on regional tours of inspection (until 1689 when the monarchy ceased to issue the appropriate writs). Hence, when devising his tables of social statistics in the mid-1690s, King drew upon his own field experience as well as his access to official tax statistics, such as they were. As a result, his estimates were much more accurate than some of the wild but vague claims about 'swarms' or 'plagues' of professional people. Indeed, if anything, it is probable that King erred on the side of caution, in tune both with his own temperament and with his desire to refute inflated claims about Britain's population and resources.[36]

Even as a minimum, however, an estimate of perhaps 28,000 men in the 'learned professions' in 1700 was quite a large figure. It greatly exceeded King's total of 16,500 landowners (lords, baronets, knights, esquires and landed gentlemen) and his 10,000 overseas merchants and traders. Nor did the lawyers, clerics and doctors exhaust the ranks of the skilled services. The state bureaucracy, although very small by later standards, itself employed a number of career civil servants, Samuel Pepys being a famous exemplar. King listed another 10,000 household heads in greater/lesser offices and places, here including courtiers as well as officials. In addition, there were the other 8,000 individuals who comprised the non-medical 'Persons in Sciences and Liberal Arts'. Among these were the teachers who were struggling to attain professional status, often in the face of public derision. In 1723 Bernard de Mandeville, for example, sniped at the 'petty Tyrants' of the schoolroom as 'Wretches of both Sexes', who were motivated by 'a natural antipathy to Working, . . . [who] perceiving within a much stronger Inclination to Command than ever they felt to Obey, . . . wish from their Hearts to be Masters and Mistresses of Charity-Schools'.[37]

Side-stepping these problems of status, King merely listed 46,000 adult male heads of household in occupations that may be defined as the civilian professions. To those were added another 5,000 naval officers and 4,000 military men. Their status was rising in the course of the eighteenth century, backed by the power of the post-1689 state.[38] A life in the armed services offered 'a fine asylum for those spirits, which are too restless for domestic life', suggested Vicesimus Knox demurely.[39] And these swash-bucklers certainly had their own specialist jargon. Thus in 1704 a satirist teasingly itemised the patter that would enable a young blood to impress the ladies as a bold fighting man:

Speak of strange Towns and Castles, whose barbarous Names, the harsher they're to the Ear, the rarer and more taking. – Still running over Lines, Trenches, Outworks, Counterscarps, and Forts, Citadels, Mines, Countermines, Pickeering [scouting], Pioneers, Centinels, Patroles, and others, without Sense or Order, that matters not.[40]

As that suggests, the satirists enjoyed laughing at professional pretensions. And indeed King confirmed that these occupations were a sizeable social target, since he estimated in the 1690s that at least 55,000 household heads were engaged in professional employments of one sort or another. In an approximate calculation, they equalled 2.1 per cent of the male population of 2.6 million (assuming those to constitute one half of the 5.2 million people then living in England and Wales).[41] At the same time, the professions were very similar in numbers to King's estimate of 40–50,000 shop-keepers and tradesmen,[42] and lagged only slightly behind his total of 60,000 artisans and craftsmen.

From this vantage point at the start of the eighteenth century, the professions then experienced three salient developments. In the first place, there was a long-term growth in their numbers. Secondly, there was a multiplication of service specialisms, as established professions were joined by new ones. For example, the work of the estate steward was often undertaken by attorneys who understood tenurial customs and leases. But, gradually, the post became a separate occupation in its own right – with the hearty encouragement of the agricultural writers who bewailed the typical lawyers' lack of skill in husbandry.[43] Other new specialisms were those of accountants,[44] surveyors and architects, scientists and engineers, opticians, and dentists – not to mention many on the fringes of professional status, such as actors, artists, writers, poets, journalists, and the 'whole Tribe of Singers and Scrapers' who made a hazardous living as musicians in 'this Musical Age', as another occupational handbook observed rather wryly in 1747.[45]

Yet the professions did not thrive upon unqualified expansion. That risked letting supply greatly outrun demand. Hence the third key development in this period was the growing realisation within the professions that some mechanism was desirable to regulate their own numbers, qualifications and performance. It was difficult to achieve; and the outcome was not the same in all cases. However, the professions increasingly recognised that the maintenance of 'mystery' entailed not only a masterful presence but some element of exclusivity as well.

Subsequent updates of Gregory King's figures suggested a gradual process of change. In his *Dictionary of Trade and Commerce* (1751–5), the economic writer Malachy Postlethwayt published fresh estimates, supplied by an anonymous 'gentleman of honour'.[46] This unknown social scientist left unchanged King's occupational groupings but modified the totals to show a modest aggregate expansion from at least 55,000 professions in 1688 to 67,300 in 1750, at a time when the total population was

Table 2.1 Estimated numbers of male heads of household with professional occupations in England and Wales, 1688, 1750 and 1803

	King 1688	Postlethwayt 1750	Colquhoun 1803
Persons in the law	10,000	15,000	11,000
Clergymen (greater)	2,000	2,000	1,000
Clergymen (lesser)	8,000	8,000	10,000
Dissenting ministers	—	—	2,500
Persons in sciences and liberal arts (medical, literary & fine arts)	16,000	18,000	16,300
Teachers (univs & chief schools)	—	—	500
Others in education	—	—	20,000
Theatre/music	—	—	500
Persons in office (greater)	5,000	5,500	2,000
Persons in office (lesser)	5,000	8,500	10,500
Naval officers	5,000	4,800	3,000
Army officers	4,000	5,500	5,000
Half-pay officers	—	—	2,000
Total	55,000	67,300	84,300

Sources: 1688 in Barnett (ed.), *Two Tracts by Gregory King*, p. 31
1750 in Postlethwayt, *Universal Dictionary*, data from vol. 2 (1755), p. 438, *sub* 'People'
1803 in Colquhoun, *Treatise on Indigence*, p. 23

growing only very slowly. The only group to be reduced in numbers were the naval officers (down by 200) while the others were either left unchanged (10,000 clerics) or increased slightly (16,000 persons in the sciences and liberal arts became 18,000). The most significant expansion was in the ranks of the legal profession. King had guessed the 'Persons in the Law' to number 10,000 in 1688, while Postlethwayt's informant raised the total of 'Law and Dependants' to 15,000. But since these figures were undocumented, they are best regarded as a loose guess rather than as indicating a veritable 50 per cent expansion in the early eighteenth century.

Fifty years later, another onlooker tried again. Patrick Colquhoun was probably unaware of the Postlethwayt variant. But he undoubtedly knew King's figures. These were reprinted in 1806 as the framework for Colquhoun's own revised estimates for England and Wales in 1803.[47] His aim in so doing was to assert the capacity of the well-to-do to help the poor. He did not conduct a fresh occupational survey and his figures were no more than the guesswork of an energetic businessman and social reformer.[48] Colquhoun began with Gregory King's categorisation of male heads of household, giving the totals in each category a modest boost. The 10,000 lawyers in 1688 were inflated to 11,000 in 1803 (much lower than the 15,000 proposed for 1750 in Postlethwayt). Similarly, King's 16,000 persons in the sciences and liberal arts were pushed up to 16,300 by Colquhoun. But he embroidered the picture rather more extensively than did Postlethwayt in 1750. For example, Colquhoun distinguished the totals for the Church of England from those of the Dissenting ministry. He added in a separate category for the small theatrical profession, and did the same for the army and navy officers on half-pay (i.e. those not in active service). Most notably, he discovered the teachers, the 'petty tyrants' against whom Mandeville had railed. King had concealed these amongst his 'persons in sciences and liberal arts'. Colquhoun instead specified 500 teachers in the universities and chief schools and 20,000 others 'engaged in the education of youth of both sexes'.

Aided by this pedagogic expansion, the number of professional heads of household had expanded to 84,300 in 1803, growing modestly but not rampantly since 1688 (see Table 2.1). Social power, of course, was not based simply upon numbers. But social frequency was. In that context, it is worth noting that the professions were much more numerous than the country's landowners, since Colquhoun listed no more than 287 temporal peers and peeresses plus 26,890 other landowning families. And there were also more skilled service specialists than the 74,500 shopkeepers and tradesmen. It is true that none of these groups in turn matched the greatly expanded estimates of 'artisans'. But in that case Colquhoun had significantly widened King's category to include wage-earners as well as employers.[49] The upshot was that the professions had become yet more socially visible without their numbers having mushroomed out of control.

Scotland and Ireland, by contrast, did not spawn their own Gregory Kings to list their own social structures. The case for diversification of their professional populations therefore rests upon circumstantial evidence. In both countries, the clergy remained culturally powerful. But other groups were also influential. Lawyers were everywhere active, encouraged by the multifarious business generated by political links with England. In Edinburgh by 1773/4 the branches of the legal profession (including advocates, clerks and writers) kept at least 653 men busy, their ranks headed by the brilliant orator Henry Erskine, who twice became Scotland's Lord Advocate and whose brother Thomas Erskine simultaneously bedazzled the English bar.[50] Ireland's capital city was another notable haven for lawyers. Fully 1,384 attorneys and others in the legal profession were listed in a Dublin Directory for 1784. Within a few years, they were joined by the young Daniel O'Connell, called to the Irish bar in 1798, who made his name as a devastating, passionate and witty cross-examiner, dubbed with reverence 'the Counsellor' long before he turned to active politics and was renamed 'the Liberator'.[51]

Ireland meanwhile saw the controversial emergence of the land steward. This occupation embraced not only devoted but incompetent old family retainers, like Maria Edgeworth's fictional Thady Quirk of *Castle Rackrent*, but also men with a sharp eye for ruthless commercial management, like Quirk's unscrupulous son.[52] By 1851 there were as many as 5,971 land stewards and land agents in Ireland. They were almost as numerous as the clergy, who numbered just over 6,000. But it was not just the social visibility of the stewards that made them notorious. It was the fact that many of them wielded unsupervised power, on behalf of absentee English landowners, that was so disliked by the tenantry.

Conversely, in Scotland the dramatic new professional arrivals were the doctors. Edinburgh in particular acquired European-wide fame as a mecca of medical teaching with the launching of its medical school in 1726. It soon vied with Leiden and later with London and Paris for predominance. Many students in fact moved on to practice elsewhere, thus diffusing Scotland's medical influence. But a proportion also remained to join the buoyant literary and professional circles of Edinburgh and Glasgow that led the Scottish Enlightenment.[53]

By 1851, therefore, all three kingdoms had generated a skilled service sector. And the qualitative impact of the professions was even more apparent than their numbers implied. That was noted explicitly in the census report of 1851. It commented that 'their importance cannot be over-rated; yet in point of mere numbers they would be outvoted by the tailors of the kingdom.'[54] Moreover, the figures themselves were far from perfect, since they undercounted part-timers and 'irregulars'. Yet the census returns can be used to indicate the range of professionals within the mid-nineteenth-century economy.[55] Table 2.2 looks at the full picture, including junior-ranking employees as well as senior: law clerks as well as lawyers, minor parish officials as well as clerics (but the low-paid rank-and-file soldiery are excluded as they were not regarded as a skilled profession).[56] Incidentally, it should be noted that this survey recorded occupations rather than employment (as did all censuses before 1931), since much labour was still casual and domestic, which meant that there was no rigid demarcation between being in work and being unemployed.[57]

Everywhere the senior professions of law, religion and medicine were dominant. They thus accounted for a significant section of all men engaged in professional occupations: 42.2 per cent in England and Wales, 42.3 per cent in Scotland and 34.4 per cent in Ireland. Also numerically important, although socially less established, were the schoolteachers. They constituted another 12.4 per cent of the male professionals in England and Wales, 18.9 per cent in Scotland and the sizeable phalanx of 22.1 per cent in Ireland.

Further details are also instructive. Ireland in 1851, for example, had no accountants (or at least none publicly identified as such). But it contained over 2,000 musicians, considerably surpassing the mere 450 male music-makers in Scotland and approaching 40 per cent of the 5,275 musicians in the much more populous England and Wales. Scotland, meanwhile, had a larger absolute number in the medical profession than did Ireland,

Table 2.2 Men with professional occupations in Great Britain and Ireland, 1851

	England/Wales*	Scotland	Ireland
Lawyers	15,980	2,442	3,351
Law clerks/law officers	16,414	2,745	2,209
Clergymen	26,235	3,812	6,241
Parish clerks/ch. officers	4,178	395	757
Medicine			
Physicians	1,817	511	1,223
Surgeons/apothecaries	13,586	1,576	1,864
Druggists/chemists	14,131	1,194	332
Others in medicine	3,970	923	230
Total (medicine)	33,504	4,204	3,649
Veterinary surgeons/farriers	6,135	395	193
Farm bailiffs/land agents	10,581	2,219	5,971
Central government officials	35,084	3,823	5,433
Local govt. officials (excl. police)	9,903	1,745	3,699
East India service	3,410	364	—
Accountants	5,711	852	—
Army officers (incl. half-pay)	5,573	678	—
Navy officers (incl. half-pay)	4,335	222	—
Civil engineers	2,589	420	2,251
Surveyors	2,778	113	—
Architects	2,698	273	257
Scientists	421	45	—
Artists (fine arts)	5,183	446	353
Authors & others in literature	2,584	282	211
Actors & others in theatre	1,333	172	115
Musicians	5,275	460	2,006
Teachers (all categories)	28,304	6,074	10,428
Total	228,208	32,181	47,124
All men with stated occs	5,787,364	864,312	1,903,438
Professional men as % of all men with stated occs	3.9%	3.7%	2.5%
Total men all age groups	8,848,079	1,375,479	3,190,630
Professional men as % of men all age groups	2.6%	2.3%	1.5%

Source: 1851 census in *British Parliamentary Papers* (1852/3), vol. 88/1 (Gt. Britain); and (1856), vol. 31 (Ireland)
Note: * Includes Channel Islands and I. of Man

although the Famine-depleted Irish population at 6.6 million was still well over twice as numerous as Scotland's 2.9 million. England and Wales, by contrast, had a disproportionate predominance over both the other kingdoms in the case of government officials – as well as in the armed services and in the fields of fine arts and literature.

Of course, these professionals still represented only a small proportion of the total workforce. The 1851 returns thus suggest that at least 3.9 per cent of the males with occupations in England and Wales were located in the professional sector of the economy; with a fractionally smaller proportion of 3.7 per cent in Scotland; and a distinctly smaller proportion of 2.5 per cent in the ravaged agrarian economy of Ireland. The 1851 figures can also be analysed in per capita terms, bearing in mind that the number with occupations was smaller than the total population (which included the very old and the very young). Thus in England and Wales the professional sector accounted for 2.6 per cent of men in all age groups, compared with 2.3 per cent in Scotland and a much smaller 1.5 per cent in Ireland, where chronic poverty and the emigration of young adults after the Famine had left a depleted population with fewer people in employment.

Long-term trends are difficult to establish on the basis of such scrappy and non-matching data. However, tentative comparisons can be made with Gregory King's estimates. His estimates suggested that at least 2.1 per cent of all English- and Welshmen in 1688 were engaged in the professions. After that, the skilled service sector expanded slightly more rapidly than the general population. However, an increase from 2.1 per cent in 1688 to 2.6 per cent in 1851 clearly was not runaway growth. The early size of the professions was thus as significant as their continuing strength. These figures stand comparison with anything before very modern times. For example, Perkin calculates that in 1881 ten leading professions accounted for 2.1 per cent of all men with occupations in England and Wales, rising to 2.6 per cent in 1911 (and that excluded engineers, accountants and surveyors).[58] In other words, the eighteenth-century professions were proportionately as significant in the workforce as were their Victorian successors. (Only in postwar Britain has the professional/managerial sector risen dramatically to constitute over 10 per cent of the workforce).[59]

Throughout all this, women played a conspicuously low-ranking role. They were not totally excluded from the professions but were clustered in the 'nurturing' branches. This state of affairs was accepted without comment by all but a few radicals. Women were allowed to have some areas of expertise (or 'expertness' as it was then termed). They had skills in housekeeping, childcare, charity, piety and sociability. Many also made a living as alehousekeepers, shopkeepers, teachers, nurses or cleaners; and a few as actors and musicians. Yet this variety remained strongly focused

Figure 2.2 Sarah Mapp from Hogarth's 'Company of Undertakers' (1737). Women in the professions also met with criticism. Hogarth brutally caricatured the osteopath, Sarah Mapp – as the middle figure (with a bone) in a sinister trio of quacks. Despite that, Mapp had many fans, one writing a eulogy to her as the 'wonder of the Age!' Detail from: W. Hogarth's print, *The Company of Undertakers* (1736/7; see also Figure 3.5)

Table 2.3 Women with professional occupations in Great Britain and Ireland, 1851

	England/Wales*	Scotland	Ireland
Lawyers	—	—	—
Law clerks/law officers	13	—	—
Clergy	—	—	—
Parish clerks/ch. officers	865	36	240
Religious orders	—	—	1,160
Ministering to charity	—	—	916
Medicine			
Physicians	—	—	—
Surgeons/apothecaries	—	—	—
Druggists/chemists	269	33	4
Others in medicine	—	—	14
Midwives	2,067	815	572
Nurses	23,923	1,543	2,783
Total (medicine)	26,259	2,391	3,373
Veterinary surgeons/farriers	—	—	1
Farm bailiffs	—	—	—
Army/navy officers	—	—	—
Central government officials	1,245	244	57
Local govt. officials (incl. charity)	1,011	115	289
Accountants	—	—	—
Civil engineers	—	—	—
Surveyors/architects	—	—	—
Scientists	24	1	—
Artists (fine arts)	528	20	30
Authors & others in literature	110	5	5
Actors & others in theatre	723	96	77
Musicians	838	61	134
Teachers (all categories)	67,551	4,415	6,979
Total	99,167	7,384	13,261
ALL women with stated occs.	2,931,464	501,397	938,185
Professional women as % of all women with stated occs.	3.4%	1.5%	1.4%
Total women all age groups	9,222,656	1,513,263	3,361,755
Professional women as % of women all age groups	1.1%	0.5%	0.4%

Source: As Table 2.2
Note: * Includes Channel Islands and I. of Man

upon domestic skills, which were not thought to need either great physical strength or much mental prowess.[60] Above all, women were not expected to hold positions of power (except, in a very few cases, by inheritance). Thus females who appeared to gain access to 'mysteries' were often denounced as unwomanly. That happened to the celebrated osteopath Sarah Mapp, despite her heyday of fame in the mid-1730s. And indeed, medicine became a crucial battle ground for female advancement in the professions.[61]

A comparison of the figures in Tables 2.2 and 2.3 highlights the limited role for British women professionals. In 1851, none were lawyers, clerics, physicians or surgeons, although there was one solitary female veterinary surgeon in Ireland. None were army officers. None were engineers or architects. Instead, there were many women midwives and nurses, plus a small number of women druggists and chemists. There were also some females employed in central and local government. And almost 2,000 women across the British Isles sought a full-time living as actors and musicians, risking the notorious fluctuations of fame and fortune that such occupations entailed. Many were recruited from families already in the business. But there were only a handful of stars to match the brilliance of the soprano, Elizabeth Billington, or on stage the impact of a Sarah Siddons – and both these women faced detractors and scandal-mongers.[62]

Above all, teaching was the predominant source of professional occupation for women. Indeed, such was their dominance in this field that there were more than twice as many schoolmistresses and governesses in England and Wales in 1851 as there were schoolmasters and tutors. By contrast, female pedagogues were not so plentiful in Scotland or Ireland. And no country had anything as startling as a women professor. Hence, the female role was limited. Women were concentrated into the lower rungs of the hierarchy and into a narrow range of occupations. Midwifery, nursing and teaching between them accounted for 94.3 per cent of all professional women in England and Wales in 1851; 91.7 per cent in Scotland; and 77.9 per cent in Ireland. It amounted to a toe-hold within the 'mystery'.

However, social power was not based upon sheer numbers. Had that been so, then the agricultural labourers would have been the single most potent occupational group in eighteenth- and early nineteenth-century Britain. Instead, they were very far from that. On the contrary, the relatively small number of men and even smaller number of women professionals derived their power from their scarcity as well as their status. That was based not upon the principle of high birth but upon an ability to command a corpus of knowledge. However, to be effective, specialist knowhow depended upon a delicate balance. It needed sufficient supply to respond to consumer demand but sufficient scarcity to safeguard the exclusivity and incomes of practitioners. Hence followed many competitive tensions.

Despite the endemic uncertainties, however, the professions represented the power of human knowledge in application to the service of
humanity. Thus was created the authority of the 'expert'.[63] That term was
already known as an adjective in the eighteenth century and by the mid-
1820s it also came into use as a noun.[64] Implicitly, the experts began to
challenge other social power-brokers. At the same time, the professions
were not remote idols to adore but ubiquitous practitioners close at hand.
Their expertise was liable to intense consumer scrutiny, in a way that the
traditional authority of an immutable hierarchy was not. Thus professional 'mystery' attracted not only awe but satire.

NOTES

1　G. Colman the Younger, *New Hay at the Old Market: an occasional drama* (London,
　 1795), p. 10; repr. as *Sylvester Daggerwood* (1808).
2　See J. Hawkes, *The Meynellian Science: or, fox-hunting upon system* (c.1808;
　 repr. Leicester, 1932), pp. 41–8; and R. Carr, *English Fox-hunting: a history*
　 (Weidenfeld, London, 1976), pp. 38–40, 68–9.
3　A 'calling, vocation, known employment' was the first of three meanings noted
　 in Johnson, *Dictionary*, vol. 2, *sub*: 'profession', the others being a declaration
　 and a public avowal of opinion.
4　E.g. C. Wheatly, *Bezaleel and Aholiab: or, men's abilities and skill the gifts of God,
　 and their professions and trades the ways of serving Him* (London, 1727).
5　*The Times*, 27 July 1786, jested: 'Sashes are at present confined to the
　 meretricious fair [i.e. prostitutes], and no emblem could be better appropriated
　 to their profession. A sash may be considered the *equinoxial line* of their
　 terrestrial globe, and all within its embrace the *torrid zone*.' This occupation was
　 not, however, the sort that the author of *Bezaleel and Aholiab* [n. 4] had in mind.
6　J. Rogers, *Ohel or Beth-Shemesh: a tabernacle for the sun* (London, 1653), p. 415.
7　For an example that did not refer to occupation, see G. Osborn, *Preparedness
　 for Christ's Appearance Recommended . . .: In a sermon, [on the] . . . death of Mr . . .
　 Parkes . . . with some account of his dying professions . . .* (Birmingham, 1786). For
　 usages that did, see citations in W. Prest, 'Why the history of the professions
　 is not written', in *Law, Economy and Society, 1750–1914: essays in the history of
　 English law*, ed. G.R. Rubin and D. Sugarman (Professional Books, Abingdon,
　 1984), pp. 307–9.
8　N. Bailey, *An Universal Etymological English Dictionary* (London, 1721), *sub*:
　 'profession'.
9　Compare Johnson, *Dictionary* (1st edn, 1755; 4th edn, 1773), vol. 2, *sub*:
　 'Profession'. After 1773, all enlarged editions of this work referred to the
　 learned professions; many short popular versions still did not – e.g. Thomas
　 Nelson's *Comprehensive Johnson's Dictionary* (London, 1847).
10　Thus J.A.H. Murray (ed.), *A New English Dictionary on Historical Principles* (11
　 vols, 1884–1928), later *The Oxford English Dictionary* (1933-) defines its specialist
　 usage, rather wordily, as 'a vocation in which a professed knowledge of some
　 department of learning or science is used in its application to the affairs of
　 others or in the practice of an art founded upon it', citing the learned
　 professions and the military as examples.
11　Anon., *The Disappointed Travellers: or, the three professions in tribulation* (Salis-

bury, 1785?), single sheet: after nineteen verses, the heroes return without having enjoyed the anticipated feast.

12 For a subtle analysis, see G. Simmel, 'The secret and the secret society' (1908), in *The Sociology of Georg Simmel*, ed. K.H. Wolff (Free Press, Glencoe, Ill., 1950), esp. p. 363.

13 V. Knox, *Essays, Moral and Literary* (2 vols, London, 1778–9), vol. 2, p. 247.

14 For a modern critique, see e.g. K. Hudson, *The Jargon of the Professions* (Macmillan, London, 1978).

15 R. Steele, *The Conscious Lovers* (1722), in *The Plays of Richard Steele*, ed. S.S. Kenny (Clarendon, Oxford, 1971), pp. 350–1.

16 C. Turner and M.N. Hodge, 'Occupations and professions', in *Professions and Professionalization*, ed. J.A. Jackson (Cambridge University Press, Cambridge, 1970), esp. pp. 23–6; and R.H. Hall, *Dimensions of Work* (Sage, Beverly Hills, 1986), pp. 40–55.

17 On the problems of translation into French, see G.L. Geison 'Introduction', in idem (ed.), *Professions and the French State, 1700–1900* (University of Pennsylvania Press, Philadelphia, 1984), p. 3 and fn. 7; and into German, J. Kocha, 'Bürgertum and professions in the nineteenth century: two alternative approaches', in *Professions in Theory and History: rethinking the study of the professions*, ed. M. Burrage and R. Torstendahl (Sage, London, 1990), pp. 62–3.

18 The concept of 'Industrial Revolution' remains fiercely debated; but few, even among its strongest protagonists, now insist that it offers a universal template. For a critique of single models of change (though not of the concept of structural growth itself), see A. Gershenkron, 'The typology of industrial development as a tool of analysis', in idem, *Continuity in History and Other Essays* (Belknap Press, Cambridge, Mass., 1968), pp. 77–97.

19 E.g. M. Burrage, 'Introduction', in *Professions in Theory and History*, ed. Burrage and Torstendahl, esp. pp. 6–20.

20 See C.M. Cipolla, 'The professions: the long view', *Journal of European Economic History*, 2 (1973), pp. 37–51; and R.M. Hartwell, 'The service revolution: the growth of services in the modern economy, 1700–1914', in *Economic History of Europe*, vol. 3: *The Industrial Revolution, 1700–1914*, ed. C.M. Cipolla (Fontana, London, 1976), pp. 358–61.

21 Ibid., pp. 368–71. E.g. Britain in 1901 had only 9 per cent of its workforce in agriculture, with 46 per cent in manufacturing and 45 per cent in services; but these estimates are 'subject to wide margins of error': P. Deane and W.A. Cole, *British Economic Growth, 1688–1959: trends and structure* (Cambridge University Press, Cambridge, 1967), pp. 141–2.

22 R.S. Turner, 'The *Bildungsbürgertum* and the learned professions in Prussia, 1770–1830: the origins of a class', *Histoire sociale/Social History*, 13 (1980), pp. 113–24. For a fine warning against universal schema, see also C.E. McClelland, *The German Experience of Professionalization: modern learned professions and their organisations from the early nineteenth century to the Hitler era* (Cambridge University Press, Cambridge, 1991), pp. 14–27, 32–50.

23 M. Sarfatti Larson, *The Rise of Professionalism: a sociological analysis* (University of California Press, Berkeley, 1977), esp. p. xvii. See also discussion, infra p. 179.

24 J. Earle, *Micro-cosmographie: or, a peece of the world discovered* (London, 1628), no. 4.

25 The early history of the professions in England is well analysed in H.C. Clough (ed.), *Profession, Vocation, and Culture in Later Medieval England: essays dedicated to ... A.R. Myers* (Liverpool University Press, Liverpool, 1982); K. Charlton, 'The professions in sixteenth-century England', *University of Birmingham*

Historical Journal, 12 (1969), pp. 20–41; W. Prest (ed.), *The Professions in Early Modern England* (Croom Helm, London, 1987); and, especially, in Geoffrey Holmes's *Augustan England: professions, state and society, 1680–1730* (Allen & Unwin, London, 1982), esp. pp. 3–42.

26 See W.J. Reader, *Professional Men: the rise of the professional classes in nineteenth-century England* (Weidenfeld, London, 1966); and H.J. Perkin, *The Rise of Professional Society: England since 1880* (Routledge, London, 1989), passim and esp. pp. 5–9, 116–23 on the impact of the professional ideal.

27 J. Addison, writing as 'Clio', *The Spectator*, no. 21, 24 March 1710/11.

28 This approach was exemplified in E. Greenwood, 'Attributes of a profession', *Social Work*, 2 (1957), pp. 45–55; and criticised notably by J.A. Roth, 'Professionalism: the sociologist's decoy', *Sociology of Work and Occupations*, 1 (1974), pp. 6–23. For a helpful summary, see also T.J. Johnson, *Professions and Power* (Macmillan, London, 1972), pp. 9–38.

29 See e.g. A. Etzioni (ed.), *The Semi-Professions and Their Organisation: teachers, nurses, social workers* (Free Press, New York, 1969).

30 I. Loudon, '"The vile race of quacks with which this country is infested"', in *Medical Fringe and Medical Orthodoxy, 1750–1850*, ed. W.F. Bynum and R. Porter (Croom Helm, London, 1987), p. 107.

31 [W. Chase, ed.], *The Norwich Directory: or, gentlemen and tradesmen's assistant* (Norwich, 1783), pp. 19, 23.

32 G. Winter, *Animal Magnetism: history of its origin, progress and present state* (London, 1801), p. 2.

33 For Addison, see *The Spectator*, no. 21, 24 March 1710/11. Other references to the 'learned professions' were numerous in the eighteenth century: see e.g. W. Blackstone, *Commentaries on the Laws of England* (Oxford, 1765–9), vol. 1, p. 13.

34 Anon., *A General Description of All the Trades* (London, 1747), pp. 6–7. This author's account of the qualities required in a lawyer was copied without acknowledgement in M. Postlethwayt, *The Universal Dictionary of Trade and Commerce: translated from the French of the celebrated M. Savary . . . with large additions and improvements* (2 vols, London, 1751–5; reissued 1774), vol. 1, pp. 152–3.

35 Data from G. King's MS 'Natural and politicall observations . . . upon the state and condition of England' (1696), publ. in G. Chalmers, *An Estimate of the Comparative Strength of Great-Britain* (London, 1802), p. 424, and in corrected format in *Two Tracts by Gregory King*, ed. G.E. Barnett (Johns Hopkins University Press, Baltimore, 1936), p. 31.

36 King's reputation as a demographer has been upheld by D.V. Glass, 'Two papers on Gregory King', in *Population in History*, ed. D.V. Glass and D.E.C. Eversley (Arnold, London, 1965), pp. 159–220. But the conservatism of King's social statistics has been highlighted, especially by G.S. Holmes, 'Gregory King and the social structure of pre-industrial England', *Transactions of the Royal Historical Society*, 5th ser., 27 (1977), pp. 41–68.

37 B. de Mandeville, *The Fable of the Bees: . . . as also an essay on charity and charity-schools* (London, 1723), p. 331. See also D. Cressy, 'A drudgery of schoolmasters: the teaching profession in Elizabethan and Stuart England', in Prest (ed.), *The Professions*, pp. 129–53; and Holmes, *Augustan England*, pp. 57–80.

38 J. Brewer, *The Sinews of Power: war, money and the English state, 1688–1783* (Cambridge University Press, Cambridge, 1989), esp. pp. 55–60, 64–85, and 88–134.

39 Knox, *Essays*, vol. 2, p. 250.

40 Young Bookwit from R. Steele's *The Lying Lover: or, the ladies' friendship* (1704), in Kenny (ed.), *Plays of Richard Steele*, p. 122.

41 This accepts David Glass's calculations, based upon King's figures: see Glass, 'Two papers', pp. 203–4.
42 King pushed his first estimate of 40,000 up to 50,000 in a revised version published by Charles Davenant in 1699: see Holmes, 'Gregory King and social structure', pp. 56, 67.
43 See G.E. Mingay, 'The eighteenth-century land steward', in *Land, Labour and Population in the Industrial Revolution*, ed. E.L. Jones and G.E. Mingay (Arnold, London, 1967), pp. 3–27, esp. pp. 8–9.
44 Interestingly, neither R. Campbell's *The London Tradesman: being a compendious view of all the trades, professions, arts. . . in the Cities of London and Westminster* (London, 1747) nor Anon., *General Description* (also 1747) listed 'accountant' as an occupation, but Postlethwayt's *Universal Dictionary* (1751), vol. 1, pp. 10–11, noted 'accountant' or 'accomptant'.
45 Campbell, *London Tradesman*, p. 93. For context, see also Holmes, *Augustan England*, pp. 28–31; and C. Ehrlich, *The Music Profession in Britain since the Eighteenth Century: a social history* (Clarendon, Oxford, 1985), pp. 1–53.
46 Postlethwayt, *Universal Dictionary*, vol. 2, p. 438, *sub* 'People'.
47 P. Colquhoun, *A Treatise on Indigence* (London, 1806), p. 23.
48 Idem, *A Treatise on the Police of the Metropolis, explaining the Various Crimes and Misdemeanours . . .* (London, 1796) had earlier put forward grossly exaggerated figures on the state of roguery in London but there he had no prior source to guide him. By contrast, his occupational data followed closely upon King's schema and probably erred on the side of caution.
49 Colquhoun, *Treatise on Indigence*, p. 23 broadened the 'artisans and handicraft' category to include mechanics and labourers in manufacturing and building, adding a marginal note to indicate that these included wage-earners as well as masters. As a result, his total of 445,726 persons was almost eight times larger than the 60,000 craftsmen proposed by Gregory King; but the categories were no longer strictly comparable.
50 See variously *Williamson's Directory for the City of Edinburgh . . ., 25 May 1773 to 25 May 1774* (facsimile edn, Edinburgh, 1889), pp. 1–85; and *Dictionary of National Biography* (subsequently *D.N.B.*) for Henry Erskine (1745–1817).
51 *Wilson's Dublin Directory for the Year 1784* (Dublin, 1784), pp. 105–22; and F. O'Ferrall, *Daniel O'Connell* (Gill & Macmillan, Dublin, 1981), pp. 16–21.
52 From M. Edgeworth's genial satire, *Castle Rackrent: an Hibernian tale* (London, 1800), esp. pp. 1–5, 130–47. In idem, *The Absentee* (London, 1812), Edgeworth returned to the theme with greater urgency, stressing the harm done by rapacious stewards to masters and tenants alike.
53 See C. Lawrence, 'Ornate physicians and learned artisans: Edinburgh medical men, 1726–76', in *William Hunter and the Eighteenth-Century Medical World*, ed. W.F. Bynum and R. Porter (Cambridge University Press, Cambridge, 1985), pp. 153–6; and N. Phillipson, 'The Scottish Enlightenment', in *The Enlightenment in National Context*, ed. R. Porter and M. Teich (Cambridge University Press, Cambridge, 1981), pp. 19–40, esp. pp. 26–9, 38–40.
54 *British Parliamentary Papers (B.P.P.)* (1852/3), vol. 88/1, p. lxxxvii.
55 The 1841 census had also recorded occupations but its coverage was poor in comparison with 1851: see J.M. Bellamy, 'Occupation statistics in the nineteenth-century censuses', in *The Census and Social Structure: an interpretative guide to nineteenth-century censuses for England and Wales*, ed. R. Lawton (Cass, London, 1978), pp. 166–8.
56 V. Neuburg, *Gone For a Soldier: a history of life in the British ranks from 1642* (Cassell, London, 1989), pp. 15–26. By 1851, there were 40,241 soldiers in the

British Isles, 5,349 of them under the age of 20 – excluding men in imperial armies overseas: see *B. P. P.* (1852/3), vol. 88/1, p. cxxvi.

57 E. Higgs, *Making Sense of the Census: the manuscript returns for England and Wales, 1801–1901* (H.M.S.O., London, 1989), pp. 78–93.

58 Perkin, *Rise of Professional Society,* p. 80. This data is fully explained in idem, 'Middle class education and employment in the nineteenth century: a critical note', *Economic History Review,* 2nd ser., 14 (1961), pp. 127–9.

59 British professionals plus administrators together constituted 12.6 per cent of the male workforce by 1951 and 11.6 per cent of the female. By 1971 the figures had risen to 21.5 per cent of the male workforce, 15.5 per cent of the female: Perkin, *Rise of Professional Society,* p. 422.

60 For example, a man of liberal (but not radical) views argued that women were not inferior but different, in Anon., *Woman: sketches of the history, genius, disposition, accomplishments, employments, customs and importance of the fair sex* . . . (London, 1790), p. 141: 'Their talents are in general not adapted to tread the horrid path of war, nor to trace the mazes and intricacies of science.'

61 See discussion below, pp. 144–6.

62 C. Ehrlich, *The Music Profession in Britain* since the Eighteenth Century: a social history (Clarendon, Oxford, 1985), pp. 13–16. For Billington and Siddons, see also *D.N.B.,* and P.H. Highfill *et al.* (eds), *A Biographical Dictionary of Actors, Actresses, Musicians, Dancers, Managers and other Stage Personnel in London, 1660–1800* (Southern Illinois University Press, Carbondale, 1973), vol. 2, pp. 122–9.

63 For discussions, see F.W. Znaniecki, *The Social Role of the Man of Knowledge* (Columbia University Press, New York, 1940), esp. pp. 83–8, 113–57; and M. Sarfatti Larson, 'The production of expertise and the constitution of expert power', in *The Authority of Experts: studies in history and theory,* ed. T. Haskell (Indiana University Press, Bloomington, 1984), pp. 28–80, esp. pp. 31–8, 60–8.

64 Johnson's *Dictionary* (1755) knew 'expert' as an adjective, and the *O.E.D.* dates its earliest use as a noun to the 1825 'Act to extinguish Feudal Tenures in Lower Canada', 6 George IV, cap. 59, sect. 3 which appointed 'Experts' to assess tenancy valuations.

3

SATIRE

How Merrily we live that Doctors be;
We humbug the Public and Pocket the Fee.
(Caption to satirical print, 1791)

As the power of knowledge was not based upon physical might, it depended instead upon social acceptance of its claims. That lay behind the care given to language and 'manner' on the part of the professions themselves. Their dignity was not ultimately sustainable if public interest in their services and acceptance of their powers faltered. Professional performance depended upon favourable client reactions. But the process was complex. There were multiple feedbacks among professionals, clientele and wider social perceptions. Over time, all parties managed to consolidate acceptable conventions of mutual behaviour. It means, however, that the emergence of the professions cannot be studied as an autonomous process. In particular, the barrage of satire that they attracted was not only a tribute to their power but simultaneously a communal goad to ensure that they lived up to their pretensions.

Humorists were quick to seize upon the comic potential of discrepancies between high claims and base reality. If the barb struck home, then the accompanying laughter acted as safety valve, mocking and scourging without destroying; but it could also be aggressive and hostile.[1] Indeed, humour is and has been as protean as power, against which it is often pitted. It can circumvent even the strictest censorship to record its point. Satire took things further and added venom to the laughter. Beneath the wit, the point was serious. Satire too was open-ended in its implications.[2] Its cultural impact could be conservative, laughing at the new, and purging errors to sustain and improve the old ways. Yet it could also be subversive, challenging outworn conventions and mocking the powers-that-be.

It thrived on caricature. That was undoubtedly present in the eighteenth-century satirical representations of the professions. Parsons of the Church of England were fat, greedy for tithes and drink-sodden – oppressing their curates, who were thin, ignorant and impoverished. At the same time, Nonconformist ministers were lank, unpleasing and sanctimonious, deluding their credulous congregations with fake piety. Doctors fared no better. They were mercenary, often brutal, and prone to hide their ignorance behind grand-sounding diagnoses. They kept company with disease and death; and (in the early nineteenth century) patronised the notorious resurrection men, who plundered graveyards to provide corpses for dissection. Lawyers were just as sinister. They were sharp, cunning, devious, protracting their legal cases for the additional fees, and obfuscating matters with long-winded and incomprehensible jargon. If the doctor consorted with death, in the form of a skeleton, the lawyer was instigated by the devil, with whom he frequently acted in concert. Meanwhile, army officers were dandified poltroons, hiding cowardice behind braggadocio and smart uniforms, whilst trifling with loose women. Sailors were more kindly viewed, as they were blunt and jovial; but they were also credulous, preyed upon by sharpers and prostitutes.

None of this was calculated to improve recruitment into the professions. That was hardly the aim of such caricatures. The chastisement of the professions instead drew attention to their generic defects, with varying degrees of laughter and anger, as a device both to warn the public and to keep the professionals on their toes. Of course, other social groups also suffered the lash of critical humour. Satire was a traditional mode of human communication – expressed at courts by fools and jesters, or voiced informally by wags and wits. Its quantity and rate of circulation were not, however, constant factors. They were crucially affected by the prevailing means of communication. The ending of press censorship with the lapsing of the licensing laws in 1695 ushered in a period of abundant publication.[3] All forms of literary and artistic output, from the weightiest of sermons to the most ephemeral of cartoon caricatures, multiplied apace, encouraged by and in turn encouraging a public that was manifestly eager to purchase these wares.

Satire was one of the most pungent forms of eighteenth-century communication. The formal ending of press censorship proved a stimulant to quality as well as quantity. In literature, in the era of Pope, Gay, Swift and their successors, it became a characteristic motif.[4] In graphic art, it fostered an abundance of satirical prints and cartoons, communicating both verbally and visually. This was the fertile context in which Hogarth, Rowlandson, Gillray and Cruikshank flourished. Even in polite conversation, a lively, bantering style of wit was acceptable, if used with due discretion, while buffoonery, coarse humour and guffawing was deprecated.[5] To scoff lightly at known targets for criticism was a viable formula for social exchange, easily understood and repeated. In that spirit, for example, the 4th Earl of Chesterfield noted that: 'Many young people think it very genteel and witty to abuse the clergy.' He rejected this as unwise but added his own quiet demystification of ministers of the cloth: 'They [the young] are extremely mistaken; since, in my opinion, parsons are very like men, and neither the better nor the worse for wearing a black gown.'[6]

Targets for satire were highly stereotyped. They included both individuals and generic characters, or (as in the case of Pope's victims in *The Dunciad*) individuals who could also be taken as prototypes. Above all, satire was used to probe at issues, actions and areas of social life that were seen as problematic. Its art required a keen awareness of the subject for critique. Freud argued that satire and invective – what he termed 'hostile wit' – acts as an indirect form of aggression, aimed at hurting not by force but by humiliation and ridicule; and it is thus well adapted for attacks by the relatively powerless against the powerful.[7] It was also enjoyable simply as humour. Certainly, in eighteenth- and early nineteenth-century Britain, a quotient of satire and irreverence was thereby incorporated into cultural traditions:

> If the knowing well how to expose any Infirmity or Vice were but a sufficient Security for the Vertue which is contrary, how excellent an Age might we be presum'd to live in! [wrote Shaftesbury in 1711]. Never was there in our Nation a time known, when Folly and Extravagance of every kind was more sharply inspected, or more wittily ridicul'd.[8]

The output of eighteenth-century satire was highly diverse, as were its targets. Time-worn jokes were frequently updated and reused; and new polemics were developed for new controversies. The genre focused especially upon social issues that provoked especial tension or conflict. Thus women with ambitions were fiercely mocked.[9] Inadequate politicians were derided.[10] All foreigners and especially the French were taunted for their oddities.[11] The affectations of social-climbers were pilloried. Fashionable dandies were ridiculed.

Amongst this galaxy, attacks upon the pretensions of the professions had a prominent and logical place. The practitioners in these occupations were distinctive enough to attract attention for their idiosyncracies and their claims were elevated enough to invite chastisement in the event of backsliding. Of course, not all criticisms were new to this period. The legal profession, for example, had often been accused of greed and duplicity. Hence Sir Thomas More's *Utopia* (1516) had hoped for a society without lawyers to teach people to lie, while Cade's rebels in Shakespeare's *Henry VI* made the ever popular suggestion: 'Let's kill all the lawyers.'[12]

Yet the notable element in eighteenth-century satire of the professions was not its absolute originality but rather its development and diffusion. That gave it extensive cultural impact. Of course, not everyone consulted the repertoire of prints, squibs, cartoons, pamphlets, essays, plays, novels, poems and songs that sustained the genre. Nor was every joke and allusion instantly comprehensible. Even Jonathan Swift, Pope's close friend and allied wit, did not recognise all the innuendoes of *The Dunciad*. Writing from Ireland on 16 July 1728, he suggested that full notes be provided, 'for I have long observed that twenty miles from London no body understands hints, initial letters, or town-facts and passages; and in a few years not even those who live in London'.[13] Ideas did not, however, depend upon perfect comprehension to get into general circulation. They were adapted and stereotyped as they were filtered and recirculated by more and more people, thus adding to their general cultural familiarity.

Repetition drummed home the point. Successful satires were recycled again and again, usually without reference to their authors. Indeed, given the confused state of case law on copyright in the eighteenth century there were few inhibitions about outright plagiarism. For instance, Swift laughed at his fellow satirists in 1710, with the comment that: 'Satire is a sort of glass, wherein beholders do generally discover everybody's face but their own.' A few years later, an anonymous poet enjoyed the jibe sufficiently to borrow it, with minor adaptations, for a doggerel poem on *The Manners of the Age: in thirteen moral satires* (1733). This did indeed speak volumes for the customs of the era, as the plagiarist wrote, without any acknowledgement to Swift: 'Satire's that mystic glass, in which are shewn/ All faults, and faces, but the reader's own.'[14] Lesser wits, in other words, happily recycled the jokes of the great for the amusement of the general public.

In that process, the evolving eighteenth- and nineteenth-century media of communication facilitated both the coinage and the recirculation of critical satire. Not only did the output of the printing presses increase dramatically after 1695 but its velocity of circulation was also speeded, as travel times were cut. In addition, the pool of potential readers of the written word was widened by the long-term spread of literacy among adults.[15] Meanwhile, songs and ballads were enjoyed by the illiterate and the literate alike.[16] Similarly, prints and cartoons vaulted over educational barriers, using pictures with or without words to convey messages to those who could not read as well as those who could. Visual material was hung up in shops, workplaces and homes, or circulated in handbills. Admittedly, the production runs for quality prints were relatively small. But there were many popular copies in circulation, and favoured motifs were sometimes reproduced on small items such as cards, fans and plates.[17]

Consequently, the professions were made aware that their generic faults and foibles were liable to public mockery. In one sense, of course, satire was a back-handed tribute to the power and influence of these occupations. The professions were valid targets for criticism if they fell below their own high ideal of disinterested professional service. At the same time, the criticisms were sharply made. Thus the many satires against the professions can also be regarded as the clients' revenge. Those with grievances could at least enjoy the critique and spread the warning to others. But there was no clear-cut dichotomy between solemn experts and satirical clients. The professions in general may have disliked criticism. Nonetheless, individual practitioners sometimes launched *ad hoc* satires and polemics against their fellows. Furthermore, much of the genre was produced by professional artists and writers, often themselves on the margins of respectability and solvency. Such men (and a few women) were quick to spot the flaws of those just above them in the hierarchy of esteem. However, they also needed to catch public attention. They did that by articulating and embellishing deeply felt cultural responses to change in the eighteenth century – which included the emergence of the aspirant professions.

If the motivations behind the production and circulation of satire were complex, the messages were equally so. It was rare to find expertise in itself derided and pure ignorance elevated. The substratum of professional knowhow was allowed to be admirable. But erudition unrelieved by common sense and practical experience was highly vulnerable to satire. The man (and, later, the woman) who was too clever by half made a popular target. A prototype was Sir Nicholas Gimcrack in Shadwell's play *The Virtuoso* (1676). This hero had learnt the technique of swimming on a table, but would not venture into the water, as he cared only for the 'Speculative' art and not the 'Practick'.[18] And Gimcrack had many successors. These ranged from Swift's other-wordly scientists in Laputa (1726) who had to be reminded to speak;[19] to Thomas Love Peacock's metaphysical Mr Flosky (1818), who was an enthusiast for truth, provided that it was 'so completely abstract as to be altogether out of the reach of the human faculties'.[20]

Similarly, professionals who sought to cloak their high learning in jargon – especially if it was couched in Latin – were admonished. *The Man of Manners* (1740) stated decidedly that: 'It is not civil in Conversation, to discourse in a Language the rest do not understand.' And this guide continued chaffingly to note that 'for which Reason *raw Clergymen*, petty *School-masters*, *Apothecaries*, and young *Attorneys* are accounted the worst Company, because they are perpetually throwing out Scraps of bad *Latin*'.[21]

Something of a paradox thus ensued. Knowledge was admired, especially when it had a practical application; but its possessors were ridiculed, if they seemed too vain of their learning or abstruse in their theories or odd in their personal behaviour. This attitude fuelled a lurking anti-intellectalism that was especially apparent in the English (rather than the Scottish) cultural tradition. Indeed, some intellectuals endorsed this viewpoint themselves.[22] However, the paradox was not as great as it seemed. The distinction between knowledge and its possessors was indeed a valid one, even if in practice it was not always easy to sustain. As a result, satirists of the clergy were able to claim sincerely that they intended no slight upon religion itself. Critics of lawyers were simultaneously able to praise the virtues of law. Scourges of 'quack' doctors were able to assert unhesitatingly the merits of modern medicine. And those who jeered at schoolteachers still wanted the nation's children to be instructed in the rudiments of learning.

Hence the functions of satire were multiple. It provided a safety vent for frustration and resentment among the clientele of the professions. It cut the pretensions of over-confident men of learning down to size. And it acted as an impromptu corrective to the power of knowledge, by indicating that it was only acceptable if it was well used. No doubt, many were too ready to trust in self-proclaimed experts. Thus, when writing of people's tendency to run after the latest medical panacea, Lady Mary Wortley Montagu deplored the 'foolish credulity of mankind'. Southey, who later quoted her, also concurred that 'Man is a credulous animal'.[23] Nevertheless, the general public was not uniformly composed of simple-minded dupes. And people could also learn from the critics and satirists to check whether their experts had feet of clay.

Within the satirical genre, there was certainly a strong element of polemical excess. Modern studies of England's lawyers, for example, have agreed that the charges against the legal profession were overblown and in practice unjustified.[24] However, satire did not seek accuracy. It exaggerated to engage attention and to make a point. In other words, the satires of the professions characteristically highlighted their worst defects in the name of an implicit ideal of what proper practice should be. But to draw blood, the critics had to aim at a substratum of recognisability. That meant that, although the satirists held up a sensationalised and distorted mirror, they trained it upon the known conventions of professional practice.

Lawyers, for example, were teased for their long-winded pedantry. A satire upon *Professional Characteristics* (1808) caught the flavour, as the attorney, Peter Positive, droned on relentlessly:[25]

> I must first premise, declare, and set forth, simply, modestly and conscientiously, that I shall expect, look for, request, and require a patient, silent, and quiet hearing, and attention, without let, hindrance, molestation, interruption, reply, or rejoinder, whilst I narrate, investigate and elucidate, all and sundry the troubles, sorrows, vexations, chagrins, crosses, delays, disappointments, rubs, and miseries, by whatever, and whichever, name, title, phrase, cant-phrase, or designation, all, any, and every one, or all of the said troubles, sorrows, vexations, cha –

At that point, the unstoppable sentence was interrupted by the lawyer's exasperated audience. But Positive resumed, to complete a sentence of well over 120 words. His fellow practitioners were similarly derided when they peppered their speech with law-French and mangled Latin. *The English Lawyer* (1736) was a popular eighteenth-century adaptation of an earlier drama, in which the legal expert, named Ignoramus, entered exclaiming: 'Fy, fy; *Tanta pressa, tantum croudum, ut fui pene trusus ad mortem*: I am almost squeez'd to death in this Croud, I'll have an Action of Intrusion against them all. Oh, how I sweat! O, hot, hot: *Meltavi meum pingue*, I have melted my Grease. Fy, fy; where are my Clerks?' His pride in his bad Latin constituted the central jest of the play. But there were also some pointed exchanges about the law. A servant requested legal advice with the proviso 'I am very poor, Sir', to which Ignoramus responded simply 'Then your Cause is bad.'[26]

Indeed, money was never far away when lawyers were satirised. The delays of the law and the mounting costs of legal advice were perennially resented. The suspicion was voiced that lawyers deliberately prolonged the business in order to increase their fees. They lived upon conflict and disputes. In 1810, George Crabbe expressed that when he hymned the men of law as 'the litigious rupture-stirring race;/ Who to contention as to trade are led,/ To whom dispute and strife are bliss and bread'.[27] The warning was often repeated. In Macklin's play *A Bone for the Lawyers* (1746), the attorney was a Mr Cormorant; in *The Pettyfogger Dramatized* (1797), he was Mr Wolf.[28] A light-hearted verse of 1698 paid tribute to legal slickness: two men quarrelled over an oyster and were assisted by a lawyer. The combatants then learnt a crucial lesson: "Twas *Law* that did the *Oyster* eat/ And left to us the *Shell*.'[29] Meanwhile, a print (c.1733) declared that 'Law is a Bottomless Pit'; it showed a wolf gazing down appreciatively upon the King's Bench Court, with its throng of attorneys and litigants, attended by a surreptitious pickpocket.[30]

Guile and knowledge of obscure case laws were seen as the basic prerequisites for legal success. 'They'll Cite you Six Hundred several *Presidents* [sic], tho' not one of them come near the case in *Hand*', complained a tract of 1708.[31] A fictional debate (1737) between three lawyers named Truman, Skinall and Dryboots – satiric ancestors of *Private Eye*'s Messrs Sue, Grabbit and Runne – penned a mock-lament over the abstruseness and complexity of English law. As a result, Truman observed sadly that: 'I often thought of a Saying of Honest Judge *Hales* [Sir Matthew Hale, the famous seventeenth-century jurist], that it was next to an Impossibility for an Attorney to be an honest Man.'[32] But the law remained uncodified. Hence a (verse) appeal for reform in 1836 demanded indignantly: 'But, shades of BLACKSTONE, LITTLETON, and HALE,/ Shall fraud again, and Gothic night prevail?'[33]

Darkness thus shrouded the imagery of the legal world. The Devil in person often appeared in cartoons of lawyers. They shared with him a reputation for smooth talking that cloaked sinister intentions. It was an appropriately sardonic custom to name the unpaid juniors who prepared briefs for senior counsel as 'devils'.[34] All these power-broking lawyers were dangerous because they went everywhere and knew everyone's secrets.[35] And barristers were doubly so because they were required to plead any case, for a fee, regardless of right or wrong. Swift was one of many who denounced their ability to argue 'that *White* is *Black*, and *Black* is *White*, according as they are paid.'[36] A sub-Swiftian broadsheet of 1749 concurred. There were too many 'subtil, greedy Attorneys who will readily undertake, for Lucre, to defend the unjustest Causes, and daringly affirm, in the Face of Justice, White to be Black, and Black White'.[37] Meanwhile, a poet in 1800 pondered the sharp practices that would be needed to get a legal expert into heaven: 'What did the Lawyer? Did he creep in?/ Or dash at once to take Possession? Oh, no, he knew his own profession . . .'. He obtained entry by subterfuge and then challenged St Peter to evict him.[38]

How many people knew such satires and found them funny is not known. However, authors manifestly expected these pedantic and/or villainous lawyers to strike a chord with the public. The great novelist of the law, Charles Dickens, drew freely upon this tradition. He himself had had experience as a young clerk in an attorney's office and later as a litigant. In his *Bleak House* (1852/3), lawyer Kenge parodied the legal style to explain that 'on the numerous difficulties, contingencies, masterly fictions, and forms of procedure in this great cause, there has been expended study, ability, eloquence, knowledge, intellect, . . . high intellect' and high costs. Meanwhile, the forlorn Miss Flite represented the eternal client, constantly awaiting the Day of Judgement, with the wards in Chancery represented by evocatively caged birds:

> With Hope, Joy, Youth, Peace, Rest, Life, Dust, Ashes, Waste, Want, Ruin, Despair, Madness, Death, Cunning, Folly, Words, Wigs, Rags, Sheepskins, Plunder, Precedent, Jargon, Gammon and Spinach![39]

Under this sort of barrage, lawyers became sensitive to their public nomenclature. A 'pettifogging attorney' was increasingly taken as a hostile description. It implied a low, rascally, quibbling trickster. Originally, in fact, a 'pettifogger' was a minor law officer, but by at least the sixteenth century the term had become controversial and it did not recover thereafter. In 1794, Lord Abingdon gave a respectable voice to criticisms of the profession, threatening a bill to reform 'those locusts in the law'.[40] A sardonic rebuttal from a stage attorney known as Mr Wolf (1797) did not mend matters: 'Let them say what they will respecting Pettyfogging, and Chicanery Quibbling, and Quirking: let them hold us up as public nuisances; still the profession of the law is a glorious one, it gives a man such opportunities to be a villain.'[41] Stung by jibes such as these, many rank-and-file lawyers had by the early nineteenth century taken to calling themselves by the alternative title of 'solicitor' instead (although in the

Figure 3.1 A Flat between Two Sharps (c. 1760). The 'flat' and bemused client is no match for the 'sharp' attorney and barrister who stand each side of him. The text below made the point in a homely metaphor: 'Law is like a new fashion, folks are bewitched to get into it – It is also like bad weather, most people are very glad when they get out of it.'
Published by permission of the British Museum, Department of Prints and Drawings

Figure 3.2 The First Day of Term: Or the Devil among the Lawyers (c. 1760). The gleeful
devil showers legal business and claims for costs upon eager lawyers, while in front
a clumsy country client obediently pays his guileful lawyer a fee. At their feet are
a bundle of deeds endorsed 'Began in 1699 – not yet finished – in Chancery'.
Published by permission of the British Museum, Department of Prints and
Drawings

51

United States the traditional name of 'attorney' survived). This shift in nomenclature was a notable tribute to the power of satire. Eventually, Parliament itself endorsed the change by referring to 'solicitors' in the 1873 Judicature Act.[42]

Clergymen too were popular targets for satire. Criticisms of the ministry were not necessarily the same as hostility to the church or to organised religion itself. However, it was sometimes easy to confuse matters. A poetic survey of *Modern Manners* in 1781 jested ponderously about a divine named Dr Cringe Croucher, who was complacent about his church duties and interested only in food. The author then added hastily: 'But think not, with sceptical malice and pride,/ The church, or the clergy, I mean to deride.' Instead, it was made clear that the intended targets were bigots, hypocrites and any with commercial motives who '*deal in* good works, whose religion's *a trade*.'[43] That offered a pertinent reminder that the ministry was viewed as a special calling or vocation in the service of God. The higher the standard, however, the greater the risk of default, and the sterner the criticisms of failure.

Preaching styles that smacked of insincerity and fake religiosity were easily ridiculed. Too much melodrama in the pulpit drew critical fire from one tract in 1708.[44] This claimed that the perfervid style of preaching was either 'perfect *Cant*' or 'meer *Stage Playing*'. The author evoked the swooping vocalisms of the fashionable modern clergymen:

> Their *Praying* is altogether as Ridiculous, as their *Preaching*; for imagining that in their Addresses to Heaven, they shou'd set out in a low and Tremulous Voice, as a Token of Dread and Reverence, they begin therefore with such a soft *Whispering*, as if they were afraid anyone shou'd overhear what they said, but when they are gone a little way, they clear up their Pipes by degrees, and at last Bawl out so loud as if with *Baal's Priests*, they were resolv'd to awake a sleeping God. And then again, being told by *Rhetoricians* that Heights and Falls, and a different *Cadency* in *Pronunciation* is a great advantage . . ., they'll sometimes . . . mutter their Words inwardly, and then of a sudden *Hollow* them out, and be sure to end in such a flat faultring [sic] Tone, as if their Spirits were *spent*, and they had run themselves out of Breath.

Laughter was one form of response from people embarrassed by excess religious fervour. Tub preaching was also satirised because it was seen as potentially dangerous. Thus eighteenth-century critics continued the tradition already exemplified by Ben Jonson's Zeal-of-the-Land Busy in *Bartholomew Fair* (1614) and Samuel Butler's *Sir Hudibras*, who objected to mince pies and plum porridge (1662/3). The zeal of the Nonconformists met with particular derision. 'Even at this Day,' noted Anthony Collins in 1729, 'the *Ridicule* is so strong against the present Dissenters, so

Figure 3.3 *The Vicar and Moses* (1784). This popular theme is illustrated by Thomas Rowlandson to show a worldly vicar stumbling home from the tavern, with his meagre clerk Moses. The ballad by the humorist George Stevens included the jovial lines: 'The Parson was *non se ipse* [not himself],/ *Non se ipse* d'ye say,/ What's that to the Lay?/ In plain English the Parson was tipsy.'
Published by permission of the British Museum, Department of Prints and Drawings

promoted by Clergy and Laity, especially in Villages and small Country Towns, that they are unable to withstand its Force, but daily come over in Numbers to the Church to avoid being *laugh'd* at.'[45] His point was exaggerated but it indicated that mockery could be used as a weapon against suspect piety. Prints and cartoons showed a series of grotesque orators holding forth before their credulous flocks.[46] And ridicule was especially excited when the sermonisers combined an elevated moralising with lowliness of birth. In *The Methodist* (1776), for example, Evan Lloyd, himself an Anglican parson, deplored the 'vulgar' enthusiasts in their modern conventicles. He sneered especially at humble tradesmen who claimed powers of spiritual leadership. One such was: 'The *Baker*, now a *Preacher* grown,/ Finds Man *lives not by Bread alone*,/ And now his Customers he feeds/ With *Pray'rs*, with *Sermons, Groans*, and *Creeds*.'[47]

Pulpit performances were not the only target. Even more than other professions, ministers of God's word were permanently on review. They were expected to set an example as well as to preach one. 'Consider you are always look'd upon/ With more regard than any other Man,/ And any Vices that appear in you,/ Look much more horrid than in us they do', as a lay author reminded the clergy firmly in 1691.[48] In consequence, there was a perennial stream of jokes, old and new, about clerics who passed their time in wining, dining, wenching and frivolity. As a poem to 'The Priest in his Cups' (1704) indicated, scandal ensued when the spiritual mentor sank to the level of his parishioners: 'Sober he kept the formal Path,/ In's Cups was not the same Man;/ But reel'd and stagger'd in his Faith,/ And Hickup'd [sic] like a *Lay-man*.'[49] A much repeated satirical print depicted 'The Vicar and Moses', rollicking back to church from the ale-house. Consequently, the bottle was often the comic *leit motif* for the eighteenth-century parson.

But all forms of clerical over-indulgence in worldly pleasures were criticised. A fable of 1796, now lost, had the promising title of *Things out of Place: or, the parson, the bear, and the butter*. But usually the charges were less obscure. George Crabbe, himself a modest country vicar, penned a sharp portrait (1783) of the sporting parson: 'A sportsman keen, he shoots through half the day,/ And, skill'd at whist, devotes the night to play.'[50] Richard Savage contributed a lurid poetic satire (1735) of the greedy cleric at table: 'See him with *Napkin*, o'er his *Band*, tuck'd in,/ While the rich Grease hangs glist'ning on his Chin.'[51] This fictional anti-hero then progressed through the vices from masturbation, to wenching, procuring an abortion, a loveless marriage, wife-beating and homosexuality, before becoming a Bishop, 'lawn-sleev'd and mitred'. Hogarth's satirical prints of fat clerical hypocrites were mild by comparison. But Savage would have appreciated one of Rowlandson's erotic prints, which lampooned sanctimonious religion in the form of a preacher whose upper torso was

Figure 3.4 The Sailor and the Field Preacher (early nineteenth century). Rowlandson satirises the itinerant preachers. The speaker cries: 'I hear a voice from Heaven', while the crowd gawps. But a sailor is sceptical: 'Come – Come – none of your fore castle gammon with me, you Swab – have not I been *aloft* this half hour, and if so be any orders of that kind came down – don't you think I should have heard them first?'
Published by permission of Princeton University Libraries, Department of Rare Books and Special Collections (Graphic Arts, Visual Materials Division: Collection of Dickson Q. Brown)

fervently engaged in prayer whilst his lower half was energetically making love with an obliging wench.[52]

Of course, if people were determined to find fault, the 'parson-hunters' could always find something to criticise, as a poem of 1731 explained. If a clergyman ate modestly, he was too 'dainty'. If heartily, he was a glutton. If he drank freely, he was a toper. If he refrained, 'He's sly, and for a Hypocrite does pass.'[53] Moreover, much of the humour was based upon the repetition of social stereotypes. However, the point was not the accuracy of the jibes but the constant reminder they gave to clergymen about their social visibility.

Money was another source of grievance. Richard Savage again derided the parson who provided perfunctory funerals for paupers since they were unable to pay the expected perquisites of gloves, rings or trinkets.[54] Above all, the Church of England clergy faced acrimony over the payment of tithes. In practice, arrangements varied from parish to parish. But that did not prevent the long-running grievance from being used as a generic excuse for complaints. For example, the amusing cartoon of 'The tythe pig' appeared in many versions. It showed a chubby parson levying one in ten of the livestock of the poor. But in this case the farmer's wife agrees to surrender the pig only if he will take her tenth child off her hands as well.[55] Popular wit thus rebuked clerical greed.

There were also problems stemming from the unequal value of church livings. Anger over that was voiced by the poet and satirist Charles Churchill. He was himself curate of St John's Westminster for a while. But his clerical career soon ended. Later in 1785, he bitterly contrasted the luxury of the bishops with the penury of the poor parsons, who were 'Condemn'd (whilst proud and pamper'd Sons of Lawn,/ Cramm'd to the throat, in lazy plenty yawn)/ In pomp of rev'rend begg'ry to appear,/ To pray, and starve on forty pounds a year.'[56] The inadequacy of many livings encouraged clergymen to become pluralists, for which greed they were again pilloried.[57] It also meant that many Anglican parsons were absentees, who left their parish duties to deputies. That prompted further satirical prints, contrasting the fat, rich and carefree pluralists with their meagre, dreary and harassed curates.[58]

Little wonder that ambitious clerics were disposed to flatter the wealthy laity who had the right of nomination to church livings. Jane Austen (who was the daughter of an Anglican rector) satirised that enjoyably in the bowings and scrapings of the eternally obsequious Mr Collins before his noble patron Lady Catherine de Bourgh.[59]

Medical doctors were just as controversial. As they rose to prominence during this period, they too attracted a growing volume of satire. Many standard jests referred to the doctors' professional interest in the spread of disease. Thus a stage physician in *Physick lies a Bleeding* (1697) complained that his patients were 'damnable healthy';[60] while one Dr Bilioso in a comic operetta of 1788 lamented: 'What a cursed neighbourhood is this for a physician to live in. . . . All the villagers are such a set of d–n'd vulgar, healthy dogs.'[61] Medical experts were also ghoulishly familiar with the physical manifestations of bodily infirmity. A satire in 1717 pilloried the doctors in earnest conclave over such evidence: 'With rev'rend Nods they hardly speak a Word,/ Because their Wisdom will not one afford;/Yet ev'ry learned Argument they vent,/ Upon the Patient's stinking Excrement.'[62] William Hogarth's 'Company of Undertakers' (1736/7) similarly laughed at a group of physicians, two of whom gaze raptly into a flask of urine, while a third dips his finger in to taste.[63] But the surgeons were even more repellently intimate with the human body. Hogarth was one among many to depict them as gruesome butchers (1750/1), unfeelingly carving up a cadaver, wrenching out its intestines and gouging out an eye.[64] Death was thus the doctor's ultimate companion and the skeleton their symbol.

No part of the medical profession escaped censure for greed and callousness. In numerous prints and cartoons, dentists wrenched teeth out brutally;[65] midwives were gross and drink-sodden;[66] physicians fought over dying patients,[67] prescribed unpleasant medicines,[68] and made clandestine love to wives and maidservants.[69] A play by Caroline Boaden in 1829 satirised the mad doctor, Dr Soothem, who was happy to confine sane people in his private lunatic asylum.[70] In 1760 Lawrence Sterne had created the famous man-midwife, Dr Slop, who mangled the nose of the hapless *Tristram Shandy*.[71] And in 1783 Crabbe characterised the village apothecary as one whose 'most tender mercy is neglect'.[72] That was probably better than many remedies on offer. Indeed, a serious tract in 1741 warned that the medical fashion for bloodletting could itself do harm: there were too many 'ignorant conceited coxcombs' within the profession, who knew no other treatment but to wield the lancet, crying fatuously, 'Egad, I must have some of your blood.'[73]

These blundering measures were often accompanied by a grandiose rhetoric, designed to blind the patient with science. A popular play of 1697 found the doctors as bad as the other professions at giving a classical veneer to pedestrian advice: 'There's several sorts of *Latin*; There's Law-*Latin*, Priests *Latin*, and Doctor's-*Latin*; as for example: *Olo Purgatum*, *Physicum*, and *Vomit-um-guts-out-um* – and so forth.'[74] A smattering of learning was likely to impress. Yet there were hazards in dealing with invalids, as one Dr Doleful (1808) discovered:

> Called in to an opulent patient, you open your approaches in the first stile [sic] of medical importance – you talk of irritability and excitement, of prognostics and diagnostics, of symptoms, sympathies, and nonnaturals, of diaphoretics, sudorifics, etc. etc. etc., when unfortunately you find your patient, in addition to his other maladies – is deaf.[75]

Figure 3.5 Hogarth's '*Company of Undertakers*' (1737). Hogarth drew a mock-heraldic shield for the medical profession as a Company of Undertakers. Three notorious 'quacks' – John Taylor the oculist, Sarah Mapp the osteopath, and Joshua Ward with his facial blemish – loom over a conclave of learned physicians. These in turn look coarse and ugly, sniffing their scented canes, while three absorbed doctors make a diagnosis by studying a flask of urine. From: Hogarth prints (1737) Published by permission of the British Museum, Department of Prints and Drawings

Charlatans found that a ready patter was able to impress and gull the public into buying their nostrums. But there was no strict dividing line between the impostor and the orthodox medical man. 'The regular and the quack have each their several schemes of imposition, and they differ in nothing so much as in the name', a hostile William Godwin decided in 1797.[76] Indeed, many respectable doctors needed to puff their skills. 'Make all the Noise and Bustle you can', advised the semi-satirical *Art of Getting into Practice in Physick* (1722).[77] In addition, doctors sometimes satirised their own rivals. The eminent Dr Mead, himself much criticised, penned tracts in 1719 to scoff at Dr Woodward's cure for digestive disorders.[78] A bitter quarrel ensued. A rousing reply in 1748 purported to convey Dr Woodward's resentment even from beyond the grave: 'Hack'd, thwack'd, and rack'd, my injur'd Ashes,/ Having receiv'd a hundred Lashes,/ From Post to rugged Pillar bounc'd,/ Keel-haul'd, and De'elhaul'd, sadly trounc'd,/ Swift-skimming thro' the rising Gloom,/ A discontented GHOST I come . . .'[79]

Meanwhile, these competitive medical men charged fees for their services and nostrums. Healers were thus not to be trusted too readily. In a play of 1697, apothecaries were shown gloating over the high profits they got from making cheap potions to sell dearly.[80] Physicians too were mere cutpurses, sang a ballad of c. 1725, as they schemed to get 'more Diseases and Money'.[81] A print of c. 1760 depicted 'The rapacious quack'. He was obviously wealthy but he still took a side of bacon as a fee from a destitute, dying patient, despite pleas from the anguished family. 'How Merrily we live that Doctors be', ran the cheery caption of another print in 1791: 'We humbug the Public and Pocket the Fee.'[82] Consequently, the medical profession liked to keep its patients alive – but unwell. In a 1797 comedy, an apothecary revealed his sincere conviction that:' A patient cur'd is a customer lost.'[83]

Such was the extent of doctors' villainy that they stood comparison even with the lawyers for iniquity. A poetic fiction in 1700 envisaged the medical and legal professions competing for supremacy in Hell. The lawyers won, but only narrowly.[84] Later, in a farce on *Love, Law and Physic* (1812), Doctor Camphor and attorney Flexible toasted their occupations jointly. After all, law and physic shared at least one skill: 'What's that?' – 'Bleeding to be sure.'[85]

Undoubtedly, the learned professions took the main brunt of satire, as they were prominent and influential. Their lesser brethren, however, did not escape entirely. As already noted, schoolteachers were often attacked as petty tyrants. Jonathan Swift in *The Tatler* (1709) mocked one vicar-cum-schoolmaster in the pulpit, who 'stretches his Jaws so wide, that instead of instructing Youth, it rather frightens them'.[86] But this teacher was an idler, whereas most others were depicted as floggers and bullies. William Somerville in 1735 wrote of 'captive Boys/ Cow'd by the ruling Rod, and

Figure 3.6 The Sailor and the Quack Doctor (1807). Isaac Cruikshank satirised the greed of the medical profession. The wounded sailor – representing sturdy British common sense – is met by a finely dressed doctor with the brisk instruction: 'Sir, my rule of practice is this, there is pen, ink, and paper – sign a certificate of your cure, and I'll take you in hand immediately on paying down two Guineas.'

Published by permission of the Wellcome Institute Library, London

The Pedagogue.

And then the Pedagogue, with formal wig,
His night gown and his cane; ruling like Turk,
All in his dusty School:

Figure 3.7 The Pedagogue (1790). The stern pedagogue with his wig and cane presides in his own classroom. His prestige outside his school might be limited; but inside its walls, his power was intimidating enough to overawe the schoolboy reciting the alphabet. Thus the verse referred to the schoolmaster 'ruling like a Turk,/ All in his dusty School'
Published by permission of the British Museum, Department of Prints and Drawings

haughty Frowns/ Of Pedagogues severe . . .'.[87] A 'professional gentleman' in 1827 added to the tale. 'The Despotic Pedagogue' was 'horrific in his look and nod' – and he wielded his 'spectral rod' so severely that he terrorised adults as well as children.[88] Dickens's Mr Wackford Squeers of Dotheboys Hall was obviously in good company here.

Governesses did not attract the same venom but they also proved easy to caricature (although their appearances in pornographic prints were, by contrast, usually quite without humour). In 1797, one hostile prototype was depicted on the London stage in the character of Mrs Rigid. She was a schemer who plotted to enrich and then to mulct her young pupil. Mrs Rigid also had an accomplice in the tutor, Veritas. But he was converted from villainy by being made drunk at the crucial moment (a joke upon the motto 'in vino veritas').[89] In general, however, women teachers were sneered at rather than excoriated. They were disdained as humble beings of lowly origins and uncertain status. Charlotte Brontë, who was of course once a governess herself, reproduced in *Jane Eyre* (1847)[90] the scorn that fine ladies often expressed for these menials – 'half of them detestable and the rest ridiculous, and all incubi' – although in her unconventional novel, the governess was allowed to triumph in the end.

By contrast with the learned professions, the officers in the armed forces made bluffer targets for satire. The naval leadership generally escaped undue criticism, since the British navy was generally both successful and popular. Individuals who presided over failures – such as Admiral Byng at the loss of Minorca in 1755 – were pilloried, to be sure; and the press-gang was denounced as a method of recruitment. But the naval officers were seen as dashing figures, amorous and good-humoured, if unduly likely to be duped by bawds and women of the town.

Army officers, however, were a more complex case. Their triumphs over foreign enemies were glorified, but disasters were as sternly rebuked. The recruitment process was also unpopular – and Farquhar's dashing Captain Plume in *The Recruiting Officer* (1706) did not have any theatrical successors. As a professional group, however, army officers were more frequently accused of vanity than of brutality. They strutted around in elaborate regimentals. One uniformed hero was depicted as a modern Narcissus (1782), in love with his own smart image.[91] It was often hinted that such dandies were poltroons under fire. A satire upon the making of an officer entitled *The Rutland Volunteer Influenza'd* recycled a traditional saying with some topical point in 1783, after the loss of the American colonies: 'I'll fight again, I'll run away,/ I'll live to fight another day.'[92] And the army volunteers in the war years of the 1790s were sternly categorised as timid civilians, who were unwilling to get their uniforms wet in the rain.[93]

Above all, however, it was agreed that the military man was a monotonous bore, endlessly talking about army life and past battles. The hero of

Macklin's *Love à la Mode* (1759) was Sir Callaghan O'Brallaghan, an Irish officer trained in the Prussian army. He was introduced with the tart comment: 'I don't suppose he has six ideas out of his own profession – garrisons and camps have been the courts and academies that have formed him.'[94] And Lawrence Sterne, the son of an amiable but not very successful army officer, created the supreme example – only this time an endearing one – in the guise of *Tristram Shandy*'s Uncle Toby who, with his devoted Corporal Trim, punctiliously re-enacted in garden miniature the sieges and battles of the Marlborough wars.

This collective barrage of wit and humour had some interesting implications. It did not halt the growth of demand for professional services. On the contrary, the force of these satires was an oblique but real tribute to the cultural power of the professions. They were not attacked simply because they were numerous and socially visible. Britain's shopkeepers and farmers – for example – were more staple to the economy and more ubiquitous; but they attracted relatively little satire – and then generally not for their working practices but for the social pretensions of their wives and daughters. By contrast, the professions constituted a serious target because they had such cultural influence and such potential power over individual lives. Thus satire, which is sometimes treated as an aberration by historians of the professions, was a recognizable response to the claims of authority.

Amidst the informal humour, too, lurked serious, if sometimes rather contradictory, criticisms. Satire contrasted the ideal professional performance with its obverse. It marked an antithesis of the form identified by anthropologist Victor Turner as the clash of 'structure' and 'counter-structure'.[95] By that means, the professions were alerted to disputable elements in their own behaviour. Moreover, satire was a knowing form of communication which depended upon an intelligent audience to comprehend the message. Thus, although the clients of the professions were themselves often represented as simple-minded and gullible dupes, the effect was to alert wide-awake members of the general public to the need for vigilance. The message was that authority figures had to earn trust rather than assume its automatic presence. Professional power was not entirely unchecked. Satire attempted, in a witty and disorganised way, to demystify their pretensions and unmask their secrets.

A new and growing genre of self-help manuals also began to help in that task, albeit from an earnest rather than satirical perspective. These works did not obviate all need for specialist help. Indeed, they were often written by members of the professions. Such guides did, however, try to bypass 'mystery' by making information public. For example, after 1736, it was possible to purchase *Every Man his Own Lawyer*. In 1773, a group of lawyers produced a rival volume; and a guide to getting probate followed in 1786, entitled *Every Man his Own Proctor*.[96] The growing corpus of

A LONG STORY

Figure 3.8 The Long Story (1782). Bunbury's satire catches impishly the utter boredom of a group of drinking companies, as the retired soldier – in full uniform – demonstrates at excessive length the details of his triumphant manoeuvres in the field. Even the dogs have lost heart and the servant boy joins in the general yawns. Published by permission of the British Museum, Department of Prints and Drawings

medical knowledge was also summarised for the lay public. Thus *Every Man his Own Physician* was published in 1787.[97] Moreover, there was some deliberate 'poaching' between rival experts, most notably by John Wesley. The founder of Methodism also wrote *Primitive Physick* (1747) which stayed in print for many years. This compendium of advice on health care was written specifically to combat the popular belief that medicine was 'an abstruse Science, quite out of the reach of Ordinary Men.'[98] It is extremely unlikely, by contrast, that Wesley would have approved of *Every Man his Own Parson*, but that escaped his displeasure since it was not published until 1851.[99]

None of this amounted to an outright rejection of all expert advice. There was no eighteenth-century equivalent of a modern Ivan Illich to argue that the professions constituted no more than a restrictive cartel designed to 'disable' ordinary citizens.[100] But satirists, critics and authors of self-help manuals helped to challenge professional pretensions. Laughter especially provided – as it still provides – a corrective goad to the solemn brokers of power/knowledge.

NOTES

1 See M. Mulkay, *On Humour: its nature and its place in modern society* (Polity, Cambridge, 1988); and A.J. Chapman and H.C. Foot (eds), *It's a Funny Thing, Laughter* (Pergamon, Oxford, 1977). For context, see also S.M. Tave, *The Amiable Humorist: a study in the comic theory and criticism of the eighteenth and nineteenth centuries* (University of Chicago Press, Chicago, 1960); and K. Thomas, 'The place of laughter in Tudor and Stuart England', 1976 Neale Lecture, *Times Literary Supplement*, 21 Jan. 1977, pp. 77–81.

2 R.C. Elliott, *The Power of Satire: magic, ritual, art* (Princeton University Press, Princeton, 1960), esp. pp. 273–5; also Mulkay, *On Humour*, pp. 144, 153–7, 197–211.

3 G.A. Cranfield, *The Press and Society: from Caxton to Northcliffe* (Longman, London, 1978), pp. 29–30, 31–57.

4 D. Nokes, *Raillery and Rage: a study of eighteenth-century satire* (Harvester, Brighton, 1987), p. 1, argues that English literature between 1660 and 1760 was positively 'dominated' by satire.

5 Tave, *Amiable Humorist*, pp. 16–22.

6 W. Ernst-Browning (ed.), *The Wit and Wisdom of the Earl of Chesterfield* (London, 1875), p. 14.

7 S. Freud, *Wit and its Relation to the Unconscious*, ed. A.A. Brill (Fisher Unwin, London, 1916), pp. 148–53, 154.

8 A.A. Cooper, 3rd Earl of Shaftesbury, 'A letter concerning enthusiasm', in idem, *Characteristicks* (2 vols, London, 1711), vol. 1, p. 9.

9 Details in F. Nussbaum, *'The Brink of all We Hate': English satires on women, 1660–1750* (University of Kentucky Press, Lexington, 1984).

10 See e.g. P. Langford, *Walpole and the Robinocracy* (Chadwyck-Healey, Cambridge, 1986) or H.T. Dickinson, *Caricatures and the Constitution, 1760–1832* (Chadwyck-Healey, Cambridge, 1986).

11 M. Duffy, *The Englishman and the Foreigner* (Chadwyck-Healey, Cambridge, 1986).

12 T. More, *Utopia*, transl. P. Turner (Penguin, London, 1965), p. 106; and W. Shakespeare, *2 Henry VI* (1594), IV. 2.

13 H. Williams (ed.), *The Correspondence of Jonathan Swift*, vol. 3: *1724–31* (Clarendon, Oxford, 1963–5), p. 293.

14 Compare J. Swift, *A Full and True Account of the Battel . . . between the Ancient and the Modern Books* (1710) in *The Prose Works of Jonathan Swift, D.D.*, ed. W.E.H. Lecky (Bell, London, 1897), vol. 1, p. 160, with Anon., *The Manners of the Age: in thirteen moral satires* (London, 1733), p. 526.

15 L. Stone, 'Education and literacy in England, 1600–1914', *Past and Present*, 42 (1969), pp. 102–26; R.A. Houston, *Scottish Literacy and the Scottish Identity: illiteracy and society in Scotland and northern England, 1600–1800* (Cambridge University Press, Cambridge, 1985), pp. 33–67, 70–83.

16 See especially R. Palmer, *The Sound of History: songs and social comment* (Oxford University Press, Oxford, 1988), esp. pp. 1–19.

17 For discussion, see T. Wright, *A History of Caricatures and Grotesques in Literature and Art* (London, c.1864), pp. 423, 426; and A. Dyson, *Pictures to Print: the nineteenth-century engraving trade* (Farrand, London, 1984).

18 T. Shadwell, *The Virtuoso: a comedy* (London, 1676), p. 30.

19 J. Swift, *Travels into Several Remote Nations of the World: in four parts, by Lemuel Gulliver* (London, 1726), pt 3.

20 T.L. Peacock, *Nightmare Abbey* (1818), in *The Works of Thomas Love Peacock*, ed. H.F.B. Brett-Smith and C.E. Jones (Constable, London, 1924), vol. 3, p. 49.

21 [Erasmus Jones], *The Man of Manners: or, the plebeian polish'd, being plain and familiar rules for a modest and genteel behaviour . . .* (London, 1737?), p. 19.

22 See discussion in B. Schilling, *Conservative England and the Case against Voltaire* (Columbia University Press, New York, 1950), pp. 60–8.

23 For Southey and Montagu on English credulity, see R. Southey, *Letters from England*, ed. J. Simmons (Cresset, London, 1951), p. 293.

24 See e.g. E.W. Ives, 'The reputation of the common lawyer in English society, 1450–1550', *University of Birmingham Historical Journal*, 7 (1960), p. 161; and M. Miles, '"Eminent Attorneys": some aspects of West Riding attorneyship, *c.* 1750–1800' (unpubl. Ph.D. thesis, University of Birmingham, 1982), pp. 19–144, and summary 134–44.

25 Anon. [J. Beresford?], *Professional Characteristics: consisting of naval squalls, military broils, physical disasters, legal flaws, and clerical lamentations, uttered by an admiral, a colonel, a lawyer, a doctor and a parson . . .* (London, 1808), pp. 54–5.

26 E. Ravenscroft, *Ignoramus: or, the English lawyer – a comedy* (London, 1736), pp. 7, 27. The play was a free adaptation of Codrington's translation of George Ruggle's *Ignoramus* (1630).

27 G. Crabbe, *The Borough* (London, 1810), Letter 6, p. 58.

28 See C. Macklin, *A Will and no Will: or, a bone for the lawyers* (1746; in Augustan Society reprint edn, Los Angeles, 1967); and [T.B.], *The Pettyfogger Dramatized: in two acts* (London, 1797).

29 Anon., *Aesop at Tunbridge: or, a few select fables in verse – by no person of quality* (London, 1698), Fable 10.

30 F.G. Stephens and M.D. George (eds), *Catalogue of Political and Personal Satires: preserved in the . . . British Museum, 1660–1830* (British Museum, London, 1978 repr.), vol. 2, no. 1990.

31 Anon., *The Art of Tickling-trouts: . . . shewing the method how all faculties and professions in the world affect the false arts of wheedle, cant and flattery . . .* (London, 1708), p. 11.

32 [J. Purves], *The Law and Lawyers laid open . . .* (London, 1737), p. 102 (correctly p. 202).

33 Anon., *The Professions: with other pieces in verse* (London, 1836), p. 37.

34 See infra, p. 90. Printers' assistants were also known as 'devils' not for their moral infamy but for their inky-black appearance.

35 Anon., *The Pettifoggers: a satire . . . displaying the . . . frauds, deceits, and knavish practices, of the pettifogging counsellors, attornies, solicitors and clerks . . .* (London, 1723), p. 18.

36 Swift skirmished against the lawyers in Brobdingnag: see *Travels*, pt 2, pp. 114–15; but kept his sharpest words for Gulliver in the land of the Houyhnhnms: ibid., pt 4, pp. 70–2.

37 Anon., *A Bone to Pick for Somebody* (Dublin, 1749), single sheet; and compare also Anon., *The Flames of Newgate: or, the new ministry* (London, 1782), p. 29: 'But lawyers will affirm that day is night,/ And shew that white is black, and black is white'.

38 Anon., *The Lawyer* (London, 1800?), p. 3.

39 C. Dickens, *Bleak House* (1853), ed. N. Page (Penguin, Harmondsworth, 1971 edn), pp. 923, 875. For context, see also W. Holdsworth, *Charles Dickens as Legal Historian* (Yale University Press, New Haven, 1928).

40 House of Lords, 17 June 1794, in *Parliamentary Register*, 39 (London, 1794), pp. 403–4.

41 [T.B.], *The Pettyfogger Dramatized*, p. 12.

42 See P.J. Corfield, 'Defining urban work', in *Work in Towns, 850–1850*, ed. P.J. Corfield and D. Keene (Leicester University Press, Leicester, 1990), p. 218.

43 Anon., *Modern Manners: in a series of familiar epistles* (London, 1781), pp. 43–4.

44 Anon., *The Art of Tickling-trouts*, p. 11.

45 [Anthony Collins], *A Discourse concerning Ridicule and Irony in Writing* (London, 1729), p. 41.

46 For example, Stephens and George (eds), *Catalogue of . . . Satires*, vol. 3, pt 1 (1), no. 2432 'Enthusiasm displayed' (1739), shows the Methodist Whitefield, accompanied by 'hypocrisy' and 'deceit'.

47 E. Lloyd, *The Methodist* (London, 1776), p. 33.

48 Anon., *The Moralist: or, a satyr upon the sects* (London, 1691), p. 20.

49 Anon., *The Tavern-frolick: or, a comical dialogue between a drunken priest, and a . . . London Quaker* (London, 1704), p. 8.

50 G. Crabbe, *The Village* (1783), in *The Poetical Works of George Crabbe*, ed. A.J. and R.M. Carlyle (Frowde, London, 1908), p. 38.

51 R. Savage, *The Progress of a Divine: a satire* (London, 1735), p. 9; and following references from pp. 9–10, 13, 17–19.

52 Rowlandson illustrated a song entitled 'The sanctifed sinner', in Anon., *The Gentleman's Bottle-companion: containing a collection of . . . songs* (London, 1768; Edinburgh reprint, 1979), p. 38.

53 Anon., *The Parson Hunter: a poem* (London, 1731), pp. 5, 6, 12.

54 Savage, *Progress of a Divine*, p. 5.

55 Stephens and George (eds), *Catalogue of . . . Satires*, vol. 3, pt 2, no. 3794 has a classic version of 'The tythe pig' (c.1760).

56 C. Churchill, *The Author*, in his *Poems* (London, 1763/5), vol. 2, pp. 16–17.

57 E.g. 'The pluralist' (1744) shows a cleric couching above four churches which support his hands and feet, while he looks around for a fifth: Stephens and George (eds), *Catalogue of . . . Satires*, vol. 3, pt 1 (2), no. 2617, and copy no. 2618.

58 E.g. 'The fat pluralist and his lean curates' (c.1733) in ibid., vol. 2 (2), no. 2003.

59 Later, when Lady Catherine is displeased, Mr Collins is given sardonic advice: 'Stand by the nephew. He has more to give': J. Austen, *Pride and Prejudice* (London, 1813), vol. 3, p. 311.

60 T. Brown, *Physick lies a Bleeding: or, the apothecary turned doctor – a comedy, acted*

almost every day in most apothecaries shops in London (London, 1697), p. 10.

61 J. Cobb, *The Doctor and the Apothecary: a musical entertainment* (London, 1788), p. 25 (adapted from an earlier German *Singspiel*).

62 Anon., *A Satyr upon the Present Times* (London, 1717), pp. 9–10.

63 S. Shesgreen (ed.), *Engravings by Hogarth* (Dover, New York, 1973), plate 40. Diagnosis by 'piss prediction' was a controversial method: for a hostile account, see Anon., *The Modern Quack: or, the physical impostor detected . . .* (London, 1718), pp. 125–46.

64 This was the final stage in Hogarth's 'Four stages of cruelty' (1750/1): Shesgreen (ed.), *Engravings*, Plate 80. Anxiety about dissection reached new heights in the early nineteenth century, as the expansion of medical training created a hunt for corpses: see e.g. Stephens and George (eds), *Catalogue of . . . Satires*, vol. 10, no. 15444 'Surgical operations' (1827); and discussion infra, p. 153.

65 On the crudity of pre-anaesthetic dental extractions, see ibid., vol. 6, nos. 6759, 6760 (c.1784), nos. 8051, 8052 (1791); vol. 7, no. 8909 (1796); vol. 10, no. 14311 (1821).

66 See ibid. vol. 9, no. 11795 for Rowlandson's celebrated 'Midwife going to labour' (1811).

67 E.g. print in ibid., vol. 7, no. 8590 I. Cruikshank?, 'Doctors differ and their patients die' (1794).

68 'Taking physick' by Gillray (1800), imitated by Cruikshank (1801) in ibid., vol. 7, no. 9584 and vol. 8, no. 9804. For the unpleasant impact of purges, see also ibid., vol. 7, no. 9094 'A sudden explosion' (1797) and vol. 8, no. 9805 'Taking an emetic' (1801).

69 For Rowlandson satires, see ibid., vol. 7, no. 9673 'The doctor disturbed' (c.1788?); and vol. 8, no. 11638 'Medical dispatch: or, doctor doubledose killing two birds with one stone' (1810).

70 In the farce by C. Boaden, *William Thompson: or, which is he?* (London, 1829).

71 L. Sterne, *The Life and Opinions of Tristram Shandy, Gentleman* (London, 1760).

72 A.J. and R.M. Carlyle (eds), *Poetical Works of . . . Crabbe*, p. 37.

73 Anon., *An Essay upon the Present Epidemic Fever* (Sherborne, 1741), quoted in C. Creighton, *A History of Epidemics in Britain*, vol. 2: *From the extinction of the plague to the present time* (Cambridge University Press, Cambridge, 1894), p. 83, n. 4.

74 E. Ravenscroft, *The Anatomist: or, the sham-doctor* (London, 1697), p. 22. This play was reprinted and adapted in 1722, 1735, 1762, 1784, 1805, 1807. Henry Fielding also recycled jokes about medical Latin via his popular translation of Molière, *The Mock Doctor: or, the dumb lady cured . . .* (London, 1732), pp. 16–17.

75 Anon., *Professional Characteristics*, p. 102.

76 W. Godwin, 'Of trades and professions', in idem, *The Enquirer: reflections on education, manners and literature* (London, 1797), p. 227.

77 Anon., *The Art of Getting into Practice in Physick* (London, 1722), p. 10.

78 Satires attributed to Mead are: Anon., *The Life and Adventures of Don Bilioso de L'Estomac* (London, 1719) and 'Momophilus Carthusiensis', *A Serious Conference between Scaramouch and Harlequin* (London, 1719).

79 'Dr Andrew Tripe' [William Wagstaffe], *Dr Woodward's Ghost* (London, 1748), p. 1. All parties to the dispute were criticised in turn by Anon., *Tauronomachia: or, a description of a bloody and terrible fight between two champions, Taurus [Mead: the bull]* and *Onos [Woodward: the donkey]* (London, 1719).

80 Brown, *Physick lies a Bleeding*, pp. 27–30.

81 Anon., Ballad to tune of 'You cut purses all' (Dublin, 1725?).

82 See Stephens and George (eds.), *Catalogue of . . . Satires*, vol. 3, pt 2, no. 3797 'The rapacious quack' (c.1760) and vol. 6, no. 8050 'How merrily etc.' (1791).

On medical profits, see also ibid., vol. 8, no. 9794 'The quack doctor's prayer!!' (1801) and vol. 8, no. 10896 'The sailor and the quack doctor!!' (1807?).

83 R. Cumberland, *False Impressions: a comedy* (London, 1797), p. 3.

84 Anon., *Hell in an Uproar, occasioned by a Scuffle . . . between the Lawyers and the Physicians for Superiority . . .* (London, 1700).

85 From J. Kenney, *Love, Law and Physic: a farce in two acts* (London, 1812), in *British Theatre, with Remarks Biographical and Critical*, ed. J. Cumberland (London, 1829), vol. 23, p. 33.

86 J. Swift in *The Tatler: by Isaac Bickerstaff Esq.*, no. 71 (20–22 Sept. 1709).

87 W. Somerville, *The Chace: a poem* (London, 1735), p. 33.

88 G.A. Rhodes, *Professional Poems: by a professional gentleman* (Wolverhampton, 1827), p. 66. Compare with Wackford Squeers in C. Dickens, *The Life and Adventures of Nicholas Nickleby* (London, 1838/9).

89 See F. Reynolds, *The Will: a comedy, in five acts* (London, 1797), passim, incl. pp. 41–5 for the drunken Veritas.

90 See C. Bell [C. Brontë] (ed.), *Jane Eyre: an autobiography,* (London, 1847), vol. 2, p. 50. Charlotte's sister Anne Brontë similarly satirised the mediocrity and heartlessness of the employing classes in *Agnes Grey: a novel* (London, 1847).

91 Stephens and George (eds), *Catalogue of . . . Satires*, vol. 5, no. 6157 (1782).

92 W. Rice, *The Rutland Volunteer Influenza'd: or, a receipt to make a patriot, a soldier, or a poet* (London, 1783), p. 6.

93 See e.g. Stephens and George (eds), *Catalogue of . . . Satires*, vol. 7, no. 9221 'Lobsters for the ladies: i.e. jessamin soldiers, or a veteran corps going on duty' (1798).

94 C. Macklin, *Love à la Mode* (1759), in *Four Comedies by Charles Macklin*, ed. J.O. Bartley (Sidgwick & Jackson, London, 1968), p. 46.

95 V.W. Turner, *The Ritual Process: structure and anti-structure* (Penguin, Harmondsworth, 1974), passim, esp. p. 193.

96 G.J., *Every Man his Own Lawyer: or, a summary of the laws of England* (London, 1736). This was produced by the compiler Giles Jacob (1686–1744), whom Pope dubbed a veritable 'Blunderbuss of Law' in *The Dunciad* (1728/9): see J. Butt (ed.), *The Poems of Alexander Pope* (Methuen, London, 1968 edn), p. 409. See also Anon., *The Lawyer's Magazine: or, . . . repository of practical law . . . by a Society of Gentlemen of the Middle Temple* (London, 1773); Anon., *Every Man his Own Proctor: . . . by a gentleman of Doctors Commons* (London, 1786); and J. Gifford (ed.), *The Complete English Lawyer: or, every man his own lawyer* (London, 1820).

97 Anon., *Every Man his own Physician: being a complete collection of efficacious remedies . . .* (London, 1787).

98 J. Wesley, *Primitive Physick: or, an easy and natural method of curing most diseases* (London, 1747), p. x. For a medical counterblast, see W. Hawes, M.D., *An Examination of the Revd Mr John Wesley's Primitive Physic: shewing that a great number of the prescriptions . . . are formed on ignorance of the medical art* (London, 1780).

99 Anon., *Every Man his Own Parson* (Bristol, 1851).

100 I. Illich, 'Disabling professions', in idem and others, *Disabling Professions* (Marion Boyars, London, 1977), pp. 11–39.

4

LAWYERS

I have read of your Golden Age, your Silver Age, etc. One might
justly call this the Age of the Lawyers.[1]

In 1712, the Scottish physician and wit John Arbuthnot put that dictum
sardonically into the mouth of his fictional John Bull – a frustrated litigant
who came to be adopted as the stereotype of sturdy English common
sense. The comment recorded a phenomenon of the times. With the
abolition of the royal prerogative courts in the seventeenth century, there
was a surge in the quantity and range of business entrusted to the common
lawyers. These experts were not only caricatured in the satirical prints of
the day; but they were often genuinely disliked. For example, in 1732 Sarah
Byng Osborn, an aristocratic widow coping with an encumbered estate,
wrote despairingly in a private letter of her dealings with the lawyers:
'Nobody that has not experience of the delays of that profession can
imagine the plague of them . . . I have bought my experience dear.'[2]

Nonetheless, clients in large numbers continued to use lawyers – even
if only to combat other lawyers. The profession did not show any signs of
faltering under the harsh public scrutiny. On the contrary, in the eighteenth and early nineteenth centuries, the lawyers collectively strengthened
their numbers and powers. In addition, they consolidated the unwritten
conventions that distributed business between attorneys and barristers.
And from 1740 onwards a group of London attorneys began the crucial
process of professional self-regulation.

Despite some hazards, therefore, lawyers were a confident social group.
They were encouraged by the high constitutional reputation of the 'law'
itself. Legal knowledge had wide-reaching scope and principles. 'In
England, Law is the paramount Science, and may be said to include all
others: it is dignified by an importance that no other profession, or science,
can reach', asserted a bullish observer in 1805.[3] By no means everyone
would have agreed with this claim. Moreover, its author was himself a
stern critic of the legal profession in action. But the law also conferred
respect upon those with the key to its mysteries. 'If it be true, that Liberty

is established by the Laws of *England*, our Freedom must then depend upon the Knowledge, Capacity, Integrity and Courage of the Professors of the Law, as well as upon the Virtue and Incorruption of the Legislature', wrote an anonymous commentator in 1759.[4] The eminent barrister and Whig politician, John Dunning, conceded in 1779 that: 'Our profession is generally ridiculed, as being dry and uninteresting.' Yet he argued that it enshrined a high cause, since the law 'has the good of the people for its basis, and the accumulated wisdom and experience of ages for its improvement'.[5] It was an avocation 'worthy of a Scholar and a Gentleman', a 1747 guidebook concurred.[6]

Nor was this merely persiflage for public consumption. Many lawyers probably did think that their profession contributed to the general good of society. By assisting in the implementation of law, they were part of the unwritten constitution. Thus when the judges and barristers travelled around the country on circuit, they were greeted as dignitaries of importance. A lawyer in 1830 recorded the excitement he felt as a young man when the Assizes came to town: 'It appeared to me, that a barrister must be the happiest person in existence. I have heard of boys and men who panted for the red or the blue coat, but to be clad in a long and flowing robe of a counsel, and to have a wig curling over my shoulders, appeared to me this earth's supremest felicity.'[7] Those emotions were recalled after the event and may have been exaggerated or fictionalised. Nonetheless, it suggests that the public welcome accorded to the men of law may have encouraged some aspirants to join the profession.

Some others were positively idealistic about the potential of legal expertise. An enthusiastic expression of this viewpoint was penned in a private letter from a young man of seventeen, who was articled to a country attorney. Writing to his father in February 1793, William Henry Ebenezer Pattisson confessed that the lengthy training was generating both idealism and headaches:

> Dear Sir,/ I think it my duty to endeavor [sic] to promote the happiness of society as far as possible & I know not in what manner I would more willingly undertake to do so than by studying the Law. The Law seems rather an abstruse Profession & it will undoubtedly require much time & study to become a Proficient in it. I must say I think I like it extremely & I hope custom will render the long confinement at my desk more & more consonant to my health, for now & then my head aches extremely.[8]

Knowledge of the law did indeed entail a lot of hard, detailed and sometimes stultifying study. The Tory politician and occasional poet, George Canning, had trained for the bar as a young man. Depressed by the experience, he penned a mournful verse about beginners who were 'condemn'd 'midst gothic tomes to pore'. As the result of such 'dull toil', he revealed that the 'indignant mind' was often tempted to wander.[9] Nonetheless, countless young lawyers were eventually initiated into an exclusive corpus of knowledge, whose intricacies were difficult for outsiders to grasp. That brought them not only status but also clients who needed guidance through the maze.

Law was already well established as a specialist subject of study. In this period, it was extensively developed and systematised. That happened in the case of the two distinctive legal traditions within Britain. In England and Ireland, the law was based upon a complex admixture of parliamentary statute and interpretative case law, while the separate 'Scots law', which continued unchanged even after political Union in 1707, was based upon Roman (civil) law as partially modified by English case law.[10] A number of eminent jurists began to provide textbooks. In Scotland, for example, Sir George Mackenzie founded an Advocates Library at Edinburgh (1682) and wrote the seminal *Institutions of the Law of Scotland* (1691).[11] This tome was later updated into a classic. Indeed, John Erskine's extended *Institute of the Law of Scotland* (published posthumously in 1773) and especially his shorter *Principles of the Law of Scotland* (1754), known as the 'little Erskine', remained in use as standard textbooks until well into the twentieth century.[12]

Similarly, in England, Sir Matthew Hale's famous summaries were published posthumously and at first anonymously as *The History of the Common Law* and *Analysis of the Law* (both 1713). These became standard works for several decades. But they were then decisively superseded by the magisterial Sir William Blackstone, who became Oxford's first Vinerian Professor of Law in 1756.[13] His four-volume *Commentaries* (1765–9) set out to analyse England's common law not merely as a corpus of precedents but as a set of principles that had evolved as an intrinsic part of English history. This study enjoyed instant fame, followed by immense long-term success.[14] The authorised text went into many editions and was popularised by countless handbooks throughout the English-speaking world. His arguments also attracted close attention in Ireland, where the legal system had many similarities with that of England.[15] Thus in 1780 Ayres's Blackstone-derived analysis (1780) made a nationalist case for Ireland's claims to legal autonomy.[16]

There were also numerous less famous works to guide the legal practitioner.[17] One example was William Bohun's handbook for *The Practising Attorney* (1724), which ran to 552 closely packed pages. The law reports of the seventeenth-century jurist Sir Edward Coke were also much consulted and in 1742 an enterprising poet put these into rhyme: the verses were laboured but they offered a mnemonic device for learning by rote.[18] Specialist conveyancers meanwhile could consult W. West's staple *Symboleographia* (1590 and many later editions) or J. Walthoe's *Modern Conveyancer: or conveyancing improved* (1697). And another poet managed another improbable feat: in 1821 the rules of conveyancing were made available for lawyers to read in verse.[19] Most prolific of all was the man dubbed by Alexander Pope as the 'Blunderbuss of Law'. Giles Jacob edited at least twenty-six different tomes, from specialist works such as *The Law Military* (1719) and *Lex Mercatoria: Or, the Merchant's Companion* (1718), to the encyclopedic *New Law-Dictionary* (1729), which was enlarged by T.E. Tomlins in 1795 and still in print in 1835.[20]

This accumulating stock of knowledge moreover had an immense range of practical applications. The barristers or 'upper branch' of the profession increasingly specialised in litigation, although they were also engaged in a variety of non-contested legal business. In addition, a small number of civil lawyers continued to concentrate upon business pertaining to the church and Admiralty courts.[21] Meanwhile, the great majority of attorneys, who constituted the 'lower branch' of the profession, were not confined to matters that led to litigation. They not only briefed barristers for court cases but also acted as family advisers, drew up wills, deeds and marriage settlements, witnessed oaths, audited accounts, held manorial courts, clerked for public bodies and acted as property conveyancers.[22] In addition, some were *de facto* election agents for patrons who had political interests in a parliamentary borough.[23] And others managed landed estates for owners who did not have the time or inclination to undertake this task for themselves. For example, that role eventually brought in much business for the quondam idealist William Pattisson, who later became the trusted agent for the DuCanes of Braxted Park in Essex.[24]

Furthermore, many attorneys acted as financial intermediaries, lending money, discounting bills of exchange, organising mortgages, collecting debts and functioning as informal deposit bankers. That made them significant players in the money markets, with sizeable sums to invest for themselves and their clients.[25] Thus, while in the early eighteenth century the number of contested civil cases before the English courts was very much lower than the proportionately all-time high of a century earlier,[26] that did not mean that the legal profession suffered a corresponding slump in business. Far from it. Not only did they deal with many disputes that did not end in court, but the attorneys in particular also carried out an immense array of other administrative and legal tasks, including many that were later undertaken by specialist bankers or land stewards.

All this gave lawyers extensive knowledge of the world. Some indeed felt that their information could go too far. The Liverpool attorney and reformer, William Roscoe, found himself saddened by the machinations of his clients. He wrote to his wife in a private letter, sometime before his early retirement from practice in 1796: 'I am almost disgusted with my profession, as it affords me a continual opportunity of observing the folly and villany [sic] of mankind.'[27] Later in 1830 Sir George Stephen, a scion of a famous legal family, sagely advised attorneys not to be too trusting when dealing with the public: 'Attention must be profound, but credulity scarce; never believe above half of what an angry client may say, but most patiently endure the whole of it.'[28] It meant that a certain amount of scepticism became an occupational hazard.

However, it was the lawyers' faults that were generally on public parade and eventually prompted various reforms. The first change was the abolition of the old custom that required legal business to be conducted in the impenetrability of law-Latin. This popular reform had already been introduced briefly between 1650 and 1660. But at the Restoration the old system was restored. Within a few decades, public resentment also returned. Lawyers were accused of mystification by concealing their trade in an alien tongue. Eventually two petitions from Yorkshire magistrates won a sympathetic hearing from Parliament. In 1731 it legislated to obviate the 'many and great Mischiefs' of law-Latin. The Act provided that after 25 March 1733 all proceedings in England's law courts (other than the Admiralty) and in Scotland's Exchequer courts were to be conducted and recorded in English.[29] For good measure, the Act added that law reports must be inscribed in full rather than abbreviated. Here, however, tradition survived and short phrases such as 'crim. con.' for 'criminal conversation' (adultery) continued defiantly in use.

Legislation of this nature showed that the British Parliament – almost 11 per cent of whose members at that date were practising lawyers[30] – was prepared to countenance moderate reform. The opposition of the Lord Chief Justice was overruled.[31] On the other hand, the 1731 statute was cautious and in 1733 it was given a yet more conservative gloss. A clarifying Act decided that the Exchequer need not use English but could keep the 'antient Method and Practice'; and another Act, also in 1733, conceded that lawyers could retain certain technical terms in Latin.[32] Thus *habeas corpus* did not become have-his-carcase (as Dorothy Sayers later splendidly rendered it) but remained *habeas corpus*. Although the language of law had been 'Englished', it retained its own esoteric style and often archaic vocabulary. That continued to bond lawyers together, while bemusing the public.

The precise number who shared in these mysteries was not recorded. Custom did, however, enforce a gender qualification. Throughout the eighteenth and early nineteenth centuries, all professional lawyers were men. Sometimes women supervised their own legal business and gave private advice. In the American colonies, a few were also attorneys.[33] But within the British Isles women did not act publicly on behalf of clients. Their exclusion was initially enforced by custom, although it was later enshrined for many years in the rules of the Law Society. Thus, in 1851, there were only a handful of female clerks in the courts. Only in 1911 was the British census first able to record any women lawyers.[34]

Meanwhile, the uncounted thousands of legal brethren in the eighteenth

The PRACTISING ATTORNEY: *Or,*

A Declaration of Slander, *for Words ſpoken againſt a* Lord.

Midd. ſ. Prehonorabilis *A.* Comes *B.* un' Procerum &
Magnat' hujus Regni *Magn' Britann',* qui tam pro Domino
Rege quam pro Seipſo ſeqr' Quer' de *C D.* in Cuſtod' Marr'
Mareſc. pro eo videlicet quod cum idem *A.* Comes *B.* (tali
die & Anno) & diu antea & continue poſtea hucuſque fuit
un' Proc' & Magn' hujus Regn' & vocem & locum in Parliament' diſti Dom' Reg. nunc *Magn' Britann'* ut un' Procerum hujus Regni habuit & adhuc habet præd' tamen *C D.*
Machinans & Malitioſe intendens contra form' Stat' in hu'-
moi caſu nuper edit' & proviſ. Magnum Scandalum excitare
de pred' comitem & al' Proceres & Magnates & al' Subditos
diſti Dom' Reg. hujus Regni *Magn' Britann'* oriri poſſin
pred' die & Anno ſupradiſt' apud, *&c.* in Com' pred' habens
Colloquium cum quodam *E F.* de et concernen' pred' Co-
mite hec falſa fiſta Scandaloſa & opprobrioſa Anglicana
verba ſequen' in preſentia & auditu diverſor' diſti Dom'
Reg. nunc fidel' Subditorum ad tunc & ib'm falſo Malitioſe & Scandaloſe dixit retulit Propalavit & Publicavit,
viz. the Earl of B. (pred' Com' innuendo) *is a pitiful Man,*
and no Body will take his Word for any Thing; and Men of Re-
putation value him (pred' Com' iterum innuendo) *no more than*
I (Seipſum *C D.* modo Defendentem innuendo) *value the*
Dirt of the Streets. Quorum quidem falſor' fiſtor' & Scan-
daloſor' Anglicanor' verbor' diccon' propalacon' Publica-
con' & Affirmacon' pretextu idem Comes maxim' Honoris
& Eſtimacon' ſuor' apud Proceres & Magnates pred' & alios
diſt' Dom. Reg. nunc Subditos leſione ſubijt & paſſus eſt
acetiam Diſplicentia diſt' Dom. Reg. erga prefat' Comitem
necnon Diverſa Magna Diſcordia & Scandala infra hoc
Reg. *Magn. Britann.* inter ipſum Com' & diverſos alios
Proc' & Magn' & alios ſubdit' diſt' Dom. Reg. hujus Regn'
oriuntur ac indies magis Magiſque occaſione prediſta oriri
veriſimilia ſunt in Magnam perturbacon' Tranquillitatis
hujus Regn', *&c.* in diſt' Dom' Reg' nunc contempt' & ipſius comitis Magn' Scandal' & gravamen & contra formam
Stat. pred'. Ad Dampnu' ipſius Com' qui tam pro, *&c.*
1000 *l.* Et inde idem Comes tam pro *G H.* quam pro
Seipſo producit Sectam, *&c.*

In Aſtions of *Scandalum Magnatum,* the Plaintiff may
proſecute in the Name of the King, and in his own Name;
and ſo he ſhall recover Damages; and the Defendant be
otherwiſe

Figure 4.1 Extract from Bohun's handbook 'The Practising Attorney' (1724). Before 1731,
legal proceedings were conducted in Latin. This specimen writ of Scandalum
Magnatum (slander) was confusing to clients, since the only words in English were
those of the alleged slander. And even after 1731 legal language remained
cumbersome
Photograph by permission of the British Library (ref. 1130 e.17)

century were difficult to control or supervise. Theoretically, there were safeguards against knavish lawyers. All those transacting legal business in England and Wales had to be enrolled in an appropriate law court, as specified since 1402 – attorneys in the common law courts and solicitors in Chancery. Hence a defaulter could be 'struck from the rolls'. But in practice the system was not operated strictly. An observer in 1724 explained that: 'None are to be *admitted* Attornies in Courts of Record, but such as have been brought up in the said Courts, or are well skill'd in soliciting of Causes, and of an honest Disposition.' But he added: 'NB. All this is very good, but the greatest part of it is wholly disregarded.'[35] In 1697, the Earl of Rochester (son of Clarendon, Charles II's Lord Chancellor) had attempted to reform the system. But that plan failed, as did similar bids in 1701 and 1706 which sought not only to regulate but also to reduce the number of attorneys.[36]

By the 1720s, anxiety was escalating. In 1725 Parliament decreed that convicted perjurers and forgers were to be debarred from acting as an attorney or solicitor in England and Wales (but not in Scotland), with a penalty of seven years transportation.[37] Then in 1729 followed the single most important piece of legislation affecting the eighteenth-century legal profession. This reform was also prompted by a petition from Yorkshire and given discreet help from the Walpole administration. The 1729 Act 'for the better Regulation of Attornies and Solicitors' made a serious attempt to clarify the mechanisms of control.[38] After 1 December 1730, all would-be attorneys were to be examined by a judge. He was to accept only honest men who had served a five-year articled clerkship with an enrolled lawyer (each lawyer being restricted to two clerks). If endorsed, the neophyte then promised: 'I, A.B. do swear, That I will truly and honestly demean myself in the Practice of an Attorney [or Solicitor] according to the best of my Knowledge and Ability. *So help me God.*'

That entitled the applicant to enrolment and he was free to practice, with the penalty of disqualification if detected in wrongdoing. This legislation also promoted a fusion of 'lower branch', since the 1729 Act empowered attorneys to act as solicitors without an additional fee, and later in 1750 another Act permitted solicitors to act as attorneys, on the same terms.[39] Thus the law established the articled clerkship as the first step on a unified professional path.

Parliament's willingness to legislate for modest reform was notable. It shows that the British government was not completely non-interventionist in its attitude towards the professions. But equally the *ad hoc* nature of these reforms indicates that there was no systematic policy. Moreover, the legislative bark of a statute was often louder than its administrative bite. As a result, the British system produced a compromise between the forces of regulation and those of *laissez faire* – if at the cost of some confusion.

Even after 1729 the vetting process remained haphazard. Judges had other matters to preoccupy them. Moreover, they did not employ attorneys and solicitors and had no direct interest in their behaviour. Hence, as long as the due fees were paid to the court, the scrutiny could be very casual. Two controversial cases were reported in 1757. One involved an attorney's footman, who had surreptitiously obtained enrolment. Both master and servant were struck from the rolls. The other involved a turnkey in King's Bench gaol who was articled as a clerk to help a lawyer get business from the prisoners. That was too scandalous. Upon complaint, it was ruled that life as a gaoler was 'a very improper education for the profession of an Attorney' and the articles were cancelled.[40]

Numerous candidates, however, seem to have been allowed through without close scrutiny. At least one noted his surprise and gratification at the ease of the process.[41] The real-life William Hickey had not been a studious clerk. He was nervous when his enrolment was arranged by his attorney father in 1775. Invited to breakfast by a friendly judge, the 26-year-old Hickey was too terrified to eat the French rolls and muffins that were on offer. Then – anticlimax. The judge's cross-examination was superficial in the extreme: 'He asked me how I liked the Law, how long I had been out of my clerkship, and two or three other questions equally unimportant.' After that, the court formalities went smoothly and, upon payment of the necessary fees and tips, Hickey was launched as a lawyer.

Others, however, managed to bypass completely the hurdles of formal clerkship and enrolment. These men were 'irregulars' in the profession – denounced as 'pettyfoggers', 'hedge attorneys', 'Wapping attorneys' (if from anywhere near east London) or 'understrappers' (underlings). The writer and magistrate Henry Fielding penned a hostile sketch of such a character in 1742:

> This *Scout* was one of those Fellows, who without any Knowledge of the Law, or being bred to it, take upon them, in defiance of an Act of Parliament, to act as Lawyers in the Country . . . They are the Pests of Society, and a Scandal to a Profession, to which indeed they do not belong, and which owes to such kind of Rascallions the Ill-will which weak Persons bear towards it.[42]

The novelist Eliza Haywood followed suit in 1751. She depicted another scoundrel 'understrapper in the law, one who knew all those quirks and evasions, which are called the knavish part of it'.[43] Since this character was cunning and impoverished, he was ready to cut every legal corner to earn a fee from his clients.

No doubt, there were real-life counterparts to these shady characters. However, by the nature of things, there is little hard evidence on their activities. The number of 'irregulars' was unknown, although they may have run into the thousands. They certainly left no working papers. It is difficult therefore to know whether they were much more machiavellian than their respectable fellows, and, if so, by how much. Instead, the role of the understrappers indicates that there was a demand for cheap legal services. Thus a reformer in 1795 claimed that all attorneys were low-grade men, frequenting taverns and fomenting strife among the topers in order to turn minor affrays into costly lawsuits: 'Many a golden harvest have they reaped from the epithets – *thief – swindler – liar* &c – or *exchanged blows*, when the parties were overheated and in liquor.'[44] That was a hostile account but it suggested that lawyers could find clients even among the less well-to-do. For the poorly educated and especially for the illiterate, a pettyfogger could be a welcome intermediary to the world of written words. Thus, while the charge in 1732 for serving a writ was the not inconsiderable sum of 5s. some 'hedge attorneys' charged as little as 3d. or 6d. for writing a letter.[45] In that way, the otherwise uninitiated got cheap access to the power of the written word, and the understrappers got their fee.

It meant that legal services were by no means available only to the very wealthy. It is sometimes argued that lawyers in this period – like the other professional groups – were essentially dependent upon the landed interest for their business. But that was not true. Lawyers did of course assist landowners. Sizeable numbers, however, also provided services for wealthy businessmen and many other 'middling' families in the towns, while the cheapest understrappers and 'hedge attorneys' aimed at an even humbler clientele, including desperate prisoners in gaol. Lawyers cannot therefore be regarded simply as a set of 'hangers-on' to the aristocracy. Already by 1700 the 10,000 people engaged in law (according to King's estimates) were far too numerous and some were too lowly to be employed exclusively or chiefly by an elite of 4,600 lords, baronets, knights and esquires.[46] Instead, lawyers increasingly saw themselves as a separate and self-referential professional group with their own separate interests, attitudes and codes of behaviour.

At the same time, the proliferation of numbers put pressure on the upholding of professional standards. No-one knew exactly how many lawyers there were. Wildly exaggerated totals such as 20,000, 60,000 or even 100,000 were sometimes claimed by contemporaries in the early eighteenth century.[47] Jonathan Swift wrote fastidiously that lawyers were almost as plentiful as verminous 'Caterpillars'.[48] There certainly had been a long process of growth throughout the seventeenth century. Whereas in the 1560s the legal profession in England and Wales had accounted for no more than about 500 practitioners, there were by 1640 at least 400 active barristers and some 1,750 enrolled attorneys in King's Bench and Common Pleas plus still more in other courts.[49] By the 1690s, as already noted, Gregory King estimated that 10,000 men made their living from law. He was referring to everyone from senior judges to junior law clerks. But his total must have included many thousand attorneys, which does confirm that a surge of growth had occurred in the later seventeenth century.

Enrolments under the new regulating legislation of 1729 also support that view.[50] All the respectable members of the 'lower branch' hastened to renew their credentials. Between 1729 and 1731, the judges on progress in England and Wales enrolled as many as 10,183 legal practices in the various law courts. Most of them were admitted into the central law courts, but Table 4.1 shows that a small proportion (5.65 per cent) were processed in the regional courts.

Table 4.1 Attorney enrolments before the law courts, England and Wales, 1729–31*

	Total	% of total
Westminster courts		
Chancery Petty Bag	2,572	25.26
Chancery	1,699	16.68
Common Pleas	2,983	29.29
King's Bench	1,157	11.36
Exchequer	1,198	11.76
	9,609	94.35
Regional courts		
Welsh Counties sessional courts	261	2.56
Lancashire Palatine courts	305	3.01
Newcastle upon Tyne Court of Record	8	0.08
	574	5.65
Total Westminster & regional courts	10,183	100.00
Number of enrolled individuals	4,825	
Mean number of enrolments per individual	2.11	

Sources: Enrolments by 16 March 1729/30 from Anon., *Lists*, pp. 1–35; and subsequent enrolments by 17 March 1730/1 in Anon., *Additional Lists*, pp. 1–260
Note: * At the time of enrolment under the new legislation, many lawyers took the precaution of enrolling their names before more than one court of law

Nevertheless, there were fewer individual attorneys and solicitors than the grand total implied. Many lawyers enrolled before more than one court. Abraham Radcliffe junior, from Birstall in Yorkshire, provides an example. He was accepted not only as an attorney in the Court of Common Pleas but also as a solicitor in the Courts of Exchequer, Chancery and Petty Bag. Discounting duplicates, therefore, a net total of 4,825 attorneys and solicitors can be identified. Since an additional number of the shadier legal fish escaped the trawl, it implies that the lower branch of the law may have totalled perhaps 5,500 to 6,000 by the early 1730s. That was indeed a dramatic increase from the number a century earlier.

Of these 4,825 individual attorneys and solicitors, 1,610 or 33.4 per cent of the total gave addresses in greater London (including Westminster, the

City, Middlesex and Southwark), while 3,185 others (66 per cent) lived in the provinces and a cautious 30 (0.6 per cent) gave no address.[51] These were the respectable members of the profession – ubiquitous and publicly recorded. At the same time, however, each lawyer was designated as a 'Gentleman' in the enrolments. That indicated their status, ranking above the toiling masses. Indeed, many lawyers preferred to describe themselves – quite legitimately – as 'gentlemen' rather than as attorneys or solicitors. That avoided the disdain that legal hacks could attract. Dr Johnson in 1770, for example, reportedly said of someone who had just left that: 'He did not care to speak ill of any man behind his back, but he believed the gentleman was an *attorney*.'[52] Thus reputable lawyers often avoided the term. As a result, many eighteenth-century occupational listings obscured the true size of the legal profession. For example, in Norwich at the 1734 parliamentary election no freeman voter called himself an 'attorney'. However, the East Anglian regional capital was not without access to legal expertise. The 1729–31 enrolments named thirty attorneys and solicitors in Norwich. Moreover, a detailed cross-check confirms that twenty two of these thirty men did indeed cast their vote in 1734 – but each was styled as 'Gentleman' without divulging an occupation.[53]

Respectability was indeed the desideratum and that could not be achieved without some regulation within the profession. Otherwise it was too easy for any enterprising fellow to set up in practice and deceive clients with some weighty law tomes and a smattering of jargon. After 1729, however, the process of enrolment began to curb the headlong expansion. A formal articled clerkship, after all, required the financial outlay of an initial fee of anything from £10 to £500.[54] It also took time to become established: five years humdrum training in articles and several years after that for maturity, 'the Generality of People not being over-fond of very young Attorneys', as the occupational handbook advised candidly in 1747.[55]

Nonetheless, even after lengthy training, there was still scope for chicanery. Critics in 1724 and again in 1795 published frank itemisations of the all too many strategems for gulling the public.[56] Moreover, even the most respectable lawyer's capacity to charge fees for 'invisible' services was a genuine source of unease. Some critics called for a drastic reduction in the size of the profession. The nation's 'commercial Community' was harmed by the spiralling cost of law, urged one tract that called in 1750 for regulation and fresh curbs.[57] The whole country suffered from the 'pestiferous Swarm' of attorneys, agreed another in 1785, proposing implausibly that numbers be cut to a maximum of 600.[58]

Regulation of good practice, however, came eventually not from Parliament but from within the profession. A group of London attornies and solicitors in February 1740 founded a 'Society of Gentlemen Practisers in the Courts of Law and Equity', indicating firmly by that name their claim to good standing. The association was run as a club, with convivial meetings in taverns and coffee-houses. One early venue was the aptly named Devil Tavern at Temple Bar – the site today commemorated by a plaque. The Society was only small, with perhaps 200 fee-paying members by the 1770s. But from the start it accepted the need for professional monitoring. It resolved 'to detect and discountenance all male [= bad] and unfair practice'.[59] Thus the Society vetted candidates for enrolment in the law courts, monitored legal changes that affected the profession, and lobbied Parliament on a wide range of legal issues. By 1792, it called itself simply the 'Law Society'.[60]

Lofty judges and barristers who sniped at the 'lower branch' were quickly rebuked. When one Sergeant Davy alleged in 1766 that barristers' mistakes were overwhelmingly due to poor briefing by attornies, the Society made a fuss. As a result, it received a full apology in February 1767. The chastened Sergeant regretted his 'unguarded and very improper expression'.[61] This prompt action asserted that the 'lower branch' was part of one legal profession.

Above all, the Society won two crucial demarcation disputes. That consolidated the attorneys' business terrain. In the first contest, the Society was on the side of liberalisation against restrictive barriers. The City of London Scriveners' Company – advised by its attorney one Jeremiah Bentham – tried to sustain a monopoly of conveyancing within the City's jurisdiction. From 1749 onwards, the Society waged a long campaign against that, in a series of test cases. Interestingly, a number of barristers assisted, giving their services free 'on behalf of the whole profession of law'. And in 1760 the Society won.[62] Thereafter the attorneys became the main agents for property conveyancing. Indeed they in turn were granted a national monopoly over this work by a clause in a regulatory statute of 1804.[63] Then it was the attorneys' turn to complain when untrained interlopers attempted to act as conveyancers.

Demarcation rather than liberalisation was the issue at stake in the second rumbling dispute conducted by the Society of Gentlemen Practisers. The custom in England was hardening that only barristers, as the 'upper branch' of the profession, were permitted to address the courts of law. In Scotland, by contrast, the dividing line was drawn differently. There, solicitors were entitled to plead at the bar of the lower courts, while the Faculty of Advocates monopolised the higher ones. In England, however, there was a recompense. Attornies and solicitors argued that only they were entitled to deal directly with clients. Thus in 1761, the buoyant Society resolved to prosecute any barrister who breached that rule.[64] This caused some initial dissension. However, before long, the two branches accepted the demarcation, which was based upon custom rather than law.[65] The effect was to establish two adjacent monopolies within one profession – a state of affairs that has survived repeated criticisms and is still proving highly resistant to change.

As regulation and enrolment began to control the profession and control the expansion of numbers, so their collective sense of identity was enhanced. Critics remained vocal but the lawyers were clearly not going to disappear. Responding to that a venturesome apothecary in 1776 decided to provide a handbook to the profession. John Browne's *General Law List* (1776–98) enjoyed a 'most rapid and extensive Sale', according to the happy editor in 1787.[66] It marked the start of a regular series, as it was followed by Hughes's *New Law List* (1798–1802) and by Clarke's *New Law List* (1803–40), which became the *Law List* of modern times (1841–1976). These early listings were not perfect. They generally omitted the nefarious understrappers, although it was alleged that some unqualified men had sent their names to the compiler.[67] For example, in 1780 the *General Law List* named 3,666 attorneys, of whom 1,236 (33.7 per cent) resided in 'greater' London and another 2,430 (66.3 per cent) in the rest of England and Wales. That underestimated the total number in the profession, although it did show that the headlong expansion had been braked. But the list offered not a complete census but geographical points of access.[68] Thus a traveller in Cumberland could ascertain that the small town of Cockermouth (population c. 2,500) housed at least eight resident lawyers, including one John Wordsworth, the father of the poet.

Practices were generally at this time run by individual lawyers, with a clerk or two in the office. But there were also some burgeoning law partnerships, not infrequently composed of a father and son. Such partnerships were relatively most common in the metropolis, as Table 4.2 indicates.

Table 4.2 Attorneys in England and Wales working singly and in partnerships,[1] 1780

Attorneys	Listed singly	Listed in two-men partnership	Listed in three-men partnership	Total
Metropolitan London[2]	958 (77.5%)	260 (21.0%)	18 (1.5%)	1,236 (100%)
Rest of England and Wales	2,213 (91.1%)	214 (8.8%)	3 (0.1%)	2,430 (100%)
Total	3,171 (86.5%)	474 (12.9%)	21 (0.6%)	3,666 (100%)

Source: Browne (ed.), *Browne's General Law-List for the Year 1780*, pp. 35–85, 86–138
Notes: 1 Partnerships listed as 'Mssrs. Smith', etc. have been counted as two attorneys and only those specifically indicating three names have been counted as threesomes
2 Metropolitan London includes the Cities of London and Westminster, the Borough of Southwark and Middlesex

Of the 1,236 London-based attorneys, 260 (21.0 per cent) worked in two-men teams – while 18 lawyers were listed as threesomes (1.5 per cent). Meanwhile, outside the capital city, a smaller proportion of practices were multiple. Of the 2,430 provincial attorneys, only 3 individuals were listed together as one firm, while another 214 (8.8 per cent) were in two-men partnerships. Notable among these was the satirically well-named firm of Messrs Friske and Wolfe, who resided in Saffron Walden.

Social visibility thus accompanied the lawyers' growing success. It also attracted the attention of the Treasury. After the short-lived poll taxes of the 1690s, the professions were not liable to any special levy, other than the standard premiums for apprenticeship indentures. However, in 1785 the Younger Pitt, himself a barrister by training, introduced an annual license for attorneys:[69] those in London/Westminster and Edinburgh were charged £5, those elsewhere £3. In 1794 there followed a heavy stamp duty of £100 upon enrolment in the Westminster courts and £50 in the regional courts.[70] The levies aroused protests. For example, Jeremy Bentham dubbed the stamp duty a *'tax upon distress'*, since it would lead to higher fees for clients. Others by contrast argued that high charges would promote the respectability of the profession by driving out the 'vile and needy pettifoggers'.[71] In the event, the stamp duties survived and were quietly raised in 1804 and again in 1815. After that, however, they were left unchanged until 1851, confirming the lawyers' taxative liability without mulcting profits too much.[72]

Throughout all this, the Society of Gentlemen Practisers had maintained a watching brief. Its early activities were often sporadic and limited in impact, although it had formalised its venue after 1772 at Clifford's Inn and later at Furnival's Inn. Yet it enshrined the principles of association and self-regulation. Significantly, too, it was matched by new provincial societies: in Bristol (1770), Yorkshire (1786), Somerset (1796), Sunderland (1800); and 14 other places in England between 1800 and 1835.[73] The advantages of self-organisation were increasingly perceived. In Ireland a brief-lived Society of Attorneys was founded in 1774, followed by the successful Law Club of Ireland in 1791.[74] In America, many colonies formed their own law societies, such as the New York lawyers' association of 1729 or the Massachusetts bar associations from the 1750s.[75] And in Scotland the influential Society of Writers of the Signet (founded 1564) was granted a royal charter in 1797, while a rival Society of Solicitors in the Supreme Courts was founded in 1784. There were also local bodies such as Glasgow's venerable Faculty of Procurators (law agents), founded in 1668 and chartered in 1796.[76] Indeed, such was their variety that a single Scottish lawyers' organisation did not emerge until the twentieth century.

Anxiety about professional practice, however, continued. In 1795, for example, another reforming lawyer, Joseph Day, proposed a Royal College of Attorneys and Solicitors to test new entrants and to regulate the membership.[77] His farsighted plan did not get support. But a generation later, a group of lawyers founded in 1825 a new London Law Institution, originally as a joint-stock company. Within a few years, in 1831 it was transformed into the Incorporated Law Institution of the United Kingdom. That quickly absorbed into its ranks the eclipsed Gentlemen Practisers.[78] And the new body assumed by custom (and, after a new charter in 1903, by law) the old name of the Law Society.

Here was a framework for a national system of supervision. By a *de facto* gentleman's agreement, which continues to this day, the new Society did not attempt to supervise the Scottish law associations, despite the fact that its name laid claim to the entire United Kingdom. Nor did it dispute with its matching institution in Ireland, the Irish Law Society, founded in 1830.[79] But within England and Wales the new body, in its imposing new headquarters in Chancery Lane, was immediately active.[80] In 1833 it instituted lectures for articled clerks. In 1836 it appointed examiners to a new Common Law Examinations Board, which set a written paper before enrolment. That notably institutionalised the hold of practising lawyers over the content of legal education.[81] Above all, in 1843 the Law Society sponsored key legislation to denominate itself, by consent of Parliament, as the registering body for all attorneys and solicitors.[82] In addition, in 1845 it changed its constitution from a joint-stock company into a voluntary association, sustained by an extensive fee-paying membership; and in 1846 it gave expert testimony to the first parliamentary enquiry into legal education.

Policing their own reputation enabled the attorneys to shed the image of low-born rascality. However Machiavellian they remained with their clients, socially they were becoming increasingly affluent members of the middle class. That did not stop Sir George Stephen from an outburst in 1846, when he described attorneys as 'inferior men, both in point of station and of education'.[83] It may have seemed so from the perspective of a solicitor who was on the brink of turning himself into a barrister (1849). But self-regulation was designed specifically to counter disparagement.

Such 'group voluntarism' on the part of the lawyers had certain similarities with both the medieval guilds and the modern trade unions. All three were non-governmental associations designed to protect the interests of specific occupational groups; and all have been roundly criticised for restrictive practices.[84] However, unlike the urban guilds, the Law Society did not operate a municipal monopoly. And, unlike the unions, its original members were self-employed, not employees. Hence the Law Society did not identify with either of these other forms of association. Instead, it stressed its own dual role. It was empowered by charter and statute not just to represent but also to register and monitor the profession. It did not operate a 'closed shop' in trade union terms, since attorneys were not obliged to become members.[85] But, with parliamentary sanction, the Law Society did operate a 'restricted shop', in the name of maintaining good service for the general public.

Professional associations in Britain gradually evolved into a hybrid format as part private society and part public institution. Much of the initiative in this case came from the lawyers themselves, under the spur of public criticism. Many of their conventions of professional etiquette were established purely by custom. But the state too played a significant part. Its tax policies and its legislation crucially helped to shape the profession at various points. No standardised blueprint, however, was contemplated. Instead, a plurality of professional associations were allowed to co-exist within the three kingdoms. Thus, while the claims of legal knowledge were strengthened as they were institutionalised in the early nineteenth century, the process was not based upon one single source of power.

Barristers followed a complementary path. As the 'lower branch' gained in status, so the 'upper branch' consolidated its supremacy. In the course of that, a mutual politeness was adopted. Barristers and judges increasingly learned not to snipe publicly at the attorneys, as Serjeant Davy had learned in 1767. Instead, the rhetoric stressed the unity of the 'one profession' – one with its own internal hierarchies but also with a shared knowledge and a common set of operating conventions. Some successful attorneys changed tracks to become barristers or even senior judges, as in the case of Lord Kenyon.[86] Family ties also bonded the profession. It was not uncommon for ambitious attorneys to send their sons to become barristers. Both branches, moreover, worked together in all cases of litigation. Attorneys were required to brief barristers and barristers were required to plead in court. Etiquette debarred any overt canvassing for business. Yet smart attorneys knew the value of contacts with barristers, just as canny barristers had long known the importance of cultivating attorneys.

Advocacy was the special art of the upper branch. Its members were distinguished in court by their dress. Barristers wore powdered wigs and long black robes – silk for senior counsel, stuff for juniors – in a style formalised in the late seventeenth century.[87] The historic order of Serjeants-at-law, who kept until 1846 a monopoly of appearing in the Court of Common Pleas, also wore a cap of white lawn.[88] Thus attired, they deployed their forensic skills. One famous preacher, James Parsons of York, was even said to woo his congregation 'as an eloquent barrister would a jury' – and Parsons had studied law in an attorney's office.[89] Oratorical styles, however, were varied. Some spoke in Ciceronian cadences, as did the 'matchless Erskine'.[90] Others preferred pure volume: 'Gristly and gruff, and coarse as Cambridge brawn,/ With lungs stentorian bawls gigantic Vaughan', ran a poetic tribute in 1825.[91] Knowledge of the technicalities was also effective, as shown by 'Starkie, than whom, none with quicker eye/ A slip, or lurking nonsuit, can espy/ Or should he fail to creep out of the flaw,/ Suggest a doubt, or raise a "point of law".'[92] In the same vein, *The Pleader's Guide* (1796) stressed the merits of appealing to recondite niceties: 'For puzzling oft becomes your duty,/ And makes Obscurity a beauty.'[93] The skills of Charles Dickens's persuasive prosecutor, Serjeant Buzfuz, fitted well within this pantheon of talents.

Trials followed strict rules of procedure to bring cases to an orderly judgement. Much was routine and highly technical, although there were some moments of drama.[94] Increasingly, from the 1730s onwards, litigants began to make use of barristers for both prosecution and defence.[95] By the later eighteenth century, it was unusual for criminal cases to be tried without specialist advocacy; and civil suits began to see the same pattern. The 'lawyerisation' of trials in turn helped to clarify the laws of evidence and to crystallise the etiquette of professional intervention.[96] For example, it was early agreed that one counsel could not appear for both sides in the same case. The unwritten convention also became firmly established in the eighteenth century that barristers could not pick and choose between the briefs that arrived before them. That was later termed the 'cab-rank rule' (although cabmen as well as lawyers have been known to breach it). It meant that every client, whether saint or sinner, was entitled to skilled advocacy, whatever the barristers' personal opinion of the merits of any case.[97] That defined the barristers' professional commitment and also provided their defence against the frequent public criticisms of the rule.

Participation in court-room procedures thus brought business and public recognition to the 'upper branch' of the legal profession. At the same time, their presence also tended to increase the average length and cost of a trial. As one sardonic observer noted in 1740, exaggerating for better emphasis:

> Formerly one or two Counsel was thought sufficient . . .; but now they are increased to such a Number, that, if it goes a little farther, we may expect to see the whole Bar, in every great Cause, drawn up in Battle array, like two Armies against each other, and . . . the Expense will be very little short of that of an Army.[98]

By the early nineteenth century, indeed, the custom had hardened into an unbreakable convention that each senior counsel should be accompanied in court by a junior. Not surprisingly, that created resentment. Winners often found the system just as costly as did losers. There were penalties, therefore, in the process of 'lawyerisation', even while it added to the dignity and good order of court-room procedures.

Dignified rituals and customs also sustained the barristers' claims to august status. Their prestige had already risen in the course of the seventeenth century.[99] They then consolidated their own way of life, their own institutions, their own habitat. All members of the 'upper branch' were required to be graduates of one of the four Inns of Court. These

Etio perpetua.

A PEEP INTO WESTMINSTER HALL ON A CALL OF SERJEANTS.

London Printed for R Sayer & J Bennett N.53 Fleet street & J. Smith N.35 Cheapside as the Act directs March 1 1781

Figure 4.2 A Peep into Westminster Hall on a Call of Serjeants (1781). This print of a fictional robing ceremony celebrated the gowned and wigged majesty of the law. Centrally, a judge invests a serjeant-at-law with a white lawn cap, which only these senior barristers were permitted to wear. The surrounding legal tribe gaze with suitable intentness, while the new candidate kneels at the judge's feet
Published by permission of the British Museum, Department of Prints and Drawings

autonomous collegiate bodies, dating from medieval times, regulated admission to the bar. They were sited in and amongst a maze of buildings, gardens, squares and alleys that constituted 'legal London', stretching from Gray's Inn via Lincoln's Inn to the Middle and Inner Temple by the riverside. The new Law Society Hall (1831) in Chancery Lane was built in its heartland. Many barristers kept chambers in or near the Inns. They also had a secondary habitat in the law courts, including the City of London's famous Old Bailey and the four high courts at Westminster (the Strand Courts were not opened until 1882). Thus during the law terms of Hilary, Easter, Trinity and Michaelmas, robed figures were habitually to be seen scurrying along the Strand between Temple and Westminster.

Outside London, furthermore, barristers frequented the regional courts and a contingent of Londoners also toured each year with the puisne (junior) judges on the Lenten and Summer circuits to conduct the provincial Assizes. These carefully scheduled progressions were greeted with much pomp. In England, there were in this period six itineraries: the Home Circuit (around London) and those to Norfolk, Oxford, the Midlands, the West and the North. A seventh contingent travelled to Wales plus Chester.[100] Ireland was similarly covered by six circuits: the Home (around Dublin), North-East, North-West, Connaught, Munster, Leinster.[101] All this further increased the social visibility of the barristers as well as their professional cohesion.

Theirs was a sociable, clubbable, self-important world. Many barristers cultivated an air of *gravitas*. The essayist Charles Lamb was himself born in the Inner Temple in 1775. As the son of a barrister's clerk, he was therefore familiar with the style. Writing of the 'Old Benchers of the Inner Temple', he mused with some disbelief: 'Lawyers, I suppose, were children once.'[102] But these august beings were ready enough to relax in the company of their fellows. Thus barristers on tour organised their own messes to arrange for dinners and conviviality. By the early nineteenth century, these groups also began informally to monitor and adjudicate their own behaviour, with fines for infractions commonly paid into the wine fund. As that happened, the circuit messes became the barristers' equivalent of the attorneys' law societies.[103] But their constitutions long remained informal, regulated only by custom. That suited the legal love of precedent and case law. It was not until 1883 that a national Bar Committee was established – the precursor of the modern Bar Council (1894) – with representatives not only from the Inns of Court but also from the circuit messes.[104]

Informality was sustained all the more readily in the eighteenth century, since the barristers remained relatively few in number. That heightened their prestige through scarcity. But no-one knew the precise total. Some gentlemen attended the Inns of Court for the social status, without obtaining any qualification. Many more were called to the bar but did not

Figure 4.3 A Limb of the Law (1802). The law also employed a vast tribe of clerks, such as this young 'limb of the law'. He looks pert and knowledgeable, as he holds his bag of barristers' briefs. Less grandly, both William Cobbett and Charles Dickens had early training as clerks in attorneys' offices
Published by permission of the British Museum, Department of Prints and Drawings

go on to practise. And others – like the Younger Pitt – had only brief legal careers. As a result, neither admissions to the Inns of Court nor the number of calls to the bar reflected the size of the active profession. It is probable, however, that there were some 300–350 working barristers in England and Wales in 1700. After that, the total declined slightly in the early eighteenth century, before slowly recovering.[105]

Growth resumed more rapidly from the 1780s onwards, as barristers extended their hold upon litigation and as consumer demand rose. The 1780 *Law List* named 257 junior barristers, 13 serjeants, 14 senior counsel and 5 law officers – a total of 289.[106] The listing was neither accurate nor comprehensive. But, allowing for errors and omissions, it suggested a working bar of some 290–300.[107] By 1805, however, the *Law List* totals had more than doubled. Then there were 690 junior barristers, 15 serjeants, and 25 seniors – in all 730. A further ninety were 'under the bar' but certificated to give legal advice.[108] Among the barristers was Thomas Trollope, the struggling equity draughtsman who was the father of the novelist. In the early nineteenth century, he was rapidly joined by many others. By 1851, England and Wales had 2,816 barristers.[109] As a result, the numerical disparity between the upper and lower branches was much reduced, since the attorneys were not by then multiplying so rapidly. (See Table 4.3.)

Competition also increased. That reduced many impecunious barristers to 'devilling' for their successful colleagues, preparing briefs at half the fee. In 1859, Charles Dickens depicted one such character in the 'fully half-insolent' Sydney Carton, the jackal to the rising lion Mr Stryver.[110] At the mid-century, there were many similar carrion-hunters. They formed the sad substratum of 'briefless barristers', known by their threadbare gowns, unpowdered wigs, and sordid chambers in the attics at the Inns of Court.

With growth and competition came eventual pressure for change of the traditional system of training. Students read for the bar at one of the four autonomous Inns of Court. There were two specialisms. Equity drafting for conveyancing and special pleading, which required a knowledge of legal technicalities and generated an 'almost universal' dislike.[111] Pupillage took seven or eight years, including attendance at a number of Inn dinners over twelve terms. In June 1762 the timetable was streamlined to three years for University graduates and five for others. That responded to the call for change made by Sir William Blackstone, who was elected Bencher of the Middle Temple in 1761.[112] There was, however, no formal programme of tuition. Some judges and counsel encouraged debate. From the 1770s onwards, too, pupils were supposed to 'read in chambers' under the supervision of an established barrister. In addition, a keen tyro could attend the informal debating clubs that met in taverns and coffee-houses near the Inns. Thus as a student in 1716, Dudley Ryder, later Walpole's Attorney General, joined one law society and yearned to join another, to which he was not invited. And in 1782/3, the Whig reformer Samuel

Table 4.3 Numbers of attorneys and barristers in Great Britain and Ireland, 1700–1851[1]

	England & Wales		Scotland[2]		Ireland[3]	
	Barristers	*Attorneys*	*Advocates*	*Others*	*Barristers*	*Attorneys*
1700	325?	?	170	?	?	?
1730	300?	at least 4,825 (ratio 1:16)	180?	?	?	?
1780	approx. 290	at least 4,000 (ratio 1:14)	180?	?	?	?
1805	approx. 730	at least 5,200 (ratio 1:7)	200?	1,600?	?	?
1851	2,816	11,350 (ratio 1:4)	220	1,832 (ratio 1:8)	840	2,428 (ratio 1:3)

Sources: Pre-1851 estimates based on estimates and contemporary law listings; 1851 census returns in *British Parliamentary Papers*, (1852/3), vol. 81/1 and (1856), vol. 31

Notes: 1 These figures refer only to the specialists and exclude the many clerks, officers, students and 'other lawyers' listed in the census under the legal profession. That means that to calculate the total size of the full profession in employment terms, the number of known barristers and attorneys at any given date should be approximately doubled, as shown by comparison with figures in Tables 2.1–2.2

2 In Scotland, the advocates had a monopoly of pleading in the highest law courts but in the lower courts they shared the task with law writers, notaries, etc; so that the dividing line between advocates and others was not the same as that between barristers and attorneys

3 Note that the English and Irish bars intercommuned, so that qualified barristers in one country were also entitled to plead at the bar of the other

Romilly as a pupil at Gray's Inn organised a small club of like-minded friends to re-enact trials.[113]

Formerly, each Inn of Court had held an elaborate system of readings, moots and exercises. Yet these procedures had either fallen into abeyance or lost meaning. The obligatory dinners in Hall provided a chance for debate and the cultivation of a communal ethos. Yet, without an educational context, these ceremonials were open to ridicule. 'A gentleman becomes learned in consequence of having eat[en] a certain quantity of mutton', sneered a critic in 1797.[114] In the eighteenth century, the oligarchic Masters of the Bench were not entirely inactive. Above all, they ensured the survival of their institutions – something that was not a foregone conclusion given their financial problems in 1700.[115] Thus the Benchers rebuilt their properties, invested their funds, expanded their libraries, and upheld their own rights of election (against rank-and-file protests at the Middle Temple in 1730). Moreover, they retained control over the old Inns of Chancery – which were once the rival institutions of the lower branch – and they kept the attorneys from membership (even though many had rooms within the precincts).[116]

Educational reforms, however, moved slowly. At Gray's Inn, the barrister Danby Pickering lectured regularly between 1753 and 1769, but the series was discontinued.[117] At the Middle and Inner Temple, there was no examination, while at Gray's and Lincoln's Inn the final exercises had become farcical. A hostile Walter Bagehot recalled that.[118] Thus the Benchers at Lincoln's Inn posed a stock case which was answered by:

> a mechanical reading of copied bits of paper, which it was difficult to read without laughing . . . If you kept a grave countenance after you had read some six words, the senior Bencher would say 'Sir, that will do'; and then the exercise was kept. But . . . if you laughed, you had to read the 'slip' all through.

Reformers in the nineteenth century were slow to make headway against the autonomous traditions of the Inns. Twice, public lectures were instituted – in 1833 and again in 1846 – and twice abandoned for want of support. Eventually, in 1851 the four Inns of Court themselves founded their own Council of Legal Education. Pupils were thenceforth required either to attend lectures or to undergo a written examination, an ordeal which was made compulsory in 1872.[119] As that happened, the Inns themselves became professionalised and the proportion of pupils who were successfully called to the bar rose steeply.[120]

Ireland followed a very similar pattern. Barristers there came under the aegis of the ancient Society of the King's Inns, which intercommuned with the English Inns. The eighteenth century saw a period of institutional decay, followed by recovery.[121] The King's Inns clung to their own traditions and were slow to accept change.[122] In 1839–42, however, the pioneering barrister Tristram Kennedy taught at a new Dublin Law Institute. And eventually, in 1850 an Irish Committee for Legal Education was founded, with lectures at the King's Inns and at Trinity College Dublin.[123] That preceded its English counterpart by a year. But in both countries, the bar's sense of its own legitimacy and its cultivation of its own traditions long preceded the processes of reform.

Scottish advocates, too, were equally confident in the value of the distinctive 'Scots law'. Chairs in the subject were founded at Glasgow and Edinburgh Universities;[124] and during the eighteenth century, the proportion of law students who remained in Scotland for their training rose dramatically.[125] A contemporary in 1714 estimated that there were as many as 200 advocates in Scotland, of whom 170 were in practice.[126] That was a high figure, compared with 300–350 barristers in the very much larger population of England and Wales. Edinburgh in particular seemed awash with lawyers. There from 1684 onwards, the Faculty of Advocates monitored admissions to the senior Court of Sessions. It also tended its fine law library, over which the philosopher David Hume presided as

Keeper from 1752 to 1757. But Scotland's legal training also showed signs of ossification over time. The stereotyped examination, which depended upon rote repetition, was a particular target of criticism. When the number of recruits grew in the early nineteenth century, complaints multiplied. After many delays the Faculty grudgingly instituted a reform committee in 1854.[127] Here as elsewhere, however, change built upon the old ways. Thus in Scotland too the structures and ethos of the bar were overhauled rather than destroyed by the Victorian reforms.

Pre-eminent over this well-entrenched profession came the judges. Seated on the bench, full-wigged and robed in crimson, girt with court-room ceremonial, and gravely pronouncing the sentence of the court – they were truly majestic figures. Technically, they were above and not of the legal profession. They no longer offered services for hire but were remunerated with official salaries, plus sundry perquisites. Judges therefore in this period always resigned from the Inns of Court upon appointment. But the judiciary was invariably chosen from among the senior barristers, who were addressed from the bench as 'Brother'.

Eighteenth-century procedures were gradually formalised into a set of professional conventions. The bedrock of judicial independence was established by law in 1701, so that judges could be dismissed only upon petition from both Houses of Parliament or after impeachment for a criminal offence.[128] The Lord Chancellor was a political appointee but retained a separate authority in legal matters. Once on the bench, judges were required to listen to counsel (some ostentatiously did not), to weigh evidence, to remain alert and awake (some also flagged here), to adjudicate on points of law, to guide barristers on procedure (some berated them too roundly), to use discretion in pronouncing sentences, and to eschew any financial interest in cases that came before them. They did that upon a regular salary, supplemented by perquisites and court fees. A High Court appointment was a freehold tenure, ended only by death or retirement. After 1799, pensions were supplied by Parliament. As a result, judges were expected not to accept bribes or *douceurs*. That was established in 1725, when Walpole's government successfully impeached Lord Chancellor Macclesfield for corruptly selling Chancery masterships. There were no more overt financial scandals, although the judges retained extensive powers of patronage. Thus the reputation of the judiciary recovered from the shadow of fiscal taint in the early Stuart era.[129]

Judges were therefore establishment figures in terms of their authority and dignity. Yet, at the same time, they represented a separate source of power within the system. In fact, the Hanoverian bench was very small in numbers, with no more than fifteen salaried judges at any one time.[130] It included, however, some distinctive figures. Legally most eminent, if politically controversial, was Lord Mansfield, whose judgements during his long stint at the Court of King's Bench (1756–88) virtually created the modern case law of insurance.[131] Others included the popular Lord Camden; the blunt Lord Kenyon; the powerful Lord Thurlow; the liberal Lord Erskine, not a great judge (despite his success as a barrister) but long toasted at Law Society dinners for raising the attorneys' fee; the intimidating Lord Eldon, that staunch bastion of conservatism; and, in Scotland, the savage Lord Braxfield, later the model for R.L. Stevenson's autocratic *Weir of Hermiston*.

Anecdotes about these personages were avidly circulated in legal circles. Such gossip interested both lesser attorneys and senior barristers. Judicial achievements were later given a scholarly memorial by the barrister John Campbell. He produced the eight-volume *Lives of the Lord Chancellors* in 1845–7 and a three-volume *Lives of the Chief Justices* in 1849–57, before himself accepting the Great Seal as Lord Chancellor (1859–61). A rival, Edward Foss, launched an alternative nine-volume *Judges of England* (1848–64) and, just to clarify the message, Campbell also published *Atrocious Judges: Lives of Judges Infamous as Tools of Tyrants and Instruments of Oppression* (1856). In that, he cited a number of examples, such as the notorious Judge Jeffreys, all dating from before 1689 – in implicit contrast with the modern bench. The 1820s and 1830s then saw some long overdue reforms, such as a streamlining of ancient legal procedures and the abolition of some obsolete offices. Judges, however, retained their august authority throughout, which in turn shed lustre upon the entire legal profession.

Critics often called – but in vain – for reform of the slow and costly law courts and a codification of law itself. Instead, it was the lawyers who controlled access to the legal system and to legal knowledge. Jeremy Bentham – the son of one attorney, the grandson of another, and himself qualified as a barrister – knew that.[132] He too denounced the 'perpetual conspiracy of lawyers against the people' (1827). The professional monopoly of the robed and bewigged experts was safeguarded by their arcane legal knowledge. 'It serves them as a fence to keep out interlopers' (1792). Hence his pithy summary (1808): 'The power of the lawyer is in the uncertainty of the law.'

NOTES

1 [J. Arbuthnot], *John Bull still in his Senses: being the third part of law is a bottomless-pit* (London, 1712), p. 27.

2 J.McClelland (ed.), *Letters of Sarah Byng Osborn (1721–73), from the Collection of the Hon. Mrs McDonnel* (Stanford University Press, Stanford, 1930), p. 13.

3 R. Holloway, *Strictures on the Characters of the Most Prominent Practising Attorneys* (London, 1805), p. 13.

4 Anon., *Reflections or Hints Founded upon Experience and Facts, touching the Law, Lawyers, Officers, Attorneys, and Others Concerned in the Administration of Justice* (London, 1759), p. 3.

5 J. Dunning, Baron Ashburton, letter of 3 March 1779, published in Anon., *A Treatise on the Study of the Law: . . . written by . . . Lords Mansfield, Ashburton, and Thurlow . . .* (London, 1797), p. 55.

6 Anon., *A General Description of All the Trades* (London, 1747), p. 6.

7 Anon., *The Life of a Lawyer, Written by Himself* (London, 1830), p. 5. Within the text, the author named himself as 'John Eagle' but his account concealed all real identities under fictional names.

8 Private family papers, quoted by permission of David Pattisson: letter from William Henry Ebenezer Pattisson (Diss, Norfolk) to Jacob Pattisson (Witham, Essex), 18 Feb. 1793.

9 'Friendship' cited in Anon. [A. Polson], *Law and Lawyers: or, sketches . . . of legal . . . biography* (London, 1840), vol. 1, p. 17.

10 Although Scotland's legal system was unchanged in 1707, its courts thenceforth came under the appellate jurisdiction of the House of Lords: J.W. Coull and E.W. Merry, *Principles and Practice of Scots Law* (Butterworth, London, 1971), pp. 6–10. For the placid contemporary acceptance of pluralism, see T.E. Tomlins (ed.), *The Law-Dictionary: explaining the rise, progress, and present state, of the English law . . .* (London, 1797), vol. 2, *sub*: 'Scotland'.

11 D.M. Walker, *The Scottish Jurists* (Green & Sons, Edinburgh, 1985), pp. 158–72.

12 Ibid., pp. 206–15.

13 H.G. Hanbury, *The Vinerian Chair and Legal Education* (Blackwell, Oxford, 1958), pp. 11–16, 18–19.

14 For Blackstone's impact, see M. Lobban, *The Common Law and English Jurisprudence, 1760–1850* (Clarendon, Oxford, 1991), pp. 12–13, 27–46; and D. Leiberman, *The Province of Legislation Determined: legal theory in eighteenth-century Britain* (Cambridge University Press, Cambridge, 1989), esp. pp. 60–7.

15 Between 1720 and 1783, appeals from Ireland went to the British House of Lords. That system was ended in 1783, but the 1800 Act of Union restored the appellate jurisdiction of the British House of Lords (thenceforth including Irish peers): see 23 Geo.III, cap. 28 (1783); and 39 & 40 Geo.III, cap. 67 (1800), 8th Article.

16 W.T. Ayres, *A Comparative View of the Differences between the English and Irish Statute and Common Law: in a series of . . . notes on the Commentaries of Sir W. Blackstone* (2 vols, Dublin, 1780).

17 See W. Holdsworth, *A History of English Law* (Methuen, London, 1938), vol. 12, pp. 101–93; and especially J.N. Adams and G. Averley (eds), *A Bibliography of Eighteenth-Century Legal Literature* (Avero Publications, Newcastle upon Tyne, 1982).

18 For example, a couplet explained Foster's case from Coke's *Fifth Report* as 'Foster, Justice of peace may warrant send/ To bring before himself such as offend': see Anon. [J. Worrall], *The Reports of Sir Edward Coke, Kt, in Verse* (London, 1742), pt 5, no. 63.

19 J. Crisp, *The Conveyancer's Guide: a poem, in two books* (London, second edn, 1821).

20 For Pope on Jacob, see above, p. 69 n. 96.

21 In 1700 there were c.500 'civilian' lawyers in England and Wales: see G. Holmes, *Augustan England: professions, state and society, 1680–1730* (Allen & Unwin, London, 1982) pp. 147–50; and G.D. Squibb, *Doctors' Commons: a history of the College of Advocates . . .* (Clarendon, Oxford, 1977), pp. 32–3, 36, 102–9.

22 See e.g. P. Aylett, 'Attorneys and clients in eighteenth-century Cheshire: a study in relationships, 1740–85', *Bulletin of John Rylands Library,* 69 (1987), pp. 326–58; R. Stewart-Brown, *Isaac Greene: a Lancashire lawyer of the eighteenth century* (Liverpool, 1921), pp. 6–25; and esp. M. Miles, '"Eminent

practitioners": the new visage of country attorneys, c.1750–1800', in *Law, Economy and Society, 1750–1914: essays in the history of English Law*, ed. G.R. Rubin and D. Sugarman (Professional Books, Abingdon, 1984), pp. 470–503, and notes pp. i–xii.

23 E.A. Smith, 'The election agent in English politics, 1734–1832', *English Historical Review*, 84 (1969), pp. 12, 17–26, 34–5; and R. Robson, *The Attorney in Eighteenth-Century England* (Cambridge University Press, Cambridge, 1959), pp. 96–103.

24 C. Shrimpton, *The Landed Society and the Farming Community of Essex in the Late Eighteenth and Early Nineteenth Centuries* (Arno, New York, 1977) pp. 123–9.

25 Examples in B.L. Anderson, 'The attorney and the early capital market in Lancashire', in *Capital Formation in the Industrial Revolution*, ed. F. Crouzet (Methuen, London, 1972), pp. 223–55; M. Miles, 'The money market in the early Industrial Revolution: the evidence from West Riding attorneys, c.1750–1800', *Business History*, 23 (1981), pp. 127–46; and P. Mathias, 'The lawyer as businessman in eighteenth-century England', in *Enterprise and History: essays in honour of Charles Wilson*, ed. D.C. Coleman and P. Mathias (Cambridge University Press, Cambridge, 1984), pp. 151–67.

26 The volume of civil cases rose again from the 1760s onwards: see statistics in C.W. Brooks, 'Interpersonal conflict and social tension: civil litigation in England, 1640–1830', in *The First Modern Society: essays in English history in honour of Lawrence Stone*, ed. A.L. Beier, D. Cannadine and J.M. Rosenheim (Cambridge University Press, Cambridge, 1989), pp. 360–7, esp. pp. 362–3.

27 H. Roscoe, *The Life of William Roscoe, by his Son Henry Roscoe* (London, 1833), vol. 1, p. 206.

28 [G. Stephen], *Adventures of an Attorney in Search of Practice* (London, 1839), p. 47.

29 4 Geo.II, cap. 26 (1731). The government gave tacit aid to this Act and the prime minister's brother, Horatio Walpole, sat on the relevant committee: *Commons' Journals, vol. 21*, 11 Feb. 1730/1.

30 74 MPs between 1727 and 1734 were lawyers, out of a total of 684 [i.e. 10.82 per cent]: see R. Sedgwick (ed.), *The House of Commons, 1715–54* (History of Parliament Trust, London, 1970), vol. 1, p. 155.

31 D. Mellinkoff, *The Language of the Law* (Little, Brown, Boston, 1963; in 1983 edn), p. 133.

32 6 Geo.II, cap. 6 and cap. 14 (both 1733): the latter Act was devised to reduce vexatious arrests but it included some clauses 'for the obviating a Doubt which has arisen' about the 1731 Act.

33 S.H. Drinker, 'Women attorneys of colonial times', in *The Legal Profession: major historical interpretations*, ed. K.L. Hall (Garland, New York, 1987), pp. 242–58.

34 W.J. Reader, *Professional Men: the rise of the professional classes in nineteenth-century England* (Weidenfeld, London, 1966), p. 181.

35 Anon., *Law Quibbles: or, a treatise of the evasions, tricks, turns and quibbles . . . used in the profession of the law . . .* (London, 1724), pp. 7–8.

36 Holmes, *Augustan England*, pp. 151–2; Robson, *The Attorney*, p. 7.

37 In the 'Act to Prevent Frivolous and Vexatious Arrests', 12 Geo.I, cap. 29 (1725), clauses 4–6.

38 2 Geo.II, cap. 23 (1729). Top government lawyers were members of the select committee on the bill: see *Commons' Journals, vol. 21*, 25 Feb. 1728/9. For debates, see Robson, *The Attorney*, pp. 9–13.

39 23 Geo.II, cap. 26 (1750).

40 See E. Freshfield (ed.), *The Records of the Society of Gentlemen Practisers in the Courts of Law and Equity, Called the Law Society* (Law Society, London, 1897), pp. 80–1, 84, 306.

41 A. Spencer (ed.), *Memoirs of William Hickey, 1749–1809* (Hurst & Blackett, London, 1913–25), vol. 1, pp. 331–2; also Robson, *The Attorney,* p. 159.

42 H. Fielding, *The History of the Adventures of Joseph Andrews, and his Friend Mr Abraham Adam* (London, 1742), vol. 2, p. 188.

43 E. Haywood, *The History of Miss Betsy Thoughtless* (London, 1751), vol. 3, p. 126.

44 A. Grant, *The Progress and Practice of a Modern Attorney: exhibiting the conduct of thousands towards millions* (London, 1795), p. 25.

45 E.B.V. Christian, *A Short History of Solicitors* (London, 1896), p. 166; Holmes, *Augustan England*, p. 157.

46 G.E. Barnett (ed.), *Two Tracts by Gregory King* (Johns Hopkins University Press, Baltimore, 1936), p. 31.

47 See W. Prest, 'Lawyers', in idem (ed.), *Professions in Early Modern England* (Croom Helm, London, 1987), pp. 72–5.

48 J. Swift, *Travels into Several Remote Nations of the World: in four parts, by Lemuel Gulliver* (London, 1726), pt 4, p. 70.

49 C.M. Brooks, *Pettyfoggers and Vipers of the Commonwealth: the 'lower branch' of the legal profession in early modern England* (Cambridge University Press, Cambridge, 1986), pp. 29–30, 112–14, 264.

50 Enrolments to 16 March 1729/30 are given in Anon., *Lists of Attornies and Solicitors, Admitted in Pursuance of the Late Act For the Better Regulation of Attornies and Solicitors* (London, 1729), pp. 1–35; and those to March 1730/1 in Anon., *Additional Lists of Attornies and Solicitors, Admitted in Pursuance of the Late Act* . . . (London, 1731), pp. 1–260. After this, the courts kept their own records (manuscripts in the Public Record Office).

51 From enrolments in Anon., *Lists* and *Additional Lists.* See discussion below, pp. 216–17; and also P. Aylett, 'A profession in the marketplace: the distribution of attorneys in England and Wales, 1730–1800', *Law and History Review,* 5 (1987), pp. 7–13.

52 R.W. Chapman (ed.), *Boswell: life of Johnson* (Oxford University Press, Oxford, 1976), p. 443.

53 Comparison of entries in Anon., *Lists* and *Additional Lists* with Anon., *An Alphabetical Draught of the Polls . . . for MPs for . . . Norwich, Taken May 15th 1734* (Norwich, 1735), pp. 5–81.

54 Robson, *The Attorney,* pp. 52–67; M. Birks, *Gentlemen of the Law* (Stevens, London, 1960).

55 Anon., *General Description,* pp. 8, 9.

56 See variously Anon., *Law Quibbles;* and Grant, *Progress and Practice of a Modern Attorney,* passim.

57 Anon., *Animadversions upon the . . . Laws of England: . . . [with] a proposal for regulating the practice, and reducing the number of attornies . . .* (London, 1750), p. v.

58 Anon. [H.C. Jennings], *A Free Enquiry into the Enormous Increase of Attornies* (Chelmsford, 1785), pp. 8, 31.

59 From the Society's oldest surviving record, dated 13 February 1739/40: see Freshfield (ed.), *Records,* pp. iii, 1. Six bound minute books are owned by the Law Society and I am grateful to the Librarian for permission to consult the originals – including the volume for 1810–19, which was not available for use by Freshfield. See also for the Society's role, Holdsworth, *History of English Law,* vol. 12, pp. 13–14; and Robson, *The Attorney,* pp. 20–34.

60 See original Law Society Minute Books, vol. 4, f. 34 (Dec. 1792).

61 Freshfield (ed.), *Records,* pp. lxxiv–lxxvi, 114–15.

62 See ibid., pp. xiv–lxxii, xxviii–xxix; and Robson, *The Attorney,* pp. 26–8, esp. p. 26, n. 5.

63 44 Geo. III, cap. 98 (1804), cl. 14 imposed a fine of £50 upon any conveyancer who was not qualified as either attorney or barrister.

64 See Freshfield (ed.), *Records*, pp. 101, 103–4, 173–4, 180–4; and also Christian, *Short History*, pp. 135–8.

65 In 1846, a test case upheld the convention but the judge refused to define it as a rule of law, since it did not date from 'time immemorial': Holdsworth, *History of English Law*, vol. 12, p. 74.

66 J. Browne (ed.), *Browne's General Law List for the Year 1787* (London, 1787), preface [unpag.] . This volume was sold for 3s.

67 J. Hughes (ed.), *New Law List* (London, 1798), preface [unpag.].

68 J. Browne (ed.), *Browne's General Law List for the Year 1780* (London, 1780), pp. 35–138. See also Aylett, 'Profession in the marketplace', pp. 13–23; and below, pp. 216–17.

69 Pitt was probably motivated by a desire to broaden Britain's fiscal base rather than by any especial hatred of lawyers, though he did dislike his pugnacious Lord Chancellor Thurlow: see J. Ehrman, *The Younger Pitt: the years of acclaim* (Constable, London, 1969), pp. 23–4, 185, 250–6; and 25 Geo.III, cap. 80 (1785).

70 34 Geo.III, cap. 14 (1794), revised 37 Geo.III, cap. 90 (1797).

71 Compare J. Bentham, *A Protest against Law Taxes, Shewing the Peculiar Mischievousness of all Such Impositions* (London, 1795; 1835), p. 8, with Anon., *A Defence of the Attornies, with Reasons for Thinking that No Attorney, . . . who has at Heart the Increasing Respectability of the Profession, will object to be Taxed* (London, 1804) as cited in Robson, *The Attorney*, pp. 16–17.

72 See 44 Geo.III, cap. 98 (1804) and 55 Geo.III, cap. 184 (1815). In 1851, the duties were consolidated at £80 upon articles, 9s. for an annual certificate for metropolitan lawyers, and 6s. for lawyers elsewhere: Christian, *Short History*, p. 218.

73 Robson, *The Attorney*, pp. 36–51. See also for the Liverpool Law Society (founded 1827), P.J. Williams, *A Gentleman's Calling: the Liverpool attorney-at-law* (Liverpool, 1980).

74 D. Hogan, *The Legal Profession in Ireland, 1789–1922* (Law Society of Ireland, Dublin, 1986), pp. 91–2.

75 See G.W. Gawalt, *The Promise of Power: the emergence of the legal profession in Massachusetts, 1760–1840* (Greenwood Press, Westport, Conn., 1979), pp. 11–15, 19–22; and M. Bloomfield, *American Lawyers in a Changing Society, 1776–1840* (Harvard University Press, Cambridge, Mass., 1976), pp. 43, 51, 139.

76 See A. Paterson, 'The legal profession in Scotland: an endangered species or a problem case for market theory?', in *Lawyers in Society*, vol. 1: *The common law world*, ed. R.L. Abel and P.S.C. Lewis (University of California Press, Berkeley, 1988), pp. 80–2, 84–5; and J.S. Muirhead (ed.), *The Old Minute Book of the Faculty of Procurators in Glasgow, 1668–1758* (Glasgow, 1948). I am also grateful for advice from Scott Galt of the Scottish Law Society.

77 J. Day, *Thoughts on the Necessity and Utility of the Examination . . . previous to the Admission of Attorneys and Solicitors* (London, 1795), pp. 6–7, 10, 22–3; and Holdsworth, *History of English Law*, vol. 12, pp. 64–5, for the Law Society's reactions to Day.

78 The Gentlemen Practisers did not oppose the new Law Society, which now holds the records of its precursor: Christian, *Short History*, p. 176; Holdsworth, *History of English Law*, vol. 12, p. 66.

79 Hogan, *Legal Profession in Ireland*, pp. 93–4.

80 H. Kirk, *Portrait of a Profession: a history of the solicitor's profession, 1100 to the present day* (Oyez, London, 1976), pp. 27–33, 35–9; Birks, *Gentlemen of the Law*, pp. 153–60; and Anon. (ed.), *Handbook of the Law Society* (London, 1938), pp. 5–6.

81 The first ever question was 'Define respectively common law and statute law': see Anon., *The Key to the Examination Questions . . . from 1835 to 1849* (London, 1849), vol. 1, p. 1. For the continuing influence of the practising lawyer tradition in England, see also D. Sugarman, 'Legal theory, the common law mind and the making of the textbook tradition', in *Legal Theory and Common Law*, ed. W. Twining (Blackwell, Oxford, 1986), pp. 26–61, esp. pp. 29, 51–2.

82 Solicitors Act, 6 & 7 Vict., cap. 73. (1843), cl. 21.

83 Evidence to Select Committee on Legal Education, in *British Parliamentary Papers*, 10 (1846), pp. 208–9.

84 See analysis in A. Black, *Guilds and Civil Society in European Political Thought from the Twelfth Century to the Present* (Methuen, London, 1984), pp. 237–41; and G. Millerson, *The Qualifying Associations: a study in professionalization* (Routledge, London, 1964), pp. 19, 24.

85 They numbered only 1,320 in 1851: see Anon. (ed.), *Handbook*, p. 7.

86 See *D.N.B.*, *sub*: Lloyd Kenyon, first Baron Kenyon (1732–1802), who was solicitor in 1749, barrister in 1756 and chief justice from 1788 to 1802.

87 J.H. Baker, *History of the Gowns Worn at the English Bar* (London, 1985), reprinted from *Costume*, 9 (1975).

88 Idem, *The Order of Serjeants at Law: A Chronicle of Creations . . . and a Historical Introduction* (Selden Society, suppl. ser. 5, 1984), pp. 118–22, 125–6, 129.

89 See *D.N.B.*, *sub*: James Parsons (1799–1877).

90 For Thomas Erskine (1750–1823), see A. Howard (ed.), *The Beauties of Erskine* (London, 1834?); and J.A. Lovat-Fraser, *Erskine* (Cambridge University Press, Cambridge, 1932), esp. pp. 68–88, 109–26.

91 Anon., *The Bar: with sketches of eminent judges, barristers, etc. . . .* (London, 1825), p. 55. This was probably Sir John Vaughan (1769–1839), who became Attorney General in 1816: see *D.N.B.*

92 Anon., *The Bar*, p. 146. He was Thomas Starkie (1782–1849), author of the standard *Treatise on Criminal Pleading* (London, 1814).

93 'J. Surrebutter, Esq.' [J. Anstey], *The Pleader's Guide: a didactic poem in two books . . .* (London, 1796), p. 74.

94 See J.R. Lewis, *The Victorian Bar* (Hale, London, 1982), pp. 13–26.

95 Discussed in J.M. Beattie, *Crime and the Courts in England, 1660–1800* (Clarendon, Oxford, 1986), pp. 352–59; and J.H. Langbein, 'The criminal trial before the lawyers', *University of Chicago Law Review*, 45 (1978), pp. 264, 282–3, 307–14.

96 Ibid., esp. pp. 307–14. See also J.H. Baker, 'Criminal courts and procedure, 1550–1800', in idem, *The Legal Profession and the Common Law: historical essays* (Hambledon, London, 1986), pp. 259–301.

97 D. Pannick, *Advocates* (Oxford University Press, Oxford, 1992), pp. 1–2, 6–7, 90–2, 105–25, 127–69.

98 *The Gentleman's Magazine*, 10 (1740), p. 388.

99 W.R. Prest, *The Rise of the Barristers: a social history of the English bar, 1590–1640* (Clarendon, Oxford, 1986) and D. Lemmings, *Gentlemen and Barristers: the Inns of Court and the English bar, 1680–1730* (Clarendon, Oxford, 1990).

100 See D. Duman, 'The English bar in the Georgian era', in *Lawyers in Early Modern Europe and America*, ed. W. Prest (Croom Helm, London, 1981), p. 97; and details in J. Whishaw, *A Synopsis of the Members of the English Bar* (London, 1835), pp. 263–74.

101 Hogan, *Legal Profession in Ireland*, pp. 42–53.

102 C. Lamb, *Elia: essays which have appeared under that signature in the London Magazine* (London, 1823), p. 193.

103 See R. Cock, 'The bar at assizes: barristers on three nineteenth-century

circuits', *Kingston Law Review*, 6 (1976), pp. 36–52; and R. Walton, *Random Reflections of the Midland Circuit* (2 vols, London, 1869, 1873), passim.

104 R. Cocks, *Foundations of the Modern Bar* (Sweet & Maxwell, London, 1983), pp. 215–20. Thanks also to the Bar Council for making available for consultation its early Minute Books.

105 Lemmings, *Gentlemen and Barristers*, pp. 10, 60–2, 123–4.

106 Browne (ed.), *Browne's General Law List for . . . 1780*, pp. 17–33. R.L. Abel, *The Legal Profession in England and Wales* (Blackwell, Oxford, 1988), pp. 482–3, Table 4.1, gives long-run figures for 1730–1981 but his pre-1851 totals are too small since they include only junior counsel and exclude serjeants and king's counsel.

107 Duman, 'The English bar', in Prest (ed.), *Lawyers in Early Modern Europe*, pp. 88–90.

108 S. Hill (ed.), *Clarke's New Law List* (London, 1805), pp. 10–42.

109 From 1851 census for England and Wales, *British Parliamentary Papers*, 88/1 (1852/3). For problems in assessing the size of the Victorian bar, see also D. Duman, *The English and Colonial Bars in the Nineteenth Century* (Croom Helm, London, 1983), pp. 2–9, 25–8.

110 C. Dickens, *A Tale of Two Cities* (Philadelphia, 1859), vol. 1, pp. 108, 112–15.

111 Anon. [J. Simpson], *Reflections on the Natural and Acquired Endowments Requisite for the Study of the Law* (London, 1764), p. 43.

112 P. Lucas, 'Blackstone and the reform of the legal profession', *English Historical Review*, 77 (1962), pp. 457–61, 477–9.

113 See W. Matthews (ed.), *The Diary of Dudley Ryder, 1715–16* (Methuen, London, 1939), pp. 190, 207, 223, 226, 363–4; and S. Romilly, *Memoirs of the Life of Sir Samuel Romilly . . . Edited by his Sons* (Murray, London, 1890), vol. 1, p. 67.

114 Anon., *A Treatise on the Study of the Law . . .* (London, 1797), pp. v–vi.

115 Lemmings, *Gentlemen and Barristers*, pp. 42–7, 49–52; Holdsworth, *History of English Law*, vol. 12, pp. 14–46.

116 H.H.L. Bellot, 'The jurisdiction of the Inns of Court over the Inns of Chancery', *Law Quarterly Review*, 26 (1910), pp. 382–99; and idem, 'The exclusion of the attorneys from the Inns of Court', *Law Quarterly Review*, 26 (1910), p. 144.

117 F. Cowper, *A Prospect of Gray's Inn* (Stevens & Sons, London, 1951), p. 90.

118 W. Bagehot, *Literary Studies* (London, 1906), vol. 3, p. 253.

119 Millerson, *Qualifying Associations*, pp. 21–2.

120 Duman, *English and Colonial Bars*, pp. 26–8. See also Cocks, *Foundations*, pp. 34–81; and overview by Duman, 'Pathway to professionalism: the English bar in the eighteenth and nineteenth centuries', *Journal of Social History*, 13 (1980), pp. 615–28.

121 See C. Kenny, *King's Inns and the Kingdom of Ireland: the Irish 'Inn of Court', 1541–1800* (Irish Academic Press, Dublin, 1992), pp. 162–82, 229–62.

122 For opposition to the 'hasty and selfish spirit of reform', see B.T. DuHigg, *History of the King's Inns: or, An Account of the Legal Body in Ireland. . .* (Dublin, 1806), p. 571.

123 Hogan, *Legal Profession in Ireland*, pp. 104–6, 109–10.

124 J.W. Cairns, 'The formation of the Scottish legal mind in the eighteenth century: themes of humanism and enlightenment in the admission of advocates', in *The Legal Mind: Essays for Tony Honoré*, ed. N. MacCormick and P. Birks (Clarendon, Oxford, 1986), pp. 262–5.

125 N. Phillipson, 'Lawyers, landowners, and the civic leadership of post-Union Scotland', in *Lawyers in Their Social Setting*, ed. D. MacCormick (Green & Son, Edinburgh, 1976), p. 194.

126 For William Forbes's 1714 estimate, see J.S. Shaw, *The Management of Scottish*

Society, 1707–64: power, nobles, lawyers, Edinburgh agents and English influences (Donald, Edinburgh, 1983), p. 31.

127 Cairns, 'Scottish legal mind', pp. 253–4; Phillipson, 'Lawyers, landowners', p. 175.

128 See the Act of Settlement, 12 & 13 William III, cap. 2 (1701) and C.H. McIlwain, 'The tenure of English judges', in idem, *Constitutionalism and the Changing World* (Cambridge University Press, Cambridge, 1939), pp. 294–307.

129 Technically, Macclesfield was impeached as ex-Chancellor since he resigned the Great Seal before the case: E. Foss, *The Judges of England, With Sketches of their Lives*, vol. 8: *1714–1820* (London, 1864), pp. 48–52. See also W. Prest, 'Judicial corruption in early modern England', *Past & Present*, 133 (1991), 67–95, esp. pp. 81–95.

130 Prosopographical details are analysed in D. Duman, *The Judicial Bench in England, 1727–1875: the reshaping of a professional elite* (Royal Historical Society, London, 1983).

131 Mansfield's verdicts were quickly consolidated into a standard textbook by J.A. Park, *A System of the Law of Marine Insurance* (London, 1787 and many later edns). See also *D.N.B., sub*: William Murray (1705–93), first Earl of Mansfield.

132 J. Bowring (ed.), *The Works of Jeremy Bentham* (Edinburgh, 1843), vol. 7, p. 270, n.; vol. 5, p. 234; vol. 10, p. 429.

5

CLERICS

Divinity is no less than the Knowledge of the true God.[1]

The vocation of the clergy was demanding. They lived in secular society alongside many temporal figures of authority, such as lawyers and magistrates. But the clergy were spiritual pastors in a profession of great antiquity. They had their own special knowledge, based upon the teachings of God and explicated by a sophisticated theology. John Wesley, whose father and both grandfathers were ministers, put it very grandly in 1756. Each clergyman was 'an Ambassador of *Christ*, a Shepherd of never-dying Souls, a Watchman over the *Israel* of God, [and] a Steward of the Mysteries which Angels desire to look into'.[2] Moreover, these pastors were sustained by solid church institutions, that framed their individual roles within wider organisational structures.

Potentially and actually, therefore, clerical authority was formidable. Throughout this period, clergymen remained one of the most numerous and important professions throughout all three kingdoms. Ordained ministers successfully contained the various challenges that were made from time to time by unordained 'irregulars', seers and prophets. At the same time, the clergy also learned to live within a pluralist system of power. Certainly, the number of avowed freethinkers and atheists in Britain before 1851 was only very small. The public denial of the existence of God was theoretically debarred by the blasphemy laws of 1697/8.[3] The clergy were thus relatively rarely subjected to a frontal assault upon religion and they lived within a culture that retained a strong Christian tradition.

At the same time, however, the clergy in this period faced a growing range of competition. Some of that was provided by rivalries between the various denominations. That undermined the spiritual dignity of God's faithful, as the ecumenical Methodist John Fletcher warned in 1777: 'Unspeakable is the mischief done to the interests of religion by the divisions of Christians: and the greater their profession [i.e. of faith] is, the greater is the offence given by their contests.'[4] But other competition came from the secular professions. Over time, these began to carry out some of the roles traditionally carried out by the churches.

As an occupation, the cure of souls required a round-the-clock commitment. A minister in clerical garb was unavoidably in the public eye. As William Hazlitt – the son of a Unitarian minister – commented waspishly in 1818: 'A full dressed ecclesiastic is a sort of go-cart of divinity.'[5] Any lapses were liable to face criticism. There was no end to the spiritual struggle, since the forces of the Devil were always ready to lure souls into danger. Admittedly, fear of the imminent rule of Antichrist was not as claustrophobically intense in the eighteenth century as it had been in earlier times.[6] Admittedly, too, hellfire was gradually becoming interpreted more as a metaphor than as a literal pit of flames.[7] But a clergyman could never relax. His pastoral duties were extensive and intensive.[8] Attendance was required at intimate moments of family history: baptism, confirmation, marriage, the deathbed. In addition, he usually officiated at public services at least once a week.

Ideally, therefore, a candidate for the ministry needed a genuine spiritual vocation or 'calling' from God. Eager parents were warned not to push unwilling sons into the office, merely to gain social status. That debased divinity into a mere trade. Instead, a clergyman should combine morality, judgement, truth and compassion, plus an ability to communicate. Someone too meretricious would not suit, advised a handbook in 1747; nor someone too melancholy.[9] Ordination required personal dedication and mental assent – or at very least a convincing outward appearance of the same. That was true to an extent of all professionals, since they undermined their own mystique if they did not take their business seriously. But it was crucial that the clergy should show their faith in the religion they upheld, hence from time to time the agony of a sincere person in holy orders who contracted 'doubts'. That happened, for example, to the historian J.A. Froude, an ordained Fellow of Exeter College, Oxford, who published an autobiographical novel on *The Nemesis of Faith* in 1849. His orthodox colleagues were outraged. The senior tutor publicly burnt the book in Exeter Hall. And Froude resigned from his Fellowship and adopted a literary career.[10]

God's ministry was therefore not just another occupation. It was the *'sacred profession'* for one writer in 1764.[11] The term 'clergy' bore special connotations of book learning, dating from the days when their order enjoyed a near monopoly of education.[12] By the eighteenth century, they no longer had an exclusive claim to learning but they still retained some signs of separate status. For example, established clergymen were exempt from jury service and disqualified from bearing arms or standing for Parliament. The radical John Horne Tooke – who had been ordained as a young man – challenged that in 1801, by getting elected for the pocket borough of Old Sarum. But his success was only temporary. Legislation in 1801 immediately ruled that ministers of the established churches in both England and Scotland were ineligible. Horne Tooke was not expelled but he did not offer himself for re-election.[13]

Furthermore, the separate status of the clergy was signalled by their ceremonial role. In the Catholic tradition, it was the priest who officiated at the mysteries of the holy mass. For Protestants, the pastor led the service and gave the weekly sermon. Each clergyman was master in his own pulpit. He was heard (usually) in respectful silence, although open-air preachers were sometimes treated more roughly. Sermons were a powerful form of spoken communication.[14] Many were also circulated in print, to reach a wider audience. Indeed, the output of the clergy was huge. They wrote countless sermons, catechisms, hymnals and homilies. And they published prayers for all eventualities, such as in 1692 special prayers for invalids at Bath; in 1712 and 1785 devotions for all condemned malefactors; and in 1850 – careful not to overtax a sensitive congregation, after the crisis of Froude's apostacy – *Occasional Prayers for . . . the Undergraduates of Exeter College Oxford*.

These writings were aimed in part at a lay readership. But the material was simultaneously available for the nervous, lazy or modest minister seeking inspiration. There were few worries about wholesale borrowing, in this age of ready plagiary. Among the most frequently repeated Anglican sermons were those of John Tillotson, Archbishop of Canterbury between 1691 and 1694, whose majestic orations did much to set the style of pulpit oratory.[15] Others indeed consciously sought the ready-made market. Thus in 1796 the Revd John Trusler set out his specimen sermons in a large flowing easy-to-read italic script, to save fellow-preachers from the labour of copying them in their own hands.[16] Meanwhile, for the clergy wishing to compose their own oratory there were also numerous handbooks to teach the appropriate techniques.

Pulpit style was a matter of choice. A rich sonorous tone was the general trademark. Handbooks advised that speech should be simple and sincere. Speaking freely from notes was better than reading aloud from a prepared text. Even the 'fanatic who mounts his stool in the corner of the streets' could extemporise effectively, warned a tract in 1792.[17] Not everyone, of course, heeded the advice. William Cowper (the son of a rector) satirised humdrum preachers as:

> The things that mount the rostrum with a skip,
> And then skip down again; pronounce a text;
> Cry – hem: and, reading what they never wrote,
> Just fifteen minutes, huddle up their work.[18]

On the other hand, too much improvisation could also provoke complaint. It could become trite; or drift into error. 'It always pleases the vulgar, probably because it conveys the idea of immediate inspiration', sniffed Vicesimus Knox in 1779.[19] But a good sermon should have depth as well as immediacy, and be delivered with economy and grace. 'Never clap your hands, nor thump the pulpit', added John Wesley.[20]

Famous sermons were widely reported and some had great impact. For example, Bishop Hoadley of Bangor's 1717 theological disquisition on the 'Kingdom or Church of Christ' began the prolonged 'Bangorian controversy' over the division of authority in church and state.[21] Some sermons reached to the philosophical heights. Those included the subtle moral analysis in the *Rolls Sermons* of Bishop Butler in 1726,[22] and, a century later, the inspirational orations of John Henry Newman.[23] Others gained fame for whimsy. James Penn became known for a 1768 sermon on *The Reasonableness of Repentance*. It was dedicated to the Devil, who was addressed as 'Tremendous Sir!' There were other surprising speakers like the young Coleridge (another vicar's son) who once planned to become a Unitarian minister and addressed a surprised congregation at Shrewsbury in January 1798.[24] And there were two extraordinary Methodist preachers, who could hold the attention of huge crowds in the open air: one was John Wesley, whose sermons had great force and immediacy; the other was George Whitefield, whose bell-like tones, expressive features, and dramatic imagery were positively startling in their intensity.[25]

Of these public preachers in this period, only a tiny number were women. Mainstream Christianity took it as axiomatic, on the authority of the Bible, that God's ministry was a male occupation. Nonetheless, it was possible to hear women testify. The young Boswell heard one at a Quaker meeting in 1763. His report prompted one of Dr Johnson's best-known ripostes: 'Sir, a woman's preaching is like a dog's walking on his hinder legs. It is not done well; but you are surprized to find it done at all.'[26] A recurrent minority, however, disagreed. That radical view was most common among the low-church Protestant sects, who stressed the importance of divine inspiration. Since the Old Testament referred both to prophetic 'sons and daughters', they argued that the Bible did after all allow women some role in the conduct of worship.[27]

Practical expression of that was undertaken most vigorously in this period by a number of redoubtable Methodist women, who travelled the country as open-air preachers. On this question, John Wesley's spiritual and organisational radicalism triumphed over his social conservatism. He gave his support, albeit cautiously, to these pioneering 'holy women'.[28] Among their ranks was Elizabeth Tomlinson, whose niece by marriage, George Eliot, gave her aunt's open-air evangelism a sympathetic portrayal in the character of Dinah Morris in *Adam Bede* (1859).[29]

However, their activities caused dispute even among the Methodists. Some congregations rejected female preachers. Hence the concept of a woman in the pulpit remained deeply controversial, even though in Britain no church contemplated the ordination of women as ministers – in contrast to a few radical Baptist and Congregational churches that actually did so in the USA in the early nineteenth century.[30] Instead, majority opinion feared that allowing people to preach as the spirit moved would simply promote hysteria, self-indulgence, fraud, blasphemy and spiritual anarchy.

Criticism was sharpened in the early nineteenth century by the extraordinary career of Joanna Southcott (1750–1814). She was a former maidservant and shop assistant turned prophetess.[31] In 1801 she published her 'spiritual communications', with the support of some respectable sponsors, including a few Church of England divines. Her revelations from God gave her 'more knowledge than the learned', she assured her readers.[32] A number of Southcottian congregations were founded, notably in the metropolis, Yorkshire's West Riding, and her home county of Devonshire. She herself officiated at some religious services, with her chosen minister, one William Tozer, and she devised dramatic rituals, based around the Anglican liturgy but with her own hymns.[33]

Orthodox opinion, already scandalised, was horrified by Southcott's distribution to her followers of signed and sealed warrants of salvation. That arrogated to herself quasi-divine powers. Then in 1813 she revealed, to some excitement, that the millennium was nigh and that in her sixty-fifth year she was pregnant with 'Shiloh' or the new Messiah. In fact, she was bloated with a fatal illness. She died in December 1814 without producing the holy child. That disillusioned her followers and ruined the reputation of those doctors who had endorsed her condition. Satirists portrayed her as a drunken fraud, sporting a bright red nose.[34] Yet one of the most remarkable features of her career was the degree of success that she achieved for over a decade and the absence of any prosecution against her. Moreover, although her support dwindled rapidly after 1814, her religious movement did not cease. She was followed by a 'false Joanna', one Mary Boon, who claimed to be Southcott reincarnated; and by two controversial male successors, John Wroe (1782–1863), founder of the Christian Israelites, and the Irish mystic John 'Zion' Ward (1781–1837), who launched the 'Shilohites'.[35] Thus, while Joanna Southcott did not have anything like the missionary powers, the organisational skills, or the theological depth of a John Wesley, she did found a continuing, if small and highly fissiparous, religious tradition that still continues mutedly today.[36]

On the other hand, the female intruders gained very little ground in the long term. Their daring behaviour caused shock and alarm; but the traditional male ministry was not easily shaken. Eventually, even the Methodists resumed an orthodox stance on this issue. The large Wesleyan Old Connexion banned women preachers in 1803; and Conference in 1835 repeated the interdict. A few, like Elizabeth Tomlinson, were not deterred. She and her husband Samuel Evans left the Wesleyans and worked with

Figure 5.1 *Detail from 'The Impostor or Obstetric Dispute' (1814) with (right) a Seal of Election issued by Joanna Southcott (1803). Well before her phantom pregnancy in 1814, Joanna Southcott was a controversial figure. To the orthodox, she was simply blasphemous. She issued manuscript Seals, such as this (right) issued to Hannah Darnborough, which promised the 'Elect Precious' that she would have permanent salvation in Heaven on Southcott's signed authority.*
Published by courtesy of University of London (Harry Price) Library

the Primitive Methodists and later the Derby Faith Methodists. But most women reluctantly acquiesced, as did Eliot's fictional Dinah Morris, 'to set th'example o'submitting'.[37] As a result, although the number of women preachers rose in the later eighteenth century, it had declined again by the mid-nineteenth century. The female evangelists left only a dwindling memory – even within Methodism – not a self-renewing tradition.

They had, however, briefly posed a professional as well as a theological challenge. One writer pointed out caustically in 1739 that female 'irregulars' were potential trade rivals. Unorthodox competition would eventually threaten clerical incomes and hence 'the united Interest of the whole Body of Men called Clergymen'.[38] In fact, it never came to that, since the female incursion never won ordination and preferment. If anything, the danger was to clerical influence rather than finances.

Similar problems were posed by the male lay preachers. In the eighteenth century, a number of radical religious groups – again most notably the Methodists – successfully deployed 'itinerants' as a means whereby a relatively impoverished evangelical church could reach new congregations, especially those in the countryside away from the big cities.[39] A few of these men were themselves ordained ministers, although most were not. They preached the gospel without pay, travelling long distances to spread God's word. Their activities were not as shocking as the phenomenon of female preachers. Yet there were still many critics of this form of improvised assistance to the ordained ministry. The itinerants were 'destitute of Greek learning, the language in which the New Testament was originally written', complained a vicar in 1802. And the laity could be ungrateful: 'I preached to about 100 people but few could hear much the opposition was so noisy, some few eggs were flung, one struck me', recorded Thomas Wastfield (a schoolmaster by occupation) during an open-air preaching tour in Wiltshire in 1797.[40]

There was, however, no direct contest between the regular clergy and the assorted 'irregulars'. It was rare to find pugnacity such as that displayed by John 'Zion' Ward, one of the unorthodox heirs to Joanna Southcott. In 1832 he roundly condemned all 'priestcraft' and circulated handbills stating that 'The Bishops and Clergy are Religious Impostors, and as such by the Laws of England liable to Corporal Punishment.'[41] He was at once imprisoned for blasphemy, despite a petition to Parliament defending his right to free speech. But John Ward was a pugnacious freelance. In general, the Nonconformist churches supervised their lay preachers closely. By the early nineteenth century, their numbers and influence were waning as the church developed a settled ministry.[42] Hence the professional clergy remained the predominant form of pastoral leadership, with only a small minority of radical churches – most notably the Quakers – preferring *ad hoc* spontaneity over an organised ministry.

Because their role was so well entrenched, the clergy attracted much attention. In majestic style, John Dryden (another child of the vicarage) penned a gracious tribute to *The Character of a Good Parson* (1700). Affectionate mockery was also directed at unworldly divines, such as the simple curate Abraham Adams in Fielding's *Joseph Andrews* (1742) or the gentle *Vicar of Wakefield* (1766), whose sermons lulled the squire to sleep. On the other hand, the clergy were, with the other learned professions, frequent targets of satire. The niceties of theology were debunked as arid and abstruse. Hence people invoked 'the old saying, that an *ounce of mother wit is worth a pound of Clergy'*, as recorded by Sydney Smith, himself both a wit and a cleric.[43] Parsons featured in popular verses with promising titles, such as *The Bishop and the Parson's Beard* (1810) and *The Parson and his Maid* (1722). That title technically applied only to Anglican rectors who held full parochial tithes. But the name of 'parson' was too often held in undue contempt through 'familiar, clownish, and indiscriminate use', as Blackstone fretted in 1765.[44]

Theoretically, there was a resident clergyman of the established church in every parish and, although practice did not live up to theory, the local church provided one point of enquiry. The eighteenth-century book trade did not therefore detect any urgent demand for clerical directories. A variety of handbooks to the valuations and patrons of Anglican benefices were available. But it was not until 1817 that the first *Clerical Guide* to the Church of England arrived, followed by the first *Irish Ecclesiastical Register* in 1818, and the definitive *Crockford's Clerical Directory* from 1858 onwards. By contrast, the Catholic priests were self-effacing before Emancipation in 1829, although an annual *Catholic Directory* for Great Britain and Ireland was later launched in 1838. And the Protestant Nonconformists throughout relied upon their own networks and there was no general guide to their separate ministries until 1883.

Consequently, no-one in the eighteenth century knew the precise total of the 'Gentlemen of the *Long-Petticoat* Tribe', as a critic wittily dubbed them in 1720.[45] Even without detailed figures, however, it was clear that the clergyman were ranked in thousands. That meant that they remained one of the most numerous of all the professions. Gregory King thought that there were 10,000 clergymen in England and Wales in the 1690s – and the smaller populations of Ireland and Scotland may have sustained another 2,500 and 1,500 respectively (a total of *c*.14,000). By 1803, Colquhoun suggested for England and Wales an expansion to 13,500, including Dissenting ministers, although his estimate may have been too cautious. The Irish and Scottish totals had also grown, with perhaps 3,500 and 1,900 respectively at the end of the eighteenth century. And the following fifty years saw a considerable acceleration. By 1851, there were 26,235 clergymen within England and Wales, plus another 6,241 in Ireland and 3,812 in Scotland. (See Table 5.1.) That total of 36,288 clergymen constituted 1 for every 737 people in the British Isles.

Table 5.1 Numbers of clergymen (all denominations) in Great Britain and Ireland, 1700–1851

	England & Wales[1]	Scotland	Ireland
1700	10,000	1,500?	2,500?
1801	13,500?	1,900?	3,500?
1851	26,235	3,812	6,241

Sources: Figures for 1700 and 1801 are estimates based on partial contemporary data and assessments
Figures from 1851 census in *British Parliamentary Papers (B.P.P.)* (1852/3), vol. 88/1, pp. ccxxii, ccxxviii and ccxxxiv (Great Britain) and *B.P.P.* (1856), vol. 31, p. 782 (Ireland)
Note: 1 Includes Channel Islands and I. of Man

Expansion signalled that the churches were indeed responsive to demand for pastoral services from the fast-multiplying population. Religion was essential to the welfare both of the individual and of society, argued one author – cannily counting the cost/benefit in *An Estimate of the Profit and Loss of Religion* (1753).[46] Few calculated the question as coolly as that. But many agreed that religion was the foundation of individual morality and the general social order. Hence there was a clear need for collective worship and pastoral care. The divine William Sherlock once described his fellow professionals as spiritual doctors, dealing in spiritual balm. With that in mind, he urged rhetorically: 'Are we careful to preserve our bodies from any hurt, from pains and sickness, from burning Fevers, or the racking Gout or Stone, and shall we not be as careful of the ease of the Mind too?'[47] Indeed, there seems to have been an unmet demand in regions of the country that were poorly served by the traditional parochial network. In Wales, for example, the marked success of the Calvinistic Methodists was aided by the organisational weaknesses of the Church of England locally as well as by the charisma of the early evangelicals.[48]

Overall, clerical numbers grew by a multiple of some 2.69 between 1700 and 1851. That was, however, somewhat slower than the four-fold expansion of the British population as a whole. It marked a further stage in the long-term secularisation of the occupational structure, as the number of men in holy orders proportionately declined.[49] After all, financial and organisational constraints placed limits upon unfettered expansion. The least expensive services were those of the smallest sects, which met in simple chapels or even in private rooms. One Scottish lawyer went so far as to suggest slyly that the Scots preferred Calvinism because it was the cheapest religion.[50] On the other hand, the Roman Catholic priesthood was celibate, while Protestant ministers were allowed to marry and often had a family to support. But, again, many clerical wives acted as unpaid parochial helpmeets. They went unnoticed, other than a few distinguished exceptions like Mary Bosanquet (1739–1815), the Methodist

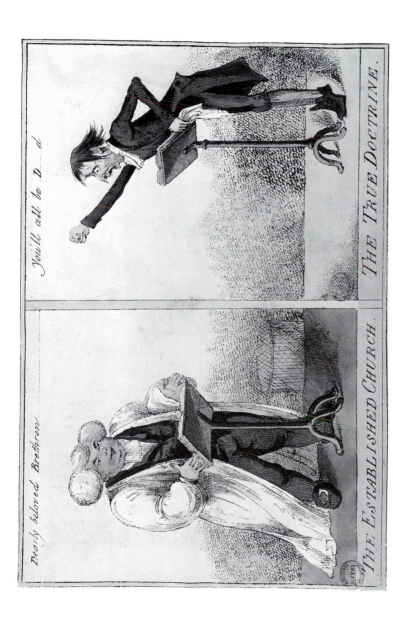

Figure 5.2 The Established Church/The True Doctrine (1818). All varieties of clerical style were subject to satire. Here a plump and complacent Church of England clergyman in flowing white addresses his flock soothingly as 'Dearly Beloved Brethren', while a lean Dissenter pronounces menacingly: 'You'll all be Damned.'

Published by permission of the British Museum, Department of Prints and Drawings

lay preacher within the Church of England who was wife of John Fletcher, the Anglican vicar of Madeley in Shropshire.[51]

Professionally, therefore, the clergy had to balance their high calling against more mundane practicalities. In that, they were sustained by their churches. Yet none held a monopoly. As a result, there was often competition between the churches and consequently between their clergymen too. A very few lone individuals did from time to time suggest an ecumenical reunion[52] – but these proposals did not command any serious attention, let alone support. Thus, unlike the lawyers who increasingly spoke of one 'legal profession' with its two complementary branches, clergymen did not see themselves as part of a single clerical profession.

Instead, there were numerous religious disputes, some measured, some very acrimonious. There were too many 'church-Hectors' ready to ride into battle, wrote the wit John Dunton (whose own father, grandfather and great-grandfather were all clerics).[53] The fierceness of theological contention was a tribute to the importance of the issues, so much so that the hatreds generated became proverbial. Thus in 1734 an anonymous Cambridge mathematician wryly referred to the 'Odium Theologicum' or 'the intemperate zeal of Divines'.[54] Of course, the disputants were often sustained by enthusiastic followers. But their devotion in turn encouraged clerics in their commitment. The nullifidian philosopher David Hume published in 1753 a cool analysis of excessive religious zeal. Clergymen argued with too much fury, he explained:

> Because all their credit and livelihood depend upon the belief, which their opinions meet with; and they alone pretend to a divine and supernatural authority . . . The Odium Theologicum, or theological hatred, is noted even to a proverb, and means that degree of rancour, which is the most furious and implacable.[55]

From the point of view of the public, however, the divisions between the churches offered an element of consumer choice in religion. That was easier to exercise in large towns with many congregations than it was in small or remote parishes with only one. But it meant that people at this time belonged to a growing number of churches worshipping side by side – each church constituting a group of co-religionists in a single organisation, who shared a common faith and form of service (liturgy).

This often fractious state of confessional pluralism was not uniform across the three kingdoms. The diversity of churches was generally greatest in the large towns, least so in the country villages. Yet, even in homogeneous rural communities, the existence of alternatives could affect attitudes towards the clergy. For example, a parishioner in Weston Longeville (a village 12 miles from Norwich) used this knowledge when in dispute with the Anglican parson. The encounter was recorded by the Reverend James Woodforde (1740–1803) in his diary for 1 October 1777:

Harry Dunnell behaved very impertinent this morning to me because I would not privately name his child for him, he having one Child before named privately by me and never had it brought to Church afterwards. He had the Impudence to tell me that he would send it to some [Nonconformist] Meeting House to be named etc. – very saucy indeed.[56]

According to this account (and Dunnell's version was not recorded), the parishioner was trying a little social blackmail. Woodforde was shocked at this uppish behaviour from a poor neighbour, whom he employed occasionally as a handyman. In fact, their confrontation did not lead to a permanent breach. Woodforde continued to hire Dunnell, and Dunnell did not defect to a rival denomination. Moreover, they compromised on the substantive issue. In 1784 Dunnell's next-born daughter was presented in the parish church, while in 1788 another son was baptised privately.[57]

Nonetheless, the episode was instructive. It showed that, even in a relatively intimate village community, a determined parishioner could pressurise the parson by threatening to defect to a rival church. Choice was here made explicit. It was equally notable, however, that Woodforde was shocked at Dunnell's 'Impudence' rather than seriously alarmed. As the local incumbent of the established Church of England for many years, he was confident in his own position. He did not approve of Methodism but he remained calm when the Methodists did convene a meeting in Weston. His diaries remained preoccupied with his daily round, his food and his ailing health. Thus on 27 April 1801 he noted simply: 'A Methodist Meeting we heard to day is held at Whisson's House on Sundays – very near us.'[58] This laconic style may perhaps have hidden some deeper emotion. Yet Woodforde made no further reference to the matter and certainly did not feud with 'Neighbour Whisson'.[59]

Contemporaries knew that there were many churches. For Voltaire, viewing the country from afar, that was a matter for approval. He claimed sweepingly that 'If one religion only were allowed in *England*, the government would very possibly become arbitrary; if there were but two, the people wou'd cut one another's throats; but as there are such a multitude, they all live happy and in peace.'[60] He exaggerated the concord. But he was correct in noting that there was more than one, or even two, denominations. This dictum was sufficiently accepted to be embellished (without attribution) by Horace Walpole in November 1789. He too wrote cheerfully: 'The more religions the better. If we had but two in the island, they would cut one another's throats for power. When there is plenty of beliefs, the professors only glean customers here and there from rival shops, and make more controversies than converts.'[61]

Britain's clergymen were therefore distributed among many churches, ranging from the majority denominations to the many small religious sects (which was a hostile term applied to any breakaway group). Within each kingdom, there was one large institution with majority support. The three were: in Ireland, the non-established Roman Catholic church; in Scotland, the established presbyterian Kirk of Scotland; in England and Wales, the established Church of England. But all of these were teased by rivals. The Protestant tradition in particular, with its appeal to the individual conscience, was notably fissiparous. Thus the leading Dissenters such as the Presbyterians, Congregationalists, Baptists and Quakers were joined by the Methodists, who left the Church of England in the early 1790s before dividing themselves into a number of rival connections. And there was a tail of very much smaller religious groups, whose numbers waxed and waned following the inspiration of charismatic preachers and prophets.

Numbering the churches was for that reason a difficult task. The sole religious census, held in 1851, produced contentious results and was never repeated.[62] A subsequent report by the Registrar General for England and Wales did list as many as seventy-eight Nonconformist groups that had been licensed with their own separate meeting house or chapels, at some point during the century and a half between 1688 and 1852.[63] But this list, summarised in Table 5.2, is purely indicative and not conclusive. The Registrar General's survey did not receive answers from all localities. Moreover, those who did reply gave very vague information, naming groups as 'Christians', 'Protestants' and 'Millenarians', or paradoxically for Nonconformists, 'Church of England' and 'Established Church'. However, the list does serve to suggest the variety of places licensed for worship between 1688 and 1852 as well as the notable imprecision of their denominational labels.

Diversity such as this sundered clergymen one from another. In this period, as already noted, none of the three British kingdoms was a single 'confessional' state with only one official church and one permitted 'confession of faith'.[64] In 1689 England's Act of Toleration insisted that no Catholic could succeed to the throne; but it also conferred freedom of worship upon all those Protestants who believed in the trinity of Father, Son and Holy Ghost. That included not only those who conformed to the established Anglican Church but also all trinitarian Protestants who did not.[65] Similar Acts followed in 1712 for Scotland and in 1719 for Ireland.[66] This legislation did not allow an unfettered religious freedom, since officially Catholics, Unitarians and non-Christians had no rights of public worship. Yet the traditional assumption that there was and should be 'one people, one church' was decisively and legally ended. That contrasted with numerous countries in continental Europe. For example, in Austria before Joseph II's 1781 Patent of Toleration, subjects were expected to conform to the Catholic church and special commissions checked that everyone held confession tickets (*Beichtzettel*) to show their attendance at the obligatory Easter confession.[67]

Table 5.2 Religious groups with licensed venues for worship in England and Wales, December 1688 – June 1852

Established Church[1]
Not   Church of England (also known as Anglicans; Conformists; Episcopalians)
listed

Leading Nonconformist churches [Protestant Dissenters]
1   Protestants and Protestant Dissenters[2]
2   Presbyterians [Calvinists]
3   Independents or Congregationalists
4   General Baptists [aggregated by Registrar General]
5   Particular Baptists
6   Quakers [also known as Society of Friends]
7   Wesleyan Methodists
8   Primitive Methodists [aggregated by Registrar General]
9   Other Arminian Methodists
10   Calvinistic Methodists

Leading non-Protestant nonconformist churches
11   Roman Catholics

Other specified denominations[3]
12   Aitkin's Christian Instruction Society
13   Arminian Bible Christians
14   Arminians
15   Baptized Protestants
16   Baxterians
17   Bethel Union Society
18   Bible Christians [Methodists; also known as Jumpers[4]]
19   Brethren
20   Bryanites [Methodists]
21   Calvinists
22   Chartist Religionists
23   Children of Sion
24   Church of England
25   Christian Believers
26   Christian Bond Society
27   Christian Pilgrims
28   Christian Revivalists
29   Christians
30   Christian Society
31   Christian Society of Harmony
32   Christian Union
33   Countess of Huntingdon's Persuasion [Methodist]
34   Disciples of Christ
35   Dissenters
36   Episcopalians
37   Established Church
38   Evangelical Arminians
39   Evangelical Unionists
40   Followers of Peace
41   Free-thinking Christians
42   Friendly Society

Table 5.2 continued

43	Holy and Apostolic Church [Catholic Apostolic Church; sometimes also known as Irvingites]
44	Home Missionaries
45	Huntingtonians [sic] [Methodist]
46	Independent Bible Christians
47	Independent Millenarians
48	Jews
49	Latter Day Saints [Mormons]
50	Millenarians
51	Moravians [United Brethren]
52	Mormonites
53	New Church [Swedenborgians]
54	New Jerusalem Church [Swedenborgians]
55	New Jerusalemites
56	Peculiar Calvinists
57	Philadelphians
58	Plymouth Brethren
59	Primitive Christian Dissenters
60	Providence Society
61	Providence Union Society
62	Ranters [Primitive Methodists][5]
63	Rational Religionists
64	Revivalist Community
65	Sandemanians [Glasites]
66	Seceders
67	Separatists
68	Shilohites [followers of the Southcottian, John Ward]
69	Social Institution
70	Sons of Sion
71	Southcottonians [sic]
72	Trinitarians
73	Unitarians [also Arians; Socinians][6]
74	Unitas Fratrum
75	United Brethren
76	United Friends
77	Universalists
78	Universal Millenarian Church

Foreign churches[7]

1	Lutherans
2	French Protestants
3	Reformed Church of the Netherlands
4	German Protestant Reformers
5	Roman Catholics
6	Greek Orthodox Church
7	German Catholics
8	Italian Reformers
9	Catholic and Apostolic Church
10	Latter Day Saints [Mormons]
11	Jews

Source: B.P.P. (1852/3), vol. 78, pp. 107–8: Registrar General's Returns relating to Dissenters' Places of Worship, as licensed between December 1688 and 29 June 1852: based on returns from municipal and clerical authorities

Notes: 1 Added to list, since the the Registrar General did not include the official Church of England in his survey.

2 So named in the Registrar General's returns, indicating that a large number of sects gave no further identification than this

3 As listed by Registrar General

4 For the Bible Christians as Jumpers, see C.M. Davies, *Unorthodox London: or, phases of religious life in the metropolis* (London, 1873), p. 89

5 Some Primitive Methodist congregations were known as 'Ranters': see ibid., p. 71. The name echoed that of the radical religionists of the 1640s, but there was no organisational connection

6 Arianism was the pre-eminent form of Unitarianism in eighteenth-century England, a doctrine that denied the Trinity and regarded Christ as subordinate to the Father, but still accepted the concept of atonement. A less common variant of anti-Trinitarianism was Socinianism, which denied both the divinity of Christ and the doctrine of atonement

7 Additional list from 1851 Religious Census for England and Wales: *B.P.P.* (1852/3), vol. 89, p. ix

By contrast, the (limited) religious freedom in England allowed full participation in the 'body politic' to all Protestant Nonconformists who were willing to pledge allegiance to the crown. If they met the relevant electoral qualifications, they were entitled to vote in local and national elections; and many did so.[68] Some also stood for parliament, such as the Unitarian dissenter William Smith, MP for Norwich 1802–5 and 1807–30. Moreover, in England the situation began slowly to be further liberalised in practice, with Catholic Relief Acts in 1778 and 1791, long before Emancipation in 1829. It was this civic pluralism that attracted Joseph II of Austria and alarmed his mother, the Empress Maria Theresa. She warned him in 1777 that even the Protestants realised that toleration would inevitably lead to religious indifference and universal destruction. Consequently, there were 'few more unfortunate and backward countries' than England, Saxony, Baden, Holland and Prussia, she urged dramatically – albeit without managing to convince her reformist son.[69]

Under Britain's Protestant monarchy, however, there was – at least in theory – a 'confessional' government or executive arm. This confusing state of affairs was the result of compromise in 1689. The Toleration Act did not disestablish the Church of England. It also left intact the old Test (1673) and Corporation Acts (1661), which survived until 1828. As a result, all office-holders were required to take oaths of allegiance and supremacy and (under the Test Act) to prove by certificate that they had taken communion according to Anglican rites. However, the rules were not operated very rigorously and were increasingly evaded. Thus some Nonconformists conformed occasionally to gain office; and after 1727 the Indemnity Acts allowed all defaulting office-holders to take extra time to comply after their appointment. That resulted in confusion, so that no-one knew exactly what the law required.[70] Furthermore, successive governments between 1722 and 1851 paid a semi-secret Treasury grant, known as the *regium donum*, to the old Protestant Nonconformist churches. The Baptists, Presbyterians and Congregationalists then used the money to supplement the income of poor ministers.[71] This helped to sustain those churches, whilst again blurring the government's confessional stance.

Anglican clerics themselves displayed a diversity of views. Theirs was a broad-based church which had no Inquisition to root out heresy or even a High Commission court to attempt surveillance, as had happened before 1641. Hence some clergymen within the established church professed a belief in the unity rather than the trinity of God. One such was Dr Samuel Clarke of Norwich. His career proceeded well, despite controversy, to the extent that in 1717 he was considered for the bishopric of Bangor (but not the archbishopric of Canterbury, as Voltaire wrongly reported). It was only at this point that Clarke was opposed, on the grounds that he had all the qualifications but one: 'He was not a Christian.'[72] Whether those words were precisely reported or not, this telling episode revealed that heterodox ministers could rise within the established church, even if not to the very top. In the event, Clarke did not become a bishop, although he did remain an officiating clergyman until his death in 1729.

Similar tensions were revived in 1776 by another Anglican parson with unitarian sympathies. In his tract *The Confessional*, Dr Francis Blackburne apologised for his 'quaint and uncouth' title, as a prelude to arguing that the Church of England should avoid any rigid confession of faith.[73] A simple declaration of belief in the Bible should suffice. Some of Blackburne's supporters (though not Blackburne himself) left the Church of England over the issue. Clearly, there were some limits to the flexibility of Anglicanism. The 39 Articles were not jetissoned. Yet the argument also showed that the capacious established church retained a considerable range of theological opinions even among its own ministry. Blackburne was not hounded from his quiet Yorkshire rectory and the stance of the Church of England remained calmly non-inquisitorial.

Ministers of the cloth therefore charted their way amidst a pluralist Christian culture. Each kingdom produced its own variations upon this theme. Ireland, for example, saw fierce three-way rivalries. The Catholicism of the majority Irish population was challenged by the Anglicanism of the established Church of Ireland and by the determined Presbyterianism of Ulster in the north.

Each set of ministers drew upon different sources of support. The Church of Ireland was backed by the institutions of the Anglo-Irish ascendancy. From 1704 until repeal in 1780, a special Irish Test Act restricted office-holding to Anglican communicants.[74] Two international figures also added lustre to the Church in the early eighteenth century, although both Dean Swift in Dublin and Bishop Berkeley in Cloyne achieved fame for their writings rather than for their patient pastoral labours. All these ministers, however, struggled against a major organisational hurdle. The Church of Ireland was funded by tithes, which were due from all parishioners whatever their religious faith (before disestablishment in 1869). Those payments were hated by the predominantly Catholic populace. Indeed, even a supporter of tithes admitted that their collectors were generally considered to be 'notorious Rogues, vigorous Exactors of illegal Dues, and Oppressors of the Poor'.[75]

Against the church of Swift and Berkeley, on the other hand, was pitted the loyalty of the Irish population to the priests of the old religion. The British state found that it could buttress Anglicanism but – without an inquisition – could not erase the rival faith. Penal laws debarred Catholics from the bench, the bar, the vote, Parliament, public office, and property ownership, before Relief Acts began to ease things in 1778, 1782 and 1793.[76] But, crucially, the 'hedge-priests' did not disappear. They remained close to their flocks, to whom they spoke in Gaelic, unlike the English-speaking Church of Ireland clergy.[77] The semi-secrecy of their mission added to the emotional intensity of the bonds. Thus the Catholic priesthood became very numerous, despite the official harassment. The names of 1,089 were recorded in 1705; and, by 1731, numbers had risen to c.1,400. After that, growth continued but less rapidly, to reach by the start of the nineteenth century some 1,800 priests and curates; and, by 1851, fully 2,464, plus 207 monks and friars.[78] Moreover, the education of these Catholic priests began to become professionalised, when in 1795 the Irish government agreed to fund St Patrick's Royal College at Maynooth, in the quiet Kildare countryside west of Dublin.[79] That inaugurated some (limited) state financial support for the Catholic church. Otherwise, the priesthood was funded by fees and by voluntary aid that was levied twice yearly.[80] Since all this was in addition to the obligatory tithes for the established church, it was not surprising to find a strong strand of Irish anticlericalism alongside Irish piety.

Meanwhile, the third group of ministers competing for popular allegiance were the Protestant Nonconformists. The Presbyterians were the best organised of these, with 130 separate congregations already in 1708[81] and strong support in Ulster. However, they too faced problems. For example, the status of marriages conducted by Presbyterian ministers was unclear before 1737, when matters were somewhat clarified.[82] More crucially, they faced internal disputes. A Presbyterian Secession Church separated in 1727 and did not reunite with the parent Synod of Ulster until 1840.[83] On the other hand, successive governments continued until 1869 to pay an Irish *regium donum* to subsidise poor Nonconformist ministers.[84] Thus Protestant pluralism survived, augmented in the later eighteenth century by the incoming missions of Irish Methodism.

Intense competition resulted. And the temperature was raised rather than abated when the Catholics gained Emancipation in 1829. A group of evangelicals counter-attacked with a new 'Protestant crusade' to combat what they saw as the triumph of 'Papist' bigotry and superstition.[85] In fact, none of these churches managed to eradicate the others. Instead, a close balance of clerical manpower helped to prolong the contest for allegiance. Thus, the 1851 census (Table 5.3) revealed, strikingly, that there were nearly as many (varied) Protestant ministers (2,627) in Ireland as there were Catholic priests in holy orders (2,671), despite the fact that the Catholic parishioners greatly outnumbered the Protestants.

Table 5.3 Men in Holy Orders in Ireland, 1851[1]

Church	No. of clergy	% of total (to 1 d.p.)
Roman Catholic		
Priests/curates (seculars)	2,464	41.2
Monks/friars (regulars)	207	3.5
All Catholics	2,671	44.7
Protestant		
Church of Ireland (Established)	1,786	29.9
Presbyterian Church	586	9.8
Methodists	232	3.9
Other Protestants[2]	23	0.4
All Protestants	2,627	44.0
Other		
Jewish rabbis	2	0.03
Unspecified[3]	679	11.4
All others	681	11.4
Total	5,979	100.1

Source: 1851 census in *B.P.P.* (1856), vol. 31 (Ireland), p. 782.
Notes: 1 In addition, there were 1,160 nuns engaged in pastoral and charitable works
2 Comprising 11 Baptists, 6 Moravians, 5 Unitarians and 1 Independent (Congregationalist)
3 This includes 669 'unspecified' plus 10 'missionaries' (denomination unspecified); but excludes other men engaged in the clerical/professional sector who were not in Holy Orders, such as clerks, sextons, and scripture readers

Theological rivalries similarly cut across any thoughts of professional solidarity amongst the clergy in Scotland. There the battle lines were different but the contests as animated. The new religious settlement left a legacy of disputes. In 1689, the old Scottish Episcopal Church – the parallel to the Anglican Churches of England and Ireland – lost its position as the established church. Instead, the majority Presbyterian Kirk of Scotland assumed that role. Its ministers were known for their forceful preaching, in a tradition derived from John Knox.[86] Voltaire could not resist teasing the stereotype. The Scottish Presbyterian 'puts on a sour look . . .; preaches thro' the nose, and gives the name of the whore of *Babylon* to all churches, where ministers are so fortunate as to enjoy an annual revenue of five or six thousand pounds'.[87] However, despite criticisms, the Presbyterian ministry enjoyed robust fame. Moreover, when they convened in their General Assembly, the meeting acted as an unofficial quasi-national forum for Scotland, after the 1707 Union had ended the country's separate Parliament.

Nevertheless, the Presbyterian ministers could not rest on their laurels. Scotland's alternative religions continued to survive and some to flourish. Throughout the eighteenth century, a quietist Catholicism continued in the northern Highlands, while in the nineteenth century a more ebullient Irish Catholicism was introduced by migrants into the west-coast industrial towns.[88] In addition, the old Episcopal Church remained broodingly unreconciled. Some of its adherents supported Jacobitism in the eighteenth century and flirted with Anglo-Catholicism in the nineteenth.[89] Meanwhile, at the other end of the theological spectrum, the Quakers, Baptists and Independents had some support, while minority sects such as the communitarian Glasites (Sandemanians) offered a radical alternative. Added to these, the pioneering Methodists drew large crowds in the 1740s and 1750s. However, the strength of the indigenous preaching tradition ensured that Methodism was notably less successful in Scotland than it was in England, Wales and Ireland.[90]

Protestantism, after all, was an argumentative faith that saw many schisms. In 1689–90, a small group of Calvinist purists refused to join the state church and set up the Reformed Presbytery, also known as the Cameronians, Convenanters or Society-Men.[91] Another row followed over the rights of lay patrons (under the 1712 Patronage Act). The dispute led to a second schism in 1733, when the minister Ebenezer Erskine founded the new Secession Church in 1737.[92] This group in turn split into two in 1747, each dividing again in 1799–1806.[93] In the meantime, a renewed dispute over patronage within the state church led to the third breakaway in 1761, to form the Relief Church. Only later did some of these groups re-amalgamate. In 1820 the United Secession Church was formed, which in 1847 merged with the Relief Church as the United Presbyterians.[94] But the fourth breakaway was the greatest. It sprang from simmering tensions between the ruling Moderates and their critics, the Evangelicals. Thus, in one sensational crisis in 1843, more than one-third of ministers and parishioners left the 'ould Kirk' to form the Free Church.[95]

No wonder that Hume, who lived among these disputants, commented upon the extent of *odium theologicum*, since the clergy were protagonists and often the leaders in these quarrels. Thus the profession in Scotland too was divided between competing churches. By 1851, the ministers of the Scottish Kirk remained the largest single group as almost 30 per cent of all clergymen. That is shown clearly in Table 5.4.

Yet the 'other' Protestant churches – which by then included the newly seceded Free Church – had between them almost twice as many clerics

Table 5.4 Men in Holy Orders in Scotland, 1851

Census description	No. of clergy	% of total (to 1 d.p.)
Church of Scotland (Presbyterian)	1,124	29.5
Other Protestant ministers	2,228	58.4
Priests and other religious teachers	460	12.1
Total	3,812	100.0

Source: Figures from 1851 census in *B.P.P.* (1852/3), vol. 88/1, p. ccxxviii – Table 26 and note * (Scotland)

(58.4 per cent), while priests and 'other religious teachers' stood at 12.1 per cent.

Clerical power was becoming increasingly fractured and in the long term muted by these divisions. However, its force clearly survived the absence of any professional monopoly or common organisational body to regulate their activities. And the influence of the clergy remained especially significant for the committed believers within each church.

Such religious pluralism also obtained in England and Wales. There the established Anglican communion held securely onto its position as the largest church. But it was accompanied by a great diversity of other faiths, including both old ones revived and new ones. The Roman Catholic priesthood in England, for example, survived the loss of royal support at the fall of James II in 1689. Their numbers fell to a nadir in the early eighteenth century. Nonetheless, the church then began to recover indigenous support and, as already noted, limited Catholic Relief Acts were passed in 1778 and 1791.[96] Irish immigrants also contributed fresh numbers and vitality in the early nineteenth century. In 1829 Catholic civil disabilities were lifted;[97] and in 1847 a full episcopate restored. Most famously, too, the defection to Rome in 1845 of John Henry Newman – from 1828 to 1843 the Anglican vicar of St Mary's Oxford – gave Popery a formidable new exponent. Indeed, his elevation as Cardinal in 1879 made him by far the most famous Catholic potentate in Britain since the Reformation.[98]

Little love was lost between these 'Papists' and the low-church Protestants. These latter were agreed in their common opposition to Rome and all its works. However, the Protestant Nonconformists or Dissenters, as they were also known, were also divided, as they met in their simple chapels, salems, bethels and tabernacles. In the early eighteenth century, the leading churches – Presbyterians, Baptists, Quakers, Congregationalists – grew in respectability rather than in great numbers. By the later 1710s they had some 2,000 congregations in England and Wales.[99] Their ministers were assisted discreetly under the *regium donum*, their schooling was promoted via the Dissenting Academies, and after 1732 they had an organised lobby in the Dissenting Deputies.[100] But the English Presbyterians had an especially chequered history. In 1719, they experienced the fierce doctrinal disputes in the Salters' Hall controversy, which foreshadowed conflicts among their Scottish and Irish counterparts; and by 1800, Presbyterianism was no longer England's largest dissenting church. Indeed, many congregations that were nominally of their persuasion had quietly become Unitarian.[101]

Ministers in these voluntaryist churches often had very close and intense relationships with their congregations. But it could make for a precarious way of life, in the event of disagreement. The restless career of one Charles Lloyd illustrated that. He caused shock by changing his theological views and his appointments several times: from a Presbyterian (Unitarian) post at Evesham in 1788 to a Baptist ministry in Sussex by 1790; on to the care of two unorthodox breakaway chapels in Cardiganshire by 1801 and back to a post as Unitarian minister in Suffolk in 1803. Eventually in 1811 he retired to make his living as a schoolmaster in London. In his autobiography, he bemoaned the poverty and uncertainty of the Nonconformist ministry, adding darkly: 'Every minister maintains his rights and independence at his peril.'[102] Few odysseys matched that. By contrast, distinguished figures were sometimes given great latitude. Dr Joseph Priestley, the polymathic political pamphleteer and research chemist, was required only to preach on Sundays when he was called in 1780 as Unitarian minister at Mill Hill in Birmingham. However, this happy posting was abruptly ended in July 1791. A crowd of 'Church and King' loyalists destroyed two Unitarian chapels and ransacked and burnt the homes of Priestley and other Dissenters, after which the sage moved to London before retiring in 1794 to Pennsylvania.[103]

Derision, invective, satire, opposition and some hostility from the crowds also faced a very different religious radical especially at the start of his career as an evangelist.[104] He was John Wesley, the founder of Methodism. As already noted, he came from clerical stock. Yet his inheritance straddled the denominational boundaries, since his father was the Anglican Rector of Epworth while both grandfathers had been Presbyterian ministers.[105] In 1725 Wesley was ordained as deacon (at the age of 22) and in 1728 as minister. He remained within the Church of England until his death in 1791. But he was a tireless evangelist for a new religious 'method' or discipline. In addition, he devised his own theology that fused Arminianism, Lutheranism and continental pietism. The irate Anglican polemicist Augustus Toplady denounced Wesley's ideas as a *'Necromantic Soup'* and one step away from Popery to boot.[106] Faced with this, senior figures within the established church were uncertain how to respond. On the one hand, Wesley was not promoted to a bishopric. On the other, no steps were taken to halt or expel him, even in 1784 when he took the dramatic step of ordaining new ministers on his own authority.

Wesley's power was therefore *sui generis*. It sprang from his unique combination of attributes. He had not only a new spiritual message and a vivid preaching style but also formidable organisational skills. Those helped to launch a vibrant new religious movement, which later separated from its Anglican parent and had became by 1851 one of the largest components within English Nonconformity. By contrast, Wesley's fellow pioneer, George Whitefield, was a messianic preacher but not a church-builder. His followers formed a much smaller group of Calvinistic Methodists. Organisationally, 'my people are a rope of sand', as Whitefield conceded.[107] Similarly low-key were the other Calvinistic networks, such as those in Wales or in the Countess of Huntingdon's Connection. Yet even the predominant Wesleyan tradition knew schisms.[108] The Old Connection did consolidate its seniority and respectability, under the firm hand of Jabez Bunting (between 1806–58 the secretary and four times president of its organising conference). However, the New Connection broke away in 1797, the Independent Methodists in 1806, the Primitive Methodists in 1812, the Bryanites or Bible Christians in 1815, the Tent Methodists in 1822, the Wesleyan Methodist Association in 1836, and the Wesleyan Reformers (later the Free Methodists) in 1849/50.

Cohesion was difficult to maintain in the voluntaryist sector. One small radical church provides a case history. In 1787/8 the Swedenborgian Society founded the New Jerusalem Church at London's Great Eastcheap, briefly supported by the poet William Blake and his wife. A leading evangelist was Robert Hindmarsh, son of a Methodist minister. By 1790, the membership were at loggerheads over church organisation as well as over questions of sexual morality. Hindmarsh was expelled, promptly to form a new Society. His group then ousted the first from the Eastcheap premises. In 1793 there were two rival Swedenborgian Conferences, while Blake lamented the return of overbearing 'Priests in black gowns'.[109]

Nor did money and a high-church theology solve the problems of building a new movement. In 1832 the millionaire banker and Tory MP Henry Drummond and some friends identified themselves as apostles. They worked with the charismatic preacher Edward Irving (a former minister of the Scottish Kirk in London) to found a new Catholic Apostolic Church. However, they lost support when a ritualistic liturgy was introduced. Only in the later 1840s did membership revive, as the apostles adopted the practice of 'sealing' – shades of Joanna Southcott – in the form of tickets of spiritual redemption.[110] But the decision not to renew the succession, as the founders died, led to the church's eventual demise.

All this encouraged a growing toleration of religious diversity. It is true that the campaigns in 1736, 1739, 1787, 1789 and 1790 to repeal the Test and Corporation Acts had all failed – although the 1789 vote was close.[111]

But adjustments were made. The *regium donum* offered some consolation. Moreover, in 1779, Dissenting teachers and ministers were given relief from various legal penalties. Concessions on Nonconformist worship followed in 1812. That marked a success for the vigorous lobbying of an alliance of the Protestant Dissenting Deputies, the Wesleyans and the newly constituted Protestant Society. In 1813, religious toleration was legally extended to the Unitarians. And in 1828 the Dissenters achieved repeal of the Test and Corporation Acts.[112]

Throughout all these perturbations, the Church of England retained its status. There was a small surviving rump of Non-Jurors, who refused to accept the political settlement of 1688/9. But their tiny church ceased with the death of their last bishop in 1779.[113] They did not seriously trouble the loyal Anglican ministry. The Church of England was, after all, the state-sponsored established church. Contempt of its ecclesiastical courts was punishable by excommunication, backed up by imprisonment, even though these penalties fell into disuse well before abolition in 1813.[114] The 26 Anglican bishops sat in *ex officio* splendour in the House of Lords.[115] Then came the ranks of deans and archdeacons, the power-brokers of the cathedral close.[116] And following them, the regular clergy.[117] Those included rectors with full tithes and vicars, who shared the tithes with the patron of the parish.

Loyalist clergymen were sometimes criticised for undue docility. The satirical ballad to *The Vicar of Bray* (1720?) ridiculed the weather-cocks who changed their views to suit each change of government. However, such tactics could succeed. 'Wou'd you rise in the *Church*, be *Stupid* and *Dull'*, advised the too brilliant Swift, who did not advance beyond an Irish Deanery.[118] Hazlitt later satirised obsequious candidates for preferment, who spent their time 'nodding to Deans, bowing to Bishops, waiting upon Lords, following in the train of Heads of Colleges, [and] watching the gracious eye of those who have presentations in their gift, and the lank cheek of those who are their present incumbents'.[119] Yet the appointments system was not simple. Senior churchmen may have discussed patronage at their favoured coffee house in London's St Paul's Yard. On the other hand, since the Reformation, many lay patrons and patronesses held the advowsons or rights of presentation to half the 11,000 Anglican livings. In 1742, 53.4 per cent were in private hands, compared with 48 per cent in 1835 – when the rest were held by the crown (9 per cent), the bishops (12 per cent) and other institutions, such as the Oxbridge colleges (31 per cent).[120]

Thus appointments were not centrally controlled. That was reinforced by the fact that advowsons and speculative 'futures' in presentations were discreetly available for sale. Individual clerics were prohibited by a law of 1713 from buying a nomination for themselves[121] but there was nothing to prevent families from obliging instead. Such a system was not ideal.

The effect, however, was to decentralise church appointments and to give power to money as well as to traditional ownership. Moreover, once installed, incumbents were not easily dismissed. Beneficed posts were considered as freehold tenure for life. As a result, the Anglican clergy included saints and sinners, wits and dullards, old and young, plus a handful famed for non-clerical activities: such as the novelist Lawrence Sterne; the reformer Christopher Wyvil; the inventor Edmund Cartwright; the demographer Parson Malthus; the polemicist Martin Madan, who created a furore in 1780 by advocating polygamy; the humorist Sydney Smith, who complained that the 'timid profession of the Church' did not promote free spirits like himself;[122] the hunting parson or 'clerical Nimrod' Jack Russell, who ran the best pack of hounds in Devonshire; and the eccentric Joshua Brookes, who knew by heart not only the Bible but the academic qualifications of all his fellow clergymen.[123]

Variations were also produced by the great diversity in the value of livings. Even the bishoprics ranged from the affluence of Canterbury with £7,000 per annum to the modesty of Bristol with only £400.[124] The state acted in 1704 to create Queen Anne's Bounty, which was a special fund to augment the revenues of the poorest livings. That began to raise the social status of the profession.[125] But the diverse valuations of Anglican livings encouraged pluralism, whereby one individual held more than one post simultaneously. Dr John Lynch was a notorious case. He was Dean of Canterbury in 1734 plus Master of St Cross Hospital, Winchester, Treasurer of Salisbury, and rector of six parishes. Moreover, he owed this success to family favouritism, since he was the son-in-law of Archbishop Wake of Canterbury.[126] In fact, some nepotism was condoned. Hence many bishops' sons routinely found employment in the Church. But criticisms were voiced if appointees were too obviously unsuitable or too young. Indeed, Parliament in 1804 ruled that twenty-three should be the minimum age for all Anglican deacons and twenty-four for Anglican priests.[127]

Most damaging was the sheer extent of clerical absenteeism, as the result of plural incumbencies. After 1803, the situation was regulated – but not resolved – by licenses for non-residence. These showed that in 1827 there was a resident Anglican parson in only 41.9 per cent of all parishes, although in another 15.1 per cent the non-resident parson lived near enough to visit and hold services.[128] The remaining 43 per cent relied upon the curates or clerical assistants. They were the subalterns of the professional phalanx. Their pay was often poor and their prospects uncertain. 'There is something that excites compassion in the very name of a Curate!!!', wrote Sydney Smith feelingly.[129] Some gained promotion, while others struggled hard to sustain gentility on relatively low incomes.

Reforms were difficult to achieve, especially against the vested interests of the lay patrons. Moreover, the church's own parliamentary body or Convocation did not meet between 1717 and 1852.[130] The clergy had no

The rising of the inferior Clergy.

Figure 5.3 The Rising of the Inferior Clergy (1768). This revolt never happened. But the print showed the resentment of the lesser clergy in the Church of England. A group of distressed curates, with their ragged families at their side, stand under the Shield of Faith and threaten to pull down their fat and indifferent seniors. In reply, the Bishops wave writs of excommunication and bags of money, while one says smilingly 'Religion is great Gain.'

Published by permission of the British Museum, Department of Prints and Drawings

forum to rebut attacks such as W. Benbow's perfervid polemic *The Crimes of the Clergy: or, the pillars of priest-craft shaken* (1823). Yet in the late eighteenth and early nineteenth centuries, there were some diocesan efforts at renewal, spurred by Protestant evangelism.[131] In addition, groups of active incumbents formed local societies, rather like the mutual-aid groups among the secular professions. By the 1830s, the restructuring process known as the 'second Reformation' had begun. Pushed jointly by external critics and internal reformers, the Church of England accepted tithe commutation (1836), overhauled its diocesan structures, greatly reduced pluralism and absenteeism – and defeated calls for its disestablishment.[132] At the same time, its grass-roots clergy began to call for the revival of Convocation as their own properly Anglican forum for regulating the church, especially as Parliament was becoming more and more multi-denominational after 1828/9. Equally, the specialist nature of the clerical vocation was stressed by low-church evangelicals and, in the 1830s, by the devotees of the Oxford Movement.[133]

It was by dint of this sort of pastoral commitment as well as state support that the Church of England triumphantly survived schisms and criticisms. The number of Anglican pastors approximately doubled from perhaps 8–9,000 in 1700 to 17,463 in 1851, as shown in Table 5.5. They made still by far the largest clerical phalanx within England and Wales – comprising two thirds of the total. However, they lived in a competitive world.

Table 5.5 Men in Holy Orders in England and Wales, 1851[1]

Census description	No. of clergy	% of total (to 1 d.p.)
Clergymen (Church of England)[2]	17,463	66.6
Other Protestant ministers[3]	6,466	24.7
Catholic priests and other religious teachers[4]	2,306	8.8
Total	26,235	100.1

Source: Aggregate figures from 1851 census in *B.P.P.* (1852/3), vol. 88/1, pp. ccxxii and ccxxxiv
Notes: 1 Includes Channel Islands and I. of Man
2 The census enumerator's 'Results and Observations' explained that those listed as 'clergymen' were ministers of the established church: see *B.P.P.* (1852/3), vol. 88/1, p. lxxxvi, note *. The census gave a variant total of 17,621 'clergymen' for Great Britain as a whole, which is sometimes cited instead: ibid., pp. cxii, cxxviii
3 The census also gave a denominational breakdown for the entire non-established ministry in Great Britain: ibid., p. cxxviii. The Presbyterians were the largest group (mainly in Scotland) followed by the Independents and the Wesleyan Methodists (chiefly in England and Wales). But the figures are not conclusive, since a large number were left unclassified simply as 'Protestant minister'
4 In Great Britain as a whole, there were 2,570 'Others' comprising 1,093 Catholic priests plus 1,477 'theological students, and various real or pretended Religious Teachers': ibid., p. lxxxvi

The non-Anglican Protestant ministry had multiplied yet more rapidly, from perhaps c. 1–2,000 in 1700 to 6,466 in 1851. By then, one out of every three clerics was not an Anglican parson.[134]

Collectively, this profession was also challenged by secular foes. These came in many guises, ranging from deism and freethinking to apathy, non-attendance, indifference, irreligion and outright atheism.[135] In times of stress, clergymen themselves were prone to alarmist statements. Bishop Butler lamented in 1751 'the general decay of religion in this nation; which is now observed by every one, and has been for some time the complaint of all serious persons'.[136] In 1796, Joseph Priestley agreed: 'Great . . . is the increase of infidelity in the present age'.[137] Meanwhile John Wesley in 1778 had curbed an enthusiast for missionary work overseas with the brusque comment: 'You have nothing at present to do in Afric[a]. Convert the heathen in Scotland.'[138] In practice, the extent of secularism was difficult to assess. It was enough that thinking clergymen were prepared for a spiritual struggle in a troubled world.

Moreover, Christianity was no longer unitary; new forms of knowledge were appearing; and the other educated professions also strove for public influence and attention. In Britain as elsewhere in the English-speaking world, tasks previously carried out by clergymen were gradually hived off to new specialists.[139] In 1700, for example, quite a number of Anglican parsons acted as land stewards and advisers to local landowners.[140] By 1800, however, that was rare. School-teaching was another occupation that was ceasing to be a clerical monopoly. Charitable work, once a special duty of the church, was becoming shared by lay agencies; and the laity played a prominent role in parish affairs too.[141] And, while some old-fashioned parsons still dosed their ailing parishioners, health care was fast becoming medicalised, despite John Wesley's eloquent warnings.

One enthusiast for good preaching nonetheless consoled the clergy in 1852 by reminding them of their role as moral mentors:

> Knowledge is power; truth is power. The preacher has power, other things being equal, just in proportion to the amount of truth he has encompassed and brought under the mastery of his faculties, so that he can use it at pleasure, for conviction, reproof, correction, and instruction in righteousness.

So wrote one Professor Shepard.[142] He was no precursor of Foucault. His aim was to praise the rightful power of the pulpit. But this was now exercised without a monopoly and within a pluralistic society.

NOTES

1 R. Campbell, *The London Tradesman, being a Compendious View of all the Trades, Professions, Arts, . . . in the Cities of London and Westminster* (London, 1747), p. 24.

2 J. Wesley, *An Address to the Clergy* (London, 1757), p. 28.
3 9 & 10 Will. III, cap. 32 (1697/8); and D. Berman, *The History of Atheism in Britain: from Hobbes to Russell* (Croom Helm, London, 1988), pp. 110–12, 134–6, 145–51.
4 J. Fletcher, *The Reconciliation: or, an easy method to unite the professing people of God* (London, 1777), p. 3.
5 W. Hazlitt, 'On the clerical character' (1818), in *Selected Essays of William Hazlitt, 1778–1830*, ed. G. Keynes (Nonsuch Press, London, 1946), pp. 780–1.
6 C. Hill, *Antichrist in Seventeenth-Century England* (Oxford University Press, Oxford, 1971), pp. 146–77; and P. Carus, *The History of the Devil . . .* (Land's End Press, London, 1969), pp. 392–406.
7 D.P. Walker, *The Decline of Hell: seventeenth-century discussions of eternal torment* (Routledge, London, 1964); and G. Rowell, *Hell and the Victorians: a study of nineteenth-century theological controversies concerning eternal punishment and the future life* (Clarendon, Oxford, 1974).
8 The standard guide was G. Burnet, *A Discourse of the Pastoral Care* (London, 1692; 14 edns by 1821). See also the helpful overview in J. Gregory, 'The eighteenth-century reformation: the pastoral task of Anglican clergy after 1689', in *The Church of England, c.1689–c.1833: from toleration to tractarianism*, ed. J. Walsh, C. Haydon and S. Taylor (Cambridge University Press, Cambridge, 1993), pp. 67–85.
9 Campbell, *London Tradesman*, pp. 26–9, 35.
10 H.W. Paul, *The Life of Froude* (London, 1905), pp. 47–9.
11 Anon., *An Admonition to the Younger Clergy* (London, 1764), p. 22.
12 'Benefit of clergy' was originally a clerical privilege, later extended to all literate adults, enabling them to avoid the worst legal penalties for a first offence: J.M. Beattie, *Crime and the Courts in England, 1660–1800* (Clarendon, Oxford, 1986), pp. 141–5, 451–2. After adaptation, 'clergy' was abolished in 1827.
13 See 41 Geo. III, cap. 63 (1801); and A. Stephens, *Memoirs of John Horne Tooke* (London, 1813), vol. 2, pp. 237–60.
14 For stylistic techniques, see R.P. Lessenich, *Elements of Pulpit Oratory in Eighteenth-century England, 1660–1800* (Böhlan, Cologne, 1972).
15 J. Downey, *The Eighteenth-Century Pulpit: a study of the sermons of Butler, Berkeley, Secker, Sterne, Whitefield and Wesley* (Clarendon, Oxford, 1969), pp. 15–16.
16 J. Trusler, *Twelve Sermons* (London, 1796).
17 Anon., *The Fashionable Preacher: or, modern pulpit eloquence displayed* (London, 1792), pp. 5, 10–12, 13–14, 17, 20–1.
18 W. Cowper, 'The Task, Bk. 2' (1785), in *The Poetical Works of William Cowper*, ed. H.S. Milford (Oxford University Press, London, 1950), p. 155.
19 V. Knox, *Essays, Moral and Literary* (2 vols, London, 1778–9), vol. 2, p. 165.
20 J. Wesley, *Directions concerning Pronunciation and Gesture* (Bristol, 1770), p. 11.
21 J. Hunt, *Religious Thought in England from the Reformation to the End of the Last Century* (London, 1873), vol. 3, pp. 32–47.
22 Downey, *Eighteenth-Century Pulpit*, pp. 32–57.
23 E.A. Abbott, *The Anglican Career of Cardinal Newman* (London, 1892), vol. 2, pp. 1–7.
24 E.K. Chambers, *Samuel Taylor Coleridge: a biographical study* (Clarendon, Oxford, 1938), pp. 86–90.
25 Downey, *Eighteenth-Century Pulpit*, pp. 165–78, 201–16.
26 R.W. Chapman (ed.), *Boswell: life of Johnson* (Oxford University Press, Oxford, 1976), p. 327.
27 *Holy Bible*, Joel, 2: 28.
28 See Z. Taft, *Biographical Sketches of the Lives and Public Ministry of Various Holy Women* (2 vols, London and Leeds, 1825, 1828); L.F. Church, *More about the Early*

Methodist People (Epworth, London, 1949), pp. 136–76; E.D. Graham, *Chosen by God: a list of the female travelling preachers of early Primitive Methodism* (Wesley Historical Society, Bunbury, Cheshire, 1989); and especially D.M. Valenze, *Prophetic Sons and Daughters: female preaching and popular religion in industrial England* (Princeton University Press, Princeton, 1985).

29 V. Cunningham, *Everywhere Spoken Against: dissent in the Victorian novel* (Clarendon, Oxford, 1975), pp. 145–71.

30 J.L. Weidman (ed.), *Women Ministers* (Harper & Row, San Francisco, 1985), p. 2.

31 The *D.N.B.* labels Southcott as a 'fanatic'; but she is discussed thoughtfully in J.F.C. Harrison, *The Second Coming: popular millenarianism, 1780–1850* (Routledge, London, 1979), pp. 86–134; and esp. J.K. Hopkins, *A Woman to Deliver her People: Joanna Southcott and English millenarianism in an era of revolution* (University of Texas Press, Austin, 1982), passim.

32 J. Southcott, *The Strange Effects of Faith* (Exeter, 1801), p. 69.

33 See P. Pullen, *Hymns or Spiritual Songs composed from the Prophetic Writings of Joanna Southcott* (London, 3rd edn, 1813), p. 223.

34 E.g. the ballad mock-lament *Johanna: or, the broken bubble* (1814).

35 Harrison, *Second Coming*, pp. 137–60.

36 One branch was the Panacea Society (1916). I am grateful to Evan Jones and Joy Dixon for advice; and to the Panacea Society of Bedford for confirmation of their continuing existence.

37 So Adam Bede explained Dinah's decision: G. Eliot, *Adam Bede* (Penguin, London, 1985), p. 583. See also Valenze, *Prophetic Sons and Daughters*, pp. 59–60, 63–4, 70–1, 188–90; and Cunningham, *Everywhere Spoken Against*, p. 145.

38 'Bernardus Utopiensis' [J. Rutty], *A Second Dissertation on the Liberty of Preaching granted to Women by the . . . Quakers* (Dublin, 1739), p. 13.

39 D. Lovegrove, *Established Church, Sectarian People: itinerancy and the transformation of English Dissent, 1780–1830* (Cambridge University Press, Cambridge, 1988), pp. 41–4.

40 Both quotations from ibid., pp. 41, 167.

41 See *D.N.B., sub*: John Ward; and Harrison, *Second Coming*, pp. 158–9.

42 Lovegrove, *Established Church, Sectarian People*, pp. 56, 142, 162, 165.

43 S. Smith, 'Persecuting Bishops' (1822), in idem, *The Works of the Revd Sydney Smith* (London, 1839), vol. 2, p. 125.

44 W. Blackstone, *Commentaries on the Laws of England* (Oxford, 1765–9), vol. 1, p. 372.

45 Anon., *Priestianity: or a view of the disparity between the Apostles and the modern inferior clergy* (London, 1720), p. 1.

46 G. Anderson, *An Estimate of the Profit and Loss of Religion* (Edinburgh, 1753).

47 W. Sherlock, *A Practical Discourse concerning Death* (London, 10th edn, 1699), p. 39.

48 O.W. Jones, 'The Welsh Church in the eighteenth century', in *A History of the Church in Wales*, ed. D. Walker (Historical Soc. of the Church in Wales, Penarth, Glam., 1976), pp. 103–4, 110–14.

49 Proportionately, the clergy were at their peak during the intensification of monasticism in the thirteenth and early fourteenth centuries: see J. Cox Russell, 'The clerical population of medieval England', *Traditio*, 2 (1944), pp. 179, 212. I am grateful to Hugh Lawrence for advice on this point.

50 Anderson, *Estimate*, p. 251, reported that remark made by Robert Cragie [i.e. Robert Craigie, Edinburgh lawyer and MP].

51 See H. Moore, *The Life of Mrs Mary Fletcher, Consort and Relict of the Revd John Fletcher, Vicar of Madeley, Salop., Compiled from her Journal . . .* (2 vols, London,

1817–18); Church, *Early Methodist People*, pp. 139–49; and T.A. Seed, *John and Mary Fletcher: typical Methodist saints* (London, 1906).

52 For example, Anon., *An Essay towards a Proposal for Catholic Communion, . . . for . . . a General Peace: by a minister of the Church of England* (London, 1704); Anon., *Religious Union: being . . . a plan for uniting the Catholics and Presbyterians within the established Church* (London, 1801); and Anon., *Sectarianism, the Bane of Religion . . . and the Necessity of an Immediate Movement towards Unity* (London, 1846).

53 J. Dunton, *The Pulpit-Fool: a satyr* (London, 1707), Pt 1, p. 23.

54 'Philalethes Cantabrigiensis', *Geometry no Friend to Infidelity: or, a defence of Sir Isaac Newton and the British mathematicians* (London, 1734), p. 13.

55 D. Hume, 'Of National Characters', essay 24, in his *Essays and Treatises on Several Subjects* (London, 1753), vol. 1, pp. 281–2, n.

56 J. Beresford (ed.), *The Diary of a Country Parson, The Reverend James Woodforde*, vol 1: *1758–81* (Clarendon, Oxford, 1968), p. 212.

57 Ibid., pp. 200, 214–15, 242, 309–10; vol. 2: *1782–7*, p. 114; and vol. 3: *1788–92*, p. 16.

58 Ibid., vol. 5: *1797–1802*, p. 312.

59 E.g. in July 1801, Whisson was on sufficiently neighbourly terms to take a letter to Norwich for Woodforde's niece: ibid., p. 325. The fact that the diary was systematically cut for publication by its editor John Beresford may possibly have excised some stronger religious emotions on Woodforde's part.

60 M. de Voltaire, *Letters concerning the English Nation* (Engl. transl., London, 1733), p. 45.

61 See W.S. Lewis (ed.), *Horace Walpole's Correspondence*, vol. 34: *With the Countess of Upper Ossory, III: 1788–97* (Oxford University Press, London, 1965), p. 83.

62 W.S.F. Pickering, 'The 1851 census: a useless experiment?', *British Journal of Sociology*, 18 (1967), pp. 382–407.

63 Registrar General's Returns relating to Dissenters' Places of Worship, in *B.P.P.* (1852/3), vol. 78, pp. 107–8. Groups that met in private, such as the Muggletonians, were not included.

64 This contraverts J.C.D. Clark, who defines England after 1689 and before 1828/9 as a 'confessional state': see Clark, *English Society 1688–1832: ideology, social structure and political practice during the ancien regime* (Cambridge University Press, Cambridge, 1985), e.g. p. 89; and idem, 'England's ancien regime as a confessional state', *Albion*, 21 (1989), pp. 450–74.

65 1 Will. & Mary, cap. 18 (1689).

66 See W. Ferguson, *Scotland, 1689 to the Present* (Oliver & Boyd, Edinburgh, 1978 edn), pp. 110–11; and J.L. McCracken, 'The ecclesiastical structure, 1714–60', in *A New History of Ireland*, vol. IV: *Eighteenth-Century Ireland, 1691–1800*, ed. T.W. Moody and W.E. Vaughan (Clarendon, Oxford, 1986), p. 102.

67 R.J.W. Evans, *The Making of the Habsburg Monarchy, 1550–1700: an interpretation* (Clarendon, Oxford, 1979), pp. 118–20.

68 Details in J.E. Bradley, 'Nonconformity and the electorate in eighteenth-century England', *Parliamentary History*, 6, pt 2 (1987), pp. 236–61.

69 S.K. Padover, *The Revolutionary Emperor: Joseph II of Austria* (Eyre & Spottiswoode, London, 1967 edn), p. 57.

70 K.R.M. Short, 'The English Indemnity Acts, 1726–1867', *Church History*, 42 (1973), pp. 366–76.

71 Idem, 'The English *Regium Donum*', *English Historical Review*, 84 (1969), pp. 59–78.

72 See *D.N.B.*, *sub*: Samuel Clarke (1675–1729); and J.P. Ferguson, *An Eighteenth-Century Heretic: Dr Samuel Clarke* (Roundwood Press, Kineton, 1976), pp. 208–9.

73 *D.N.B., sub*: Francis Blackburne (1705–87).

74 J.G. Simms, 'The establishment of Protestant supremacy, 1691–1714', in *Eighteenth-Century Ireland*, ed. Moody and Vaughan, pp. 24–5.

75 Anon., *The Rights of the Clergy of Ireland . . .: by a friend to the constitution* (Dublin, 1767), p. 8. See also D.H. Akenson, *The Church of Ireland: ecclesiastical reform and revolution, 1800–85* (Yale University Press, New Haven, 1971); and R.E. Burns, 'Parsons, priests and the people: the rise of Irish anti-clericalism, 1785–9', *Church History*, 31 (1962), pp. 151–3.

76 S.J. Connolly, *Priests and People in Pre-Famine Ireland* (Gill & Macmillan, New York, 1982), pp. 6–11.

77 B.O'. Cuív, 'Irish language and literature, 1691–1845', in *Eighteenth-Century Ireland*, ed. Moody and Vaughan, pp. 378–81.

78 Connolly, *Priests and People*, pp. 32–3, 284–6.

79 R.B. McDowell, 'Ireland in 1800', in *Eighteenth-Century Ireland*, ed. Moody and Vaughan, pp. 688–9; and details in Anon., *The Case of Maynooth Considered: with a history of the first establishment of that seminary . . .* (Dublin, 1836).

80 J.A. Murphy, 'The support of the Catholic clergy in Ireland, 1750–1850', *Historical Studies: papers read before the sixth Conference of Irish Historians*, 5 (1965), pp. 103–21; D.J. Keenan, *The Catholic Church in Nineteenth-Century Ireland: a sociological study* (Barnes & Noble, Totowa, N.J., 1983), pp. 226–30.

81 D. Baillie (ed.), *A History of Congregations of the Presbyterian Church in Ireland, 1610–1982* (Presbyt. Hist. Soc. of Ireland, Belfast, 1982), p. 808.

82 J.C. Beckett, *Protestant Dissent in Ireland, 1687–1780* (Faber & Faber, London, 1946), pp. 116–23.

83 J.M. Barkley, *A Short History of the Presbyterian Church in Ireland* (P.C.I., Belfast, 1959), pp. 31, 49–52.

84 Beckett, *Protestant Dissent*, pp. 28–9, 60–1, 106–15.

85 See D. Bowen, *The Protestant Crusade in Ireland, 1800–70: a study of Protestant–Catholic relations between the Act of Union and disestablishment* (Gill & Macmillan, Dublin, 1978), pp. 83–123; and e.g. polemic by 'Clericus Hibernicus', *Superstition: or, the perils of Ireland in the projects of Rome* (London, 1823), p. 19.

86 W.M. Taylor, *The Scottish Pulpit from the Reformation to the Present Day* (London, 1887), esp. pp. 49–62, 139 ff.

87 Voltaire, *Letters concerning the English Nation*, pp. 42–3.

88 C.G. Brown, *The Social History of Religion in Scotland since 1730* (Methuen, London, 1987), pp. 19, 44–7.

89 Ibid., pp. 48–51. See also a Dissenter's rebuke in the ironically entitled Anon., *An Historical Account of the Bitter Sufferings . . . of the Episcopal Church in Scotland . . .* (Edinburgh, 1707).

90 Brown, *Social History of Religion*, pp. 43–4, 51–3.

91 Ibid., pp. 41–2. Most of these united with the Free Church in 1876 but a small group still retains an independent organisation.

92 See T. Stephen, *The History of the Church of Scotland from the Reformation to the Present Time* (London, 1845), vol. 4, p. 265; and J.H.S. Burleigh, *A Church History of Scotland* (Oxford University Press, London, 1960), pp. 280–2.

93 Ibid., pp. 323–4.

94 Brown, *Social History of Religion*, pp. 36–8; and for the theological debates, see I. Hamilton, *The Erosion of Calvinist Orthodoxy: seceders and subscription in Scottish Presbyterianism* (Rutherford House, Edinburgh, 1990), pp. 15–18, 22–4.

95 A.L. Drummond and J. Bulloch, *The Scottish Church, 1688–1843: the age of the moderates* (St. Andrews Press, Edinburgh, 1973), pp. 231–2, 242–56; Burleigh, *Church History*, pp. 334–58. In 1900, the Free Church merged with United

Presbyterians as the United Free Church, while a resistant minority remained the 'Wee Free Kirk'.

96 18 Geo. III, cap. 60 (1778) and 31 Geo. III, cap. 32 (1791).

97 10 Geo. IV, cap. 7 (1829). See also W. Hinde, *Catholic Emancipation: a shake to men's minds* (Blackwell, Oxford, 1992).

98 J. Bossy, *The English Catholic Community, 1570–1850* (Darton, Longman & Todd, London, 1975), pp. 295–322, 361–2, stresses the pre-Newman revival, whereas Newman saw the 1840s as pivotal. See also E. Duffy, *Peter and Jack: Roman Catholics and Dissent in eighteenth-century England* (Dr. Williams Trust, London, 1982), pp. 3–21.

99 Based upon the survey of 1715–18, known as the Evans list: see M.R. Watts, *The Dissenters* (Clarendon, Oxford, 1978), pp. 267–89.

100 The Deputies represented London's Baptist, Presbyterian and Congregationalist churches: B.L. Manning, *The Protestant Dissenting Deputies* (Cambridge University Press, Cambridge, 1952).

101 Watts, *The Dissenters*, pp. 371–82. See also H. McClachlan, *The Unitarian Movement in the Religious Life of England . . . 1700–1900* (Allen & Unwin, London, 1934); and R.E. Richey, 'Did the English Presbyterians become Unitarian?', *Church History*, 42 (1973), pp. 58–72.

102 Anon. [C. Lloyd], *Particulars of the Life of a Dissenting Minister, Written by Himself* (London, 1813; repr. 1911), p. 175.

103 F.W. Gibbs, *Joseph Priestley: adventurer in science and champion of truth* (Nelson, London, 1965), pp. 188–211; and R.B. Rose, 'The Priestley riots of 1791', *Past & Present*, 18 (1960), pp. 68–88.

104 E.M. Lyles, *Methodism Mocked: the satiric reaction to Methodism in the eighteenth century* (Epworth Press, London, 1960); T.B. Shepherd, *Methodism and the Literature of the Eighteenth Century* (Epworth Press, London, 1940), pp. 189–248; R. Green (ed.), *Anti-Methodist Publications issued during the Eighteenth Century* (London, 1902).

105 S. Ayling, *John Wesley* (Collins, London, 1979) and M. Edwards, 'John Wesley', in *A History of the Methodist Church in Great Britain*, vol. 1, ed. R. Davies and G. Rupp (Epworth Press, London, 1965), pp. 37–79.

106 A. Toplady, *A Letter to the Revd Mr John Wesley . . .* (London, 1771), p. 13.

107 Ayling, *Wesley*, p. 201. See J. Walsh, 'Methodism at the end of the eighteenth century', in *History of the Methodist Church*, ed. Davies and Rupp, pp. 292–3; and *D.N.B.*, *sub*: George Whitefield (1714–70).

108 See R. Currie, *Methodism Divided: a study in the sociology of ecumenicalism* (Faber & Faber, London, 1968), pp. 54–76; and M. Edwards, *After Wesley: a study of the social and political influence of Methodism in the middle period, 1791–1849* (Epworth Press, London, 1935), pp. 153–64. For the total of Methodist ministers, see also R. Currie, A. Gilbert and L. Horsley, *Churches and Churchgoers: patterns of church growth in the British Isles since 1700* (Clarendon, Oxford, 1977), pp. 203–6.

109 E.P. Thompson, *Witness against the Beast: William Blake and the moral law* (Cambridge University Press, Cambridge, 1993), pp. 129–73, esp. pp. 136–7, 140–4; and A. Morley, 'William Blake and the great Eastcheap orthodoxy', in *Protest and Survival: the historical experience*, ed. J. Rule and R. Malcolmson (Merlin Press, London, 1993), pp. 139–73.

110 D. Tierney, 'The Catholic Apostolic Church: a study in Tory millenarianism', *Historical Research*, 63 (1990), pp. 289–315, esp. pp. 292–6, 300–1, 303.

111 Manning, *Protestant Dissenting Deputies*, pp. 28, 31, 218.

112 See respectively 19 Geo. III, cap. 44 (1779); 52 Geo. III, cap. 155 (1812); 53 Geo. III., cap. 160 (1813); and 9 Geo. IV, cap. 17 (1828).

113 T. Lathbury, *A History of the Non-Jurors* (London, 1842), pp. 362–5, 410.

114 53 Geo. III, cap. 127 (1813).

115 See N. Sykes, *Church and State in England in the Eighteenth Century* (Clarendon, Oxford, 1932), pp. 41–146.

116 Their powers were defined by A. Trollope, *Clergymen of the Church of England* (1866; repr. Leicester University Press, Leicester, 1974), pp. 31–53.

117 P. Virgin, *The Church in an Age of Negligence: ecclesiastical structure and problems of church reform, 1700–1840* (Clarke, Cambridge, 1989); P.C. Hammond, *The Parson and the Victorian Church* (Hodder & Stoughton, London, 1977); and A. Haig, *The Victorian Clergy* (Croom Helm, London, 1984).

118 J. Swift, 'Advice to a parson: an epigram' (1732), in *Swift: Poetical Works*, ed. H. Davis (Oxford University Press, London, 1967), p. 535.

119 Keynes (ed.), *Selected Essays of William Hazlitt*, p. 788.

120 D.R. Hirschberg, 'The Government and church patronage in England, 1660–1760', *Journal of British Studies*, 19 (1980), pp. 111–17; and M.J.D. Roberts, 'Private patronage and the Church of England, 1800–1900', *Journal of Ecclesiastical History*, 32 (1981), p. 202.

121 12 Anne, stat. 2, cap. 12 (1713). See also Haig, *Victorian Clergy*, pp. 252–62; Virgin, *Church in an Age of Negligence*, pp. 181–5.

122 H. Pearson, *The Smith of Smiths* (Hamilton, London, 1934), p. 234.

123 Joshua Brookes (1754–1821) was lightly disguised in the 'Brief sketch of the Revd Josiah Streamlet', *Blackwood's Edinburgh Magazine*, 8/48 (March 1821), p. 364.

124 N. Sykes, 'The Church', in *Johnson's England: an account of the life and manners of his age*, ed. A.S. Turberville (2 vols, Clarendon, Oxford, 1933), vol. 1, p. 18.

125 2 & 3 Anne, cap. 11 (1703/4). For the Bounty Board (1704–1948), see esp. G.F.A. Best, *Temporal Pillars: Queen Anne's Bounty, the Ecclesiastical Commissioners, and the Church of England* (Cambridge University Press, Cambridge, 1964), pp. 28–34, 78–136, 537–8.

126 N. Sykes, *William Wake, Archbishop of Canterbury, 1657–1737* (Cambridge University Press, Cambridge, 1957), pp. 241–2. See also critique by 'A Yeoman of Kent', *The Life of Dean L—ch* (London, 1748).

127 44 Geo. III, cap. 43 (1804). This gave the traditional Anglican canons the force of law and expressed concern at breaches in the rule, especially among the Church of Ireland clergy.

128 An Act of 43 Geo. III, cap. 84 (1803) created a system of licenses for non-residence. See also details in Virgin, *Church in an Age of Negligence*, pp. 160–4, 196–202, and p. 290 (Table 18); and for a case study of London, see V. Barrie-Curien, 'The clergy in the diocese of London in the eighteenth century', in *The Church of England*, ed. Walsh, Haydon and Taylor, pp. 90–4.

129 Pearson, *Smith of Smiths*, p. 232. For curates, see also Best, *Temporal Pillars*, pp. 16–17, 207–9; Haig, *Victorian Clergy*, pp. 218–40; and Virgin, *Church in an Age of Negligence*, pp. 215–46.

130 T. Lathbury, *A History of the Convocation of the Church of England* (London, 1842); and G. Roberts, *A Plain Tract Showing the History and Nature of Convocation* (London, 1850).

131 See esp. R.A. Burns, 'A Hanoverian legacy? diocesan reform in the Church of England, c.1800–33', in *The Church of England*, ed. Walsh, Haydon and Taylor, pp. 265–82. See also K. Hylson-Smith, *Evangelicals in the Church of England, 1734–1984* (Clark, Edinburgh, 1989); and W.R. Ward, *The Protestant Evangelical Awakening* (Cambridge University Press, Cambridge, 1992).

132 For the 1830s reforms, see E. Evans, *The Contentious Tithe: the tithe problem and English agriculture, 1750–1850* (Routledge, London, 1976), pp. 6–12, 16–37,

115–32; Best, *Temporal Pillars*, pp. 296–47; and K.A. Thompson, *Bureaucracy and Church Reform: the organisational response of the Church of England to social change, 1800–1965* (Clarendon, Oxford, 1970), pp. 56–82. By 1879, clerical absenteeism had fallen sharply to only 11.9 per cent of all parishes: Virgin, *Church in an Age of Negligence*, p. 290 (Table 18).

133 O. Chadwick, *The Spirit of the Oxford Movement: tractarian essays* (Cambridge University Press, Cambridge, 1990), pp. 1–53.

134 See also K.S. Inglis, 'Patterns of religious worship in 1851', *Journal of Ecclesiastical History*, 11 (1960), pp. 74–86; Currie, Gilbert and Horsley, *Churches and Churchgoers*, pp. 2–4, 23–9.

135 C.J. Sommerville, *The Secularization of Early Modern England: from religious culture to religious faith* (Oxford University Press, Oxford, 1992); J. Champion, *The Pillars of Priestcraft Shaken: the Church of England and its enemies, 1660–1730* (Cambridge University Press, Cambridge, 1992); and A.D. Gilbert, *The Making of Post-Christian Britain: a history of the secularization of modern society* (Longman, London, 1980), pp. 4–39.

136 J. Butler, 'A charge . . . to the clergy . . . of Durham', in idem, *The Works of Joseph Butler* (2 vols, Edinburgh, 1804), vol. 2, p. 27.

137 J. Priestley, *Observations on the Increase of Infidelity* (London, 1796), p. x.

138 J. Telford (ed.), *The Letters of the Revd John Wesley* (Epworth Press, London, 1931), vol. 6, p. 316.

139 E.g. D.M. Scott, *From Office to Profession: the New England ministry, 1750–1850* (Pennsylvania University Press, Philadelphia, 1978), pp. 148–55. See also M. Hawkins, 'Ambiguity and contradiction in "the rise of professionalism": the English clergy, 1570–1730', in *The First Modern Society: essays in English history in honour of Lawrence Stone*, ed. A.L. Beier, D. Cannadine and J.M. Rosenheim (Cambridge University Press, Cambridge, 1989), pp. 241–69; C. Dewey, *The Passing of Barchester: a real-life version of Trollope* (Hambledon Press, London, 1991), pp. 1–6; and B. Heeney, *A Different Kind of Gentleman: parish clergy as professional men in early and mid-Victorian England* (Archon Books, Hamden, Conn., 1976).

140 D. Hainsworth, *Stewards, Lords and People: the estate steward and his world in later Stuart England* (Cambridge University Press, Cambridge, 1992), pp. 19–21.

141 For lay elders in Scotland, see Brown, *Social History of Religion*, pp. 118, 121, 127; and for the 'laicisation of religion' in the Anglican Church, see also Sykes, *Church and State*, pp. 379–80.

142 Prof. Shepard, *Pulpit Outlines: 120 sketches of sermons preached to evangelical congregations* (London, 1852), p. xxiii.

6

DOCTORS

> Ah, my dear doctor, you are of a profession which will endure
> for ever; no revolution will put an end to Synochus and Synocha
> [Latin = continuing fevers].

So wrote the Reverend Sydney Smith to a medical friend in 1805.[1] For once, the celebrated wit was not joking. Since disease and death were unavoidable, demand for health care was perennial. Provided that people had confidence in the medical profession, their role was assured. Thus doctors could entice customers to pay for care – unlike the clergy who faced growing difficulty in collecting tithes, as Smith wryly noted.

This was a key period in which the status of 'medicine' rose. The still-continuing traditions of household doctoring and self-medication were pushed into subsidiary roles. Demand for good health, after all, was not difficult to stimulate. But, increasingly, the diversifing medical profession was identified as the source of assistance in achieving that goal. If therefore the years around 1700 were the 'age of the lawyer', then the later eighteenth and nineteenth centuries belonged to the doctor. That process was closely related not only to the growth of a corpus of medical knowledge – power/knowledge in Foucaultian terms – but also to the defining role of the many medical institutions.

Certainly, in these years medicine was identified as an independent subject with sub-specialisms such as dentistry and ophthalmics. Its name was also clarified. For many years, 'medicine' and 'physic' were both used. They were interchangeable terms. Thus a 1728 handbook defined medicine as 'an Art, ordinarily call'd *Physic*', while 'physic' was 'the Art of Healing; properly called *Medicine*'.[2] But 'physics' also meant the science of matter and energy. Hence by the mid-eighteenth century, 'medicine' was becoming the preferred (though not universal) term. In 1771, the editor of the *Encyclopaedia Britannica* had no doubts. He described 'physic' with the simple instruction: 'see MEDICINE'.[3]

At the same time, this corpus of knowledge was increasingly defined as a science. A Scottish pioneer William Graeme argued that in 1729. 'Physick is a Science that may be taught by a Master', he wrote.[4] The concept was quickly accepted and indeed glorified. Medicine was 'the science which proposes the noblest object for its end, the preservation and restoration of health', Dr Lettsom opined in 1773; Samuel Ferris studied the *Establishment of Physic as a Science in England* in 1795; and the Edinburgh-trained American doctor Samuel Bard agreed in 1812 that: 'Medicine is a comprehensive and intricate science, founded on numberless facts '.[5] The subject thus conferred its own lustre. A divine in 1794 happily noted that 'the medical profession in Great Britain enjoyed that degree of estimation and credit, which a science, conferring on mankind the greatest of all comforts except those of religion, justly deserves.'[6] Medicine united therapeutic practice with precise knowledge. Thus a letter in *The Lancet* in 1826/7 put both art and science together to remark that: 'the professors of the healing art, that godlike science of restoring health to man, have ever received the veneration and esteem of mankind'.[7]

Some cautious doctors still collected fees for very little. They maintained that 'Nature should be left to do her own Work, while the Physician stands by, as it were to clap her on the Back, and encourage her when she doth well', as Henry Fielding wrote chaffingly in 1749.[8] But interventionism was increasingly advocated. Crabbe's *Parish Register* (1807) imagined the clash of cultures between a brash young town doctor and a traditional midwife. The newcomer, Dr Glibb, was ready to conquer all: 'No slave to Nature, 'tis my chief delight/ To win my way and act in her despite.'[9] And his optimism led to social, if not medical, success: 'The wealthier part, to him and science went;/ With luck and her the poor remain'd content.'

Part of the pressure for intervention came from public demand, which encouraged doctors to respond. This process has been described as 'medicalisation', whereby expectations were raised and a fatalistic acceptance of illness retreated. In the eighteenth century, pioneers began to call for programmes of preventive medicine. The earliest ventures – such as the campaigns against smallpox – began modestly but gained increasing support as techniques were refined. By 1767, Dr Giles Watts declared that inoculation reflected credit upon 'the art of medicine in general'.[10] He was followed in 1785 by Dr Haygarth of Chester with a bullish *Enquiry how to Prevent the Small-Pox*, which by 1793 was extended into a *Plan to Exterminate the Casual Small-Pox from Great Britain*. Passivity was abandoned. Jenner's new technique of vaccination then followed upon inoculation. Thus, despite controversies at every point, a loathsome disease began to be combatted (and by 1977–200 years later – has disappeared world-wide, outside the laboratory).

Medical experts took confidence from this. They were also boosted by studies of the heroic evolution of their own discipline. An early example was John Freind's *History of Physick* (1729). Such writings offered a picture of 'progress', although William Black's *Historical Sketch of Medicine and Surgery* (1782) also advised the pundits to study reliable data in preference to vain theorising.[11] Doctors could also consult the specialist journals launched from the 1750s onwards. Celebrated examples included in Edinburgh Dr Andrew Duncan's *Medical and Philosophical Commentaries* (1773–95); the *Dublin Journal of Medical and Chemical Science* (later *The Irish Journal of Medical Science*) from 1832; and the *British Medical Journal* in 1840. A new magazine called *The Scalpel* (1822/4) failed; but Thomas Wakley's *The Lancet* (1823-) became required reading as a crusading weekly journal. Before 1800, at least 31 new medical periodicals – many short-lived – had appeared; by 1850 another 148 followed.[12] All reported research and case histories.

Close observation of both patient and malady was advised. That was stressed in the later seventeenth century by the 'English Hippocrates' Dr Thomas Sydenham: 'You must go to the bedside. It is there alone you can learn disease.'[13] In practice, of course, it was impossible to test and observe everything; and many doctors did not try. The subject remained full of rival theories, some still invoking the old Galenic teaching of bodily 'humours'. Yet such eclecticism left scope for experimentation by bold spirits. Medicine remained a practical discipline, with great stress upon communication and reportage. That also generated many wrangles and disputes, which linked British scientists into an eristic medical community – and one that existed within an increasingly international framework, as Leiden and Edinburgh, and later London and Paris, vied for medical supremacy. By 1850, the new prestige of medicine was based upon better anatomical understanding, refined surgical techniques, a developing classification of diseases (nosology), a battery of powerful drugs (often over-used) and the formulation of the principles of public and private health.

Admittedly, doctors in practice often blundered. They understood symptoms at this time much better than they did causes.[14] Thus both the theories and therapeutics of eighteenth-century medicine contained many flaws, especially when compared with the dramatic improvements of the later nineteenth century (although of course, the profession has still made errors thereafter). Some mistakes were very public, as when Dr Reece in 1814 wrongly confirmed that the 64-year-old prophetess Joanna Southcott was pregnant.[15] And the medical community was divided and uncertain before the ravages of cholera in the 1830s.[16]

However, doctors in every era have offered care and treatment rather than guaranteed diagnosis and cure. In this period, their therapeutic healing was offered with new confidence on the basis of a subject that was being systematised, tested and communicated. Doctors increasingly stressed that scientific knowhow aimed not at sectional gain but at the general good. For that reason, opposition to secrecy was a point of principle. The first issue of the *Lancet* in 1823 accordingly revealed the hitherto unknown ingredients of twenty-four popular patent medicines.[17] And Samuel Bard had earlier propounded a classic statement of this ethos in 1769:

> Do not pretend to Secrets, Panacea's, and Nostrums, they are illiberal, dishonest, and inconsistent with your Characters, as Gentlemen and Physicians, and with your Duty as Men – For if you are possessed of any valuable Remedy, it is undoubtedly your Duty to divulge it, that as many as possible may reap the Benefit of it; and if not, (which is generally the case) you are propagating a Falsehood, and imposing upon Mankind.[18]

Enlightened doctors reported their own cases and discussed those of their fellows. Thus the 'scientific revolution' in nineteenth-century medicine – including the adoption of anaesthetics (first used in Britain in 1846), antiseptics (pioneered by Joseph Lister in 1867) and immunology (with the microbacteriology of Louis Pasteur and Robert Koch) – occurred within an international scientific community that was already interested in these problems long before the 'breakthrough' came.[19]

One index of the rising prestige of the medical practitioners was their successful capture of the scholarly title. A 'doctor' officially referred to one with a higher university degree – whether in physic, law, divinity or music. That was the first reference in Johnson's *Dictionary* in 1751.[20] But the medical meaning became ever more predominant in popular parlance, while the old name of 'leech' or blood-sucker survived only in jocular usage. One author in 1749 did indeed worry about the upgrading of occupational labels. Just as the 'meanest pettifogger' had become a *'lawyer'*, so 'every farrier, little apothecary, or surgeon's mate, is also commonly honoured with the title of *doctor'*.[21] It meant that practitioners were able in effect to 'graduate themselves' in the sardonic phrase of Tobias Smollett, who did have a medical doctorate from Aberdeen.[22] The learned title conferred status. As one physician grumbled in 1735: 'There is not a poor Peasant or Mechanick, but if he has two Sons, one of them must be a *Doctor*, as they call them.'[23] Moreover, a single occupational title bridged over technical distinctions. Thus when a London Medical Society was planned in 1773, its members were to include 'Physicians, Surgeons, and Apothecaries; and others versed in sciences connected with medicine'. Only the commercial proprietors of patent medicines were excluded.[24]

Here then was an ancient occupation, with many branches, in process of consolidation as one profession. Medical dress among the physicians expressed their eminence with a black coat, knee breeches, tie-wig and gold-topped cane. Later the stereotype evolved. From the 1820s onwards (following the pioneering Laennec in France) the cane was replaced by the stethoscope.[25] But the image remained strong and dignified. A growing interest was expressed in the lives of these powerful beings. In 1740 Dr Edward Milward called for biographies of famous British doctors (physicians and surgeons alike) to record their collective history.[26] Soon his call was abundantly answered. Surveys such as the surgeon John Aikin's

Biographical Memoirs of Medicine in Great Britain ... (1780) or Benjamin Hutchinson's *Biographia Medica* (1799) were augmented by many individual studies. In addition, portraits, engravings and sculptures were produced for sale and also collected in Thomas Pettigrew's four-volume *Medical Portrait Gallery* (1840). Such works saw the history of medicine as a progression of great men, leavened by famous eccentrics such as the blunt-talking long-lived Dr Messenger Monsey.[27] Moreover, the role of the profession was seen as part of the nation's destiny. Thus Dr Cooper's poem on *The Progress of Physic* (1743) boasted:

> From *East* to *West*, hence Physic boasts her *Sway*,
> And darts on *All* a more propitious *Ray*;
> But Fix'd her *Throne* on fair *Britannia*'s Isle,
> To whom she owes a *Harvey* – and a *Boyle*.[28]

Admiration on that scale was also likely to provoke concern. It was not surprising, for example, that John Wesley in 1747 worried that leading doctors were too often viewed 'as Persons who were something more than Human'.[29] His attitude reflected a real distaste for doctor-worship as well as jealousy from a rival profession. That lay behind the production of his famous self-help manual of 'God-given' folk remedies, although Wesley was not hostile to all forms of doctoring and he experimented with new medical treatments, such as 'electrification'. These hesitations before the advance of medical authority were shared by others. Hence there were fears that the doctors' growing control over the secrets of health care conferred too much power over a credulous public.

Indeed, that view has reappeared, buttressed by Foucaultian theory, in some recent studies. Instead of a Whiggish stress upon the emergence of a disinterested and benevolent profession, the doctors' role in health care is viewed in less than glowing terms. The advent of the 'expert' meant that the 'patient' lost control.[30] Doctors were seen as generally confident and determined, while their clients were weak, ill and depressed. Indeed, the identification of someone as a 'patient' or 'invalid' tended to tilt the balance of power in favour of the fit, active healer rather than the anxious, passive sufferer. For some ultra-liberal analysts, doctors are but tyrants under the mask.[31]

It is certainly wise not to be too starry-eyed about any of the professions, since they had their own sectional interests as well as those of their clients to serve. But their power was limited. Satirists and critics supplied a countervailing dose of scepticism, while (as will be seen) the doctors were themselves divided organisationally. Most importantly, patients were not all the passive creatures of mythology. Indeed it has even been argued that physicians, who treated the aristocracy, generated the matrix of medical theory among the prevailing ideas of the ruling class.[32] That in fact exaggerates the reliance of the senior medical men upon the elite, since

THE DOCTOR TOO MANY FOR DEATH.

Figure 6.1 The Doctor too many for Death (1787). This print praises the power of the medical profession. A confident physician in wig and sword, plus gold-headed cane, wields his full syringe to repel the skeleton of Death. Meanwhile, the patient has sufficient strength to drink soup and point to his medical saviour.
Published by permission of the Wellcome Institute Library, London

medical services were available to a broader range of clients than that implies, and it also exaggerates the role of the physicians in spearheading medical thought. But it does point to the positive input from patients. They gave or withheld trust in doctors and the latest medical knowhow, just as they followed or ignored the medical advice they were given.

Moreover, there was a continuing tradition of self-medication.[33] Pills and elixirs were readily on sale, including popular opiates such as the Kendal Black Drop to which Coleridge became addicted.[34] People were also helped by family and friends, while, in country villages, some grandees continued to dispense aid. Farquhar drew a fictional portrait in 1707 of the old-fashioned Lady Bountiful, busy with the 'spreading of plaisters, brewing of diet-drinks, and stilling rosemary-water'.[35] And the real-life Parson Woodforde dosed not only himself but also his niece and his servants, although at times he consulted a local doctor too.[36]

Because the resources available to patients were variegated, the medical profession had to earn trust in a competitive world. The famous Dr Radcliffe (1650–1714) once recommended that doctors should either cajole or bully their patients.[37] But bluffness was not tyranny and even bluffness could be taken too far. The ideal manner was the discreet sympathy of a wise family friend. It took time to build up a practice and young doctors – like junior lawyers – often struggled.[38] Regular church-going was one means to prove respectability: 'I intend being there [at the Cathedral] every Sunday morning as attention of this kind is necessary in a professional man, he must accommodate himself in some degree to the manners & principles of those he expects to employ him', decided a weary young and radical doctor in Norwich in 1783.[39] Careers were also boosted by a smart gimmick or new treatment.

Durable success took longer to obtain and required greater solidity of achievement. The visible trappings of wealth worked wonders to help a career. Tobias Smollett, who was a surgeon as well as author, stressed the value of a carriage. It was a 'travelling sign post to draw in customers'.[40] A later observer in 1839 confirmed that perception: 'a physician who is able to drive his own carriage, is considered extremely clever in his profession, and is patronised accordingly.'[41]

Crucial in the doctors' quest for respectability was the need to distance themselves from the untrained 'empirics' and outright 'quacks'. These latter were the commercial 'irregulars' of the medical business. In origin, they were named for the fast 'quacking' patter with which they hawked their cures, although some were eloquent speakers.[42] They were difficult to count or even to define, since orthodox doctors were not above abusing each other with the title.[43] But all who peddled infallible potions or cures enraged the regular profession, as universal panaceas offended against the basic medical rule that enjoined careful attention to each specific case history. *The Modern Quack* was an impudent fraud who deluded both rich and poor, warned a London physician in 1718.[44] That was repeated by every generation of doctors, fuelled by conservatism and genuine concern. Another physician, this time in Leeds in 1844, added for good measure that many quacks were foreigners. Thus he warned that 'a gang of crafty adventurers thrive richly on English credulity and chuckle in their sleeve at English stupidity'.[45]

Quackery, however, was buoyed by public demand, which outstripped the supply of qualified men. Moreover, the diverse and ill-coordinated systems of medical regulation before 1858 proved quite unable to control matters. Quacks in many guises continued to flourish. Some were rogues; some were commercial vendors; while others were well-intentioned healers; and others were simply unorthodox. A few were highly talented publicists. For example, mid-eighteenth century audiences were treated to richly rhetorical lectures on the human eye, given by the self-styled 'Chevalier' John Taylor 'Ophthalmiater; Pontifical, Imperial and Royal', who was the son of a Norwich apothecary and had received an orthodox training.[46] Or in 1779–82 patients could attend James Graham's lavish Temple of Health for electro-magnetic treatment and mud baths. He also hired out his 'Celestial Bed' to couples who wished to conceive children of 'the most perfect beauty'.[47] This venture made him briefly the 'Emperor of Quacks' before the Temple failed, leaving Graham in debt.

Two at least among the eighteenth-century 'irregulars' – both lampooned by William Hogarth – had supporters as well as critics. Sarah Mapp (d 1737) was the osteopath daughter of a Wiltshire bone-setter. She was later dismissed contemptuously by the surgeon Percivall Pott as 'an ignorant, illiberal, drunken, female savage' (1773).[48] But she had some attested successes in the early 1730s, before her career nosedived into obscurity. Another controversial figure was Joshua 'Spot' Ward (1685–1761), so named after his large facial birthmark.[49] His pills were very popular, although critics alleged that the dosage contained arsenic. He amassed a fortune and treated many influential people, including King George II. Moreover, Ward received an unusual tribute in 1748, when the Commons voted to exempt his potions from proposed new controls, although the bill with this clause did not pass into law.

Since the system of regulation was incomplete and confusing, however, the regular doctors found it impossible to patrol the outer boundaries of the medical profession. Quacks continued to flourish, including among their number quite a few women healers. Sarah Mapp was one of the most famous but there were other she-doctors and surgeonesses.[50] There were also many female vendors of pills and potions, often in the guise of widows or daughters of medical men. Much the most financially successful of these women was Joanna Stephens. In 1739 the secret recipe for her 'lithontriptic [stone-dissolving] nostrum', which combined powdered eggshells and snails with other ingredients to mask the taste, was purchased for the nation by an impressed Parliament for a sensational fee of £5,000.[51] Critics at once complained that the money was wasted on an unproven remedy from an untrained female.[52] Yet the episode indicated that at least some women could gain a foothold in medical matters. Male doctors were potentially challenged both for their fees and prestige, as a stage song about Sarah Mapp pointed out gleefully in 1736:

What signifies learning, or going to school,
When a woman can do, without reason or rule,
What puts you to nonplus, and baffles your art,
For petticoat-practice has now got the start. *Derry-down*, etc.

Dame nature has given her a doctor's degree,
She gets all the patients, and pockets the fee;
So if you don't instantly prove it a cheat,
She'll loll in her chariot whilst you walk the street. *Derry-down*, etc.[53]

Galling as that was to struggling male doctors, however, Sarah Mapp proved to be more of an annoyance for them than an immediate portent. The scattered female practitioners did not form a lobby or establish a rival tradition within the profession.[54] Of course, it was accepted that women had a role in nursing and in home medication. But those activities were traditionally confined within the household and the local community as female support services. Medical handbooks such as John Maubray's *Female Physician* (1724) or *The Ladies Dispensatory* (1740) were designed to help women to help their families. Doctors often felt superior to that. Yet a commentator in 1736 urged male doctors to appreciate the importance of female assistance. Women were important consumers of health care, since they often called in specialist help. Thus 'it's commonly observed, that notable Doctorizing good Women are commonly the best Friends, and bring Business to the Profession.'[55] One textbook in 1770 tried to cater for all markets simultaneously. Thus *The Female Physician: or, every woman her own doctress* was aimed, despite its title, not only at women readers at home but also at novice medical practitioners throughout Britain and the colonies.[56]

Of course, the growing professionalisation of medicine did not end the older traditions of female health care both inside and outside the household. However, in the long term the role of women changed.[57] Their unpaid part-time labour was not ousted but it was pushed into a subsidiary role by the advent of paid professionals, as housewifery itself was streamlined by the commercial supply of domestic services.

The most dramatic eighteenth-century instance of that was the advent of the man-midwife or accoucheur. This hero was trained in anatomy and used surgical instruments, especially the new obstetrical forceps. Many well-to-do women thus opted for his services in lieu of the traditional female midwife.[58] Of course, the change was not universally welcomed. The clumsy but self-important Dr Slops with their new-fangled instruments were much satirised. Nor did traditional female midwifery disappear. In the 1830s, for example, village women sometimes consulted Betsey Tomlinson as a midwife, while she toured as a Methodist lay preacher.[59] And many poor women continued to rely upon a local Sairey Gamp – the experienced but untrained midwife and hired nurse, depicted in unflattering stereotype by Charles Dickens (1843) as heartless, garrulous, 'snuffy', and hard-drinking to boot.[60]

Gradually, however, as childbirth came to be defined as a condition needing expert attention, the status and number of independent female midwives declined. In 1760 Elizabeth Nihell, herself trained at a Paris hospital, complained bitterly that the men, armed with new instruments, were taking over the field. The glib man-midwife deceived many a trusting woman patient: 'what with [his] scientific jargon, through the cloud of which it was impossible for persons unversed in the matter to discern the truth, what with an air of importance, and what with especially her own weak prepossession in favour of the superiority of men to women-practitioners'.[61] In fact, obstetric training did improve during this period. But that further encouraged women to seek attention from a surgeon or accoucheur, leaving the supporting care to a midwife. By the 1820s, delivering babies had become one of the staples of ordinary general practice. It did not pay very well but it brought even poor families into the orbit of the profession.[62]

Full-time male doctors thus tended to marginalise the unpaid part-time care formerly provided by women. Female involvement in regular practice also remained concentrated in the foothills of the profession. It was therefore accepted without comment when the 1851 census listed in the British Isles as a whole 306 women druggists, 3,454 full-time midwives and 28,249 nurses but no female physicians, surgeons or apothecaries.[63] Indeed, the first register of medical practitioners in 1859 listed only one woman – and that was by virtue of an overseas qualification from an American university.[64]

Yet the concept of female doctoring was not unthinkable by the 1850s. There were memories of earlier women healers, even if there was no fully fledged tradition. There was the young Elizabeth Garrett and others like her, eager for training. Moreover, there was no absolute theological or legal bar. Hence, the female campaigners managed within two decades to establish the principle of equal access. In 1876 Parliament passed an Enabling Act which allowed qualified persons of either sex onto the register.[65] That then heralded a long struggle, in both Britain and America, to turn the principle into effective practice.

Registration, as that suggests, had become the new benchmark of professionalism. The formation of the General Medical Council of Great Britain in 1858 with its list of *bona fide* practitioners clarified the definition of a medical doctor.[66] The profession's growth in prestige had begun well before

1858. But its expertise became more potent when its possession was confined within specified boundaries. Only those on the register were entitled to style themselves as medical doctors, and 15,000 promptly did so in 1859. Registration also supplied a means of control. Backsliders, upon a justified complaint, could be struck from the register, just as defaulting lawyers were struck from the rolls. The law before that had offered no safeguards against medical malpractice. For example, in 1830 when the fashionable and wealthy Irish quack John St John Long, who specialised in treating tuberculosis, was prosecuted for causing a patient's death, the courts were sympathetic to the defendant. He was fined only £250 and, aided by the publicity, proceeded to yet greater fame. His further prosecution for felonious assault upon a patient (who had later died) met with an outright acquittal.[67]

Such incidents worried the respectable profession and gave powerful ammunition to reformers. The campaigning surgeon Thomas Wakley, who became the radical MP for Finsbury (1835–52), led the charge – not only against St John Long but against a wide range of abuses. Writing in his new medical journal *The Lancet*, he savaged the failure of the existing medical oligarchies to exercise proper control.[68] Others too offered suggestions for improvement. In 1844, *A Dose of Physic for the Doctors!* urged the need for a strong purgative in the form of a Council of Superintendence to vet medical treatments and to examine all doctors annually.[69] That proved too drastic to swallow. Reformers argued both with traditionalists who defended the *status quo* and with libertarians who opposed all regulation on free-trade grounds. Numerous medical reform bills were defeated, including Wakley's plan in 1846 for three Registrars to supervise England/Wales, Scotland and Ireland.[70] However, rank-and-file doctors began to grumble. The various medical establishments thus decided to accept the 1858 Medical Act, which was – after all – much more modest than many of the proposed alternatives.[71]

Many reformers were bitterly disappointed. The Act did not lead to systematic state supervision. Britain did not emulate revolutionary France, where the medical profession had been gradually standardised – with the abolition in 1791 of the medical institutions, the introduction in 1795 of national training, the issue in 1798 of certificates of qualification, and the adoption in 1803 of a uniform licensing system.[72] Instead, Parliament delegated regulation to the doctors themselves. However, because there was no single authority to take control, a new forum was created. Table 6.1 shows how the constitution of the General Medical Council carefully included all the nineteen autonomous medical corporations and degree-giving bodies in the three kingdoms. As a result, seventeen members of the new body were chosen independently of the government. The crown nominated six more, while the president was chosen by the assembled Council. Registration was thus left in the hands of the existing medical

Table 6.1 Initial composition of the 'General Council of Medical Education and Regulation of the United Kingdom', known as the General Medical Council, 1858

No. of Members	Appointing authority (each position for term of 5 yrs)
England and Wales	
1	Royal College of Physicians
1	Royal College of Surgeons of England
1	Apothecaries Society of London
1	University of Oxford
1	University of Cambridge
1	University of Durham
1	University of London
—	
7	
Scotland	
1	[Royal] College of Physicians of Edinburgh
1	[Royal] College of Surgeons of Edinburgh
1	Faculty of Physicians and Surgeons of Glasgow
1	University of Edinburgh PLUS Aberdeen's 2 University Colleges (merged 1860 as Aberdeen University)
1	Universities of Glasgow and St Andrews together
—	
5	
Ireland	
1	King's and Queen's [Royal] College of Physicians in Ireland
1	Royal College of Surgeons in Ireland
1	Apothecaries Hall of Ireland
1	University of Dublin
1	Queen's University in Ireland
—	
5	
6	The crown on the advice of the Privy Council, choosing 4 members from England/Wales, 1 from Scotland and 1 from Ireland
1	Chosen by General Medical Council, to be president[1]
—	
24	Total[2]

Source: An Act to Regulate the Qualifications of Practitioners in Medicine and Surgery, 21 & 22 Vict., cap. 90 (1858), known as the Medical Act, cl. 4
Notes:
1 The first president was the venerable Sir Benjamin Brodie (1783–1862), former president of the Royal College of Surgeons of England. After 1886, the Council was required to fill the post of G.M.A. president from among its own membership
2 Under the authority of the 1983 Medical Act (1983 Eliz. II, cap. 54), the modern General Medical Council is composed of 102 members = 54 elected; 35 appointed by the universities and regulatory bodies; and 13 nominated by the crown (constituting 11 lay people and 2 medical members): see General Medical Council, *Constitution and Functions* (London, 1991), pp. 304

oligarchies, since before 1886 the ordinary general practitioner had no vote. Significantly, the first meeting of the new body was held in the palatial building of the elite Royal College of Physicians, then in Pall Mall East.

Parliament's sole stipulation was that registration must be an ecumenical process. It was to depend upon formal qualifications and not upon adherence to any particular theory or special school of thought. Even a highly unorthodox practitioner was entitled to appear on the medical register, if he was orthodoxly qualified. It was a prudent proviso, in view of the profession's tendency to internal disputes. As a result, reformers turned their attention instead to the confused state of medical education, as the new pathway to registration. Here too the historic legacy was highly complex, since before 1886 the nineteen independent corporations and universities on the General Medical Council had between them a variety of separate licensing and examining powers.[73]

Originally, the organisational sub-divisions within the profession had been based upon a tripartite vision of medical care. The physicians dealt in theory, diagnosis and prescription – at a physical distance from the patient; the surgeons studied anatomy and treated all external disorders; and the apothecaries were tradesmen who dispensed drugs. In principle, this was a straightforward system with roots in an ancient division of labour. Moreover, these medical 'estates' were long a-dying, being upheld by law, vested interests and tradition. For example, in 1814 an agitated Oxford don declared that any criticism of the division of medicine into its 'Therapeutic, Chirurgical, and Pharmaceutical Branches' was tantamount to subverting the social order.[74]

On the other hand, actual medical practice had begun by Tudor and Stuart times – if not long before – to blur the tripartite model.[75] The plural strands were converging into one ecumenical profession, even while the organising institutions were slow to change.[76] Increasingly, the old distinctions between a physician, a surgeon and an apothecary meant less than the new status divisions between an emergent elite of specialist hospital consultants and the broad rank-and-file of 'general practitioners'. Indeed, that new composite noun (first used in 1714) was rapidly coming into currency in the early nineteenth century, especially among the medical community itself.[77] It offered an alternative to the confusing old terminology, which, however, continued in parallel usage.

Grandest in the tripartite model were the physicians. Like the barristers, they regarded their payment as an honorarium rather than as a crude pecuniary reward. 'A physician should take his fee without letting his left hand know what his right hand was doing; it should be taken without a thought, without a look, without a move of the facial muscles', noted Anthony Trollope in 1858.[78] With their University training, these were the gentlemanly consultants at the pinnacle of academic medicine. One author penned a mock recipe in 1747: 'To acquire this Art of Physic, requires only

Figure 6.2 The College of Physicians (1808–10). The Royal College of Physicians of London (founded 1518) was the senior medical corporation and it guarded its privileges jealously. Here some Fellows are quizzing a candidate for admission, while others chat unconcernedly. The Royal College was a magnificent but traditionalist club. Eventually, it became but one among many medical institutions that elected to the General Medical Council (1858)

From aquatint print by A. Pugin and T. Rowlandson, in Rudolph Ackermann's *Microcosm of London* (1808–10), vol. 1

being acquainted with a few Books, to become Master of a few Aphorisms
. . . to purchase a *Latin* Diploma from some Mercenary College, to step into
a neat Chariot and put on a grave Face, a Sword, and a long Wig.'[79]
Theoretically, physicians confined themselves to observation and prescription. However, the barriers were often breached. Not only did
apothecaries treat patients but a number of physicians also made and sold
medicines. For example, in the early eighteenth century, the west-country
physician Dr Claver Morris supplied his own potions, as well as cosmetics
and a pomade of 'hair butter'.[80] Hence an anonymous tract claimed
chirpily in 1739 that *One Physician is E'en Just as Good as T'other, . . . Surgeons
are not Less Knowing: [and] Apothecaries are as Good as Any; if not Best of All.*

Nonetheless, the old distinctions survived, chiefly because they were
institutionalised. The physicians, for example, were represented by their
own corporate bodies. These were the Royal Colleges of Physicians in
London (1518), Dublin (1667) and Edinburgh (1681). The first of these
institutions was the most venerable. It was the senior medical corporation
in the British Isles, founded under Henry VIII and acquiring its 'Royal'
title in the later seventeenth century.[81] In theory, its powers were great.
All physicians within seven miles of central London were to be either its
Fellows or Licentiates and those outside the capital needed an extra-licence
from the College or from a bishop. The provincial practitioners had,
however, long evaded this yoke, and those in the metropolis followed their
lead. Thus the Royal College had a highly selective membership and did
not constitute a full guild. The number of both Fellows and Licentiates
declined steeply in the early eighteenth century, although the total number
of physicians did not.[82]

Significantly, too, the Royal College lost a decisive battle with London's
apothecaries. These were potent medical rivals, especially as their fees
were relatively low. In the 1690s a number of Fellows from the College of
Physicians had counter-attacked. They opened a Dispensary for the Sick
Poor, which continued until 1725.[83] That angered the apothecaries, whose
pharmaceutical business was thereby undercut. A lively war of polemics
followed, including some in verse. However, the law courts were un-
moved. A test case followed in 1703/4 relating to the apothecary William
Rose, who had prescribed as well as supplied medicines. He lost round
one in King's Bench. Upon appeal, however, the Lords ruled in favour of
the apothecary's right to engage in business freely.[84] In other words, the
law endorsed the *de facto* reality.

After that, the Royal College of Physicians of London retreated into
exclusive dignity. Attempts at reform were made from time to time. In
1751, for example, one doctor proposed to hold annual lectures in obstetric
training for women.[85] Later, the College did license a few men-midwives
in the 1780s but voted in 1804 to bar them. Discontent with this exclusivity
produced some memorable battles. For example, in September 1767 a

deputation of angry Licentiates stormed the buildings to assert their right to join the College meeting. A poet commemorated the event as *The Battle of the Wigs*, even while he wondered what the fuss was about, since 'In this one point ye never disagree –/ Ye're all unanimous – about the fee'.[86] At any rate, the reformers lost. The College remained select, dominated by Anglican graduates from Oxbridge. By 1851, only 1 in 12 of the grand total of 2,300 physicians in England and Wales were Licentiates or Members of the Royal College.[87] The survival of the institution, however, upheld their separate status.

Disputes also ruffled the authority of the Royal College in Edinburgh. In 1804, a modest relaxation in the entry regulations was proposed, only to be vehemently attacked by the combative Dr James Gregory. After heated arguments, he was suspended from his Fellowship in 1809 for his pains.[88] But there was no sustained pressure to give the Edinburgh College real powers of supervision. Physicians relied instead upon their collectively high reputations. They were held to embody wisdom, learning, knowledge of the world, kindness, moderation and self-control, as Dr Gregory's father sagely affirmed in 1770,[89] even though the son's excitability did not quite match this discreet ideal.

Dublin physicians also basked in high status without wishing to be subject to close controls. That led to simmering disputes. In the early nineteenth century, Ireland's Royal College (founded 1667) tried to insist that all practising physicians should obtain a College license for a substantial fee. One Dr Brennan (known as 'Turpentine Brennan' since that was his universal remedy) penned a witty ballad to give the rival arguments of 'The Licentiate and Non-Licentiate Doctors':

LICENTIATE

And it's Oh! Doctor dear, will you be of our College,
And then none can doubt of your learning and knowledge,
When licensed by us you can fear no attack, Sir,
For an action would lie if they call you a quack, Sir.

ANTI-LICENTIATE

And it's oh! doctor dear, do you think us such ninnies,
That to be of your club I would pay fifty guineas?
Your College adds nothing to medical fame, Sir,
And half of its members stupidity shame, Sir.[90]

In the event, neither side won. Controls were not imposed but the College retained its separate grandeur. As in many other instances, the British system accepted a complex overlapping of theoretical powers and divergent practices. That preserved distinctions within the profession but left other doctors free to develop their own parallel institutions.

Surgeons were increasingly unworried by old hierarchy. It was indeed in this period that their old manual craft was transformed into a new and skilled profession. In 1747 *The London Tradesman* agreed that 'The Surgeon is the Second Branch of the Medical Art; very little inferior to the first in point of Utility, but founded upon Principles much more certain, and less precarious in its Success.'[91] The name too was streamlined. Thus the cumbersome 'chirurgeon' became the 'surgeon'. He treated not only external injuries but also a number of illnesses, including venereal disease. In 1763, for example, the surgeon Andrew Douglas cured his friend James Boswell, who had been visited by 'Signor Gonorrhoea'. But there was a cost. Boswell discovered that friendship took second place to other imperatives. When it came to fees, 'I have to do not with him but his profession', he wrote ruefully.[92]

Celebrated pioneers, however, helped to raise the surgeon's prestige. In the early eighteenth century, William Cheselden – wearing his famous silk cap in lieu of a wig – was famed for the speed and skill of his surgery,[93] while in later decades the surgeon–scientist John Hunter devoted a lifetime to research, teaching and collecting scientific exhibits.[94] But public repugnance at the invading knife was not quickly overcome. Anatomical dissection for training purposes was particularly controversial. A key source of fresh bodies was the gallows. In London, the hangman provided the Surgeons Company with four corpses from Tyburn annually and in 1752 Parliament decided that all executed murderers could be dissected.[95] However, there were soon not enough criminal cadavers to meet demand. Fresh graves were emptied by 'Resurrection-Men' and corpses discreetly sold to respectable surgeons, until things went too far. In 1827–9, Mssrs Burke and Hare embarked upon a series of murders in Edinburgh to boost their trade. Parliament riposted with the 1832 Anatomy Act, which set up a licensing system under a salaried inspectorate but also permitted the use of unclaimed pauper bodies from workhouses and hospitals.[96] The legislation meant that surgeons thenceforth had state protection and a regular supply of corpses, even though opinion among the poor was still sullenly hostile.

With the importance of status in mind, the 'sawbones' had already begun to upgrade their own institutions. In Britain as in France, the surgeons' occupation historically overlapped with that of the barbers, with whom they were grouped as barber–surgeons. But their joint London Livery Company (founded in 1540) had become irksome to the specialist surgeons, led by Cheselden. The physicians, meanwhile, had no interest in a mutual organisation, despite the example of Glasgow. There a joint Faculty of Physicians and Surgeons had existed since 1599.[97] But that model was not emulated and the few scattered proposals for ecumenical amalgamations were ignored. Furthermore, there was no outside force to insist upon change, since the state, which intervened with legislation from time to time, had no general policy for the medical institutions.

Instead, the surgeons in each of the three kingdoms created their own autonomous Colleges. The change came first in Edinburgh, the early home of medical innovation. The surgeons there won their own charter in 1695 and built a dedicated Surgeons' Hall in 1697. Their severance from the barbers was finally confirmed in 1722.[98] That was followed by change in London, where in 1745 the surgeons got statutory backing for an independent Surgeons' Company, seceding from the Barber–Surgeons.[99] The assets of the old guild were divided, although its library and a spare skeleton were sold off privately. The new body retained guild status but saw itself as 'being now of no trade but of the profession of Surgery only'.[100] A new Surgeons' Hall was built, close to the London College of Physicians. In Dublin, a campaign for separation also followed. A composite urban guild of barbers, surgeons, apothecaries, and wigmakers had survived since medieval times. But in 1780 the Dublin surgeons seceded to form their own Society. That was incorporated into a non-denominational Royal College by charter in 1784.[101]

London's surgeons thereupon decided that they too would like to have collegiate status and control of entry into the profession. A bill to that effect was promoted in Parliament in 1797. However, at its third reading in the Lords the plan was halted, when its oligarchic provisions were roundly denounced by Lord Thurlow.[102] One nettled surgeon asked in a pamphlet why a lawyer objected to tough qualifications when his own profession was so restrictive.[103] Thurlow did not deign to reply. Yet the Surgeons' Company realised that it had to change tactics. In 1800 it obtained a royal charter instead of a statute and became a Royal College by that means. It then built its stately headquarters in Lincoln's Inn Fields. However, it remained selective and unpopular. In 1818, there were renewed disputes. Only in 1843 was its membership broadened and then its jurisdiction was extended to cover the whole of England.[104]

Constitutionally, these early Colleges were self-recruiting closed corporations. They were not guilds, although some had originated from that milieu; nor were they primarily pedagogic institutions, although some did promote teaching. The Dublin surgeons in 1784, for example, sought incorporation 'to establish a liberal and extensive system of surgical education' and by 1789 they had instituted a successful medical school.[105] The main functions of the early Colleges were to examine candidates, to license practitioners – which they did only imperfectly – and to sustain their calling. As they did so, they preserved the old tripartite divisions. Moreover, their separate roles survived the advent of registration in 1858, since the Colleges still survive as select professional bodies, recruiting membership by advanced examination.

Besides such grandeur, the eighteenth-century apothecaries at first lacked clout. In theory, they were the humblest sector of the profession, forerunners of the general practitioner. Yet already by the seventeenth century, most were more than drug-dispensing shopkeepers. In 1747 it was noted that 'the Army of Apothecaries of this Age, scorn to confine themselves to the dull Scene of their Profession: They are no sooner equipp'd with a Shop, than they commence Doctor.'[106] Many still traded under the sign of the painted gallipot; but they were now medical as well as pharmaceutical experts.[107] They also gained much popular custom since their fees were lower than those of the physicians. A directory in 1763 listed 312 senior apothecaries and concluded:

> Certain it is, that in by far the greatest number of families, the Apothecary now acts in the threefold capacity of Physician, Surgeon, and Apothecary; and therefore his employment may not improperly be ranked among the Genteel Professions.[108]

The change was also reflected in nomenclature. Many medical men styled themselves as joint 'surgeon-apothecaries'. And the doctor's consulting room became known as the surgery – a usage that still survives.

From medieval times, the apothecaries in London and Dublin had been members of separate guilds. (In Scotland, by contrast, institutional control rested with the Colleges of Physicians and Surgeons.) The medical elite often disparaged the apothecaries. However, they too grew in status and were quick to assert their claims. London's Apothecaries Company (founded 1617) had been subtly upgraded into a Society by the 1680s.[109] It won the Rose case (1704) against the Royal College of Physicians, as already noted. That upheld the apothecary's right to prescribe as well as to sell medicines. Then, in the later 1720s, the Society effectively sabotaged the Royal College's supervisory tours to inspect the quality of drugs on sale.[110] Two decades later, however, the Physicians took revenge. They successfully opposed a bill sponsored by the Apothecaries Society in 1748 to regulate the rising number of chemists and druggists.[111] As a result, no single institution was able to exert control. But the Society remained watchful to tend the dignity of its own membership. In 1727, it refused to admit one Mrs Read, an apothecary's daughter who sought admission by right of patrimony. The Society paid her costs to join the Glass-sellers Company instead.[112]

Irish doctors saw a markedly similar rise in status, followed by conflicts of authority. In 1745, the Dublin apothecaries separated from the composite Guild of St Mary Magdalene (which included barbers and surgeons) to form their own Guild of St Luke.[113] This body was keen to assert its professional status and in 1766 successfully opted out of the annual civic parade of craft guilds. Reformers in the later eighteenth century then transformed its role. In 1791, the Dublin Apothecaries Society was reincorporated with a new name as the Apothecaries Hall, with pioneering powers to examine and license all Irish apothecaries. Up-to-date lectures in medicine were also provided.[114]

Reform had been simultaneously canvassed in London in the 1790s, initially without success. But in 1812/13 a new pressure group, the Associated Apothecaries and Surgeon-Apothecaries, led by George Man Burrows, revived the campaign, lobbying for a proper examining agency. The Royal Colleges severally and jointly opposed. Hence the reformers turned to the Apothecaries Society. In 1815, that body was empowered by parliament to examine and license apothecaries throughout England and Wales.[115] However, the new law included many compromises. Above all, the license was not made obligatory for all practitioners. Consequently, an indignant author complained in 1824 that many untrained 'irregulars' were still at work, instancing a motley crew of 'midwives, herbalists, cuppers, barbers, electricians, galvanisers, dentists, ferriers [sic], veterinary surgeons, village wisemen, and cow-leeches'.[116]

Apothecaries once licensed were, however, allowed under the new legislation to uphold their fees at law. Henceforth they no longer had to hide their charges amongst a bill for drugs. Most crucially, too, the principle of qualification before practice was established. That greatly encouraged the formalisation of medical education. Eager reformers still scorned the cautious leaders of the Apothecaries Society as the 'ladies of Rhubarb Hall'.[117] But successful student doctors became Licentiates of the Society (LSA), many being also members of the Royal College of Surgeons (MRCS). Qualification brought status. Thus in 1826 the Irish Apothecaries Hall ruled that 'the appellation of "Master Apothecary" is degrading to the profession, and that the word "Licentiate" be the term used for the future.'[118] The rank-and-file doctors had their own admirers. One argued in *The Lancet* (1826/7) that 'the public are grossly imposed upon by the belief that the physician has a greater stock of medical knowledge than the general practitioner, when it is a notorious fact, that nine-tenths of the physicians have infinitely less opportunities of observing diseases than the general practitioner.'[119] The local doctor, called out at all hours for modest fees, was the real '*missionary* of his profession', wrote another fan in 1843.[120]

Meanwhile, to make the confusion yet more confusing, the apothecaries in turn faced new competition from the dispensing druggists and chemists. These were surging into the foothills of the profession, as the apothecaries had done themselves two hundred years earlier. The druggists sold cheap medicines, gave over-the-counter advice to the poor, and some began to attend patients. Urban records show that the number of pharmacists began to multiply from the later eighteenth century onwards.[121] Most were small dealers, content with a purely local trade. But in the nineteenth century, a few made fortunes out of the insistent public demand for cheap medicaments. One such was the Nottingham herbalist John Boot (1816–60), a staunch Methodist who was inspired by Wesley's *Primitive Physick* and whose son expanded the business into a nation-wide chain.[122] Another success story was that of the self-taught Thomas Holloway (1800–83), founder of Royal Holloway College (1886) – who for a time advertised as 'Professor Holloway'.[123]

There were problems, however, in the lack of supervision. After 1783, vendors of medicines had to be licensed and pay Stamp Duty; but before 1868 there were no general controls upon the sale of drugs.[124] The need for an organised lobby to promote responsible pharmacy and also to defend the pharmacists' interests was increasingly canvassed in the early nineteenth century. Thus, after several short-lived organisations had come and gone, the Pharmaceutical Society of Great Britain was founded by a group of London-based reformers in 1841. The new institution launched a school in 1842 and was incorporated by charter in 1843.[125] Moreover, in 1852 it was entrusted by Parliament with the task of maintaining an official register of all pharmaceutical chemists across the country. That device foreshadowed the Medical Register of 1858 – and the two registers between them regulated the respective professional roles of the pharmacist and the doctor.[126]

Public demand for health care was, throughout all this, tempered by financial realism. Thus, although the number of doctors rose, there were limits to that expansion. Before 1858, estimates remain imprecise. For Gregory King in the 1690s, the medical profession was subsumed within the 16,000 heads of household engaged in the 'Sciences and liberal Arts'.[127] On that basis, there may then have been some 3–4,000 doctors in England and Wales. A national handbook followed many decades later (1779), compiled by a young physician, Dr Simmons. In 1783 his *Medical Register* named 4,592 doctors in England and Wales: comprising a small elite of 516 physicians and as many as 4,077 surgeons/apothecaries.[128] These were the respectable leaders of the profession. However, probably at least as many again (including the numerous 'irregulars') were not included. After that, the *Register* lapsed and had no successor until the *Medical Directory of Great Britain and Ireland* in 1845.

Growth was, however, undoubtedly accelerating from the later eighteenth century onwards. There were complaints that the profession was overstocked. By 1851, there was one man or woman providing medical services for every 302 people in England and Wales – a very high level – although only a minority of those were qualified doctors. Table 6.2 shows that, while there were no more than 1,817 physicians, there were also 13,586 surgeons/apothecaries, and as many as 14,131 men and 269 women who were dispensing chemists or druggists, plus another large group of 25,990 women nurses and midwives. The medical profession was one of '*unequal qualifications* and a *multiplicity of titles*', as a handbook exclaimed in exasperation in 1860.[129]

Ireland meanwhile had proportionately a much smaller medical profession than did England/Wales, as the figures in Table 6.2 indicate. Hence it may be inferred that the effective demand for commercial medicine was restricted, coming chiefly from the affluent landowners and the urban

Table 6.2 Composition of the medical professions in Great Britain and Ireland, 1851

	England/Wales*	Scotland	Ireland	TOTAL
Men				
Physician	1,817	511	1,223	3,551
Surgeon/apothecary	13,586	1,576	1,864	17,026
Druggist/chemist	14,131	1,194	332	15,657
Others in medicine	3,970	923	230	5,123
Total	33,504	4,204	3,649	41,357
Women				
Physician	—	—	—	—
Surgeon/apothecary	—	—	—	—
Druggist/chemist	269	33	4	306
Others in medicine	—	—	14	14
Midwife	2,067	815	572	3,454
Nurse	23,923	1,543	2,783	28,249
Total	26,259	2,391	3,373	32,023
Men & Women				
Physician	1,817	511	1,223	3,551
Surgeon/apothecary	13,586	1,576	1,864	17,026
Sub-total	15,403	2,087	3,087	20,577
Druggist/chemist	14,400	1,227	336	15,963
Others in medicine	3,970	923	244	5,137
Midwife	2,067	815	572	3,454
Nurse	23,923	1,543	2,783	28,249
Total	59,763	6,595	7,022	73,380
Total pop.	18,070,735	2,888,742	6,552,385	27,511,862
Ratio of physicians, surgeons & apothecs. to total pop.	1:1,173	1:1,384	1:2,123	1:1,337
Ratio of all providers of medical services to total pop.	1:302	1:438	1:933	1:375

Source: From Tables 2.2–3, above pp. 32, 34
Note: * Includes Channel Islands and I. of Man

middle class. However, the doctors' social and geographical 'reach' was beginning to be extended in the mid-nineteenth century by the growth of medical charities and Poor Law institutions, which employed medical men to treat the poor *gratis*.[130] Furthermore, the Irish doctors had their own collective lobby from 1839 onwards, in the form of the new Irish Medical Association, sponsored by the reformer Arthur Jacob who had also founded the *Dublin Medical Press*.[131]

By contrast, Scotland with its much smaller population was a major driving force in the emergent British medical profession. Its relatively literate and educated population proved well poised to develop a service specialism that was exported throughout the expanding empire. Medicine was everywhere in demand, whereas Scottish law was too specialised and Scottish Presbyterianism too sectarian to find an international market. In the early eighteenth century, a series of local initiatives, learning from the Dutch universities, began the process. Edinburgh University, backed by the City, created a broad-based, low-cost, non-residential, non-denominational school of medicine in 1726. It rose to great fame, based upon inspired teaching and direct clinical experience.[132] Students, especially from the English-speaking world, hastened to study there – so that non-Scots constituted 898 (79.1 per cent) of Edinburgh's 1,135 graduates between 1726 and 1799. Other Scottish Universities followed suit and the cycle became self-reinforcing. By the early nineteenth century, however, Paris, London and Dublin had also come to the fore as new medical centres, while there were scandals in Scottish medicine, not least the inadequate state of the medical degree at St Andrews.[133]

Nevertheless, with its large graduate output, Scotland was well supplied with services. In 1851, the country had one person employed in the provision of health care per 438 inhabitants (see Table 6.2). A high proportion (64 per cent) of those medical workers were men (see Table 6.3), which – given the lower status of women – indicates a profession of much prestige. However, status did not curb irreverence. Robert Burns had already written the jesting ballad of *Death and Doctor Hornbook* (1787), in which Death complained at unfair competition from the new-fangled

Table 6.3 Gender of the medical professions in Great Britain and Ireland, 1851

Engaged in provision of medical services	England/Wales* %	Scotland %	Ireland %	Total %
Men	56.1	63.7	52.0	56.4
Women	43.9	36.3	48.0	43.6
Total	100.0	100.0	100.0	100.0

Source: From Table 6.2
Note: *Includes Channel Islands and I. of Man

pills and treatments of the Doctor, who saved patients from Death's clutches only to kill them off himself.[134]

Jibes like that drew the medical profession together. Group identity was also encouraged by the doctors' clubbability. Not only did they participate in the many societies that sprang up pervasively in this period but numerous specifically medical associations also emerged, combining conviviality with mutual assistance.[135] These ranged from student fraternities to dining-clubs to serious study groups. One of the earliest was Edinburgh's Medical Society (1737) which gained a royal title and charter in 1778. Another was the 1746 association of Naval Surgeons, catering for an important sub-group within the profession. Some organisations were relatively short-lived, such as John Hunter's Society for the Improvement of Medical and Chirurgical Knowledge (1783–1818). But others still survive, including – among the early examples – Liverpool's Medical Book Society (1770), later the Liverpool Medical Institution (1837) and the London Medical Society (1773) which was transmuted into the Medical-Chirurgical Society in 1805 and later became the Royal Society of Medicine (1911).

Local groups of doctors began to meet regularly to promote their professional interests. Early societies were founded in Colchester (1774), Gloucestershire (1788), Huntingdonshire (1792), Plymouth (1794), Leicester (1800) and Huddersfield (1814). A reformer Dr Edward Harrison founded a caucus in Lincolnshire in 1804 to defend the regulars against the quacks. By 1832 there were at least forty local organisations. In that year, Dr (later Sir) Charles Hastings (1794–1866) convened at Worcester the Provincial Medical and Surgical Association. This eventually established itself as the professional body or quasi-trade union for all British doctors. The new group had a slow start. But its membership grew to c.2,000 by 1853, when for the first time London doctors were invited to join. In 1855, it was renamed as the British Medical Association and began to recruit throughout the United Kingdom.[136] Thus the ecumenical weft of the voluntary societies counter-balanced the traditional warp of the medical corporations. That was signally recognised in 1858 when Sir Charles Hastings, the founder of the BMA, was chosen as one of the first batch of crown nominees onto the new General Medical Council.

Other networks also cut across status divisions. Prominent among these were the teaching institutions. Surgeons and apothecaries had been traditionally apprenticed to a master (for up to seven years).[137] That often gave good direct one-to-one training but it was *ad hoc* in content and sometimes in execution too. In this period, there was a snowballing of interest in the formalisation of medical education. In the early eighteenth century, numerous Britons went abroad to study under Herman Boerhaave (1668–1738) at Leyden University.[138] But things changed rapidly. There was a dramatic flowering of medical education across Britain. The Scottish Universities pioneered the way; but there were also many new private medical schools as well as the foundation of the great teaching hospitals.[139] In London in 1721, for example, the pioneering surgeon William Cheselden taught comparative anatomy, while from 1746 to 1783 William Hunter, the older of the Hunter brothers, ran his famous Great Windmill Street School for anatomy and dissection.[140]

Conspicuously, the system that emerged was decentralised and *ad hoc*. It had the merits, however, of flexibility and access to leading figures in the world of medicine. In England, it was particularly the great teaching hospitals that formed the heartland of medical training. Here senior doctors supplemented their incomes by lecturing to a melange of apprentices, fee-paying pupils and dressers (skilled assistants), who gained clinical experience from 'walking the wards'. From the 1690s, one of London's oldest hospitals, St Thomas's had permitted doctors to teach on site. Others followed suit. By 1850 London had eleven teaching hospitals, each generating great *esprit de corps*.[141] Outside the capital, there were parallel developments. Birmingham, Bristol, Exeter, Hull, Leeds, Liverpool, Manchester, Newcastle, Nottingham, Sheffield and York all had at least one medical school by the mid-nineteenth century, of which seven later became university medical faculties.[142]

Oxford and Cambridge meanwhile continued to confer medical degrees, and to reform their courses only slowly in the nineteenth century.[143] In Ireland, Trinity College Dublin instituted a new school of medicine and surgery in 1710/11 but as a denominational (Anglican) establishment did not have the same success as did non-sectarian Edinburgh. Indeed, except in Scotland, the initiatives began outside the portals of higher education. Only later, in 1828, did the newly founded University College London create a new school of medicine, attached to its own hospital; followed in 1845 by the Queen's College of Ireland (which became a University in 1850); and in 1852 by Durham University, which adopted Newcastle's two medical schools as a new medical faculty. A nation-wide – if far from standardised – structure of teaching slowly evolved. In acknowledgement, all universities awarding medical degrees were represented on the General Medical Council in 1858 (see Table 6.1).

Hospitals, however, became the landmark institutions – the secular cathedrals – of the emergent medical science. A very few (such as St Bartholomew's) had old endowments but the great majority were funded by voluntary subscriptions. They became significant foci for local pride and patronage.[144] Many famous hospitals date their foundation from this period: in the metropolis, the Westminster (1720), Guy's (1724), St George's (1733), the London (1740) and the Middlesex (1745); elsewhere, the Lying-In Hospital (1745) later the Rotunda in Dublin (1757), Addenbrooke's Hospital in Cambridge (1766) and the Radcliffe Infirmary at Oxford (1770), to name but a few. These places dealt with both in-patients and out-patients, and the latter were also tended by the dispensaries, following the pioneering London Aldersgate clinic established by the Quaker John Coakley Lettsom in 1770. Table 6.4 indeed shows that Britain's growing population was easily outpaced by these fast-growing new institutions between 1783 and 1852.

Prudently, the hospitals did not claim to provide miracles or an instant reduction in mortality. Indeed, some critics alleged that they made things worse. But such claims distorted the statistics.[145] Moreover, the public was not deterred from attending hospitals in increasing numbers. That immediately extended the clientele for medical services, especially when the

Table 6.4 Number and distribution of institutions providing medical treatment (excluding lunatic asylums) in Great Britain and Ireland, 1783 and 1852

	London and Middlesex	Rest England and Wales	Scotland	Ireland	Total
1783					
Hospitals/ infirmaries[1]	14	29	3	10	56
Dispensaries	10	8	2	0	20
Other[2]	2	2	0	0	4
Total	26	39	5	10	80
Pop. (in millions)	0.8	7.0	1.4	4.0	13.2
1852					
Hospitals/ infirmaries[1]	41	127	21	55	244
Fever hospitals	—	—	—	62	62
Dispensaries	36	72	9	341	458
Other[2]	9	9	1	2	21
Total	86	208	31	460[3]	785
Pop. (in millions)	2.5	15.4	2.9	6.6	27.4
Multiplier to show:					
Extent of institutional growth, 1783–1852	3.3	5.3	6.2	46.0	9.8
Extent of population growth, 1783–1852	3.1	2.2	2.1	1.7	2.1

Sources: 1783 from Anon., *Medical Register for . . . 1783*, pp. 31–6, 51–126, 132–51, 167–9.
1852 from Anon., *The London and Provincial Medical Directory* (London, 1852), pp. 189–232, 614–34; *The Medical Directory for Scotland, 1852: uniform with the London and provincial . . .* (London, 1852), pp. 133–7; and *The Medical Directory for Ireland, 1852: uniform [etc.]* (London, 1852) pp. 158–96.
Notes: 1 All hospitals and infirmaries, including those that were also Dispensaries. These included a (small) number of hospitals with wards for insane patients; but excluded the asylums
2 'Other' include specialist institutions providing medical help that were not hospitals or dispensaries: e.g. lying-in charities for home confinements, or vaccination institutions
3 The exceptionally high figures for Ireland reflected the creation of emergency fever hospitals and dispensaries in the crisis of the 1846/7 Famine and its aftermath. By 1861, the number of hospitals had fallen to 62, and dispensaries were no longer recorded separately after amalgamation under the Poor Commission by 1851 Medical Charities Act (see n. 130)

sick poor were treated *gratis*. A doctor could see many in one place while he did not have time to visit them at home individually. Mass medicine also began to encourage the conceptual transition whereby the focus of enquiry moved from the whole person of the 'sick man' towards specific illnesses, analysed by hospital- and later laboratory-based research.[146] However, in Britain that shift took some time and clinics were slow to standardise.[147]

CERTIFICATE

To be signed by *two* Medical Practitioners, each being a Physician, Surgeon, or Apothecary, who shall have *separately* visited, and *personally* examined the Patient: to contain the separate dates on which he, or she, shall have been examined: also, the following particulars.

Patient's Name and Age. — *Charles William North Single*

Place of Residence. *Hastings Sussex Late of Bombay*

Former Occupation. *Minister of the Church of England*

The Asylum (if any) in which such Patient shall have been confined. } *nil*

Whether found Lunatic, or of Unsound Mind, under a Commission issued by the Lord Chancellor, or Lord Keeper or Commissioner of the Great Seal. } *under no Commission*

Christian and Surname of Person on whose Authority the Patient was examined. } *Frederick North*

Place of Abode of ditto. *Hastings*

Degree of Relationship, or other Circumstance of Connexion. } *Brother of the Invalid*

Special Circumstance (if any) which shall have prevented the Patient being separately examined by two Medical Practitioners. }

Special Circumstance (if any) which exists to prevent the Insertion of any of the above Particulars. }

I, the undersigned, hereby Certify, that I separately visited, and personally examined, with reference to the above Particulars, the above named *Charles William North* on *9th* day of *May* 18*31*, and that the said *Charles William North* is of Unsound Mind, and a proper Person to be confined in a House licenced for the Reception of Insane Persons.

* Signed *Robert Hawkins Surgeon*

I, the undersigned, hereby certify, that I separately visited, and personally examined, with reference to the above Particulars, the above named *Charles William North* on *2d* day of *May* 18*31*, and that the said *Charles William North* is of Unsound Mind, and a proper Person to be confined in a House licenced for the Reception of Insane Persons.

* Signed *R Batty M.D.*

* Add Physician, Surgeon, or Apothecary, as the Case may be.

Figure 6.3 *Certificate of Insanity* (1831). Under 9 Geo. IV, cap. 41 (1828), a patient could be certified insane on the affidavit of two qualified practitioners after a full medical examination. That gave the doctors the awesome power to draw the line between sanity and madness. In this example dated May 1831, Charles North, a minister of the Church of England, was committed to an asylum, after his brother had given authority for the examination. Other records show that North was at that time 33 years old and remained in the asylum for eighteen months
From the Ticehurst House Asylum Papers (Western Manuscripts), by permission of the Ticehurst House Trustees and the Wellcome Institute Library, London

Nor did hospital consultants have anything like complete control over the people they saw. Most were out-patients. The hospital inmates were only a tiny proportion of the population, although a larger number had been inmates at some stage or other. Moreover, those who were admitted did not remain for years. For example, the mean length of stay among 2,973 patients in the Edinburgh Infirmary between 1770 and 1800 was just over one month (31.3 days).[148] Medical control was thus far from total. In terms of public prestige, however, the hospitals did enhance the fame of the physicians and surgeons who worked there as consultants. They became a new medical elite, admired for their skills and service. For example, one poem to *The Hospital* (1810) dubbed its doctors as 'ministers of health' and addressed them fulsomely as: 'Distinguished Characters!/ You ask no fee to ransom from the grave/The Indigent . . .'.[149]

Very similar changes accompanied the advent of the lunatic asylum. That was another civic institution that drew upon the services of the doctors. The growing view that mental disorders were illnesses needing treatment was a component of 'medicalisation' that also created more business for the medical profession. These included obscure local practitioners, such as Mrs Spouncer of Hull who was in business from c.1806 to 1815 offering to cure insanity.[150] But the economies of scale fostered the advent of specialist 'mad-houses'. Many of these were owned by private proprietors (an increasing number of them doctors), who after 1774 were licensed by a sub-committee of London's Royal College of Physicians or by local magistrates.[151] In addition, there were a few public institutions, such as the capital's Bethlem or Bedlam (rebuilt 1676, 1815), plus charitable foundations such as the Norwich Bethel (1713) and, after new legislation in 1808, some local authority asylums.

Inmates within these places did lack power and were sometimes harshly treated, especially if they lacked family or friends.[152] Horrific scandals ensued. But eighteenth-century attitudes to insanity were more eclectic, the treatments more diverse and the institutions more variegated in size and regimens than critics allowed.[153] Most patients were inmates for less than a year;[154] and many of the insane were not immured in mad-houses at all. A survey in 1844 found that 44.7 per cent of all 'lunatics' in England and Wales were paupers in workhouses.[155] Only in 1845 did parliament decree a nation-wide system of confinement in asylums. That systematised arrangements, even though some localities were slow to accept the new law.[156] As a result, the inmates at any one time constituted only a tiny proportion of Britain's population.

Power was thus not suddenly seized by an avid medical profession. Doctors were not motivated solely by therapeutic 'progress' but they were not exclusively self-interested either. Social and civic expectations helped to form their role, as well as their own multiple quests for authority, money, knowledge and the welfare of their patients. As a result, doctors of all complexions had already begun to gain prestige by the later seventeenth century. In Britain by the later eighteenth century, they had already significantly extended their knowledge, clientele and institutional strongholds, as well as their sense of identity as an ecumenical profession, long before the boundaries were defined by medical registration in 1858.[157] The definition of lunacy, for example, had been delegated by Parliament in 1828 to the wisdom of any two physicians, surgeons or apothecaries, who were entitled (after a separate examination) to sign a certificate to consign a disordered individual to an asylum.[158]

All this took some custom from other nearby professions, especially from the clergy. There was no overt confrontation between organised medicine and religion, although medical students had by the nineteenth century gained a reputation for godlessness. However, amateur doctoring by the parish clergy was being ousted, just as Biblical literalism was gradually eclipsed by scientific explanations of the universe. That generated new optimism. Lady Mary Wortley Montagu, herself a noted lay campaigner for inoculation, saw similarities between hopes of religious and medical salvation. She wrote in April 1748 that the English had an exaggerated trust in quack remedies: 'We have no longer faith in Miracles and Reliques, and therefore with the same Fury run after receits [sic] and Physicians.'[159]

For the increasingly confident doctors themselves, however, it was – at least in theory – a matter of rational enlightenment. That was expressed with clarion confidence by the campaigning Thomas Wakley in the first issue of *The Lancet* (1823):[160]

> We hope the age of '*Mental Delusion*' has passed, and that mystery and concealment will no longer be encouraged. Indeed, we trust that mystery and ignorance will shortly be considered synonymous. Ceremonies, and signs, have now lost their charms; hieroglyphics, and gilded serpents, their power to deceive.

NOTES

1 S. Smith to Dr Henry Reeve, in *Selected Letters of Sydney Smith*, ed. N.C. Smith (Oxford University Press, Oxford, 1981), p. 36.

2 E. Chambers, *Cyclopaedia: or, an universal dictionary of arts and sciences* (London, 1728), vol. 2, pp. 523, 809.

3 W. Smellie (ed.), *Encyclopaedia Britannica: or, a dictionary of arts and sciences . . .* (Edinburgh, 1771), vol. 3, p. 478.

4 W. Graeme, *An Essay on the Method of Acquiring Knowledge in Physick* (London, 1729), p. 4.

5 See J.C. Lettsom, 'Hints for the establishment of a medical society in London' (1773), in idem, *Hints Designed to Promote Beneficence, Temperance, and Medical Science* (London, 1801), vol. 3, pp. 257–8; S. Ferris, *A General View of the Establishment of Physic as a Science in England* (London, 1795); and S. Bard, *A Discourse on the Importance of Medical Education* (New York, 1812), pp. 7–8.

6 T. Gisborne, *An Enquiry into the Duties of Men in the Higher and Middle Classes*

of Society in Great Britain, resulting from their Respective Stations, Professions and Employments (London, 1794), p. 383.

7 Letter from 'Hygeiaphilos', *The Lancet*, 11/165 (1826/7), p. 125.

8 H. Fielding, *The History of Tom Jones, a Foundling* (London, 1749), vol. 1, p. 148.

9 G. Crabbe, *The Parish Register* (1807) in *The Poetical Works of George Crabbe*, ed. A.J. and R.M. Carlyle (Frowde, London, 1908), p. 77.

10 G. Watts, *A Vindication of the New Method of Inoculating the Smallpox* (London, 1767), p. 66. See also J.R. Smith, *The Speckled Monster: smallpox in England, 1670–1970, with particular reference to Essex* (Essex Record Office, Chelmsford, 1987), pp. 40–67, 173–4; and J.C. Riley, *The Eighteenth-Century Campaign to Avoid Disease* (Macmillan, Basingstoke, 1987), pp. 145–54.

11 W. Black, *An Historical Sketch of Medicine and Surgery from their Origin to the Present Time* (London, 1782), pp. 298–300, 306–7.

12 From W.R. LeFanu (ed.), *British Periodicals of Medicine: a chronological list* (Johns Hopkins University Press, Baltimore, 1938), pp. 5–18.

13 For Thomas Sydenham (1624–89), see G.B. Risse, 'Medicine in the age of Enlightenment', in *Medicine in Society: historical essays*, ed. A. Wear (Cambridge University Press, Cambridge, 1992), p. 167; and quotation from G. Holmes, *Augustan England: professions, state and society, 1680–1730* (Allen & Unwin, London, 1982), p. 182.

14 N. Jewson, 'Medical knowledge and the patronage system in eighteenth-century England', *Sociology*, 8 (1974), pp. 370–3, 377–8.

15 For claims and counter-claims, see R. Reece, *A Correct Statement . . .* (London, 1815), pp. 18–19; and Anon. [E. Carpenter?], *The Extraordinary Case of a Piccadilly Patient: or, Doctor Reece physick'd by six female physicians* (London, 1815).

16 See R.J. Morris, *Cholera 1832: social response to an epidemic* (Croom Helm, London, 1976), pp. 159–95; and M. Pelling, *Cholera, Fever, and English Medicine, 1825–65* (Oxford University Press, Oxford, 1978), esp. pp. 295–310.

17 *The Lancet*, vol. 1, no. 1 (1823), pp. 30, 62–3, 89, 138.

18 Bard, *Discourse*, p. 10.

19 A.J. Youngson, *The Scientific Revolution in Victorian Medicine* (Croom Helm, London, 1979), esp. pp. 42–72, 127–56.

20 S. Johnson, *A Dictionary of the English Language*, (2 vols, London, 1755) vol. 1, *sub*: 'doctor'. Dr Johnson himself did not often use the title by which he is known to posterity but he was an honorary Doctor of Law (LL.D.) at both Trinity College Dublin (1765) and Oxford University (1775): see *D.N.B.*

21 *Gentleman's Magazine*, 19 (1749), p. 66.

22 T. Smollett, *The Adventures of Ferdinand Count Fathom* (London, 1753), vol. 2, p. 135; and Holmes, *Augustan England*, pp. 168–9. I am grateful to Dr Margaret Pelling for advice on this point.

23 J. Armstrong, *An Essay for Abridging the Study of Physick . . .* (London, 1735), p. 35.

24 Lettsom, 'Hints for . . . a Medical Society' (1773), in idem, *Hints . . . to Promote Beneficence*, vol. 3, pp. 262–3.

25 P. Cunnington and C. Lucas, *Occupational Costume in England from the Eleventh Century to 1914* (Black, London, 1967), pp. 300–18.

26 E. Milward, *A Circular Invitatory Letter to All Orders of Learned Men, but More Especially to the Professors of Physick and Surgery, in Great Britain* (London, 1740), esp. pp. 47–63.

27 R.W. Ketton-Cremer, 'Dr. Messenger Monsey' (1693–1788), in idem, *Norfolk Portraits* (Faber & Faber, London, 1944), pp. 85–95.

28 A. Cooper, *The Progress of Physic* (London, 2nd edn, 1743), p. 24. See also *D.N.B.*

for William Harvey (1578–1657), the discoverer of the circulation of the blood, and for Robert Boyle (1627–91), the experimental chemist/physicist.

29 J. Wesley, *Primitive Physick: or an easy and natural method of curing most diseases* (London, 1747), p. x. For context, see also A.W. Hill, *John Wesley among the Physicians: a study of eighteenth-century medicine* (Epworth Press, London, 1958).

30 See for example Mary Fissell, 'The disappearance of the patient's narrative and the invention of hospital medicine', in *British Medicine in an Age of Reform*, ed. R. French and A. Wear (Routledge, London, 1991), pp. 92–109.

31 Esp. T.S. Szasz, *The Manufacture of Madness: a comparative study of the Inquisition and the mental health movement* (Routledge, London, 1971).

32 Jewson, 'Medical knowledge', pp. 369–85.

33 See D. and R. Porter, *The Patient's Progress: doctors and doctoring in eighteenth-century England* (Polity, Cambridge, 1989), pp. 28–9, 33–52; and R. Porter, 'The patient in England, c.1660–c.1800', in *Medicine in Society*, ed. Wear, pp. 91–118.

34 V. Berridge and G. Edwards, *Opium and the People: opiate use in nineteenth-century England* (Yale University Press, New Haven, 1987), pp. 27–8, 30–4, 45, 97–105.

35 G. Farquhar, *The Beaux Stratagem* (A. & C. Black, London, 1976), p. 26.

36 J. Beresford (ed.), *The Diary of a Country Parson, The Reverend James Woodforde*, vol. 1: *1758–81*, pp. 252, 298 (home dosage), 192, 331–2 (visits from doctor).

37 F. Winslow, *Physic and Physicians: a medical sketch book* (London, 1839), vol. 1, pp. 84–5, 345.

38 See D. and R. Porter, *Patient's Progress*, pp. 118–21; and esp. A. Digby, *Making a Medical Living: doctors and patients in the English market for medicine, 1720–1911* (Cambridge University Press, Cambridge, 1994), pp. 107–34.

39 B. Cozens-Hardy (ed.), *The Diary of Sylas Neville, 1767–88* (Oxford University Press, London, 1950), pp. 312–13.

40 Smollett, *Ferdinand Count Fathom*, vol. 2, p. 143.

41 Winslow, *Physic and Physicians*, vol. 1, p. 353.

42 See esp. R. Porter, *Health for Sale: quackery in England, 1660–1850* (Manchester University Press, Manchester, 1989), pp. 1–10; and idem, 'The language of quackery in England, 1660–1800', in *The Social History of Language*, ed. P. Burke and R. Porter (Cambridge University Press, Cambridge, 1987), pp. 73–103.

43 See essays by M. Neve, 'Orthodoxy and Fringe: medicine in late Georgian Bristol'; R. Porter, '"I Think Ye Both Quacks": the controversy between Dr Theodor Myersbach and Dr John Coakley Lettsom'; and I. Loudon, '"The Vile Race of Quacks with which this Country is Infested"', in *Medical Fringe and Medical Orthodoxy, 1750–1850*, ed. W.F. Bynum and R. Porter (Croom Helm, London, 1987), pp. 40–55, 56–78, 106–28.

44 Anon., *The Modern Quack* (London, 1718), pp. iii, viii.

45 'A Medical Practitioner', *Quacks and Quackery: a remonstrance against the sanction given by the government, the press, and the public to the . . . quackeries of the day* (London, 1844), p. 9.

46 See Taylor's self-puffing autobiography, whose unabbreviated title ran to 240 words: J. Taylor, *The History of the Travels and Adventures of the Chevalier John Taylor . . . Written by Himself . . .* (London, 1761/2). Taylor's son and grandson, both also named John Taylor, followed in the family tradition as oculists: see *D.N.B.*

47 C.J.S. Thompson, *The Quacks of Old London* (Bretano, London, 1928), pp. 333–4.

48 P. Pott, *Some Few General Remarks on Fractures and Dislocations* (1773), in idem, *The Chirurgical Works of Percivall Pott* (London, 1775), p. 632. Mapp got some slight posthumous revenge when Pott in turn was denounced (1786) as 'butcher Pott': Porter and Porter, *Patient's Progress*, p. 53.

49 See Thompson, *Quacks of Old London*, pp. 285–9; and M.H. Nicolson, 'Ward's "pill and drop" and men of letters', *Journal of the History of Ideas*, 29 (1968), pp. 183–4.

50 A.L. Wyman, 'The surgeoness: the female practitioner of surgery, 1400–1800', *Medical History*, 28 (1984), pp. 22–41.

51 By the statute of 12 Geo. II, cap. 23 (1739); also A.C. Wootton, *Chronicles of Pharmacy* (London, 1910), vol. 2, pp. 199–203.

52 See e.g. Anon., *Mrs. Stephens's Receipt for the Stone and Gravel . . . [and] Some Few Thoughts how Most Properly to Encourage Valuable Discoveries . . . in Physick or Surgery* (London, 1739).

53 J. Caulfield, *Portraits, Memoirs, and Characters of Remarkable Persons . . .* (London, 1819–20), vol. 4, pp. 74–5.

54 The first committee to advance the medical education of women in England was founded in 1858: see E.M. Bell, *Storming the Citadel: the rise of the woman doctor* (Constable, London, 1953), pp. 44–5.

55 Anon., *A Letter on the Origin, Nature and Dignity, of the Degrees of Doctor, more Particularly in Physick . . .* (London, 1736), p. 30.

56 J. Ball, *The Female Physician: or, every woman her own doctress . . .* (London, 1770), p. iv.

57 P.J. Corfield, 'Defining urban work', in P.J. Corfield and D. Keene (eds), *Work in Towns, 850–1850* (Leicester University Press/Pinter Press, Leicester, 1990), pp. 219–20.

58 See variously J. Donnisson, *Midwives and Medical Men: a history of inter-professional rivalries and women's rights* (Heinemann, London, 1977), pp. 23–61; B.B. Schnorrenberg, 'Is childbirth any place for a woman? the decline of midwifery in eighteenth-century England', *Studies in Eighteenth-Century Culture*, 10 (1981), pp. 393–408; and A. Wilson, 'The perils of early modern procreation: childbirth with or without fear?', *British Journal for Eighteenth-Century Studies*, 16 (1993), pp. 1–19.

59 D.M. Valenze, *Prophetic Sons and Daughters: female preaching and popular religion in Industrial England* (Princeton University Press, Princeton, 1985), p. 72.

60 C. Dickens, *Martin Chuzzlewit* (London, 1843).

61 E. Nihell, *A Treatise on the Art of Midwifery* (London, 1760), pp. 158–9.

62 Porter and Porter, *Patient's Progress*, p. 183. See also I. Loudon, *Medical Care and the General Practitioner, 1750–1850* (Clarendon, Oxford, 1986), pp. 88–92, 99; and J. Lane, 'A provincial surgeon and his obstetric practice: Thomas W. Jones of Henley-in-Arden, 1764–1846', *Medical History*, 31 (1987), pp. 333–48.

63 For the 1851 census figures, see above Chapter 2, Table 2.3 (p. 34).

64 Bell, *Storming the Citadel*, pp. 26–45.

65 Ibid., pp. 53–84; and 39 & 40 Vict., cap. 41 (1876). See also A. Witz, *Professions and Patriarchy* (Routledge, London, 1992), pp. 97–101; and for the American context, M.R. Walsh, *'Doctors Wanted – No Women Need Apply': sexual barriers in the medical profession, 1835–1975* (Yale University Press, New Haven, 1977).

66 21 & 22 Vict., cap. 90 (1858), known as the Medical Act, with minor revisions in 22 Vict., cap. 21 (1859).

67 E.S. Turner, *Call the Doctor: a social history of medical men* (Michael Joseph, London, 1958), pp. 184–6.

68 See C. Brook, *Battling Surgeon* (Strickland Press, Glasgow, 1945), pp. 146–9.

69 Anon., *A Dose of Physic for the Doctors! or, a plan for the reformation of the medical profession . . .* (London, 1844), pp. 4–6.

70 Brook, *Battling Surgeon*, pp. 132–4; also S.S. Sprigge, *The Life and Times of Thomas Wakley* (London, 1897), pp. 431–3.

71 For the reform campaign, see I. Waddington, *The Medical Profession in the*

Industrial Revolution (Gill & Macmillan, Dublin, 1984), pp. 53–132. I am grateful to Angela Dunn at the General Medical Council for advice relating to its history.

72 See M. Ramsey, *Professional and Popular Medicine in France, 1770–1830: the social world of medical practice* (Cambridge University Press, Cambridge, 1988), pp. 74–9; and T. Gelfand, 'The decline of the general practitioner and the rise of a modern medical profession', in *Doctors, Patients, and Society: power and authority in medical care*, ed. M.S. Staum and D.E. Larsen (Wilfrid Laurier University Press, Waterloo, Ontario, 1981), p. 107.

73 M. Heseltine, 'The early history of the General Medical Council, 1858–86', *The Medical Press*, 222 (1949), pp. 10–53.

74 Anon., 'Observations on medical reform by a member of the University of Oxford', in *The Pamphleteer*, 3, no. 6 (May 1814), ed. A.J. Valpy, pp. 414–31.

75 See M. Pelling, 'Medical practice in early modern England: trade or profession?', in *The Professions in Early Modern England*, ed. W. Prest (Croom Helm, London, 1987), pp. 90–128; and R.S. Roberts, 'The personnel and practice of medicine in Tudor and Stuart England: part 1, the provinces', *Medical History*, 6 (1962), pp. 363–82, and 'part 2, London', ibid. 8 (1964), pp. 217–34.

76 Four key studies confirm this theme: Holmes, *Augustan England*, pp. 166–235; Loudon, *Medical Care and the General Practitioner*, passim; Waddington, *Medical Profession in the Industrial Revolution*, esp. pp. 176–205; and M.J. Peterson, *The Medical Profession in Mid-Victorian London* (University of California Press, Berkeley, 1978), passim. But for conflicting datings, see below, n. 157.

77 J. Bellers, *An Essay towards the Improvement of Physick, in Twelve Proposals* (London, 1714), p. 10; and comment in Loudon, *Medical Care and the General Practitioner*, pp. 1–2.

78 A. Trollope, *Doctor Thorne* (1858), ed. D. Skilton (Oxford University Press, Oxford, 1980), pp. 32–3.

79 R. Campbell, *The London Tradesman, being a Compendious View of all the Trades, Professions, Arts . . . in the Cities of London and Westminster* (London, 1747), p. 41.

80 E. Hobhouse (ed.), *The Diary of a West Country Physician (C. Morris), A.D. 1684–1726* (Simpkin Marshall, Rochester, 1934), p. 27.

81 G.N. Clark, *A History of the Royal College of Physicians of London* (Clarendon, Oxford, 1964–72), vol. 1, pp. 58, 304 and n. 4.

82 Holmes, *Augustan England*, pp. 170–1.

83 A. Rosenberg, 'The London dispensary for the sick-poor', *Journal of the History of Medicine*, 14 (1959), pp. 41–56. Poets joined the debates, most notably S. Garth, *The Dispensary: a poem* (1699).

84 See details in H.J. Cook, *The Decline of the Old Medical Regime in Stuart London* (Cornell University Press, Ithaca, 1986), esp. pp. 246–51.

85 Donnisson, *Midwives and Medical Men*, pp. 32, 40; Clark, *Royal College*, vol. 2, pp. 504–5.

86 B. Thornton, *The Battle of the Wigs* . . . (London, 1768), p. 22. See too I. Waddington, 'The struggle to reform the Royal College of Physicians, 1767–71: a sociological analysis', *Medical History*, 17 (1973), pp. 107–26.

87 Clark, *Royal College*, vol. 3, p. 803.

88 For Dr James Gregory (1753–1821), see W.S. Craig, *History of the Royal College of Physicians of Edinburgh* (Blackwell, Oxford, 1976), pp. 419–36.

89 John Gregory, *Lectures on the Duties and Qualifications of a Physician* (1st publ. 1770; rev. edn, Edinburgh, 1805), pp. 2–27.

90 J.H.D. Widdess, *A History of the Royal College of Physicians of Ireland, 1654–1963* (Livingstone, Edinburgh, 1963), p. 130.

91 Campbell, *London Tradesman*, p. 47.

92 F.A. Pottle (ed.), *Boswell's London Journal, 1762–3* (Heinemann, London, 1950), pp. 157–8, 172–3.

93 V.Z. Cope, *William Cheselden, 1688–1752* (Livingstone, Edinburgh, 1953), passim.

94 See *D.N.B.*; S. Paget, *John Hunter: man of science and surgeon, 1728–93* (London, 1897); and W.D.I. Rolfe, 'William and John Hunter: breaking the Great Chain of Being', in *William Hunter and the Eighteenth-Century Medical World*, ed. W.F. Bynum and R. Porter (Cambridge University Press, Cambridge, 1985), pp. 297–319.

95 32 Hen. VIII, cap. 42 (1540), cl. 2; extended under the Act 'for better preventing the horrid crime of murder': 25 Geo. II, cap. 37 (1752), cl. 2. See the excellent study by R. Richardson, *Death, Dissection and the Destitute* (Routledge, London, 1987); and details in J. Fleetwood, *The Irish Bodysnatchers: a history of body snatching in Ireland* (Tomar Publishing, Dublin, 1988).

96 2 & 3 Will. IV, cap. 75 (1832).

97 Much later, in 1909, the Faculty also became a Royal College: see T. Gibson, *The Royal College of Physicians and Surgeons of Glasgow* (Macdonald, Edinburgh, 1983), p. 11.

98 C.H. Creswell, *The Royal College of Surgeons of Edinburgh: historical notes from 1505–1905* (Oliver & Boyd, London, 1936), pp. 52, 130, 140.

99 18 Geo. II, cap. 15 (1745). See also V.Z. Cope, *The Royal College of Surgeons of England: a history* (Anthony Blond, London, 1959), pp. 5–6, 9; and S. Young, *The Annals of the Barber-Surgeons of London . . .* (London, 1890), vol. 1, pp. 229–32.

100 B. Hamilton, 'The medical professions in the eighteenth century', *Economic History Review*, 2nd ser., 4 (1951), p. 150.

101 J.D.H. Widdess, *An Account of the Schools of Surgery, Royal College of Surgeons, Dublin, 1789–1948* (Livingstone, Edinburgh, 1949), pp. 1, 3–4, 9–10.

102 The speech was reported in the *Parliamentary Register* (Debrett, London, 1797), vol. 3, pp. 227–9; and later reprinted in *The Lancet*, 11, no. 182 (24 Feb. 1826/7), pp. 679–82.

103 Anon., *A Dressing for L—d T—r—w, Prepared by a Surgeon* (London, 1797), p. 3. For the debates and manoeuvres, see Hamilton, 'Medical professions', pp. 157–9; Cope, *Royal College of Surgeons of England*, pp. 18–21, 27.

104 Ibid., pp. 37–40, 42–56, 65–71.

105 See Widdess, *Royal College of Surgeons, Dublin*, pp. 10, 17; and J. Fleetwood, *A History of Medicine in Ireland* (Browne & Nolan, Dublin, 1951), pp. 89, 92, 95–8.

106 Campbell, *London Tradesman*, p. 64.

107 See J.G.L. Burnby, *A Study of the English Apothecary from 1660 to 1760, Medical History*, suppl. 3 (1983), pp. 1–116.

108 T. Mortimer, *The Universal Director: or, the nobleman and gentleman's true guide to the . . . liberal and polite arts and sciences . . .* (London, 1763), pt 1, pp. 57–68, esp. p. 57.

109 C. Wall, H.C. Cameron and E.A. Underwood, *A History of the Worshipful Society of Apothecaries of London*, vol. 1: *1617–1815* (Oxford University Press, London, 1963), p. 19. I am grateful to Colonel R.J. Stringer, Clerk to the Society, for advice on its history.

110 The Physicians' right of search (dating from 1540) was amplified by 10 Geo. I, cap. 20 (1724), which required the Apothecaries Society to assist. The Act was extended in 1727 but lapsed in 1730: Clark, *Royal College*, vol. 2, pp. 493–7.

111 See Wall, Cameron, and Underwood, *Apothecaries of London*, pp. 186–7; and *Commons Journals, vol. 25*, pp. 592–5. It was from this proposed legislation that the quack Joshua Ward was exempted by special vote of Parliament, see above p. 114.

112 C.R.B. Barrett, *The History of the Society of Apothecaries of London* (London, 1905), p. 130.

113 J.C. McWalter, *A History of the Worshipful Company of Apothecaries in the City of Dublin* (Dublin, 1916), pp. 21–3, 36, 40–1, 43.

114 Ibid., pp. 36, 44–6, 48, 80.

115 55 Geo. III, cap. 194 (1815), revised 6 Geo. IV, cap. 133 (1825). For a critique, see S.W.F. Holloway, 'The Apothecaries' Act, 1815: a reinterpretation', *Medical History*, 10 (1966), pp. 107–29, 221–36; and the more favourable assessment in S.C. Lawrence, 'Private enterprise and public interests: medical education and the Apothecaries' Act, 1780–1825', in *British Medicine*, ed. French and Wear, pp. 45–73.

116 S.F. Gray, *Supplement to the Pharmacopoeia: being a treatise on pharmacology . . .* (London, 1824), p. xxix.

117 *The Lancet*, 1 (1842/3), p. 686.

118 McWalter, *Apothecaries in . . . Dublin*, pp. 84–5, 143.

119 Letter from 'A Radical Reformer' in *The Lancet*, 11, no. 175 (1826/7), pp. 455–6.

120 W.A. Greenhill, *Address to a Medical Student* (London, 1843), p. 26.

121 See L.G. Matthews, *History of Pharmacy in Britain* (Livingstone, Edinburgh, 1962); and case study in H. Marland, 'The medical activities of mid-nineteenth-century chemists and druggists, with special reference to Wakefield and Huddersfield', *Medical History*, 31 (1987), pp. 415–39.

122 S.D. Chapman, *Jesse Boot of Boots the Chemist: a study in business history* (Hodder & Stoughton, London, 1974), pp. 32–8.

123 For advertisement by 'Professor Holloway', see *Punch: or, the London charivari*, 28 (Feb.–March 1855), inside back page.

124 See 23 Geo. III, cap. 62 (1783); and the Pharmacy Act, 31 & 32 Vict., cap. 121 (1868).

125 J.K. Crellin, 'The growth of professionalism in nineteenth-century British pharmacy', *Medical History*, 11 (1967), pp. 215–27; revised and updated by S.W.F. Holloway, 'The orthodox fringe: the origins of the Pharmaceutical Society of Great Britain', in Bynum and Porter (eds), *Medical Fringe*, pp. 129–57.

126 See 15 & 16 Vict., cap. 56 (1852); and S.W.F. Holloway, *Royal Pharmaceutical Society of Great Britain, 1841–1991: a political and social history* (Pharmaceutical Press, London, 1991), pp. 147–84, esp. pp. 181–2.

127 For King's estimates, see Table 2.1 above, p. 29.

128 From Anon. [S.F. Simmons], *The Medical Register for the Year 1783* (London, 1783), pp. 5–126. See also J. Lane, 'The medical practitioners of provincial England in 1783', *Medical History*, 28 (1984), pp. 353–71. Invaluable modern listings for the whole of the British Isles have revealed the names of some 35,000 practitioners between 1700 and 1800: see P.J. and R.V. Wallis, *Eighteenth-Century Medics: subscriptions, licenses, apprenticeships* (Project for Historical Biobibliography, Newcastle upon Tyne, 1988), p. xi.

129 W. Dale, *The Present State of the Medical Profession in Great Britain and Ireland . . .* (London, 1860), pp. 24–5.

130 See R.D. Cassell, 'The Medical Charities Act of 1851 and the growth of state medicine in Mid-Victorian Ireland' (Ph.D. thesis, University of North Carolina, 1977), pp. 9–10, 20–98.

131 J. Fleetwood, *A History of Medicine in Ireland* (Browne & Nolan, Dublin, 1951), pp. 160, 346–7.

132 D. Hamilton, *The Healers: a history of medicine in Scotland* (Canongate, Edinburgh, 1981), pp. 96–7, 111–45, 147–57, 167–55; esp. p. 119 for origins of Edinburgh graduates. See also L. Rosner, *Medical Education in the Age of Improvement: Edinburgh students and apprentices, 1760–1826* (Edinburgh University Press, Edinburgh, 1991).

133 Royal Commission into the State of the Universities of Scotland, *British Parliamentary Papers* (1831), vol. 12, p. 522.

134 R. Burns, *Poems, Chiefly in the Scottish Dialect* (Edinburgh, 1787), pp. 55–65.

135 Details in A. Batty Shaw, 'The oldest medical societies in Great Britain', *Medical History*, 12 (1968), pp. 232–44; D. Power (ed.), *British Medical Societies* (Medical Press, London, 1939); H. Rolleston, 'Medical friendships, clubs, and societies', *Annals of Medical History*, n.s., 2 (1930), esp. pp. 253–60; and Peterson, *Medical Profession*, p. 268.

136 P. Vaughan, *Doctors' Commons: a short history of the British Medical Association* (Heinemann, London, 1959), pp. 1, 7–10, 40–6.

137 Contrast the sympathetic account in J. Lane, 'The role of apprenticeship in eighteenth-century medical education in England', in *William Hunter*, ed. Bynum and Porter, pp. 57–103; with the more hostile survey in Z.V. Zwanenberg, 'The training and careers of those apprenticed to apothecaries in Suffolk, 1815–58', *Medical History*, 27 (1983), pp. 139–50.

138 See variously R.W. Innes Smith, *English-Speaking Students of Medicine at the University of Leyden* (Oliver & Boyd, Edinburgh, 1932), amplified by E.A. Underwood, *Boerhaave's Men at Leyden and After* (Edinburgh University Press, Edinburgh, 1977) and A. Cunningham, 'Medicine to calm the mind: Boerhaave's medical system and why it was adopted in Edinburgh', in *The Medical Enlightenment of the Eighteenth Century*, ed. A. Cunningham and R. French (Cambridge University Press, Cambridge, 1990), pp. 40–66.

139 S.C. Lawrence, 'Entrepreneurs and private enterprise: the development of medical lecturing in London, 1775–1820', *Bulletin of the History of Medicine*, 62 (1988), pp. 171–92; and also C. Singer and S.W.F. Holloway, 'Early medical education in England', *Medical History*, 4 (1960), pp. 1–17.

140 See Cope, *William Cheselden*, p. 5; and for William Hunter (1718–83) and his school (which survived until 1831), see S.C. Thomson, 'The Great Windmill Street School', *Bulletin of the History of Medicine*, 12 (1942), pp. 377–91.

141 P.K. Wilson, 'Sacred sanctuaries for the sick: surgery at St Thomas's Hospital, 1725–6', *London Journal*, 17 (1992), pp. 36–53; and for London medical schools in 1850, see Singer and Holloway, 'Early medical education', pp. 7–9.

142 J.A. Shepherd, 'The evolution of the provincial medical schools in England', *Transactions of the Liverpool Medical Institution* (1980/1), pp. 14–39, esp. pp. 30–5; and S. Anning, 'Provincial medical schools in the nineteenth century', in *The Evolution of Medical Education in Britain*, ed. F.N.L. Poynter (Pitman, London, 1966), p. 124.

143 A.H.T. Robb-Smith, 'Medical education at Oxford and Cambridge prior to 1850', in ibid., pp. 19–52, esp. pp. 40–52.

144 See L. Granshaw, 'The rise of the modern hospital in Britain', in *Medicine in Society*, ed. Wear, pp. 197–218; M. Fissell, *Patients, Power and the Poor in Eighteenth-Century Bristol* (Cambridge University Press, Cambridge, 1991), passim; and R. Porter, 'The gift relation: philanthropy and provincial hospitals in eighteenth-century England', in *The Hospital in History*, ed. L. Granshaw and R. Porter (Routledge, London, 1989), pp. 149–78.

145 For warnings against the misuse of statistics, see J. Woodward, *To do the Sick No Harm: a study of the British voluntary hospital system to 1875* (Routledge, London, 1974), pp. 123–42.

146 See esp. M. Foucault, *The Birth of the Clinic: an archaeology of medical perception* (1963), transl. A.M. Sheridan (Tavistock, London, 1973), pp. 64–87, 124–48, 195–7; N. Jewson, 'The disappearance of the sick-man from medical cosmology, 1770–1870', *Sociology*, 10 (1976), pp. 225–44; and Fissell, *Patients, Power and the Poor*, pp. 148–70.

147 C. Lawrence, 'Incommunicable knowledge: science, technology and the clinical art in Britain, 1850–1914', *Journal of Contemporary History*, 20 (1985), pp. 503–20.

148 G.B. Risse, *Hospital Life in Enlightenment Scotland: care . . . at the Royal Infirmary of Edinburgh* (Cambridge University Press, Cambridge, 1986), pp. 172–3.

149 Anon., *The Hospital: a poem* (London, 1810), p. 6.

150 J.A.R. and M.E. Bickford, *The Medical Profession in Hull, 1400–1900: a biographical dictionary* (Hull City Council, Hull, 1983), p. 123.

151 14 Geo. III (1774), cap. 49. For the role of doctors, see W.L. Parry-Jones, *The Trade in Lunacy: a study of private madhouses in England in the eighteenth and nineteenth centuries* (Routledge, London, 1971), passim, esp. p. 284; and A.T. Scull, *The Most Solitary of Afflictions; madness and society in Britain, 1700–1900* (Yale University Press, New Haven, 1993), pp. 41–2, 178–266.

152 See esp. Michel Foucault, who posited a 'great confinement' followed by medical control within the asylum, in his *Madness and Civilisation: a history of insanity in the age of reason* (1961), transl. R. Howard (Tavistock, London, 1971), esp. pp. 38–64, 241–78.

153 R. Porter, *Mind-Forg'd Manacles: a history of madness in England from the Restoration to the Regency* (Penguin, Harmondsworth, 1990), pp. 7–9, 110–19, 155–64, 225, 280–1. See also Scull, *Most Solitary of Afflictions*, pp. 5–8, 21–4; J. Andrews, '"Hardly a hospital, but a charity for pauper lunatics"? Therapeutics at Bethlem in the seventeenth and eighteenth centuries', in *Medicine and Charity before the Welfare State*, ed. J. Barry and C. Jones (Routledge, London, 1991), pp. 63–81; and A. Digby, *Madness, Morality and Medicine: a study of the York Retreat, 1796–1914* (Cambridge University Press, Cambridge, 1985).

154 Parry-Jones, *Trade in Lunacy*, pp. 207–11.

155 *Report of the Metropolitan Commissioners in Lunacy* (London, 1844), p. 194.

156 The Act of 8 & 9 Vict., cap. 126 (1845) superseded the permissive legislation of 1808 (48 Geo. III, cap. 96). For implementation, see Scull, *Most Solitary of Afflictions*, pp. 267–9.

157 Historians agree the trend but disagree about the key turning points. Thus Holmes, *Augustan England*, pp. 166–235, highlights 1680–1730; Loudon, *Medical Care*, pp. 1–6, 48–53, 299–300, stresses the later eighteenth century, as does this account; while Waddington, *Medical Profession*, pp. 48–9, 176–205, prefers 1858; and Peterson, *Medical Profession*, pp. 5–6, 36–9, stresses fragmentation both pre- and post-1858.

158 See Geo. IV, cap. 41 (1828), cl. 30. (Cl. 31 added that pauper lunatics who were subject to an order from local magistrates could be certificated by only one medical practitioner.)

159 R. Halsband (ed.), *The Complete Letters of Lady Mary Wortley Montagu*, vol. 2: *1821–51* (Clarendon, Oxford, 1966), p. 397.

160 *The Lancet*, 1, no. 1 (October 1823), p. 2.

7

TREND

> The word [profession] was understood well enough throughout the
> known world. It signified a calling by which a gentleman, not born
> to the inheritance of a gentleman's allowance of good things, might
> ingeniously obtain the same by some exercise of his abilities.

Such were the views expressed in Anthony Trollope's novel *The Bertrams*
(1859) by one Sir Lionel Bertram, a gentlemanly sponger who lounged
through life.[1] This indolent character explained to his son that the best
profession was the one that brought in the most money for the least work.
The diligent Trollope wryly satirised this example of worldly wisdom. By
contrast, his impecunious hero, young George Bertram, desired to find a
profession that would allow him to spend his life worthily. The problem
was that he could not decide which one to adopt. 'If his father was too
mundane, he was too transcendental', as Trollope depicted their contrasting characters. But the general point was agreed by both. A liberal
profession was a potential route to social status – and an independent
income.

In other words, it was a respectable calling that was fit for the elusive
but desirable character of a 'gentleman'. Professional work was dignified
and not menial. It was untainted since it did not deal directly in 'filthy
lucre' or entail toiling at dirty manual labour (although the gory aspects
of the surgeon's job posed some problems here). At the same time, a
'profession' was in principle an active occupation. That began to broaden
the connotations of 'gentility'. From the sixteenth century onwards,
professional men were routinely styled as 'gentlemen', so that the social
accolade was increasingly applied not only to the 'idle' landed gentry who
derived their income from rentals but also to the active urban gentry who
worked for a living.[2] Here was scope for those with ability even if they
lacked blue blood or an estate in the country.

One great attraction of a professional occupation was its freedom from
close daily supervision. There were fixed points in the calendar – such as
the weekly service for the clergyman or the date in court for the barrister.

Figure 7.1 The Hope of the Family (c.1770). Bunbury's print gently satirised the young hopeful of the family, brought by his doting family to display his educational attainments to the imperious don. Father and dog urge encouragement, brother gazes expectantly, while mother clutches some talismanic books. But the pressures of leading the family's advancement into the ranks of learning seem rather too much for the confused young numbskull.

Published by permission of the British Museum, Department of Prints and Drawings

But most of the work was not scheduled to a tight timetable. That was particularly so when many professionals were self-employed, as they were in Britain at this time – in contrast with professional life in the twentieth century when the proportion of corporate professionals, employed by government or by institutions, has risen substantially.[3] Of course, the self-employed often had to hustle to make a living. And they often had to kowtow to patrons, to clients and to senior figures within their own occupational hierarchy. At the same time, however, an appeal to professional judgement encouraged a sense of professional autonomy, which was reinforced by contact with other professionals.

That generated a sense of independence. Indeed, it was sometimes invoked to defend the right to inactivity. A stalwart example of that occurred in 1799. One unnamed Anglican clergyman in the Chester diocese was rebuked for not residing in his parish. But the unabashed minister responded to a letter from his Bishop with the words: 'Upon my honour, I did not know that a bishop had anything to do with me until upon receipt of your letter I looked into Burn [the authority on *Ecclesiastical Law* (1763/5)].' The defiant legalism and sturdy sense of autonomy in this response indicates some of the problems faced by reformers, since the church had no system of direct line management. Little wonder that the exasperated Bishop snorted that, unless Parliament provided more support and unless the clergy were more zealous, 'established religion cannot exist much longer in the country'.[4] In this case, the culprit did not invoke his professional judgement. He would probably have argued instead that his beneficed living was his freehold. The point, however, was one of independence from the claims of management – an issue that is still very much a live one for modern professionals within corporate bodies.

Meanwhile, another attraction was the possibility of reasonable lifetime earnings. Adam Smith for one had observed in 1776 that the exclusive professions generally were very much better remunerated than were labouring jobs. That was in part because the skilled services classically required long and expensive training, so that higher earnings in later career carried an element of compensation for deferred income in youth. But, above all, Smith pointed out that the work of the professions entailed trust. Hence in order to guarantee that, the professions had to be financially secure enough to avoid dependence.[5] By contrast, Smith thought that confidence could not safely be reposed in 'people of a very mean or low condition'. Later, however, he agreed that the professions had very varying rates of remuneration. The wretched curates of the Church of England often had incomes that were no higher those of skilled artisans. Yet here Smith reversed the argument, to note that 'the respect paid to the profession too makes some compensation even to them for the meanness of their pecuniary recompense'.[6]

Hence their status was based upon more than money. The professions derived confidence from their shared access to a specialist arena of knowledge. And their prestige was simultaneously boosted by the public endorsement. Critics and satirists were a vital goad and corrective. But they did not destroy public approval of professional knowhow, even while professional practice might be mocked or disparaged. Self-regulation therefore became increasingly central to the definition of a profession. That was because a proportion of individual remuneration and personal gratification was paid in the form of unquantifiable social respect.

As a result, the professions commanded assets that were both more and less than financial capital. The kernel of their power was their command of expert knowhow and skilled services that were in relatively short supply and great demand. Hence the professions collectively owned mental capital. That gave them a somewhat ambivalent position in terms of socio-economic classification. They did not fall neatly into any one of the three organising categories that were identified by the pioneers of economic analysis. Adam Smith had proposed a threefold division among owners of land, owners of capital and owners of labour. These groups then formed the basis of three separate social orders or classes, with an upper class of landowning rentiers, a middle class of capitalist merchants and manufacturers, and a working class of wage-labourers. It was, he argued, a pattern found in all advanced economies. Thus he noted: 'these are the three great, original and constituent orders of every civilised society, from whose revenue that of every other order is ultimately derived.'[7] Moreover, Smith was followed in this not only by other classical economists such as his successor David Ricardo but also by Karl Marx, the founding father of revolutionary communism.[8]

But the professions complicated this threefold model. They matched neither the working class of labourers nor the upper class of landowners. The bulk of the professions were thus seen as members of the 'middle class'. Indeed, some of those engaged in the skilled services did own capital assets from the start and others, who began without much, gained substance during their careers. That was not, however, the essential basis of the professions' economic role. Thus the expert providers of skilled services were not owners of finance capital and did not fit the image of the middle-class 'capitalist'. In practice, of course, this stereotype was too limited. Instead, the social group that identified itself as 'middle class' had a broad economic base of professional, commercial and manufacturing occupations. Hence sociologists have suggested other variants. In the early twentieth century, Max Weber, who studied law and joined the professoriat, stressed the diversity of social identifiers. For him, the 'liberal professions' were not a 'property' class but an 'acquisition' class, who founded their privileged position upon ability and technical training.[9] However, the relationship between this 'intelligentsia' and the other social classes remained unclear. Thus the professions were a puzzle in terms of simple class categorisations.

Moreover, since they did not manufacture or sell visible and tangible commodities, they also posed a problem for economic analysts. The pioneers of the subject generally underestimated the impact of the 'invisible' service economy. Thus, crucially, Adam Smith in 1776 defined the professions as 'unproductive' since their efforts did not generate any tangible new goods of permanent value. In an amusing section of *The Wealth of Nations*, he tweaked the noses of the great and the good, when he argued that all providers of skilled services, even at the very highest level, had no significant economic worth:

> The labour of some of the most respectable orders in the society is, like that of menial servants, unproductive of any value, . . . The sovereign, for example, with all the officers both of justice and war who serve under him, the whole army and navy, are unproductive labourers. . . . In the same class must be ranked, some both of the gravest and most important, and some of the most frivolous professions: churchmen, lawyers, physicians, men of letters of all kinds; players, buffoons, musicians, opera-singers, opera-dancers, etc. . . . Like the declamation of the actor, the harangue of the orator, or the tune of the musician, the work of all of them perishes in the very instant of its production.[10]

This formulation proved enduringly influential. But in fact Adam Smith left a complex issue for his successor economists to ponder, since the allegedly 'unproductive' service sector was continuously expanding rather than declining with increasing economic diversification. It was difficult to regard all that as neutral or even parasitic in its impact, since it was evidently not halting growth.[11] Marx for one eventually proposed a revision that went some way to accommodating the role of the service industries. Those who worked for capitalists were 'productive', he argued, since they added surplus value to capital. On the other hand, the services provided by the self-employed did not generate any gain. Thus he concluded wryly enough that 'Milton, who wrote *Paradise Lost*, was an unproductive worker. On the other hand, the writer who turns out factory-made stuff for his publisher is a productive worker.'[12] This did accept that some professional services could generate value. However, it left a paradox that the very same work could be analysed as either parasitic or the reverse, according to the nature of its employer.

The economists' hesitations about the role of the professions, as the leading exemplars of the skilled services, matched the social ambivalence about their status and role. Neither area of uncertainty went away. On the contrary, the analytical challenge had been progressively strengthened by the mid-nineteenth century, as the professions themselves grew in numbers, social esteem and, especially, in self-organisation. The knowledge-based services had come to stay.

Here was a long-term trend of the times. It did not mean that all skilled service occupations were successfully able to control their own numbers and professional performance. Some manifestly were not. The teaching profession, for example, then and later has faced repeated difficulties in co-ordinating and controlling its own ranks. However, it was noticeable that, in field after field, there were pressures towards professional organisation and regulation. In Britain, furthermore, the changes often occurred in a common pattern, with informal arrangements considerably preceding formal ones.

'Professionalisation' in a wider sense also influenced a number of other occupations that were not strictly organised. The clergy in Britain and America constituted one obvious example. They were one of the senior professions, with a highly influential ethos of service. Yet they did not create any over-arching professional organisations, they did not establish a common set of qualifying examinations, and they did not manage to exclude self-appointed preachers and new messiahs. Rather, the clergy remained divided by their rival church institutions and often by disputes over religious principle as well. There was therefore no automatic progression from disunion to collective control of the market.

Instead, the position of different groups varied according to their sense of collective identity or otherwise and also according to their bargaining power. And that in turn depended upon the interaction of supply with the state of effective demand for professional services, whether that was generated by the state, by other institutions, by individual consumers, or by all these.

Consequently, the input of demand greatly complicates the model of change that has been proposed by Sarfatti Larson. As already noted, she posits a long-term and powerful 'professional project', undertaken by a sector of the rising middle class. It was not the result of a formal policy. Yet, she claims, it motivated key groups of skilled service workers to establish professionally regulated monopolies of knowledge and skills. That gave them control of scarce resources, which enabled them to advance their own upward social mobility.[13] In many ways, this analysis is a polite sociological replication of the satirical accounts that depicted the professions as conspirators, out to dupe the lay public for their own ends. Such a viewpoint justly points to the social power of regulation (although in some countries it should be noted that regulation was initiated by the state rather than by the professions themselves). Yet there was also a powerful demand for professional services, which became increasingly effective as consumer purchasing power grew. Without that, Larson's interpretation leaves unresolved the question of how such a 'project' could begin in the first place. Indeed, she conspicuously excludes from analysis the professions that did not organise professional associations, but which still managed to achieve social status and respect.

Furthermore, it might be added that collective organisation in the market place was not a tactic uniquely adopted by one sector of the middle class. By the eighteenth century, the old trade guilds had indeed largely vanished. There were, however, numerous other forms of organisation. At various times, skilled labourers combined in trade union activity, despite the legal hazards under the restrictive Combination Acts between 1799 and 1824.[14] Businessmen also managed to form unofficial 'rings' and cabals, and some became publicly grouped into syndicates and cartels.[15] And the landowners, who at that time eschewed any sectional organisation, nonetheless used the power of Parliament to uphold the Corn Laws that effectively subsidised the agricultural interest between the first Bounty Act of 1673 and Repeal in 1846.[16]

Thus the trend that Larson defines as the 'professional project' was not unique to the professions. It was instead part of a much wider jostling for competitive economic advantage, in which the state also played a part – either by intervening directly as employer or by setting the ground rules. Moreover, as already amply noted, there were often fierce rivalries within and between the different professions, which by no means constituted a monolithic bloc.[17]

All forms of sectional associations in the labour market were a source of grief to economic liberals like Adam Smith. He did not believe that occupational organisation might help to regulate performance in the economy. Instead, he sought to free labour from group entanglements. As a result, he was hostile to 'the exclusive and corporation spirit of all thriving professions'. That led him into dispute with an eminent Scottish physician. In 1774 Adam Smith argued in a letter to Dr William Cullen that the sale of medical qualifications without examination (as then practised by some lesser Scottish universities) was reprehensible but not important. Patients could judge for themselves and were not deceived by mere titles. Indeed, Smith added sardonically: 'That doctors are sometimes fools as well as other people, is not, in the present times, one of those profound secrets which is known only to the learned.'[18]

William Cullen's immediate reply to this jibe was not recorded. But in 1776 he devoted his university oration to arguing the rival case.[19] People found it difficult to assess medical expertise and could be misled by rogues or incompetents. Hence properly supervised qualifications were essential to protect the public. Individuals could then choose among *bona fide* practitioners. Eventually, it was Cullen's viewpoint that prevailed – but not in all circumstances or for every aspirant occupation. The path to professionalisation was often a winding one, and it was emphatically not identical for all would-be professional groups. That can be seen in the contrasting experiences of a number of other skilled services.

Some specialist occupations in the early nineteenth century did certainly progress towards self-organisation and the definition of a national standard qualification. Moreover, their official regulation often followed a prior experience of unofficial group affiliation. The veterinary surgeons formed a case in point. From 1783 onwards, a private society of practitioners who were enthusiasts 'for the Encouraging of Agriculture and Industry' met in Odiham (Hampshire) and developed a collective interest in farriery. This group then founded in 1791 a Veterinary College in London – ahead of the medical surgeons, whose College of Surgeons was not inaugurated until 1800. Later, the Highland Agricultural Society of Scotland took up the challenge. In 1823, it launched its own Veterinary College in Edinburgh. Eventually, in 1844, the two institutions were merged by charter to form the Royal College of Veterinary Surgeons.[20] That began to consolidate the profession, although it was not until 1881 that the College was empowered by Parliament to hold qualifying examinations and to maintain a register of practitioners.[21] Here then was a gradual century-long progression: from a voluntary society to formal organisation to national incorporation to full professional regulation, with the backing of the state.

Civil engineers were another group with an emergent identity, who moved rather more rapidly towards institutionalisation. Their occupation had its prosaic side. That was expressed in worthy tomes such as *The Theory and Practice of Warming and Ventilating Public Buildings ... By an Engineer* (1825) or a tract advocating *The Broad Gauge ... [as] Best Adapted to the Commercial Wants of the Nation ... By an 'Engineer'* (1846). Yet as their tracts also suggested, these experts had access to knowhow with significant practical applications. Their work was in great demand and their status was gradually rising.[22] The 'civil engineer' indeed gained his specialist name in the later eighteenth century, to differentiate practitioners from military 'engineers' who devised or handled 'engines of war'. Numerous sub-divisions then followed. By the mid-nineteenth century there were mechanical, electrical and mining engineers. Moreover, famous practitioners like Isambard Kingdom Brunel did wonders for their collective image; and there were also local heroes who devised the arched bridge or the railway cutting or the new road.[23]

However, the public needed to trust as well as to admire their skills. A social club for elite engineers, known as the Society of Civil Engineers had been formed in 1771. Just over twenty years later, in 1793, it was transformed into the Smeatonian Society which remains its modern name – in homage to the pioneering John Smeaton (1724–92).[24] But this body had no formal powers. In 1818 a group of young engineers took the highly significant step of forming a new and independent Institute of Civil Engineers, which received a royal charter in 1828.[25] This was a significant moment. The Institute was in fact the first case of conscious professional consolidation outside the traditional learned professions.

From the start, the new body was confident. It established its head-quarters in Whitehall and moved in 1837 to its present site in Great George Street, in the heart of the political world, just off Parliament Square. The profession also prided itself upon its robust practicality, in contrast with the effete and book-bound learning of the old professions. Indeed, engineers were sometimes depicted as young and vigorous intruders into traditional authority structures.[26] Another permutation was to define the profession as the key cultural intermediary between brains and brawn. That was the theme of an eloquent speech by the youthful engineer Henry Robinson Palmer (1795–1844), then aged 23, at the inaugural meeting of the Institute of Civil Engineers in 1818:

> The Engineer is a Mediator between the Philosopher and the Working Mechanic, and like an interpreter between two foreigners, must understand the language of both, hence the absolute necessity of possessing both practical and theoretical knowledge.[27]

It was a bold speech that captured the confidence of the new field, even if in practice the new subject did not play such a uniquely crucial cultural role. Britain's knowledge systems were themselves expanding and becoming pluralised. Many engineers remained culturally cautious and careful.[28] Moreover, their own organisation rapidly became fragmented. Numerous branches of engineering evolved, each with their own separate professional body. Thus, within a few decades, the 'Civils' faced competition from a new Institution of Mechanical Engineers (1847) and from the numerous other sectional bodies that followed in the course of the nineteenth century.[29] In general, the I.C.E. made no attempt to halt these changes. However, it did lobby successfully against the plan to give a royal charter to a new and multi-disciplinary rival, in the form of the Society of Engineers (founded in 1854).[30] This lack of cohesion was strikingly paralleled in Germany and the United States.[31] Nonetheless, a new and visible field of applied knowledge, albeit with many sub-specialisms, had arrived within the professional pantheon.

Architects shared a similar pride in manifest achievement. They did not reject theory, since they valued their own developing corpus of specialist knowledge. But they sought to apply it to 'the Elegant and Necessary Art' of building. That was the specific objective of a society of gentlemen practitioners, which first met in London in 1774 to promote the improvement of architecture.[32] Many builders began to covet the new occupational title. A poem in 1786 noted the uppishness of the workforce, exclaiming sardonically that even 'The Carpenter, turn'd architect, *designs!*'[33] At the same time, the occupation was notoriously fractious. One reason was the perennial competition for commissions and patronage. Yet that was true of many professions. In this case, the rivalry seems to have been exacerbated by the growing sub-division of construction into many specialist elements. Tasks were shared between architect–designers, surveyors, draughtsmen, engineers and building contractors. There were no hard-and-fast rules. In that uncertain environment, the architectural profession proved difficult to define and to organise.[34] There were numerous sectional meetings from 1791 onwards, when the Architects' Club was first founded. But this was essentially a dining society. For many years, no single group managed to gain hegemonic status.

Concern was expressed, however, about the need for a code of professional conduct. After abortive discussions with the surveyors, a group of architects in 1834 launched their own separate Institute of British Architects as a nationwide body, which was chartered in 1837.[35] Its membership was initially small and its powers limited. In addition, architectural training remained disorganised and unsystematic. The profession continued to be characteristically fissiparous. In 1847, an independent Architectural Association was founded, to campaign for improvements in education.[36] Later, too, a major schism occurred within the R.I.B.A. when another breakaway group, impatient with the delay in achieving compulsory registration, founded a rival Society of Architects (1884; incorporated 1893). Eventually the rebels reamalgamated with the parent body in 1925. But the statutory registration of architects was not introduced until 1931 nor rendered compulsory until 1938.[37]

Patterns of professionalisation were thus very far from uniform. An *ad hoc* society often but not invariably preceded institutionalisation. But, again, the subsequent creation of a corporate body did not necessarily imply immediate regulation. The importance of organisation as a sign of status and self-discipline was, however, becoming apparent. An element of emulation also came into play, once the trend was established.

For example, a group of London surveyors in 1834 formed the Land Surveyors' Club. Their aims were to improve educational standards, to enhance their collective professional image, and to establish an agreed scale of charges. They failed, although the Club survived as a convivial dining group.[38] Fully thirty-four years followed before the launch in 1868 of the Institution of Chartered Surveyors; and that body did not introduce examinations until 1881, when it gained a Royal Charter.[39] Hence the trend towards professional self-organisation and regulation cannot be described as either overwhelming or rapid. Nonetheless, a pointed editorial in the *Building News* in 1860 had already reflected the pressures towards change. Thus it asserted roundly that:

> It will scarcely be deemed credible, when architects, builders, engineers, and even their subordinates, clerks of works, and foremen engineers, have their institutions, and when every trade down to the most mechanical handicraft has its mutual benefit association or provident club, that a profession which is in close connection with

the practice of construction and engineering, standing midway between the two, should have no common centre for the reception and radiation of professional intelligence and assistance.[40]

Emulation, status and the need to control quality were linked aspirations. Once a model of organisation had been created, other groups were able to follow suit. Numerous professional institutions were founded throughout the nineteenth century and more still in the twentieth century.[41] The complex world of specialist work required specialist validation.[42] That was particularly the case as consumer markets began to widen decisively. Already by the eighteenth century, the professions had moved away from exclusive dependence upon a handful of noble patrons.[43] There were simply too many specialists at work to be all employed by the tiny elite of aristocrats and the very rich.[44]

Indeed, the widening of the market was a better safeguard than exclusive organisation, decided the architectural journalist J.C. Loudon. As a result, he argued in 1835 that: 'The surest foundation on which these gentlemen [architects] can found their hopes of future employment is on the taste of the middling classes. The time for building palaces, castles, and cathedrals is gone by, or nearly so.'[45] Moreover, his general point applied to the other professions too. Engineers and architects may have required clients of some substance. But others, such as those at the popular end of the medical or clerical professions, also habitually served among the working-class population. Silently and decisively, the 'patron' had turned into the 'client'. Of course, aristocratic consumption of specialist services in the grand style did not disappear. Yet, as the expansion into middle-class and then into mass markets grew ever more important, the scale of professional work changed. And that in turn encouraged the move towards impersonal and official validation rather than personal and *ad hoc* vetting.

Not every group of professional specialists was, however, able to regulate its own entry qualifications and to establish its own separate organisation. There were a number of 'near-misses' and 'failures'. Of course, it was not the case that all skilled occupations had a historic duty to professionalise. It was not always possible to generate a collective identity, let alone to achieve organisational unity. Thus there were a number of occupations – like those of authors and performers – which came to be seen as 'professional' without being organised into professions and without controlling access to their own special field.

'Knowledge has no value or use for the solitary owner; to be enjoyed, it must be communicated', asserted Lord Camden grandly, in a House of Lords debate on copyright in February 1774.[46] That was in the context of his attack upon the booksellers-cum-publishers for restricting or monopolising the circulation of books. Authors, he asserted, wrote for 'glory' not for gain. But his olympian claim about the status of the literary profession lacked realism. It was certainly not appreciated by those dismissed by Camden as mere 'scribblers for bread'. One of them had already pointed out in 1758 that 'a Man may plead for Money, prescribe or quack for Money, preach and pray for Money, marry for Money, fight for Money, do anything within the Law for Money'.[47] Why therefore should not authors write for financial gain? In practice, an uneasy balance was struck between the public interest in a free and cheap press, and the writers' need for protection against pirated copies of their work. A law of limited (not permanent) copyright was passed in 1709/10; and eventually, with many twists and turns, it was endorsed and updated by an international law of copyright in intellectual property.[48]

Publishers and a few leading writers of the day were consequently able to do very well. But they coexisted with a sizeable rank-and-file of relatively impoverished 'Grub Street' hacks. It was an 'AGE OF AUTHORS', announced Dr Johnson in 1753, adding wryly that the rush to get into print was joined not only by men but also by plenty of female 'Amazons of the pen'.[49] All these writers, however, inhabited a very competitive 'republic of letters', which generated very unequal rewards. That made it difficult to generate a strong group ethos, especially as writing was usually a solitary process. Moreover, the business was open-ended and fluid, without any obvious training procedures or entry qualifications or career ladders.[50] There were also many part-timers and amateurs.

Gradually, however, the disparate but increasingly commercialised literary world began to assert its freedom from noble patronage. Dr Johnson's famous 1755 letter to Lord Chesterfield (which was published in 1790) was taken as the classic authorial declaration of independence; and Johnson's own acceptance of a state pension of £300 in 1762 was not able to cloud the vigour of that assertion.[51] However, it proved in-superably difficult to translate literary freedom into the trappings of formal professionalism. The celebrated Literary Club (1764) remained a private group. Similarly, the first Society of Authors (1843) and the Guild of Literature and Art (1850) were voluntary associations with very limited support.[52] Where the field was disparate with such weakly demarcated boundaries, it proved impossible to introduce systematic regulation.

Rather the same general point applied in the case of actors, artists, and musicians. To make a living from these precarious occupations required some luck and much professional dedication. A patron might help to launch a career but success required skill and application. For example, the histrionic gifts of the triumphant actor–manager David Garrick (1717–79) were sustained by his 'constant, and unremitted attention to his profession', as noted by an admiring friend.[53] On the other hand, few were able to emulate his success. The general status of many 'players' was lowly.

'Let nice logicians tell us, if they can,/ Why a profession, which, it is confessed,/ Requires more talents, both in mind and body/ Than any other, fails to meet respect?', asked a plaintive and distinctly uninspired actor–poet in 1810.[54] But in fact the work was haphazard, the training informal, and the level of skills and rewards exceptionally variegated. That made it very difficult to forge a collective identity, let alone a professional closed shop.

Others in the arts and performing arts were similarly placed. They worked in increasingly commercialised markets.[55] A small number gained great fame and fortune. But their world was fragmented and insecure. Although many clubs and societies raised their public profile, they remained minority associations. For example, the Society of Artists (1761–91) provided rooms for members to exhibit paintings and gained a royal charter in 1765, while a rival Free Society of Artists of Great Britain provided an alternative show until 1779. Neither, however, managed to organise their fellows. Moreover, the elite Royal Academy of London (1768–) sponsored exhibitions and a drawing school, which issued diplomas signed by George III. Yet this body remained consciously an exclusive society, declining to seek a universal membership.[56]

Making a living from the arts remained, therefore, a disorganised occupation. Interestingly, however, it was coming to be interpreted in professional terms. Clearly, the absence of self-regulatory organisations did not preclude such an identification. Thus, for example, the popular song-writer Charles Dibdin entitled his autobiography *The Professional Life of Mr Dibdin, Written by Himself* (1803). He was more certain than many of his contemporaries, who remained uncertain as to how to classify the performing arts. However, in 1861 the British census decided for the first time to list the disparate artists, authors and musicians with the learned professions and the engineers in the Professional Class. By contrast, at this date, the architects and the veterinary surgeons (both groups that did have their own professional institutions) were located in the Industrial and the Agricultural Classes respectively.[57] In this case, the census officials seem to have focused upon economic role rather than social ranking. These contrasts, however, indicate that the 'professions' were interpreted both generously and variously.

Teachers, above all, illustrated the quandaries of occupational identity. At the most advanced levels, they clearly had access to a significant body of knowledge. From that, senior educational figures represented a certain cultural power. But they found it difficult to ringfence their knowledge, since their task was to educate others into the mysteries of learning. Lesser lights in the profession often held only a lowly status. Their command of knowledge did not in itself command an automatic awe. When, for example, a Sussex schoolmaster in 1750 refused to take an additional number of free pupils into his school, his diary recorded how he was graphically denounced by a local worthy:[58]

> Among other abusive and scurrilous language, he said I was an upstart, runnagate [renegade], beggarly dog; that I picked his pocket, and that I never knew how to teach a school in my life. He did not strike me [after threats of physical violence], . . . but withdrew in a wonderful heat, and ended all with his general maxim, 'The greater scholler, the greater rogue'.

Against episodes like that, teachers were not able to counterpose a professional solidarity. Their numbers were growing substantially; but they did not constitute a homogeneous interest. On the contrary. They ranged from the select ranks of Oxbridge's Anglican dons [59] and the learned Nonconformist masters at the Dissenting Academies,[60] through to the many schoolmasters, private tutors, crammers and governesses, to the humble dames who kept day-schools for young children. One of these is known to history as the woman who taught the young Samuel Johnson to read. Indeed, the widowed Dame Oliver of Lichfield paid her former pupil a handsome tribute: 'When he was going to Oxford [in 1728], she came to take leave of him, brought him, in the simplicity of her kindness, a present of gingerbread, and said, he was the best scholar she had ever had.' Johnson was delighted both with the compliment and its form.[61]

Diversity of status and style, however, prevented the teaching profession from achieving organisational unity. Some schoolmasters owned and ran their own schools but many were employees and lacked contractual independence. The teachers in charity schools, for example, were often monitored closely.[62] In addition, many male schoolmasters were clergymen, owing loyalty to their churches rather than to a secular profession. Meanwhile, the profession was also open to women. Some directed schools for girls, like the Bristol boarding-school for 'young ladies' founded in 1758 by Mary, Elizabeth and Sarah More, where their younger sister Hannah More studied Italian, Spanish and Latin.[63] Other women, however, were governesses in private households. There they were isolated and had an ambivalent social position, above the ordinary servants but not part of the family.[64]

Training was generally minimal at all levels in the teaching profession in this period. As a result, the overall level of skills was not great; and entry into teaching was not difficult. There were, nonetheless, some schemes for reform. In the 1800s, the Revd Andrew Bell (1753–1832) and the young Quaker Joseph Lancaster (1778–1838) both introduced rival training schemes and certification. These were portents for the future. Yet their initial impact was only limited.[65]

Given these various divisions by religion, employment status, pedagogic skills, levels of knowledge and gender, it was not surprising that teachers found it difficult to organise professionally and were fragmented when they did so.[66] Their differences were felt to outweigh their common interests. That was not inevitable. For example, it has been argued that in Germany reform-minded teachers developed a much stronger sense of themselves as a professional corps.[67] However, in Britain, there was no common cause to promote unity. Thus, although many teachers shared an ethos of service and although in the long term their training and role has been gradually professionalised, they did not formally envisage themselves as a single profession. Nor did the state intervene to promote that end. Thus no General Teaching Council, on a par with the Bar Council or the General Medical Council, was proposed in this period. Nor indeed has one yet been established in Britain, although it can be readily predicted that it will not be too long before that happens.

Women were notably involved in many of the occupations that were no more than semi-professionalised in organisational terms. Their abilities were employed – for example, as teachers, midwives, nurses, authors, musicians and actors[68] – where their participation was not overly constrained by social conventions or by the need for formal entry qualifications.

By contrast, women played a minimal role in 'heavy duty' occupations such as civil engineering, which was early to gain self-regulation. It was therefore sometimes assumed that the professions were automatically male-dominated and (a separate point) that professionalism was inimical to the interests of women. In fact, neither proposition was valid for all time. Conceptually, there is no reason to suggest that women were or are harmed by the professional virtues of service, commitment, expertise and vocational dedication. And historically, although men dominated the early professions, these occupations were based upon skills and knowledge, not upon gender as such. Thus, eventually, the meritocratic ethos of the professions proved the trojan horse that admitted the claims of able women. Indeed, the radical 'Sophia' had already argued in 1739 that the exclusion of women from positions of power and leadership was justified only by custom, and not by logic or justice.[69] Hence as skilled occupations became more and more reliant upon brain than upon brawn, there was less and less reason to confine these positions only to men.

Why indeed should not women be generals? Military leaders no longer scuffled in the dust of battle personally, continued 'Sophia'.[70] Hence there was no reason why a woman could not direct an army. This logic did not overcome the strongly held traditional belief in fighting as man's work. A handful of females did manage to enlist in disguise. In the mid-eighteenth century, one Hannah Snell reported her five years' service, first in the army and then the navy.[71] Yet no women as yet sought a position of military command. The general point, however, was prescient. In the very long term, all the specialist professions, not excluding the leadership of the armed forces, are finding it increasingly difficult to justify a bar upon the recruitment of qualified women.

Army and naval command in this period, however, was not yet troubled with these debates. Such posts were viewed as the ideal occupations for lively young men of good family. Temperament rather than formal knowledge was the key. 'I would recommend the Army, or the Navy, to a boy of warm constitution, strong animal spirits, and a cold genius', remarked Lord Chesterfield, perhaps thinking of the need for coolness under fire.[72] Vicesimus Knox agreed. Some energy was required. The army was ideal for 'those spirits, which are too restless for domestic life', while the navy suited those willing to live 'without ease and tranquillity'.[73]

Both these expanding services, however, had a distinctly ambivalent attitude towards recruitment. In practice, there were recurrent tensions between the claims of aristocratic status and an emergent professional ethos. In the Royal Navy, that took the form of rivalries between the 'gentlemen' officers and the sea-going 'tarpaulins'. The old hands were especially aggrieved when experienced men were overtaken by raw recruits, who were sometimes commissioned under the required age of twenty one. The young Horatio Nelson was one of these. A clergyman's son and a distant relation of the Walpoles, he became a second lieutenant at the age of eighteen.[74] But, as his career indicates, some men of status also had ability. Moreover, there were a few cases of outstanding sailors of modest background who managed to rise from the ranks of the ordinary seamen, 'through the hawse-hole' as it was termed. The navigator Captain Cook (1728–79), who began life as the son of an agricultural labourer, was the most famous case of such promotion.[75]

Naval command did therefore acknowledge the need for a modicum of technical knowhow and professional identity. Some moves were early made to provide some formal training. From 1677 onwards, senior officers at the level of lieutenant and above were examined by the Navy Board; and after 1729, the Naval Academy at Portsmouth (renamed the Royal Naval College in 1806) provided formalised instruction for some cadets.[76] In addition, uniforms were standardised from 1748 onwards.[77] Training and appearance did not, however, override the importance of practical experience. Most officers were educated via the harsh realities of life at sea. One Admiral in 1773 excused his errors in grammar with blunt pride: 'A Man of War was my University'.[78] Thus naval officers cherished a specialist knowhow that largely bypassed book learning. It led to a swashbuckling and risky way of life, in which the fortunate were rewarded by prize money from captured enemy ships, while the sick and wounded languished on half-pay.[79] Indeed, the hazards were recognised by Parliament, which legislated in 1733 to establish a special fund for poor widows of naval officers.[80] Money was thenceforth raised by the accounting expedient of listing one in every hundred sailors as a dummy entry. These

Figure 7.2 The Second Cadet Barracks in the Arsenal (later eighteenth century). The army did not claim or appreciate great learning; but like most of the professions it began gradually to formalise its training in this period. The Royal Military Academy at Woolwich was founded in 1741 and began to test candidates in 1764. Here the smart cadets leave for vacation from their simple barracks, known as 'The Warren' with its tree-lined parade ground.

Illustrated from print in W.D. Jones (ed.) *The Records of the Royal Military Academy, 1741–1840* (1851), based upon drawing held by the Royal Military Academy Sandhurst were lugubriously known as the 'widows' men', since their pay went directly into the widows' fund.

Military commanders, meanwhile, faced similar tensions about their role. They exercised a legal monopoly of organised might, which was sanctified as a crucial reserve power of the state.[81] Their service to king and country, moreover, was defined as the honourable 'profession of arms', which brought them social credit. Indeed, it was 'happy for the commonwealth that the acknowledged gentility of the profession obliterates the sense of its hardships', noted Vicesimus Knox.[82] On the other hand, the army officers of Hanoverian Britain were only patchily 'professionalised'. Some of these gallants were more at home in the salons and gaming-rooms than on the field of battle.[83] Certainly, they did not seek to establish a separate regulatory body, since their status was already validated by the organisation in which they served. In that they resembled the clergy, another non-market-oriented group that abstained from creating their own special professional association.[84]

Strikingly, too, the officers in the British army throughout this period were appointed by a combination of purchase, patronage and merit. It was not until 1871 that the sale of commissions was finally abolished. Before that, two-thirds or more of all posts were held by purchase, although the proportion fluctuated over time.[85] Eventually, it became obvious that military effectiveness required appointment by merit and not by wealth. But the purchase system did have some practical advantages. It was defended by some famous generals, such as Marlborough and Wellington, as well as by civilians. For Parliament, it confirmed the political independence of the armed forces, since the monarch could not hire and fire at will. James II in 1685–8 had, for example, found it impossible to pack his army with Catholic officers. Despite his efforts, seven-eighths of his senior military command in 1688 were Protestants.[86] Thus the army officers were drawn from the socially conservative ranks of a monied 'aristocracy' – 'that term being understood to refer to the possession of wealth as well as of rank', as Lord Palmerston wrote approvingly in 1827.[87] For the Treasury, too, the system was economical. It meant that the government did not have to provide pensions for army officers, since most acquired a lump sum on retirement by selling their commissions.

Purchase of office had, however, begun to be regulated long before 1871. The result was another British compromise. By 1760, all senior posts of colonel and above had been excluded from sale, as were technical posts in artillery and engineering. In addition, for posts that went on sale, tariffs were specified, profiteering was controlled (though only slowly among the adventurers in the Indian army) and purchasers were restricted to men in the ranks immediately below.[88] There were still many anomalies. Some experienced men without money endured years without promotion, while even teenage boys of good family had commissions purchased for them.

Here the famous example was Major-General James Wolfe (1727–59). He began his career by being commissioned at the age of 14 into his father's regiment.[89] Yet, at the same time, a number of officers were promoted for their military skills. 'Thus station and fortune in the service are sometimes obtained by humble meritorious men, who otherwise must have for ever remained in poverty', noted Serjeant Lamb approvingly in 1811, himself a humbly born non-commissioned officer.[90] These career soldiers were particularly in demand for service overseas, where there was a serious likelihood of fighting.

Additional moves towards professional identity were also gradually introduced. In 1751, army dress regulations were codified and individual officers were banned from using their own personal insignia on regimental crests or livery.[91] Furthermore, a number of engineering cadets had begun from 1741 onwards to attend the Royal Military Academy at Woolwich, known as 'The Shop'. A reforming governor instituted passing-out examinations there in 1764 and strove to enforce discipline. And later, in 1799, the Royal Military College at High Wycombe was founded, moving in 1812/13 to Sandhurst in Berkshire.[92] Officers could also consult the growing corpus of advice books and manuals to help them,[93] although the pioneering theorists of military tactics and strategy were generally viewed with some scepticism.[94] Instead, the British tradition stressed character and discipline. But, while the military ethos was staunchly anti-intellectual, it did at least promote an *esprit de corps* and a strong sense of professional honour, generally focused upon the regiment.

Recruitment, meanwhile, remained unreformed. The semi-regulated purchase system proved very difficult to dislodge, especially when the army was victorious.[95] Partial reforms proved counter-productive. For example, new regulations in 1840 had attempted to remedy the poverty of non-purchase officers, by providing a lump sum on retirement according to length of service. But, since the scheme was funded by the sale of their commissions, that further cut the pool of non-purchase posts available for appointments by merit.[96] This tangle of competing vested interests, however, became difficult to defend once the army ceased to carry all before it on the battlefield. The bungled British campaign at Sebastopol in 1854/5 sharpened, though it did not initiate, the criticisms.[97]

A few bold military men also voiced complaints. In 1855 an anonymous officer berated the system as unfair and incompetent. He called instead for 'the generous and ennobling rivalry of merit'.[98] But a special Royal Commission in 1857 failed to resolve the issue. Then in 1861 the liberal Sir Charles Trevelyan renewed the attack with a rousing call for reform.[99] Ambitious high-flyers were wrongly excluded:

The large and important class of well-educated young men who depend for their advancement upon their own exertions, and not upon their wealth and connexions, and who constitute the pith of the Law, the Church, the Indian civil service, and other active professions, are thus ordinarily excluded from the army.

But, above all, a principle was at stake:

Purchase and professional qualification are antagonistic and incompatible principles. We must take our choice of them. The army cannot be constituted upon both at the same time.

Defenders of the purchase system faltered before this barrage. Thus in 1871, the principle of professionalism won its famous victory. The implementation of reform was slow in practice, as reforms often are. Yet the case for professional efficiency and for careers open to merit had officially triumphed.

State power played an explicit role in all this. Whereas in the case of the other professions, Parliament had wielded a reserve authority – intervening with charters or statutes at particular moments to confirm or direct change – in the case of the army and navy, the role of the state was formative. Its sanction upheld the authority of the officers, as they paraded in the uniforms of the crown. Moreover, they headed a genuinely British force. High-ranking officers (Protestant before 1828) were recruited from all three kingdoms, just as were the rank-and-file soldiery. Scotland in particular produced a notable contingent of senior army commanders, including among their ranks in the early eighteenth century 43 (17.8 per cent) of the 242 Scottish peers.[100] A sense of collective professional interest among the military began to override sectional loyalties to provide a national force, with its internal allegiances focused upon ship or regiment rather than upon region or locality.

Advancement thus progressed via a diversity of paths and forms. The state did not initiate the process but presided over a long-term trend that filtered back to influence its own praxis. One manifestation of that was the growing professionalisation of the civil service. The state, in other words, could not itself remain immune to change. Officers under the crown did not organise themselves into their own separate institutions; and many of them were indeed appointed through patronage rather than merit. Yet from the 1780s onwards, a more business-like ethos was officially inculcated. The administration became more autonomous; regular salaries were paid; and blatant profiteering was discouraged.[101]

Critics, however, remained dissatisfied. In 1853/4 the influential Northcote/Trevelyan report – under pressure from Gladstone – recommended that civil service recruits be selected by competitive examination.[102] A group of reform-minded businessmen and professionals (including Charles Dickens) then formed the Administrative Reform Association, which urged in 1855 that open qualifying examinations with a practical syllabus should be held outside London in the leading provincial cities.[103] Existing civil servants were outraged, Anthony Trollope among them. He thought it unfair to subject grown men to schoolboy tests and in 1857 he lampooned Trevelyan as Sir Gregory Hardlines – which became Trevelyan's family nickname.[104] Nonetheless, competitive examinations were eventually introduced in 1870. Thus the British state also paid obeisance to professional meritocracy, even while the established departments within the civil service long retained their own styles and traditions.

Of course, the trend was not uniform. It was initially slow-moving and sometimes circuitous; it was often perplexing; but its meritocratic ethos was also increasingly triumphant.

NOTES

1 A. Trollope, *The Bertrams* (1859), ed. S. Michell (Sutton, Gloucester, 1986), p. 88.
2 P.J. Corfield, 'The rivals: landed and other gentlemen in eighteenth-century England', in *Land and Society in Modern Britain, 1700–1914*, ed. N.B. Harte and R.E. Quinault (Manchester University Press, Manchester, 1996).
3 For this key change, see H.J. Perkin, *The Rise of Professional Society: England since 1880* (Routledge, London, 1989), pp. 86, 436–40.
4 Bishop Cleaver of Chester to Lord Grenville, 13 November 1799, in Historical Manuscripts Commission, *Report on the Manuscripts of J.B. Fortescue, Esq.*, vol. 6, p. 21.
5 A. Smith, *An Inquiry into the Nature and Causes of the Wealth of Nations*, ed. R.H. Campbell, A.S. Skinner and W.B. Todd (Clarendon, Oxford, 1976), vol. 1, pp. 119, 122.
6 Ibid., vol. 1, p. 148.
7 Ibid., vol. 1, p. 265.
8 Marx specifically disclaimed any credit for discovering the existence of classes: P.J. Corfield, 'Class by name and number in eighteenth-century Britain', in *Language, History and Class*, ed. P.J. Corfield (Blackwell, Oxford, 1991), p. 127 and n. 72.
9 M. Weber, *Wirtschaft und Gesellschaft, I* (Tübingen, 1922), transl. as *The Theory of Social and Economic Organisation*, ed. T. Parsons (Free Press, New York, 1964 edn), pp. 424–7. For Weber's training and academic career, see also H.H. Gerth and C. Wright Mills (eds), *From Max Weber: essays in sociology* (Routledge, London, 1970), pp. 6, 9–11.
10 Smith, *op. cit.*, vol. 1, pp. 330–1.
11 R.M. Hartwell, 'The service revolution: the growth of services in the modern economy, 1700–1914', in *Economic History of Europe*, vol. 3: *The Industrial Revolution, 1700–1914*, ed. C. Cipolla (Fontana, London, 1976), pp. 358–61.
12 K. Marx, *Theories of Surplus Value*, transl. G.A. Bonner and E. Burns (Lawrence & Wishart, London, 1951), pp. 148–97, esp. p. 186.
13 M. Sarfatti Larson, *The Rise of Professionalism: a sociological analysis* (University of California Press, Berkeley, 1977), pp. xvi–xvii, 8–9, 14–18, 54, 66–7.
14 Compare J. Rule, *The Experience of Labour in Eighteenth-Century Industry* (Croom Helm, London, 1981), pp. 147–93; and C.R. Dobson, *Masters and Journeymen: a prehistory of industrial relations, 1717–1800* (Croom Helm, London, 1980).
15 Tensions between business competition and the role of cartels (e.g. in coal and other mining industries) are well documented by H. Levy, *Monopolies, Cartels*

and Trusts in British Industry (Jena, 1909; Engl. transl., Macmillan, London, 1927), pp. 97–166.

16 D.G. Barnes, *A History of the English Corn Laws from 1660–1846* (Routledge, London, 1930).

17 For a critique of Larson on those grounds, see A. Abbott, *The System of Professions: an essay on the division of expert labor* (University of Chicago Press, Chicago, 1988), esp. pp. xiii, 1–2, 316.

18 Adam Smith to William Cullen, 20 September 1774, repr. in A. Smith, *An Inquiry into the Nature and Causes of the Wealth of Nations, with a Life of the Author . . . and Supplemental Dissertations*, ed. J.R. McCulloch (Edinburgh, 1850), vol. 2, pp. 588–91, esp. pp. 589, 591.

19 Engl. transl. of the Latin oration by William Cullen (1710–90) in ibid., vol. 2, pp. 593–4.

20 See L.P. Pugh, *From Farriery to Veterinary Medicine, 1785–95* (R.C.V.S., Cambridge, 1962); and O.C. Bradley, *History of the Edinburgh Veterinary College* (Oliver & Boyd, Edinburgh, 1923). But G. Millerson, *The Qualifying Associations* (Routledge, London, 1964), pp. 61–3, incongruously renders the Odiham Society as Oldham.

21 44 & 45 Vict., cap. 62 (1881).

22 This was sealed by S. Smiles's admiring *Lives of the Engineers, with an Account of their Principal Works . . .* (London, 1861–2), 3 vols.

23 For the impact of Brunel (1806–59), see A. Vaughan, *Isambard Kingdom Brunel: engineering knight errant* (Murray, London, 1991); and for some of his humbler fellows, see T. Ruddock, *Arched Bridges and Their Builders, 1735–1835* (Cambridge University Press, Cambridge, 1979).

24 G. Watson, *The Smeatonians: the Society of Civil Engineers* (Telford, London, 1989) provides a sympathetic account.

25 Idem, *The Civils: the story of the Institution of Civil Engineers* (Telford, London, 1988), esp. pp. 7–30.

26 See e.g. speech at the 1866 annual dinner of the I.C.E. by the MP Robert Lowe: quoted as frontispiece in *The Architect's, Engineer's, and Building-Trades' Directory . . .* (London, 1868).

27 Watson, *The Civils*, p. 9.

28 R.A. Buchanan, *The Engineers: a history of the engineering profession in Britain, 1750–1914* (Kingsley, London, 1989), esp. pp. 15–16, 208–12.

29 Eighteen separate engineering institutions were founded between 1818 and 1930: Millerson, *Qualifying Associations*, pp. 227–30.

30 Hence the Society was not formally incorporated until 1910: see Watson, *The Civils*, p. 46.

31 Compare K. Gispen, *New Profession, Old Order: engineers and German society, 1815–1914* (Cambridge University Press, Cambridge, 1989), pp. 1–9, 15–43; and M.A. Calvert, *The Mechanical Engineer in America, 1830–1910* (Johns Hopkins Press, Baltimore, 1967), passim.

32 Unpaginated preface to first issue of *The Builder's Magazine: or monthly companion for architects, carpenters, masons, bricklayers, etc. as well as for every gentleman who would wish to be a competent judge of the . . . art of building . . . By a Society of Architects* (London, 1774).

33 T. Busby, *The Age of Genius! a satire on the times . . .* (London, 1786), p. 41.

34 J.M. Crook, 'The pre-Victorian architect: professionalism and patronage', *Architectural History,* 12 (1969), pp. 62–78, esp. pp. 62–4, 66–8. See also B. Kaye, *The Development of the Architectural Profession in England: a sociological study* (Allen & Unwin, London, 1960), pp. 44–53, 57–67; F. Jenkins, 'The Victorian architectural profession', in *Victorian Architecture*, ed. P. Ferriday (Cape,

London, 1963), pp. 39–49; and J. Wilton-Ely, 'The rise of the professional architect in England', in *The Architect: chapters in the history of the profession*, ed. S. Kostof (Oxford University Press, New York, 1977), pp. 180–208.

35 J.A. Gotch 'The Royal Institute of British Architects', in idem (ed.), *The Growth and Work of the R.I.B.A., 1834–1934* (R.I.B.A., London, 1934), pp. 1–50. See also Millerson, *Qualifying Associations*, pp. 23, 58–9, 66–7.

36 J. Summerson, *The Architectural Association, 1847–1947* (A.A., London, 1947), pp. 19–22. From the 1860s this body ran informal classes in architecture, which in the 1890s were systematised to form an independent School of Architecture, which still flourishes.

37 H. Barnes, 'The R.I.B.A. and the statutory registration of architects', in Gotch (ed.), *The R.I.B.A.*, pp. 68–84.

38 F.M.L. Thompson, *Chartered Surveyors: the growth of a profession* (Routledge, London, 1968), pp. 94–100.

39 Ibid., pp. 128–47, 182–201.

40 Ibid., p. 134, quoting editorial in the *Building News*, no. 6 (8 June 1860), pp. 447–8.

41 These are listed in Millerson, *Qualifying Associations*, pp. 221–58, though Thompson, *Chartered Surveyors*, p. 177, n. 6, notes that the College of Preceptors (1849) has been omitted. A comparable listing of Scottish and Irish associations is still awaited.

42 On the role of organisation, see Perkin, *Rise of Professional Society*, pp. 85–6, 439–40; and T.R. Gourvish, 'The rise of the professions', in *Later Victorian Britain, 1867–1900*, ed. T.R. Gourvish and A. O'Day (Macmillan, Basingstoke, 1988), pp. 13–35.

43 For widening demand even pre-1700, see e.g. W. Prest (ed.), *The Professions in Early Modern England* (Croom Helm, London, 1987), pp. 7–17; and G. Holmes, *Augustan England: professions, state and society, 1680–1730* (Allen & Unwin, London, 1982), pp. 11–18.

44 This disagrees with the view that the pre-industrial professions were still heavily reliant upon aristocratic patronage and recruitment: see P. Elliott, *The Sociology of the Professions* (Macmillan, London, 1972), pp. 20–2, 24–31, 40–3.

45 J.C. Loudon (1783–1843), in *The Architectural Magazine*, 2 (1835), p. 472.

46 J. Campbell, *The Lives of the Lord Chancellors and Keepers of the Great Seal of England* (London, 1846), vol. 5, p. 297.

47 Anon. [J. Ralph], *The Case of Authors by Profession or Trade Stated . . .* (London, 1758), p. 2.

48 See E. Plowman and L.C. Hamilton, *Copyright: intellectual property in the information age* (Routledge, London, 1980), pp. 12–14; and A. Collins, *Authorship in the Days of Johnson: being a study of the relation between author, patron, publisher and public, 1726–80* (Holden, London, 1927), pp. 53–113, 221–32.

49 [S. Johnson], *The Adventurer*, 2, no. 115 (11 Dec. 1753), p. 266.

50 See variously J.W. Saunders, *The Profession of English Letters* (Routledge, London, 1964), pp. 136–45, 162–4, 176–98; V. Bonham Carter, *Authors by Profession*, vol. 1: *from the introduction of printing until the Copyright Act of 1911* (Society of Authors, London, 1978), pp. 25–32; and J. Todd, *The Sign of Angellica: women, writing and fiction, 1660–1800* (Virago, London, 1989), pp. 36–51, 125–45, 218–35.

51 J. Boswell (ed.), *The Celebrated Letter from Samuel Johnson, LL.D. to Philip Dormer Stanhope, Earl of Chesterfield, now first Published . . .* (London, 1790), pp. 3–4.

52 Bonham Carter, *Authors by Profession*, vol. 1, pp. 80–9. A second Society of Authors followed (1884–present): ibid., pp. 119–20.

53 P. Stockdale, *The Memoirs of the Life and Writings of Percival Stockdale* . . . (London, 1809), vol. 2, p. 151.

54 J. Wilde, *The Hospital: a poem in three books* (Norwich, 1810), p. 7.

55 See M. Foss, *Man of Wit to Man of Business: the arts and changing patronage, 1660–1750* (1971; repr. Classical Press, Bristol, 1988); and C. Ehrlich, *The Music Profession in Britain since the Eighteenth Century: a social history* (Clarendon, Oxford, 1985), pp. 1–50.

56 A. Shirley, 'Painting and engraving', in *Johnson's England: an account of the life and manners of his age*, ed. A.S. Turberville (2 vols, Clarendon, Oxford, 1933), vol. 2, pp. 49–55.

57 *British Parliamentary Papers* (1863), vol. 53, pt 1, pp. 390–4.

58 R.W. Blencowe, 'Extracts from the journal of Walter Gale, schoolmaster at Mayfield, 1750', *Sussex Archaeological Collections*, 9 (1857), p. 204.

59 See S. Rothblatt, *The Revolution of the Dons: Cambridge and society in Victorian England* (Faber & Faber, London, 1968), pp. 181–208; and A. Engel, *From Clergyman to Don: the rise of the academic profession in nineteenth-century Oxford* (Clarendon, Oxford, 1983), pp. 14–54.

60 H. McLachlan, *English Education under the Test Acts: being the history of the Nonconformist Academies, 1662–1820* (Manchester University Press, Manchester, 1931), esp. pp. 16–44.

61 R.W. Chapman (ed.), *Boswell: life of Johnson* (Oxford University Press, Oxford, 1976), p. 32.

62 E.g. W.D. Smith, 'The status of eighteenth-century schoolmasters: the case of the Norwich charity schools', in *The Social Role and Evolution of the Teaching Profession in Historical Context*, ed. S. Seppo (University of Joensuu, Finland, 1988), vol. 3, pp. 33–43.

63 See *D.N.B.*, *sub*: Hannah More (1745–1833); and M.A. Hopkins, *Hannah More and her Circle* (Longmans, New York, 1947), pp. 16–18, 19–23.

64 See the admirable survey in K. Hughes, *The Victorian Governess* (Hambledon, London, 1993).

65 H.C. Dent, *The Training of Teachers in England and Wales, 1800–1975* (Hodder & Stoughton, London, 1977), pp. 1–22.

66 See A. Tropp, *The School Teachers: the growth of the teaching profession in England and Wales from 1800 to the present day* (Heinemann, London, 1957), pp. 44–57; and P.H.J.H. Gosden, *The Evolution of a Profession: a study of the contribution of teachers' associations to the development of school teaching as a professional occupation* (Blackwell, Oxford, 1972).

67 A.J. La Vopa, *Grace, Talent, and Merit: poor students, clerical careers, and professional ideology in eighteenth-century Germany* (Cambridge University Press, Cambridge, 1988), esp. pp. 287–302.

68 See e.g. T.C. Davis, *Actresses as Working Women: their social identity in Victorian culture* (Routledge, London, 1991).

69 'Sophia', *Woman Not Inferior to Man* (London, 1739), pp. 4–20, 35–8.

70 Ibid., pp. 48–56.

71 Anon., *The Female Soldier: or, the surprising life and adventures of Hannah Snell* . . . (London, 1750). I am grateful to Dr Timothy Hitchcock for this reference.

72 Lord Chesterfield to Solomon Dayrolles, 27 June 1756, in J. Bradshaw (ed.), *The Letters of Philip Dormer Stanhope, Earl of Chesterfield* (London, 1892), vol. 3, p. 1152.

73 Knox, *Essays, Moral and Literary* (2 vols, London, 1778–9), vol. 2, pp. 250–1.

74 H. Richmond, 'The navy', in *Johnson's England*, ed. Turberville, vol. 1, pp. 57–8. And for Horatio Nelson (1758–1805), see *D.N.B.*

75 See M. Lewis, *England's Sea-Officers: the story of the naval profession* (Allen & Unwin, London, 1939), pp. 120–1; and *D.N.B.*, *sub*: James Cook.

76 I. Roy, 'The profession of arms', in Prest (ed.), *The Professions*, pp. 194–6, 200–6; Lewis, *England's Sea-Officers*, pp. 87–93; and N. Elias, 'Studies in the genesis of the naval profession', *British Journal of Sociology*, 1 (1950), pp. 291–309.

77 W.L. Clowes, *The Royal Navy: a history from the earliest times to the present* (1898; repr. AMS Press, New York, 1966), vol. 3, pp. 20–1.

78 Admiral Pye to the Earl of Sandwich, 28 April 1773, in G.R. Barnes and J.H. Owen (eds), *The Private Papers of John Earl of Sandwich, First Lord of the Admiralty, 1771–82*, vol. 1: *1770–8* (Navy Records Society, 1932), p. 36.

79 Lewis, *England's Sea-Officers*, pp. 122–42.

80 6 Geo. II, cap. 25 (1733), cl. 18.

81 See J.W. Hackett, *The Profession of Arms* (Times Publishing, London, 1963), pp. 3, 63–5; and S.P. Huntington, *The Soldier and the State: the theory and politics of civil–military relations* (Belknap Press, Cambridge, Mass., 1957), pp. 11–18.

82 Knox, *Essays, Moral and Literary*, vol. 2, p. 251.

83 E.g. see E.S. Turner, *Gallant Gentlemen: a portrait of the British officer, 1600–1956* (Michael Joseph, London, 1956), pp. 59–232.

84 Since the military and clerical professions do not fit market models of professionalisation, they are for that reason excluded from Larson's analysis: Larson, *Rise of Professionalism*, p. xvii.

85 J.A. Houlding, *Fit for Service: the training of the British army, 1715–95* (Clarendon, Oxford, 1981), p. 100. For details of the purchase system, see ibid., pp. 99–116; A. Bruce, *The Purchase System in the British Army, 1660–1871* (Royal Historical Society, London, 1980), esp. pp. 14–64; E. Robson, 'Purchase and promotion in the British army in the eighteenth century', *History*, 36 (1951), pp. 57–72; and G. Harries-Jenkins, *The Army in Victorian Society* (Routledge, London, 1977), pp. 59–102.

86 I. Roy, 'The profession of arms', p. 207.

87 Cited in Bruce, *Purchase System*, p. 176. For the pros and cons of the system, see also ibid., pp. 65–94; and Roy, 'The profession of arms', pp. 207, 210–12.

88 See Bruce, *Purchase System*, pp. 22–40; A.J. Guy, *Oeconomy and Discipline: officership and administration in the British army, 1714–63* (Manchester University Press, Manchester, 1985), pp. 1–2, 53–87. But for the booty system in India: see R. Callahan, *The East India Company and Army Reform, 1783–98* (Harvard University Press, Cambridge, Mass., 1972), passim.

89 Turner, *Gallant Gentlemen*, pp. 128–32; and see *D.N.B*, *sub*: James Wolfe.

90 G. Lamb, *Memoir of his Own Life* (Dublin, 1811), p. 104.

91 Guy, *Oeconomy and Discipline*, p. 149.

92 See F.G. Guggisberg, *'The Shop': the story of the Royal Military Academy* (Cassell, London, 1900), pp. 1–2, 14; J. Smyth, *Sandhurst: the history of the Royal Military Academy, Woolwich, . . . and the Royal Military Academy Sandhurst, 1741–1961* (Weidenfeld, London, 1961), pp. 27–40, 44–51; and for nineteenth-century training, Harries-Jenkins, *Army in Victorian Society*, pp. 103–32.

93 See e.g. 'An Officer' [S. Bever], *The Cadet: a military treatise* (London, 1756).

94 Harries-Jenkins, *Army in Victorian Society*, pp. 133–8.

95 Bruce, *Purchase System*, pp. 95–171.

96 Ibid., p. 48.

97 O. Anderson, *A Liberal State at War: English politics and economics during the Crimean War* (Macmillan, London, 1967), pp. 51–68, 107–9.

98 'An Officer', *The Purchase System and the Staff* (London, 1855), p. 28.

99 C.E. Trevelyan, *The Purchase System in the British Army* (London, 1867), pp. 1–3.

100 J.S. Shaw, *The Management of Scottish Society, 1707–64: power, nobles, lawyers, Edinburgh agents and English influences* (Donald, Edinburgh, 1983), p. 9.

101 J. Torrance, 'Social class and bureaucratic innovation: the Commissioners for Examining the Public Accounts, 1780–7', *Past & Present*, 78 (1978), pp. 56–81; and H. Parris, *Constitutional Bureaucracy: the development of British central administration since the eighteenth century* (Allen & Unwin, London, 1969), pp. 39–79.

102 See J. Hart, 'The genesis of the Northcote–Trevelyan report', in *Studies in the Growth of Nineteenth-Century Government*, ed. G. Sutherland (Routledge, London, 1972), pp. 63–81; and D.W. Armstrong, 'Sir Charles Edward Trevelyan, Assistant Secretary to the Treasury, 1840–59' (unpub. Ph.D. thesis, London University, 1975), pp. 158–63.

103 O. Anderson, 'The janus face of mid-nineteenth-century English radicalism: the Administrative Reform Association of 1855', *Victorian Studies*, 8 (1965), pp. 231–42, esp. p. 235.

104 A. Trollope, *The Three Clerks* (1857), ed. W.T. Shore (Oxford University Press, Oxford, 1978), p. ix.

8

ETHOS

The importance of the professions, and the professional classes can hardly be over-rated, they form the head of the great English middle class, maintain its tone of independence, keep up to the mark its standard of morality, and direct its intelligence.

These striking words, written in 1857,[1] are often quoted by historians of the professions – and justly so, since this confident assertion epitomised the increasingly unabashed self-righteousness of this sector of society. It is no surprise to find that their author, Byerley Thomson (1822–67) came from a professional background. He was himself a barrister and the son of a professor of medical jurisprudence at the new University of London (now University College).[2] Thomson wrote these bold words in his handbook to the professions. He documented carefully the advantages and pitfalls of a career in a wide range of expert posts – not only in the church, army, navy, law and medicine but also in the civil service, the arts, architecture, engineering, science, music, education, theatre and literature. On the strength of that, he invited his readers to salute a new social force for good.

Naturally, Thomson's assertions about the intelligence and morality of the professional middle class were partisan. They were certainly not accepted without question. Not only did many professionals fall short of the high standards confidently attributed to them but there were other claimants to social and moral pre-eminence, even within the middle class. Manufacturers and inventors, for example, had their own advocates. Samuel Smiles's famous tract on *Self-Help* (1859) praised the great 'captains of industry' as well as the achievements of a miscellany of scientists, engineers, artists, musicians and soldiers.[3] That diversity mirrored Smiles's own eclectic career: he began as a practising surgeon, before becoming a reforming journalist, a railway company secretary, and a successful author.[4] But his message was always clear. Energy, courage, will-power and self-discipline – rather than pure learning – would help people from modest backgrounds to 'rise from the ranks'. He was sure that there were plenty of opportunities at the top, and in the middle too.

200

Thus there were many heroes in the social pantheon to admire. Indeed, historians who stress the impact of one group to the exclusion of all others underestimate the growing diversity of British society. But the professions were beginning to play a powerful role within that heterogeneity. They exercised influence both directly, through their occupational roles, and indirectly, as opinion-formers. That included the propagation of their own high self-esteem. Professional people were, after all, committed to a specialised way of life. Their long training and shared knowledge generated strong bonds of loyalty and of group identification.

On the strength of that, it became possible to talk of a wider professional ethos or 'spirit'. Insider knowledge was to be used in the service of the general public. Thus the advancement and power of the professions were justified by an appeal to civic morality. This was, of course, an ideal,[5] and an unwritten one at that. Sceptics could point to many defaulters in practice. Indeed, as noted earlier, some of the most carping criticisms came from within the ranks of the professions themselves. Many saw the motes in the eyes of their opponents. Already in December 1726, *The Craftsman* recognised the style. It noted teasingly that 'There is a general Complaint of abuses and corruptions in all Professions, which is most frequently urged by those men themselves, who are the chief authors and occasions of them' – instancing especially the lawyers and doctors.[6] However, the sense of superiority conferred by insider knowledge could induce an annoying complacency *vis à vis* the general public. One early nineteenth-century observer thought that smugness was an especially characteristic expression of the solicitor: 'From being continually consulted and appealed to, he attains a certain look of self-satisfaction, a perfect reliance on his own acumen.'[7]

Yet, despite these imperfections, the professional ethos imposed an orderly viewpoint upon an unruly world and gave its protagonists confidence in their own position. They were able to present themselves in lofty terms as purveyors of specialist knowledge in disinterested service to the community. The clergy had long been depicted as shepherds concerned to watch over their flocks. Now other professions viewed themselves – and hoped they were viewed by others – in the same way. Of course, fallible mortals did not always live up to the ideal. Critics responded by rending the temple veils. In 1720, de Mandeville sharply urged his readers not to be impressed by high-sounding declarations:

> Those who understand the World know, that there is a Mysterious part in every Trade and Profession, beneficial to those only that are of it, and which moreover is absolutely useless, if not detrimental to all the rest of the society.[8]

He was later echoed by *A Dose for the Doctors* (1789), which urged 'the absolute necessity of professional reformation'.[9] However, the public's

propensity to be impressed by expertise was not shaken by such de-
nunciations. Faith in the professional ethos continued to win adherents,
just as belief in religion survived the existence of sinners.

It was accepted, moreover, that power brought responsibilities in its
train. A new *savoir oblige* was superadded to the old *noblesse oblige*.[10]
'Professions and Arts, as well as Estates, are charg'd with a Debt of Succour
and Service to the Poor; Especially This of Physick', wrote a 1715 handbook
on the duties of the physician.[11] In other words, quasi-paternalist duties
were attached to key civil occupations as well as to landownership. And
some socially responsible doctors did indeed provide medicine or services
free to the poor. For example, some apothecaries reduced their charges for
pauper families and needy prisoners.[12] Thus, as the modern literary critic
Lionel Trilling has observed, the professional ideal began to gather around
itself some of the moral prestige traditionally accorded to the gentleman.[13]
However, it was a working ethos based upon skill and expertise rather
than upon the inheritance of blue blood or landed patrimony. Indeed, the
new ideal contributed itself to the middle-class colonisation and updating
of the concept of the gentleman into a more active and less 'idle' model.[14]

As a result, the growing number of professional organisations were able
to disclaim a purely sectional interest. Instead, they presented their
authority as globalised and universal. It was an adroit argument, which
the trade unions and business cartels could well have emulated to good
effect. In practice, of course, organisation certainly did augment the
professions' control over their own markets. As the architectural writer J.C.
Loudon forewarned in 1835, when criticising the new Institute of British
Architects: 'The object of every association, either exclusive or open to all
the public, is to accumulate power and to direct it to such objects as cannot
be attained by individuals alone.'[15] However, the motive of creating a
vested interest was rarely admitted by the professions. Their qualifying
associations kept their distance from any obviously sectional groups such
as the trade unions. Instead, the professional lobbies stressed their own
disinterested contribution to the greater good. It became virtually a tenet
of faith. One modern observer – himself risen from the ranks of the
academic profession – has noted the professions' chronic propensity to
identify their own interests with those of the nation. He adds: 'There is
nothing odd about this. All professional men [sic] think this way.'[16]

However, the cultural usages remained complex. The concept of 'professionalism' did not immediately sweep all before it. Some remained
obdurately suspicious of the 'expert'. As the anonymous 'Candidus' noted
in 1840: 'there certainly are two sets of prejudices – those of pro-
fessionalists, and those of non-professionalists.'[17] This was written in a
review of a new book that set out to reveal the mysteries of architecture
to the public. But 'Candidus' feared that would prove to be a serious
mistake: 'That which has hitherto been the task of a higher order of intellect

is now to become the amusement of women – perhaps the play-thing of children.' Amateurs should cultivate good taste but leave the real business to 'plodding professional exactness'.[18]

Disputes were yet fiercer in the context of organised sports and leisure activities – especially when mass sports became increasingly commercialised from the later nineteenth century onwards. At that point what had been rather flexible distinctions became encrusted in formal regulations. The 'professionals' were commercial players. They often came from a modest social background. By contrast, the amateurs were technically unpaid, even if they were actually given generous expenses. The career of W.G. Grace, who was a surgeon by profession, was a notable example of 'shamateurism' in action, since he also got financial help to pay for a locum to tend his practice.[19] Nonetheless, in the traditional social calculus, those playing for love of the game ranked above those working for filthy lucre. Hence the amateur was superior to the 'pro'. However, that was the viewpoint of the man of leisure, looking down the social hierarchy from on high. It ignored the *de facto* arrangements behind the non-monetised facade.

Instead, the working world was developing a different perspective. There the concept of a profession emerged as a superior form of toil, since it entailed a 'calling' to a specialist occupation. It came to represent a form of employment that was dignified, expert and socially admired. Thus, as modern sport has become a source of work, so the cult of the amateur has progressively given way to the notion of the professional sportsman. Moreover, in other employments, 'amateurish' became a term of disparagement. It implied a dilettante approach and slapdash execution. 'Amateurism is the curse of the nineteenth century', snorted a satirical journal dismissively in 1868.[20] 'Professionalism', on the other hand, was acquiring connotations of careful training, organisation, dedication, sleek efficiency and *esprit de corps*.[21]

Awareness of these issues was encouraged by the voluminous output of the press. There was a torrent of writing about and by the professions. Each occupation produced its own handbooks to its own conventions. These were also supplemented by general guides. Slender essays, such as that by Vicesimus Knox in 1778, were succeeded by large tomes. Thomas Gisborne's *Enquiry into the Duties of Men in the Higher and Middle Classes* (1794) included sections on all the leading professions.[22] *Essays on Professional Education* followed in 1809, from the pen of the effervescent author, inventor and Irish landowner Richard Edgeworth. He discussed careers in the church, the army and navy, medicine, law – and put these occupations in good company, with chapters on the education of a country gentleman, a statesman and a prince. The book was reviewed favourably by Sydney Smith, who applauded Edgeworth's comments on the need to diversify education away from excess concentration upon the classics.[23]

But the details were less important than the general tenor of the survey. It ushered in a new genre, of which Byerley Thomson's *Choice of a Profession* (1857) was one example.

Much of this literature stressed the importance of the ethical dimension. They urged professionals to deserve the confidence that was vested in them. Adam Smith for one pointed out how extensive that was. 'We trust our health to the physician', he wrote, 'our fortune and sometimes our life and reputation to the lawyer and attorney.'[24] He decided that no professional should be so poor or lowly that his independence was jeopardised. But it was not left solely to money and social background. There were also moral constraints upon unprofessional behaviour. Clergymen at their ordination promised to put duty to their faith before personal inclination; physicians endorsed the Hippocratic Oath;[25] and attorneys vowed before the courts to act honourably.[26]

This period therefore did not invent professional ethics. But it did see the start of an important new specialist literature, which extended both the theory and the practical applications of the subject. A pioneering manual on *Medical Ethics* was written in 1792, circulated privately in 1794, and finally published in 1803. It was written by Thomas Percival, a senior physician, who wished to provide an antidote to unseemly quarrels among his fellow doctors in Manchester. His title was to have been *Medical Jurisprudence* but, after friends objected, he changed it to a much more memorable one. He recommended that doctors should strive 'so to unite *tenderness* with *steadiness*, and *condescension* with *authority*, as to inspire the minds of their patients with gratitude, respect, and confidence'. In other words, power was to be tempered with kindness. Much of Percival's detailed commentary referred to professional etiquette between doctors but he did also deal with doctor–patient relations. For example, he offered the pertinent advice that 'The *feelings* and *emotions* of the patient . . . require to be known and to be attended to, no less than the symptoms of their diseases.'[27]

Writings such as these marked the advent of an explicit code. Unwritten understandings were to be updated and clarified. An expanding volume of publications followed. These included the anonymous *Religio Medicorum: a critical essay on medical ethics*, which was published in Edinburgh in 1855; and many, many more. Logically enough, too, ethical problems had made their way onto the agendas of the new professional bodies by the mid-nineteenth century. For example, the Manchester Medico-Ethical Association was founded in 1848; and the Provincial Medical and Surgical Association (which later became the B.M.A.) established its own medico-ethical committee in 1853.[28] Thus the expanding numbers of knowledge-brokers gradually accumulated their own field of specialist enquiry and debate – a field whose vitality of output shows no sign of abating.

One strong ethical presumption related to money. True professionals were not supposed to be unscrupulous and greedy in their dealings with the public. Mere mercenaries might seek the largest amount of money in the shortest possible time. Instead, professionals were to be honest brokers. For that, their recompense was a good conscience and public esteem. That perception was used, for example, in the long campaigns from the 1780s onwards to eradicate corruption within the developing Indian and British civil services.[29] Here the emergent new ethos very much preceded its full implementation. It was inculcated, however, from 1806 onwards at Haileybury, the training college for the Indian civil service. Reformers such as Lord Macaulay and Charles Trevelyan used the ideal of professional probity in their campaigns against corruption and sinecures. It was legitimate to want due reward for fair services rendered. Indeed, proper rates of pay were necessary to eliminate fraud. But excess greed was defined as beyond the professional pale.

An example from the memoirs of the impulsive lawyer, William Hickey, indicated how these attitudes were internalised. In 1790, he found himself in India, where he wished to reserve a plot in a Calcutta cemetery so that he could eventually lie beside his adored dead mistress. Hickey willingly paid for the construction of a burial vault but was outraged when the local clergyman demanded an additional 'permission fee' for the favour. Such a demand flouted all propriety. It was not the size of the sum but the principle that mattered. Moreover, as Hickey recounted the incident, his friends agreed with him:

> This demand struck me as so blackguard and disgraceful in a clergyman to make, independent of it being unjust, that I had at first determined to resist the payment, but upon further consideration I did not think it was worth contending about, and therefore sent the fifty rupees required. I, however, mentioned the circumstance to several of my friends, who all agreed in pronouncing it very disreputable in Mr Blanchard, as a professional man, to act in such a manner.[30]

No other witness accounts survive to confirm or deny the details of this imbroglio; but clearly Hickey's own sense of grievance was still vivid to him when he wrote his *Memoirs* in 1809–10.

Another trait that was much recommended was mutual solidarity. Professionals were not supposed to disparage one another before the general public; nor to disclose professional secrets. Their mystique was best preserved by dignified solidarity. It is true that a guide to *Medical Etiquette* warned in 1839 that exclusive knowledge could be used unfairly. For example, the use of technical terms simply to baffle and impress the laity was a misuse of power.[31] Yet the ideal of mutual co-operation and support remained attractive to many practitioners. It provided camaraderie and it also bolstered their confidence against satire and criticism from outsiders.

Professional co-operation in action was interestingly captured in the records of a local medical society that flourished for a decade from 1793 to 1803.[32] A small group of doctors in Huntingdonshire and south Lincolnshire met regularly for several years. They formed an *ad hoc* organisation that amounted to something between a group practice and an intermittent research seminar. Their rules are reproduced in Table 8.1. Mutual education was the main business at their half-yearly meetings, when difficult cases were debated (Rule 2). Furthermore, no-one could join the Society unless he had produced a satisfactory thesis on a medical subject (Rule 3). Once admitted, the members guaranteed each other mutual assistance (without charge) in the event of need (Rules 1 and 5). In addition, they agreed to petition for access to criminal corpses for dissection (Rule 7). And these doctors agreed that, if a second consultation was requested, they would call in others from the Society (Rule 6). This organisation illustrated both the real merits of mutual education and support in case of difficulty and at the same time the potential for collusion and restrictive practices. However, it was not a closed shop, since membership was very far from obligatory. Moreover, it is not known how successfully the rules were upheld, before the Society lapsed (for unknown reasons) in 1803.

Group identity was not always organised as systematically as in this example from Huntingdonshire. Yet it was very much a feature of professional life. Their clubs and societies did not eliminate personal rivalries but they helped to contain disputes within a common framework of assumptions. Professional solidarity was also encouraged by the prolonged training that their careers increasingly entailed. The system of pupilage – which long persisted in engineering and architecture, for example – could have pedagogic disadvantages when the master was lax. But it generated quasi-familial bonds. The effect was to mesh novices into the ethos and knowhow of the senior professions in a very personal way, even if their formal training was limited. Moreover, this attitude continued even when professional education was institutionalised. Medical students developed strong loyalties to their teaching hospitals; barristers to their Inns of Court; clerics to their colleges.

Education of their young recruits was after all a matter for the professions themselves. There was no state blueprint. Even when Victorian reformers instituted parliamentary enquiries, the outcome still depended upon delegation to professional and other institutions. The educational system was left to evolve in a characteristically *ad hoc* fashion. As a result, the emergence of the new professions had little immediate impact upon the traditional universities in eighteenth-century England, although the Scottish universities by contrast did forge a dramatic new reputation as centres for medical training.[33]

Expectations, however, became sharpened. The professions themselves

206

Table 8.1 Rules of the Huntingdonshire Medical Society, 1793–1803

I	That each Member of this Society shall pledge himself to assist every other Member of the same, upon all Occasions, and in all Cases of Surgical Operations, or any other Case of Surgery in which the safety of a patient may be affected, or the Character of any individual Member concerned by the misrepresentation of circumstances, without Fee or Reward.
II	That this Society meet twice in the Year for the express Purpose of communicating the different Medical and Surgical Cases which have occurred in their Practice, and to arrange such as may be worthy of Publication.
III	That any Gentleman wishing to become a Member of this Society, must be proposed by a Member at one of the Half-yearly Meetings, who is expected then to produce a Thesis, written by the Candidate, upon some Medical or Surgical Subject, which Thesis shall be immediately read and discussed, and the Candidate ballotted for at the next Half-yearly Meeting, when one dissenting voice shall exclude him.
IV	That *Peterborough*, *Bourn*, *Stamford*, and *Stilton* be the places for holding Half-yearly Meetings, that each Place be taken in Rotation, and the day fixed by the Members present at the preceding Meeting.
V	That if any Accident happens to a Member of this Society, so as to prevent him from attending the Duties of his Profession, then the different Members shall alternately assist him as far as they are able.
VI	That in case a Patient is in Circumstances to pay a consulting Surgeon, and requests one to be called in on his own account, then each Member pledges himself to call in one of this Society. ·
VII	That, as the advantages to be derived from the examination of Bodies after Death must be acknowledged by all, so the difficulty of procuring Subjects in the Country must be equally confessed, therefore in the Case of the condemnation of any Criminal with orders for Dissection, either in the Counties of Lincoln, Huntingdon, Rutland or the City of Peterborough, a petition be presented to the Sheriff or Magistrates in the name of the Society for the Body by some one of its Members, giving a concise history of the plan of the establishment and the advantage which will certainly accrue from being supplied with the Bodies of Criminals for Dissection.
VIII	That a Book be procured at the joint expense of the Society for the Purpose of inserting Cases, Medical Information, the Minutes of each Meeting, etc.
IX	That a Secretary be appointed annually at whose House the Book shall be left to insert such medical Information, as he may have received through the Channel of his Medical Correspondents.

Source: Surviving minute book, transcribed by A. Rook, 'General practice' pp. 240–4

gradually realised the need for systematic education, especially as the corpus of specialist knowhow continued to grow apace. For the churches, the change was spearheaded by the Methodists. The pioneering institution was the evangelical Trevecca College, founded by Lady Huntingdon in 1768. It was followed later by other academies and colleges, including the Wesleyan Theological Institution (1835).[34] In Ireland, training for the Catholic priesthood was given modest state funding at Maynooth (founded 1795).[35] And the Church of England proceded cautiously, with

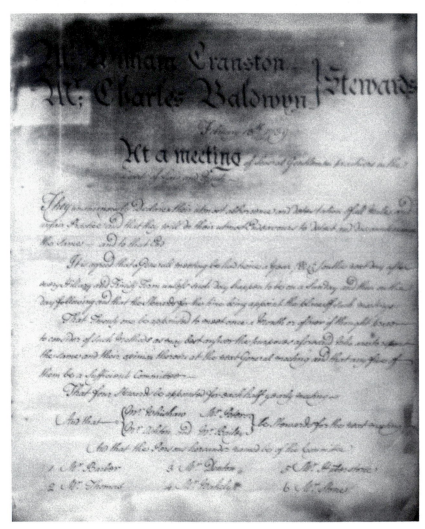

Figure 8.1 Earliest record of the Society of Gentlemen Practisers in the Courts of Law and Equity (1740). From 1740, the society of London attorneys began to campaign actively against professional malpractice. Their historic resolution in Feb. 1739/40 stated that 'They unanimously Declare their utmost adhorrence and detestation of all Male [bad] and unfair Practice, and that they will do their utmost Endeavours to detect and discountance the same.' This was a forerunner of the devolved system of professional self-regulation that emerged in Britain and was eventually endorsed by the state

Published by permission of the Law Society (photograph: Anthony Quiney)

its specialist theological Colleges at St Bees (1816) and Lampeter (1822).[36] From the 1830s onwards, the accumulating pressures for reform encouraged the creation of new universities,[37] while there were also some reforms at Oxford and Cambridge.[38] The sons – and later the daughters – of the professional middle class were prominent among the students at these institutions. There were then fears that the job market risked overcrowding by too many qualified candidates.[39] However, the effect of professional regulation and training tended rather to squeeze out the untrained 'quacks' and irregulars.

Characteristically, the British state maintained a benign but low-key approach to these changes. No government seriously attempted to halt the process. On the contrary, the state was a major employer of professional skills – in the nascent civil service, in the army and navy, in its legal services, and so forth. That was true both at home and in the expanding overseas empire. Nor did the British state simply look on passively. Parliament was ready to intervene on occasion, such as the 1729 legislation to regulate the admission of attorneys. It became, however, a British tradition to devolve controls, when required, to professional bodies, such as the existing Law Society in 1843 or the newly created British Medical Council in 1858. Such a process had the great merit of flexibility. It enabled the professional associations to monitor standards with the legal sanction of Parliament, while allowing the state to avoid the administrative costs.

Accommodation rather than confrontation was the keynote. The professions were a radicalising force in British society but not a revolutionary one. The individuals within these occupations had a range of political views across the spectrum. While some clerics, lawyers and doctors had radical views, many established figures were socially and politically moderate. Another proportion was highly conservative. Even within their own special fields, the professions were often divided. For example, some doctors were energetic campaigners for health and sanitary reforms but there were always others to dispute the efficacy of any proposed innovation.[40]

The impact of the professions was, however, a cumulative and long-term one. In France it was wryly observed in 1849 that 'plus ça change – plus c'est la même chose'.[41] That famous paradox indicated accurately and amusingly that traditional ways can outlast apparently great political upheavals. But the converse could also become true. Apparent continuity sometimes masks or underpins evolutionary changes. A good case can be made for that in eighteenth- and nineteenth-century Britain. It was an open and adaptive society, one that was becoming a major world power – not without stress and turmoil but without a political cataclysm. Its catch-phrases were 'improvement' and 'progress'[42] rather than 'upheaval' or 'revolution', which became a problematic concept in Britain after 1789.

Gradual economic and cultural diversification was well represented by the advent of the professions. Their role did not lead to a frontal attack upon the aristocracy or upon the institutions of state. Yet the impact of professional knowhow was eventually significant. It operated indirectly as well as directly, in an intertwining process of change that incorporated multiple feedbacks. By the later nineteenth century, even the most aristocratic of politicians recognised the implications of new professional skills. A gracious compliment was paid in 1889 by Lord Salisbury at the inauguration of the Institute of Electrical Engineers. He saluted the power of their science in application. Electricity had a greater effect, he argued, 'not only upon the large collective destinies, but upon the daily life and experience of multitudes of human beings, than [did] even the careers of the greatest conquerors or the services of the greatest statesmen'.[43] This was greeted with cheers.

Knowledge and applied skills were therefore a different source of power. They encapsulated the fruits of human understanding and were applied to produce social goods. On those grounds, the professions were increasingly seen as representing the principle of merit. Their authority rested on the strength of ability rather than of inherited position or ancient family. Arguments of this sort were promulgated with growing enthusiasm in the nineteenth century. An aristocracy of talent was required to right the nation, Thomas Carlyle (1795–1881) declared in 1843. Wisdom was required in lieu of bad faith and stupidity:

> We will demand of our Governors, with emphasis, and for the first time not without effect, that they cease to be quacks, or else depart; that they set no quackeries and blockheadisms anywhere to rule over us, that they utter or act no cant to us, – it will be better if they do not.[44]

Such words came proudly from the pen of a social prophet and historian, who prospered on the strength of his pen and his intellect, from humble origins as the son of a poor stonemason in Ecclefechan. Carlyle warned that there was no easy pill to cure social discontents. An aristocracy of talent was not easy to find. He hinted that literary genius might provide the answer: 'I conclude that Men of Letters too may become a "Chivalry", an actual instead of a virtual Priesthood, with result immeasurable, – so soon as there is nobleness in themselves for that.'[45] He accepted that the English seemed slow to endorse change. 'Nevertheless, new epochs do actually come', he reminded readers.[46]

Meritocracy was thus promoted within the interstices of the old world of patronage. For some observers, it had already arrived. One tract explained cheerfully in 1793 that English society was notably harmonious. That was because careers were open to talents; people of ability were appointed to offices in church and state; while 'the Advantages arising from commerce, or from professional excellence, are at least equally free of access.' Consequently, he asserted that great talents, when exercised with zeal and integrity, seldom failed. This eulogy was written by a well-meaning clergyman who took the pseudonym of 'peace-lover' in an effort to soothe social tensions in the turbulent 1790s.[47] It was interesting that he felt able to write in this way. However, he undoubtedly exaggerated in order to put the best possible gloss upon an utterly unsystematic system in which both patronage and merit played a part.

In practice, therefore, advancement could be slow and difficult for people without wealth or social connections. 'The stream of true merit, like that of true love, perhaps, never did run smooth', as it was noted tritely enough in 1827.[48] Aspirants without powerful patrons could be disappointed. For example, numerous ecclesiastical appointments in the Church of England were subject either to the political interests of ministers exercising crown patronage or to the personal quirks and caprices of lay patrons.

For those with merit who were nonetheless thwarted, it was easy to feel resentful. Dr Johnson was one literary sage who had known the travails of early penury and obscurity. As his early poem warned: 'This mournful truth is ev'rywhere confess'd,/ Slow rises worth by poverty depress'd.'[49] In 1755 he produced a famously bitter insight: 'Is not a Patron, my Lord, one who looks with unconcern on a man struggling for life in the water, and, when he has reached ground, encumbers him with help?'[50] For the radical Charles Pigott in 1795, too many appointments were made on political lines. He angrily defined a patron as 'one who countenances the apostate, protects the informer, and supports the dependant; whose patronage extends not to the friend of virtue, the opposer of tyranny, or the lover of justice'.[51] Given the potential for abuses, it was noted when patrons acted disinterestedly – as of course some did. Thus the family of the Reverend Daniel Watson, Vicar of Lecke in Yorkshire, was reportedly so proud of his promotion on 'his merits alone' that this was engraved on his tombstone in Bath Abbey. Moreover, the story was related in 1839 to the credit of his patron, the admirable Bishop Butler, who endeavoured to appoint 'none but clergymen of approved character and zeal'.[52]

Criticisms of patronage began to gain public and political support. By the 1830s, the old system was on the defensive.[53] The middle-class stress upon the importance of individual ability became more widely voiced. A dashing novel in 1784 had offered the *Original Love-Letters between a Lady of Quality and a Person of Inferior Station*. Its high-born heroine did not worry about the class divide. 'My ancestors may have quitted the plough-share and the pruning-hook a century before yours', she told her humble lover, 'and there is all the mighty difference between us. In *China*, where superior learning and virtue procure nobility, you would have been a noble of the first class. There is no rank to which superior merit and great talents may not aspire.'[54] This was fighting talk, although the novelist cautiously allowed the hero to die before the wedding. In practice, mixed-class marriages were not unknown in this period, although the participants were generally silent on the experience in print. But a survey shows that, of the 826 married peers (out of a total of 954) in eighteenth-century Britain, as many as 224 or 27.1 per cent made first marriages to commoners from families that were below the rank of baronets and knights.[55] A new literary tradition began to identify true virtue not in the landed gentry but in 'nature's gentleman'.[56] Social rank was not abolished; but it was becoming more diversified and accessible.

Here the emergent ethos of the professional middle class coincided with that of the commercial middle class. Reformers attacked purchase and patronage with increasing confidence. Such methods offended the principle of merit. This was an issue especially in the army, the civil service and the Anglican Church, with its numerous lay patrons. These institutions did not follow the new norms. *Promotion by Merit Essential to the Progress of the Church* urged E. Bartrum's reformist tract in 1866. Without such a policy, talented men would desert to other professions. The modernisers' preferred alternative for selecting candidates was the competitive examination.[57] Hence that procedure was recommended in 1855 for the civil service and implemented, after delays, in 1870. The nature of merit and how the meritorious should exercise power were solemnly debated.[58] It was increasingly assumed that the advance of men of ability would produce general benefits for the community at large. The aim was 'to clear the way in the country's cause for merit everywhere: accepting it equally whether it be aristocratic or democratic, and only asking whether it be honest and true', as Charles Dickens thundered in a barnstorming speech in favour of administrative reform in June 1855. This too prompted enthusiastic cheering.[59]

Doubters still worried about the new mechanism of selection. 'Examinations are formidable even to the best prepared, for the greatest fool may ask more than the wisest man can answer.' So wrote, truly enough, a literary vicar who had left his church to become a wine merchant, only to plunge into debt and run away to America.[60] This came from a clever man who had no success in finding his own vocation. But such reservations were shared – if put less eloquently – by a number of businessmen. They often valued practical experience and knowhow more highly than speculative intellect and success in 'bookish' examinations.[61] This indeed became a continuing source of tension between the professional and the commercial middle class. However, no satisfactory alternative system for establishing formal credentials was proposed. Moreover, training in the skilled services required some cultivation of independent judgement on the part of the practitioners. Thus the modern diffusion of the professional ethos has gone hand-in-hand not with a Gradgrindian stress upon rote learning or the mechanical testing of 'facts' but instead with intensive training, specialist qualifications, book learning and competitive examinations.

Impersonal adjudication also began very gradually to open doors for women. As already noted, they were not entirely excluded from the professions, although they were generally restricted to lowly posts or to special sectors, such as nursing. They could do this without formal training. However, it provided a hazardous living, especially for those who relied upon this as their full-time source of income. Merit alone was not decisive. One of the eighteenth century's most learned ladies was Elizabeth Elstob, the famed Anglo-Saxonist, who had been taught by her clerical brother. She, however, could not take holy orders and become a scholar–don. Instead, she struggled as a schoolteacher and then a governess in a noble household.[62]

Yet in the long run, the principle and gradual practice of meritocracy made it increasingly difficult to exclude women from education and the professions, once it was admitted that they had abilities and rationality.[63] Die-hards (male and female) fought hard – as they still fight today. The long run has not yet concluded. However, the consuming demands of a knowledge-based meritocracy for people with abilities that they can put into practice are proving collectively stronger than traditional expectations about gender roles.

All this was a compound process. Economic supply and demand fused with political acceptance, cultural promotion, educational expansion, social mobility, the growth of specialist knowledge and professional self-organisation to create a social trend that triumphed over satire, hostility, resentment and ancient patronage. At the same time, there were many diversities within the process. The professions were not monolithic as a social grouping. Even in ages, they spanned all generations from the young students to the venerable seniors. In 1851, the professional groups with relatively large numbers of practitioners aged under 20 were the medical students, schoolteachers, law clerks and (interestingly) the druggists.[64] Thus among all the other sources of tension, there were also possibilities of inter-generational disputes as well as rivalries over the religious and political issues of the day.

Power and influence were not, however, solely predicated upon unity. Most social groups, viewed closely, have internal complexities. The professions were important for these diversities, not despite them. Their own compound emergence was part of the emergent pluralism of British society. Hence the case for their importance does not imply the un-importance of other social forces. For example, the power of bankers and financiers was also rising silently but persistently during this period. Indeed, the professions did not overthrow existing authority figures within society, such as the monarch or the paterfamilias. But the claims of specialist knowledge were gaining ground. The professions were becoming power-brokers and opinion-formers within an emergent poly-archy or plurality of elites.[65] Of course, all such groups were not completely equal. There were hierarchies and nuances of power among the great. But Jeremy Bentham noted the hegemonic diversity in 1828 when he denounced 'cold, selfish, priest-ridden, lawyer-ridden, lord-ridden, squire-ridden, soldier-ridden England'.[66] And, had he been so minded, he might also have challenged a Scotland that was lawyer-, teacher- and kirk-ridden; or an Ireland dominated by land-agents and hedge-priests, whilst many landowners were absentees.

Geography also helped to strengthen the impact of the professions. They were ubiquitous throughout the settled areas of the three kingdoms. Indeed, their success depended upon their accessibility. The greatest concentrations were found in the capital cities. London, above all, was the supreme focus. Professional men also played dominant roles in Edinburgh[67] and Dublin,[68] providing a clubbable social leadership in the absence of a resident monarchy. And there were other regional concentrations. Clergymen were especially plentiful in the cathedral cities; academics in the university towns; medical men at the spas;[69] lawyers at the provincial sessions. Visiting Preston with its palatine courts in 1722, Daniel Defoe pronounced that: 'the town is full of attorneys, proctors, and notaries, . . . it being a dutchy [sic] and county palatine.'[70]

Moreover, an urban centre did not need a special role to attract a basic core of professionals to serve the town and the adjacent hinterland. Dundee provides an example. In 1818 it was a small royal borough, without any particular professional specialism; but it housed at least 19 clergymen, 20 doctors, 4 druggists (1 a woman), 30 lawyers, 2 musicians, 1 architect, 3 accountants and 40 teachers (4 of whom were women who kept their own schools).[71] At that time, the total population of Dundee was approximately 30,000 inhabitants. Elsewhere, too, the professions clustered into towns, where they participated strongly in the local economy and society. They formed – with their counterparts among the urban merchants, manufacturers, bankers and shopkeepers – a genuine civic leadership for the 'urban interest'.

Networks of contacts additionally linked the professions across the country. Information and ideas were transmitted between town and town, town and countryside. Students at Universities and teaching hospitals wrote home. A fine example is found in the letters between Hampton Weekes, a medical student at St Thomas's in London, and his father, a Sussex surgeon–apothecary, in which domestic and medical news were commingled. The elder man wanted advice on the latest techniques and instruments from his son, while sending his own commentaries on medical training in return. For example, in November 1801 the father wrote: 'Let me have one of those Tourniquets that is used in the Hospital with leather Pad &c. very exact'; but he followed that with the genial suggestion: 'get into the little dissecting room as much as possible – when I was there some times a pot of Porter would do a good deal, but perhaps they don't drink Porter now in the dissecting room –.'[72]

But, whether related on not, professionals everywhere consulted one another and frequently travelled to meet in clubs and societies. Their business also brought them together. Clergymen gathered for church functions. Country attorneys had organised links with barristers in London. All this activity kept news and gossip in circulation. Thus a minor local attorney, Nicholas Brown of Alnwick in Northumberland, recorded in his diary items of interest from legal London over three hundred miles away. In January 1786, for example, he had heard reports of the indifferent speaking style but formidable presence of Lord Chancellor Thurlow. In August 1786, Brown knew that Thurlow was visiting a spa for his gout; and in February 1787 Brown confidently noted in his diary that the rumour of Lord Mansfield's resignation was a false one.[73] Such quotidian information helped to forge a sense of common endeavour. It also very positively counteracted the isolation which was sometimes felt by those far from the headquarters of professional life.

That sentiment could be acute. In 1823, one indignant Anglican cleric bemoaned the lack of recognition for the virtuous incumbent who spent a lifetime in an out-of-the-way parish. Military heroes got ribbons and stars. But 'three times eighteen YEARS residence on a country living in the most desolate part of England or Wales establishes no claim whatsoever to anything further!'[74] Given that many country livings were poorly endowed, it was not surprising that the Church of England faced serious problems of non-residence. The objective of a parson in every parish was no more than a dream. Nonetheless, the clergy were the most locationally diffused of the professions in this period. An active missionary role was the key to a flourishing congregation, as the Methodists agreed when they sent out their own itinerant preachers.

Other professionals also went on tour. Barristers and actors went on circuit. Quacks and dentists journeyed to fairs and markets. Tutors and governesses travelled with their employers. Architects and engineers visited development sites across the country, while army and naval officers went on tours of duty at home and overseas. In addition, many others settled permanently in the countryside. Access to a sufficiently affluent clientele was the key. Thus, while barristers lived in range of the urban law courts, large numbers of rank-and-file attorneys lived outside the towns. Similarly, while leading doctors worked in the great hospitals, there were many unglamorous village sawbones. Thus the knowledge-brokers worked in both town and countryside and, via their ever increasing mesh of social and occupational contacts, became social intermediaries between the two.[75] The numerous rural contingent was strongly counterbalanced by its urban and metropolitan fellows. As a result, the professions cannot be categorised as exclusively or even chiefly confined to one type of location. Instead, it was their geographical range that was so significant. They were local power-brokers precisely because they lived and worked across the country.

No region therefore lacked resident professionals. It is true that some areas were relatively poorly supplied. Wales, the Scottish Highlands and the west coast of Ireland did not attract large numbers. The distribution of the professions was not simply a question of population resources, since the pattern of professional dispersal in England did not match exactly the distribution of the national population.[76] It meant that people often had to travel for a consultation, just as many professionals also journeyed to meet their clients. But, crucially, it was not necessary to go as far as London, Edinburgh or Dublin for initial access to basic services, even if complex issues were subsequently referred on to metropolitan experts.

Detailed data confirm this key point. For example, the enrolments of 4,825 accredited attornies in 1729–31 showed that every county in England and Wales had some lawyers. Table 8.2 shows that metropolitan London housed a huge phalanx (33.4 per cent) while Wales had fewer than 5 per cent of the total. But the rest were shared evenly among the south-east, the south-west, the midlands and the north.

In 1780, the distribution remained strikingly similar. 'Greater' London still had one-third of all the respectable attornies in the *Law List*; Wales still had very few (4.5 per cent); and the remainder were distributed throughout the English regions – with a slight percentage decrease in the south-west and a slight rise in the north. The geographical location of doctors in 1783 also showed a concentration in London, with 30.4 per cent of the total, and a very sparse showing in Wales with only 2.7 per cent. As for the rest, they were spread throughout the English counties, although this time not so evenly, with a high proportion of 22.6 per cent in the south-east.

Subsequently, this pattern of mixed concentration and dispersal was maintained throughout the continued growth of the professions. It reflected a twofold process. On the one hand, there were advantages in the locational concentration of expertise, for informal consultations and for institutional collaboration. On the other hand, there were pressures for dispersal, which conferred greater accessibility. Thus the professions eventually settled in cities, towns and villages across Britain. Light-hearted corroboration of the importance of all regions was provided in 1888 by the young Arthur Conan Doyle. His survey of 'The geographical distribution of British intellect' was hardly scientific. It was based upon the birthplaces of 1,151 mid-Victorian celebrities in the fields of 'literature, poetry, art, music, medicine, sculpture, engineering, law and other intellectual walks of life' (essentially the professions).[77] That would not have convinced Sherlock Holmes. Nonetheless, Conan Doyle, who had trained as a medical man himself, was happy to equate the professions with intellect. On that basis, he demonstrated that all regions of the British Isles contributed to the production of intelligence. London did best, with the highest number of celebrities born in relation to its total population, while he suggested that the 'mental nadir' was found in western Ireland. But

Table 8.2 Geographical distribution of attorneys and doctors in eighteenth-century England and Wales[1]

	Attorneys 1729–31 %	*Attorneys* 1780 %	*Doctors* 1783 %
'Greater' London[2]	33.4	33.7	30.4
South-East[3]	18.1	18.5	22.6
South-West[4]	16.1	13.8	14.3
Midlands[5]	15.2	15.0	15.6
North[6]	12.0	14.5	14.4
Total England	94.8	95.5	97.3
Wales[7]	4.6	4.5	2.7
No data	0.6	—	—
Total England and Wales	100.0	100.0	100.0
No. in survey	4,825	3,666	4,593

Sources: From Attorney Enrolments before the Law Courts, 1729–31 (see above p. 79); J. Browne (ed.), *Browne's General Law List for the Year 1780* (London, 1780), pp. 35–138; and Anon. [F.S. Simmons], *The Medical Register for the Year 1783* (London, 1783), pp. 5–126
Notes:
1 Includes Channel Islands and I. of Man
2 'Greater' London: London, Westminster, Middlesex, Southwark
3 South-east (home counties plus East Anglia): Bedfordshire, Berkshire, Buckinghamshire, Cambridgeshire, Essex, Hampshire, Hertfordshire, Huntingdonshire, Kent, Norfolk, Oxfordshire, Suffolk, Surrey, Sussex
4 South-west: Cornwall, Devonshire, Dorset, Gloucestershire, Somerset, Wiltshire
5 Central Midlands: Cheshire, Derbyshire, Herefordshire, Leicestershire, Lincolnshire, Northamptonshire, Nottinghamshire, Rutland, Shropshire, Staffordshire, Warwickshire, Worcestershire
6 North: Cumberland, Durham, Lancashire, Northumberland, Westmorland, Yorkshire
7 Wales: Anglesey, Brecknockshire, Caernarvonshire, Cardiganshire, Carmarthenshire, Denbighshire (plus Flint), Glamorgan, Merionethshire, Monmouthshire, Montgomeryshire, Pembrokeshire, Radnorshire

other places outside London also did well, notably Dublin and the Scottish lowlands (where Conan Doyle himself was born).

Able young recruits for the professions thus came from all three kingdoms. As a result, mobility in pursuit of career advancement was a common experience. In particular, the number of Irish and Scottish 'adventurers' trying to make their mark in London was often noted. James Boswell, who was one of them, resented the frequent jibes at his fellow-countrymen even while resolving to curb his own Scotticisms.[78] But neophytes did not confine their careers to London. Professional qualifications increasingly constituted a passport to travel – not just in Britain but throughout its expanding empire. Their shared values and terminologies constituted one of the cultural influences that helped to knit far-flung English-speaking communities together and to link them with the 'home country'.

Potentially, indeed, their scope was worldwide. The extent to which such international solidarity was achieved in this period was only limited. For instance, the Roman Catholic priesthood in Ireland and the Presbyterian ministry in Scotland and northern Ireland certainly did not attempt to intercommune on the basis of their common clerical status. And there were other divisions that made co-operation difficult – for example, the rival traditions of the English and the Scottish legal systems. The world of learning had also lost Latin as its *lingua franca*. Yet in the very long run, the ethos and organisations of the professions are generating an international and cosmopolitan community of values, which are likely to be strengthened rather than weakened in the future.

Hence fears of a conspiracy against the laity can take on a global scope. Such anxieties have been expressed in both ancient and modern times. Ivan Illich's onslaught upon the professions includes as a prime charge the allegation that the knowledge specialists constitute 'a new kind of cartel'. They are, he argues, 'more deeply entrenched than any Byzantine bureaucracy, more international than a world church, more stable than any labour union, endowed with wider competencies than any shaman, and equipped with a tighter hold over those they claim as victims than any mafia'.[79]

Those sweeping charges are clearly exaggerated. The professions have never achieved a global unity either of aim or of organisation. Nor have they achieved anything like complete control over their clientele. Their powers have emerged only slowly, alongside other independent sources of social influence and authority. And the trends often point in more than one direction. The emergence of the professions has followed upon long centuries of growth, reverses, and consolidation, all keenly debated. Certainly, in the course of the eighteenth, nineteenth and twentieth centuries, the institutionalisation of their self-organisation has strengthened their position. An expanding world of skilled and secularised knowledge that was no longer confined to the traditional clergy was in process of development.

Samuel Taylor Coleridge in 1818 coined a neologism for these new tribes of learned men, whom he termed the 'clerisy'.[80] He was thinking of poets, writers and philosophers, as proxies for the modern practitioners of the liberal arts and sciences. There were now many secular experts, not just one band of clergymen. And these new professional specialists also sought public esteem in the name of service to the community. Furthermore, the new clerisy, like the old clergy, is not ultimately constrained within national barriers. The ethos and organisations of the modern professions have a potentially international application. That is a clear portent for the future – whether as threat or promise.

NOTES

1 H. Byerley Thomson, *The Choice of a Profession: a concise account and comparative review of the English professions* (London, 1857), p. 5.

2   See *D.N.B., sub*: H.W.B. Thomson (1822–67) and Anthony Todd Thomson (1778–1849).

3   S. Smiles, *Self-Help: with illustrations of character and conduct* (London, 1859).

4   *D.N.B., sub*: Samuel Smiles (1812–1904).

5   See the classic exposition in E. Durkheim, *Professional Ethics and Civic Morals*, transl. C. Brookfield (Routledge, London, 1957); and fruitful case studies in S. Haber, *The Quest for Authority and Honor in the American Professions, 1750–1900* (University of Chicago Press, Chicago, 1991); and B. Kimball, *The 'True Professional Ideal' in America: a history* (Blackwell, Cambridge, Mass., 1992).

6   Caleb D'Anvers (ed.), *The Craftsman: being a critique on the times* (London, 1727), no. 3, p. 21.

7   Leman Rede as quoted in E.B.V. Christian, *Leaves of the Lower Branch: the attorney in life and letters* (London, 1909), p. 322.

8   B. de Mandeville, *Free Thoughts on Religion, the Church, and National Happiness* (London, 1720), p. 262.

9   'G. Glyster' [pseud.], *A Dose for the Doctors: or, the aesculapian labyrinth explored* . . . (London, 1789), p. 74.

10   M. Sarfatti Larson, 'The production of expertise and the constitution of expert power', in *The Authority of Experts: studies in history and theory*, ed. T. Haskell (Indiana University Press, Bloomington, 1984), p. 36.

11   Anon. [S. Parker], *An Essay upon the Duty of Physicians and Patients, the Dignity of Medicine, and the Prudentials of Practice* (London, 1715), p. 70.

12   See examples cited in G.M. Watson, 'Some eighteenth-century trading accounts', in *The Evolution of Pharmacy in Britain*, ed. F.N.L. Poynter (Pitman, London, 1965), p. 57.

13   L. Trilling, *The Opposing Self: nine essays in criticism* (Secker & Warburg, London, 1955), p. 215.

14   P.J. Corfield, 'The rivals: landed and other gentlemen in eighteenth-century England', in *Land and Society in Britain, 1700–1914*, ed. N.B. Harte and R.E. Quinault (Manchester University Press, Manchester, 1996).

15   J.C. Loudon in *The Architectural Magazine*, 2 (1835), p. 471.

16   This came from Lord Annan, who offered as corroboration a jibe at the ever-unpopular legal profession: 'Consider the worst and most selfish and ruinous to the public of all professions, consider the lawyers': N.G. Annan, 'The reform of higher education in 1986', *History of Education*, 16 (1987), p. 223.

17   Review of G. Wightwick, *The Palace of Architecture: a romance of art and history* (London, 1840), in *Fraser's Magazine for Town and Country*, 22 (Sept. 1840), p. 363. The *Oxford English Dictionary, sub*: 'professionalist' uncharacteristically errs by misquoting 'non-professionalist' as 'anti-professionalist'.

18   Review in *Fraser's Magazine* (1840), pp. 360, 366–7.

19   See V. Wamplew, *Pay up and Play the Game: professional sport in Britain, 1875–1914* (Cambridge University Press, Cambridge, 1988), pp. 17, 183–203 on sport generally; and p. 201 for W.G. Grace (1848–1915).

20   *Tomahawk: a Saturday journal of satire*, 3 (Dec. 1868), p. 249.

21   But 'professional' can still be used reproachfully when an action is undertaken from lesser motives: such as the 'professional foul' in competitive sport.

22   T. Gisborne, *An Enquiry into the Duties of Men in the Higher and Middle Classes of Society in Great Britain, resulting from their Respective Stations, Professions, and Employments* (London, 1794). His chapter on the physicians was later reprinted as a separate publication: idem, *On the Duties of Physicians Resulting from their Profession* (Oxford, 1847).

23   S. Smith in *Edinburgh Review* (1809), reprinted in *Selections from the Writings of the Revd Sydney Smith* (London, 1855), pp. 19–41.

24 A. Smith, *Wealth of Nations*, ed. R.H. Campbell, A.S. Skinner and W.B. Todd (Oxford, 1976), vol. 1, p. 122.

25 W.H.S. Jones, *The Doctor's Oath: an essay in the history of medicine* (Cambridge University Press, Cambridge, 1924); and historic text in L. Edelstein, 'The Hippocratic oath: text, translation and interpretation', *Bulletin of the History of Medicine*, Suppl. I (Johns Hopkins Press, Baltimore, 1943), pp. 3–64.

26 See above, p. 76.

27 T. Percival, *Medical Ethics: or, a code of institutes and precepts adapted to the professional conduct of physicians and surgeons* (Manchester, 1803), pp. x, 9, 10. For context, see also I. Waddington, 'The development of medical ethics: a sociological analysis', *Medical History*, 19 (1975), pp. 36–51.

28 Ibid., p. 37.

29 See variously E.W. Cohen, *The Growth of the British Civil Service, 1780–1939* (Allen & Unwin, London, 1941), pp. 45–81, 84–103; W. Rubinstein, 'The end of Old Corruption in Britain, 1780–1860', *Past & Present*, 101 (1983), pp. 55–86; and H.J. Perkin on 'the professionalisation of government' in his *Origins of Modern English Society, 1780–1880* (Routledge, London, 1969), pp. 319–39.

30 A. Spencer (ed.), *Memoirs of William Hickey, 1749–1809* (Hurst & Blackett, London, 1913–25), vol. 3, p. 372.

31 A. Banks, *Medical Etiquette: or, an essay upon the laws and regulations which ought to govern the conduct of members of the medical profession in their relation to each other* (London, 1839), pp. 10–11.

32 A. Rook, 'General practice, 1793–1803: transactions of a Huntingdonshire medical society', *Medical History*, 4 (1960), pp. 236–52, 330–47.

33 See above p. 159.

34 G.F. Nuttall, *The Significance of Trevecca College, 1768–91* (Epworth Press, London, 1969); and D.A. Johnson, 'The Methodist quest for an educated ministry', *Church History*, 51 (1982), pp. 304–20.

35 See above, p. 119.

36 P. Virgin, *The Church in Age of Negligence: ecclesiastical structure and problems of church reform, 1700–1840* (Clarke, Cambridge, 1989), pp. 133–4.

37 R.D. Anderson, *Universities and Elites in Britain since 1800* (Macmillan, Basingstoke, 1992), esp. pp. 12–17; also idem, *Education and Opportunity in Victorian Scotland: schools and universities* (Clarendon, Oxford, 1983), pp. 27–69.

38 S. Rothblatt, *The Revolution of the Dons: Cambridge and society in Victorian England* (Faber & Faber, London, 1968), pp. 86–93.

39 That view is supported in F. Musgrove 'Middle class education and employment in the nineteenth century', *Economic History Review*, 2nd ser., 12 (1959/60), pp. 99–111, esp. pp. 108–11; but convincingly rebutted in H.J. Perkin, 'Middle-class education and employment', *Economic History Review*, 2nd ser., 14 (1961), pp. 122–30.

40 Examples in M.E. Rose, 'The doctor in the Industrial Revolution', *British Journal of Industrial Medicine*, 28 (1971), pp. 22–6; and F.B. Smith, *The People's Health, 1830–1910* (Weidenfeld, London, 1979). See also J.V. Pickstone and S.V.F. Butler, 'The politics of medicine in Manchester, 1788–92: hospital reform and public health services in the early industrial city', *Medical History*, 28 (1984), pp. 227–49.

41 Alphonse Karr, *Les Guepes* (Jan. 1849; repr. Paris, 1859), p. 305.

42 These concepts were increasingly pervasive, although of course not everyone believed in them: see L. Whitney, *Primitivism and the Idea of Progress in English Popular Literature of the Eighteenth Century* (Johns Hopkins Press, Baltimore, 1934); and D. Spadafora, *The Idea of Progress in Eighteenth-Century Britain* (Yale University Press, New Haven, 1990).

43 *The Electrician* (1889), as quoted in A. Briggs, *Victorian Things* (Batsford, London, 1988), p. 373.

44 T. Carlyle, *Past and Present* (London, 1843; in 1894 edn), pp. 27–33, 35.

45 *Ibid.* p. 293.

46 Ibid., p. 268.

47 'Eirenophilos', *A Discourse on the Advantages, which Accrue to this Country from the Intimate Connexion which subsists between the Several Ranks and Orders in Society* (London, 1793), pp. 18–19. (The text indicates that the author was a clergyman.)

48 Anon., 'Introduction', in Percival, *Medical Ethics* (1827 revised edn), p. xxxv.

49 Johnson's early poem *London* (1738) was evocative of his early struggles, for which see J. Wain (ed.), *Johnson on Johnson: a selection of the personal and autobiographical writings of Samuel Johnson, 1709–84* (Dent, London, 1976), pp. 17–29.

50 J. Boswell (ed.), *The Celebrated Letter from Samuel Johnson L.L.D. to Philip Dormer Stanhope, Earl of Chesterfield, now first Published . . .* (London, 1790), p. 4.

51 C. Pigott, *A Political Dictionary: explaining the true meaning of words* (London, 1795), p. 100.

52 T. Bartlett, *Memoirs of the Life, Character and Writings of Joseph Butler* (London, 1839), p. 198.

53 For the growing sway of the professional ideal, see Perkin, *Origins of Modern English Society*, pp. 252–70; and for the matching defensiveness of the old system, see Rubinstein, 'The end of Old Corruption', pp. 78–9.

54 Anon. [W. Combe], *Original Love-Letters between a Lady of Quality and a Person of Inferior Station* (Dublin, 1784), pp. 276–7.

55 J. Cannon, *Aristocratic Century: the peerage of eighteenth-century England* (Cambridge University Press, Cambridge, 1984), pp. 82–5.

56 Examples are cited in P.J. Corfield, 'The rivals: landed and other gentlemen in eighteenth-century England', in *Land and Society in Britain, 1700–1914*, ed. N.B. Harte and R.E. Quinault (Manchester University Press, Manchester, 1996).

57 On these campaigns, see J.P.C. Roach, *Public Examinations in England, 1850–1900* (Cambridge University Press, London, 1971), pp. 3–34.

58 E.g. Anon., *What is Merit? A question . . . freely answered by an old crown officer* (London, 1855); Anon., *Appointments for Merit: discussed . . .* (London, 1855); and Anon., *Merit v. Patronage: or, . . . the question of civil service competitions* (London, 1858). G.O. Trevelyan's novel, *The Competition Wallah* (London, 1864), esp. pp. 7–17, 135–8, portrayed similar issues within the Indian civil service.

59 C. Dickens, *Speech of Charles Dickens, Esq., Delivered at the Meeting of the Administrative Reform Association . . . June 27 1855* (London, 1855), p. 10.

60 C.C. Colton, *Lacon: or, many things in few words, addressed to those who think* (London, 1820), vol. 1, p. 152: section 322. For Charles Colton (1780?–1832) and his chequered career, see *D.N.B.*

61 Searle, *Entrepreneurial Politics*, pp. 115–20, 124. See also N. McKendrick, '"Gentlemen and players" revisited: the gentlemanly ideal, the business ideal and the professional ideal in English literary culture', in *Business Life and Public Policy: essays in honour of D.C. Coleman*, ed. N. McKendrick and B. Outhwaite (Cambridge University Press, Cambridge, 1986), pp. 119–36, esp. pp. 115–22.

62 For Elizabeth Elstob (1683–1756), see S. Pegge, *An Historical Account of . . . the Textus Roffensis; Including Memoirs of the Learned Saxonists, Mr William Elstob and his Sister . . .* (1784), in J. Nichols (ed.), *Biblioteca Topographica Britannica*, vol. 1 (London, 1780–90; Kraus reprint, New York, 1968), pp. 21–8; and M. Reynolds,

The Learned Lady in England, 1650–1760 (Riverside Press, Boston, London, 1920), pp. 169–85.

63 See M. Bryant, *The Unexpected Revolution: a study in the history of the education of women and girls in the nineteenth century* (Institute of Education, London, 1979), passim.

64 1851 census data in *British Parliamentary Papers* (1852/3), vol. 88/1, pp. cxxviii–ix, cxl–li: Table 54.

65 This unlovely but useful term is analysed in R.A. Dahl, 'Does polyarchy matter?', in idem, *Polyarchy: participation and opposition* (Yale University Press, New Haven, 1971), pp. 17–32.

66 Letter from Jeremy Bentham to Daniel O'Connell, 15 July 1828, in *Works of Jeremy Bentham*, ed. J. Bowring (Edinburgh, 1843), vol. 10, p. 595.

67 J. Clive, 'The social background of the Scottish renaissance', in *Scotland's Age of Improvement: essays in Scottish history in the eighteenth century*, ed. N.T. Phillipson and R. Mitchison (Edinburgh University Press, Edinburgh, 1970), esp. pp. 228–37; and A.A. MacLaren, 'The "forgotten middle class", 1760–1860', in *The Making of Scotland: nation, culture and social change*, ed. D. McCrone, S. Kendrick and P. Straw (Edinburgh University Press, Edinburgh, 1989), pp. 123–42.

68 Dublin's professional life has been less well studied; but for a chatty account, see C. Maxwell, *Dublin under the Georges, 1714–1830* (Faber, London, 1936), pp. 181–251.

69 See e.g. B.S. Schorrenberg, 'Medical men of Bath', *Studies in Eighteenth-Century Culture*, 13 (1984), pp. 189–203.

70 D. Defoe, *A Tour through the Whole Island of Great Britain* (1722), ed. G.D.H. Cole and D.C. Browning (2 vols, Dent, London, 1962), vol. 2, p. 268.

71 A. Abbot, *The Dundee Directory for 1818* (Dundee, 1818), pp. 13–58, 136–8, 140, 147.

72 J.M.T. Ford (ed.), *A Medical Student at St Thomas's Hospital, 1801–2: the Weekes family letters*, *Medical History*, suppl. 7 (Wellcome Institute, London, 1987), p. 66 [punctuation added] .

73 J.C. Hodgson (ed.), 'The diary of Nicholas Brown', in *Six North Country Diaries* (Surtees Society, 118, 1910), pp. 269, 280.

74 'It Matters not Who', *Heraldic Anomalies*, vol. 2, p. 84.

75 By contrast, P. Aylett, 'A profession in the marketplace: the distribution of attorneys in England and Wales, 1730–1800', *Law and History Review*, 5 (1987), pp. 10, 13, 23–30, argues that the lives of the country attorneys were dominated by rural interests.

76 That has been shown in the case of the lawyers in 1729–31: see ibid., pp. 2–6.

77 A. Conan Doyle, 'On the geographical distribution of British intellect', *The Nineteenth Century: A Monthly Review*, 24 (Aug. 1888), pp. 184–95. I am grateful to Professor Lajos Timar of the University of Debrecen, for providing the reference to this curious essay.

78 Clive, 'Social background of Scottish renaissance', pp. 239–40.

79 I. Illich, 'Disabling professions', in idem and others, *Disabling Professions* (Marion Boyars, London, 1977), p. 15.

80 C. Woodring (ed.), *The Collected Works of Samuel Taylor Coleridge: table talk, I* (Bollingen Series 75, Routledge, London; and Princeton University Press, Princeton, N.J., 1990), p. 285: entry for 7 April 1832. See also B. Knights, *The Idea of the Clerisy in the Nineteenth Century* (Cambridge University Press, Cambridge, 1978), pp. 1–42.

9

ADVANCEMENT

MACAHONE: . . . I was going to *London* to make my Fortune.
CAPTAIN: How, Sir?
MACAHONE: Why, by the Law, Friend, or Phisick, or a Merchant's Wife, or Backgammon, or any of these honourable professions, 'tis all the same to Macahone . . .

Thus George Farquhar's Irishman adventurer in *The Stage-Coach* (1705) breezily reviewed the possibilities for social advancement.[1] He could win money at play; he could marry a merchant's widow and inherit the business; or he could go into the liberal professions. This litany had some piquancy, since Farquhar was himself an impoverished Ulsterman struggling to make a living in England – in his case, as a dramatist.

But the stage Irishman did jokingly make two important points. One was undoubtedly that the learned professions offered an avenue for advancement for the able and ambitious outsider. In this case, Macahone listed the law and medicine. He might also have mentioned the church. In medieval Europe, that had been one of the chief pathways to social promotion that was potentially open to able men of relatively lowly social position. Indeed, even the most rigidly hierarchic communities have generally had some safety-valve of this sort. In Britain, a potential element of social flexibility had long been conferred by recruitment into the professions. And that continued to increase with the growth of many skilled services and their sub-specialisms.

At the same time, however, Macahone's second point was a reminder that the professions were not the only means to advancement. There were other routes to success in eighteenth- and nineteenth-century Britain that were available to those not already born in the purple. Banking and financial services proved lucrative for some; trade, manufacturing or emigration to the colonies provided opportunities for many; while others hoped to flourish via speculation, gambling or a lucrative marriage. It was a notable characteristic of the diversifying economy of Britain that the opportunities for social promotion were so relatively varied.

The professions thus offered a significant but not the sole ladder of advancement. Indeed, theirs was a competitive world, with risk as well as opportunity, and without an automatic safety net. The prospect of success concealed the real possibility of failure. Commentators often warned that the service sector could readily become over-stocked with labour. For example, Addison in 1710/11 had already mused publicly on the propensity of parents to put their children into the professions, despite the fact that in such occupations even 'the greatest probity, learning, and good sense may miscarry'.[2] However, the outright losers tended to remain silent about their misfortunes, and generally did not seek to prevent others from joining the race.

Failure was also relative. Trollope in 1859 dubbed his era as not only an 'age of humanity' but 'an age of extremest cruelty'. He was referring in the latter case not to the experience of outright bankruptcy or starvation – but to the bitterness of coming second for those who had keenly hoped to come first. Quite a number experienced that galling fate. Indeed, the young Anthony Trollope had seen at first hand the struggles of his own parents to keep the family fortunes afloat. Thus he had witnessed both the stalled career of his irascible lawyer father and the fluctuating fame of his adventurous novelist mother. Hence Trollope mused in *The Bertrams* (1859) on the theme of competition and the dashed hopes of those who came second. And he concluded that 'There is something very painful in these races, which we English are always running, to one who has tenderness enough to think of the nine beaten horses instead of the one who has conquered.'[3]

Trollope's advice to consider society's also-rans as well as the winners is one that modern historians endeavour to follow. In practice, however, it is difficult to find data about the competitive experiences of the professions in this period – let alone to uncover information about their inner feelings on the subject. There might well have been large mismatchs between private hopes and outward status. Especially in a competitive environment, it could be very galling not to get the top prize. However, it should be noted that the ethos of professional solidarity went some way towards soothing the pains of relative failure, by meshing all professionals into a communal identity. To an extent, therefore, the success of one 'star' subtlely helped the lesser practitioners who were toiling with less glory but in the same field.

Hence the prospect of improved status was undoubtedly one of the attractions of a professional career, even if all did not advance equally. Charles Edward Trevelyan, for example, had pointed that out in the debates over army recruitment in the mid-nineteenth century.[4] A professional occupation was attractive to those able and educated young men who otherwise lacked wealth and great connections to propel them forwards. Indeed, Trevelyan's own career provided a classic exemplar. He came from an old Cornish family that had clambered into the local gentry. His father had also achieved a modest eminence as the Archdeacon of Taunton. Yet Charles Edward Trevelyan (1807–86) did not inherit land or wealth, since he was the younger son of a younger son. Instead, he joined the Bengal civil service, as a young man of 19. He made his name there, before becoming assistant secretary to the British Treasury (1840–59), briefly governor of Madras (1859–60) and, at the apogee of his career, a reforming Indian finance minister (1862–65). He was knighted in 1848. For most of this time, however, he lived on a professional salary. Only late in his life, at the age of 69, did he inherit landed property from a cousin, melding merit with a 'stake in the country'. This provided the foundation of a new family tradition. With his wife Hannah – a sister of the Whig historian and MP, Lord Macaulay – Trevelyan launched a wealthy and well-connected civic dynasty into the liberal intelligentsia of nineteenth- and twentieth-century Britain.[5]

Needless to say, not all professional careers were as glittering or as variegated as that. As already noted, competition could lead in a number of directions – to outright failure or to struggling survival as well as to moderate success or sometimes to great social glory. The problem is to determine which outcome was the most common. However, it is difficult to put successive generations of the entire professional population between 1700 and 1850 under the microscope. Contemporaries did not contemplate, let alone amass, a comprehensive compilation of detailed social statistics. Historians therefore have to work with fragmentary data. Patient investigations have nonetheless begun to fill in the picture. Thus the 'advancement' of the professions can be analysed in three guises: in terms of their social origins; the degree of financial security gained; and their social destinations.

Undoubtedly, there was no universal saga of progression from rags to riches, since many were not in rags at the start. Many high-ranking professional positions tended to attract high-ranking recruits. Judges, bishops, physicians, generals and admirals were not commonly the sons of agricultural labourers. The explorer Captain Cook, who did come from such a 'lowly' background, was very much the exception – and Cook did not achieve supreme naval command. It was instead a mark of the social allure of the senior professions that their members were often recruited from highly respectable families. A career at the bar classically attracted younger sons of the landed gentry.[6] So did the richer livings of the Church of England.[7] Those of its lordly parsons who doubled as squires of the village were teasingly known as 'squarsons' in the early nineteenth century.[8] Equally, a command in the Guards was socially acceptable for even the grandest of mortals. In 1838, for example, fully 729 (over 12 per cent) among Britain's 6,000 active officers in the home army were drawn from families in the peerage and baronetage.[9]

Across the board, however, the professions were certainly not socially exclusive. If 12 per cent of the army command were drawn from the highest ranks, then 88 per cent were not. All the professions in fact contained large contingents of social 'climbers'. Thus, for example, William Blackstone in the 1760s worried that the law was attracting 'obscure or illiterate men'. He hoped that his *Commentaries* would encourage the respectable gentlemen back instead.[10] His fear was voiced in exaggerated terms,[11] but the general point was unmistakeable. No profession was able to exclude low-born newcomers.

One notable social 'rise' was that of John Hutton (d.1712). He was a shepherd boy from Dumfries, who prospered to become court physician to William III and Queen Anne.[12] Another talented – and unrelated – Hutton also experienced dramatic social betterment. Born the son of a Newcastle colliery labourer, Charles Hutton (1737–1823) had limited schooling and flourished as an auto-didact. In 1773 he became a celebrated professor of mathematics at the Woolwich Academy, holding the post until 1807.[13] Such careers were not wildly raffish or glamorous. They were, however, solidly and respectably successful. They indicated clearly that there was leeway in the social system for the talented. Even the British army high command, which had the most marked reputation for exclusivity, recruited outside the ranks of landowning society. For example, General Thomas Perronet Thompson (1783–1869) was a military commander to defy all stereotypes: the son of a Hull banker, he became successively a sailor, an army officer, a radical journalist and a reformist MP with Chartist sympathies, while remaining on the Army Lists throughout his controversial political career.[14]

No doubt, in practice the pace of social advancement was not as rapid as jeremiahs like Blackstone feared or optimistic liberals like Trevelyan assumed. Moreover, there were gradations of status within each profession. Thus officer recruits to Britain's home army were generally from grander families than were their freebooting counterparts in the Indian army.[15] In medicine, there was not much social difference between the physicians and surgeon–apothecaries, as these traditional distinctions were melting away.[16] On the other hand, by the nineteenth century, a hierarchy of esteem differentiated the grand consultants from the rank-and-file general practitioners, who in turn ranked above the multitude of medical 'irregulars'.[17] Among the churches, Anglican clerics tended increasingly to be drawn from the respectable middle class, while their dissenting brethren were often recruited from the ranks of artisans and shopkeepers on the margins of real affluence.[18] The Catholic priesthood in Ireland was even less fashionable. Its recruits were derided for their 'very low class'. However, in fact the elite trainees at nineteenth-century Maynooth began to attract sons of tenant farmers and small traders[19] – a reminder that generalised social 'smears' against unpopular groups were not always accurate.

There was sufficient diversity in all this to indicate that the social demarcations within and between these specialist occupations were not rigid. Those at the top drew proportionately more recruits from the higher social ranks. However, the occupational peaks were relatively few in numbers. By contrast, there were very many other positions among the professions that drew upon a wider social range. In particular, there were numerous modest posts in the foothills of the professions. The occupations of the rank and file, including many poor curates, town druggists, hedge attornies, hack tutors, jobbing architects and their equivalents did provide relatively open access for ambitious newcomers of humble origins, who had talent but lacked capital and status.

Overall, therefore, there was extensive upwards social mobility, even while it was not evenly distributed at all levels within the professions. Certainly, the growing number and range of specialist services indicated that there must have been considerable diversity of recruitment. There were simply not enough younger sons of the landowners to provide recruits for this expansion on their own.

It is difficult, however, to quantify these trends precisely when the surviving data are so scrappy. To take one example: a study of 272 leading architects – defined as those who gained sufficient fame to appear subsequently in the *Dictionary of National Biography* – has suggested that there was a marked decrease in the proportion of working-class recruits between the 1770s and the 1870s, as the profession grew more respectable and the training more costly.[20] That may well have happened. Yet the survey must be ruled as ultimately inconclusive, since no information was available for the parental occupation of fully one-third of these famous architects, who anyway constituted only a small sample of the wider profession. Moreover, details of the classification that was adopted for this survey can be contested: such as, for example, the assumption that Anglican vicars and rectors were members of the upper class; while curates and Nonconformist ministers were middle-class; and all grocers were working-class.[21]

That highlights one major problem in studies of social mobility over time. There are difficulties in allocating individuals into rigidly defined 'classes' – not least because contemporaries were themselves often confused as to how many classes there were[22] – but especially when the only information available is an occupational description. Job titles in this period were often very generalised. A 'weaver' might be a master manufacturer, an independent artisan or a journeyman employed on daily piece-work rates. Hence, wherever possible, simple occupational labels need to be supplemented by evidence of wealth, life styles and self-identification, although such additional information is hard to deploy systematically.

Crucially, too, the 'gentleman' was particularly difficult to gauge. This social hero was undoubtedly a person of status. But he was not invariably an upper-class landowner. Several historians have commented upon this problem.[23] Indeed, a study of recruitment into the Church of England specifically notes that different results can easily be obtained by varying the classification of the gentleman.[24] That is an important warning. In fact, there were very many urban gentlemen, including many professional men, who did not own country estates.[25]

Thus, one study of the recruitment of attorneys' apprentices in the eighteenth century has argued that the legal profession encouraged less advancement than had been thought, on the grounds that many more recruits came from gentry backgrounds than from the middling and lower classes.[26] But that conclusion was built into the classification. Over one-third of these cases were sons of 'gentlemen' who were all assumed to be upper-class 'gentry'. Even so, another 34 per cent of the attorneys' apprentices were drawn from the 'middling sort'; and in Yorkshire the figure was higher at 40 per cent. However, in practice it is highly likely that the proportion of middling and lower-class recruitment into the legal profession was greater than this survey suggested. Many of these apprentices were probably sons of town rather than landed gentry. And, above all, a large number were probably sons of lawyers who were styled as 'gentlemen', since the professions often recruited from families within the same profession. To take one example among very many: Jeremy Bentham was called to the bar as the son of a 'gentleman'. But his father was an attorney, not a landowner. Hence, although Bentham senior was described perfectly legitimately as a 'gentleman', it would indeed be misleading to classify his background as landed gentry.[27]

Social advancement, as that indicates, was not confined to a single generation. Families rose and consolidated their status over many years. For example, Hutton senior, an otherwise unknown Newcastle miner, not only had a son who became the celebrated professor of mathematics at the Woolwich Academy in the eighteenth century but a grandson who was promoted to lieutenant-general in the Royal Artillery in the 1820s and a great-grandson who was instituted as rector of St Paul's Covent Garden in the mid-nineteenth century.[28] This was an example not of endless dynastic 'rise' but of advancement followed by entrenchment.

As already noted, a very striking feature of the professions was their propensity to recruit directly from within their own ranks or from the neighbouring professions. That often happens in the case of prestige occupations with a strong sense of identity. Offspring became accustomed to the parental life style and motivated to follow suit. Hence historians of the professions often note the hereditary element in professional recruitment.[29] There were famous army families, such as the Scottish baronial family of the Cathcarts, who provided a veritable posse of noted generals: the 8th, 9th and 10th Lord Cathcarts all attained that rank, as did two sons of the 10th Lord Cathcart (who became the first Earl), the later of these being Sir George Cathcart (1794–1854) who died in battle at Inkermann in the Crimean War.[30]

Clerical families were also well known. Two contrasting examples show links across denominational boundaries: the Methodists John and Charles Wesley were sons of an Anglican vicar, while a leading Welsh Methodist Biblical scholar, Peter Williams, had two sons who both became Anglican vicars in Wales.[31] Different generations steadily followed one another in the same profession or diversified into closely related occupations. Thus among legal families, for example, one David Pollock, a well-to-do London saddler in the reign of George III, had six judges among his direct descendants in the nineteenth and early twentieth centuries, while a great-grandson was Sir Frederick Pollock (1845–1937), the legal historian and Oxford professor of jurisprudence.[32]

Medical families were also common.[33] Again, one famous example from Scotland can stand as exemplar for many lesser cases. The Monro clan was famously dedicated to medicine. As many as sixteen descendants of Sir Alexander Monro of Bearcrofts in Stirlingshire (d.1704) became doctors in the eighteenth and nineteenth centuries. Three of them, moreover, became leaders in their profession. They were the celebrated trio of Alexander Monro Primus (1697–1767), Secundus (1733–1817) and Tertius (1773–1859) – the father, son and grandson who in succession became professors of medicine at Edinburgh University.[34] However, the path of dynastic success was not entirely smooth. The third of these Monros cut a controversial figure, and onlookers unkindly suggested that the wellsprings of dynastic talent were running dry.

Family advancement within the professions was therefore not always unchequered. It was, however, quite common. In particular, fathers of relatively lowly status within a given profession often hoped that their sons would climb higher up the same ladder. That was sufficiently notorious to attract some gentle mockery in a stage comedy of 1787. *The Man-Milliner* featured a plain country apothecary – satirically named Galen Dobbin – who sent his son to town to become a medical apprentice. The honest father confided that: 'the joy of seeing my son Bob a scientific, regular-bred surgeon, will repay all my labours, all my expense.'[35] But his plans misfired. Young Dobbin was apprenticed as a man-milliner instead. Numerous jokes ensued, including one with a modern ring as the deluded father was startled to find that the city doctors had apparently renamed their 'patients' as 'customers'. At last, the imbroglio was resolved by Bob Dobbin's love match with an heiress. The father's ambition was satisfied, although not in this case by the expected mechanism of the son's progress within the parental profession.

With this diversity of aims and achievements, it was not surprising to find that earnings in the skilled services remained unstandardised. They were potentially lucrative enough to attract newcomers but, at the same time, they were not sufficiently certain that they fostered unthinking complacency. Success or failure were subject to the vagaries of skill and reputation, as refracted by local patterns in supply and demand. Furthermore, earnings waxed and waned throughout individual life cycles. Fledgling professionals often had a long wait to establish themselves, while those with declining powers in old age also faced problems – unless they had an appointment for life, as in the case of the clergy with a freehold benefice. As a result, living standards were not constant and insurance schemes had a justifiable appeal.

Optimists, meanwhile, were encouraged by the fact that a few did make huge fortunes. An enthusiastic barrister in 1716 listed 'our Beneficent Clergy [and] our Munificent Lawyery [sic]' among Britain's 'Insatiable Rich Men' in 1716.[36] Poor curates and minor pettifoggers must have smiled wryly, for these pinnacles of success were by definition not for all. Exceptional fortunes were made, nonetheless, when scarce skills in lucrative fields met high demand. Medicine was particularly subject to fashionable crazes. But it took skill and persistence to stay at the top. Spectacular fortunes were gained in the early eighteenth century by a handful of physicians. These included Sir Hans Sloane and Dr John Radcliffe. The latter of these left a famous benefaction to the University of Oxford.[37] In the nineteenth century, some enterprising chemists also did spectacularly well. Thus Thomas Holloway with his munificent endowment of Royal Holloway College was a latter-day successor to Radcliffe, as a university patron based on the profits of marketing medicine.[38]

Similarly, successful barristers were sometimes able to corner the market as forensic stars. The great 'Counsellor' Daniel O'Connell began as a minor barrister, making £346 18s. in 1802. But his income had surpassed £5,000 per annum by the 1820s.[39] That was an immense sum in comparison with the £40 or so earned annually by a south-of-England builder's labourer in full-time employment,[40] even though the exuberant O'Connell himself remained chronically in debt. Moreover, it was still nowhere near the peak of professional earnings. For instance, Thomas Erskine in his heyday at the bar in the early 1790s made some £10,000 annually.[41] The surgeon Sir Benjamin Brodie, later the first president of the General Medical Council, provides another case history. In the 1810s he was making some £250 per annum in private practice. His reputation then grew rapidly. By 1823, his practice had soared to £6,500, which was augmented by large earnings from lectures and publications. Moreover, unlike O'Connell, Brodie was financially prudent and, before long, he was able to command another £2,000–2,500 annually in interest on money he had saved during his rise to fortune.[42]

Reaping the rewards, however, was not always easy. Self-employed professional men often had to devote extensive attention to obtaining payment of their bills. A provincial boarding-school master in 1739 went on a week's tour each June (with his sister for company) to visit the parents of his schoolboys and to obtain payment.[43] He was entertained civilly. But clients were sometimes unwilling or unable to pay, especially as fees were often augmented by 'extras'. Indeed, a proportion of all bills were never paid. For instance, between one-quarter and one-third of the sums owed to William Broderip, a leading Bristol apothecary in the later eighteenth century, were written off as bad debts.[44] It was neither gentlemanly nor wise to dun people too ruthlessly. A certain professional hauteur was recommended. On the other hand, too many unpaid bills, if pending too long, became a serious liability. The web of interlocking debts and credits was dependent upon confidence. Once shaken, it was difficult to recover. This remained a perennial problem. So George Eliot's Dr Tertius Lydgate of *Middlemarch* (1871/2) found it only too easy to spend money although fees were paid only slowly. Moreover, although of 'good family', he was a third son (as his name indicated) with no independent patrimony. Thus he informed his wife glumly: 'we are getting deeper every day, for people don't pay me the faster because others want the money.'[45]

Countless households across the country must also have learned this essential truth. Lawyers certainly had become sufficiently alert to this problem that they had developed a legal remedy against defaulting clients. An emergent convention was confirmed in 1779 by a ruling from Lord Mansfield in the test case of Wilkins v. Carmichael. As a result, an attorney was entitled to keep possession of the client's documents until the account was settled.[46] This right, known as the 'solicitor's lien', improved the financial security of lawyers, although of course it did little to enhance their popularity with the general public.

Meanwhile, at the apex of the professions, it was considered unworthy to haggle over money. Barristers and physicians in particular did not levy fees. Instead, their clientele offered an honorarium for services rendered. That amounted to the same thing financially but was socially more dignified. It also entailed mutual trust between doctor and patient, since honorary payments were not recoverable at law. The barristers were more sceptical or more realistic – and insisted upon payment in advance.[47] Gradually, however, the distinction between fees and honoraria lost its meaning, as business generally became routinised and commercialised. In medicine, that was made abundantly clear in 1858, when the Medical Registration Act gave every newly registered doctor the right to sue in order to obtain payment of all reasonable charges for professional advice, visits and medicaments, plus legal costs.[48]

By one means or another, therefore, most of those with a command of specialist skills and knowledge managed to bring in a reasonable income. Earnings often came from many sources. Eminent medical men gained fees from lectures and consultancies (though some appointments were purely honorary) as well as from their private practices.[49] Army officers were by reputation particularly creative as accountants. They were paid neither lavishly nor promptly; and had many expenses. Consequently, they were quick to claim their allowances and perquisites, while there were some cases of sharp practices, such as false mustering, and outright fraud.[50] But most self-employed professionals did not have such opportunities. Instead, those with low incomes tended to diversify. For example, chemists traded as tea dealers and grocers.[51] Lesser clergymen took in private pupils to augment a poor living.[52] Meanwhile, the Wiltshire boarding-school master, who had a school for 20–30 boys in the mid-eighteenth century, was also a small farmer who, like a good countryman, kept careful notes on the weather.[53] Thus while the successful professionals increasingly tended to specialise in one occupation, the process was far from universal and those at the foot of the ladder were ready to seek a variety of sources of income.

Numerous minor professional men found themselves clinging onto the margins of financial success. Young beginners also had a hard time, since it often took time, as well as luck and ability to gain a viable practice. For all these, it was a perpetual struggle to maintain a respectable life style. The plight of the poor curate was often canvassed as a classic case of professional poverty. But the friendless tutor or the put-upon governess from a shabby genteel family in the nineteenth century could also audition for the role. So too could the poor medical man in the provinces, struggling to help an impoverished clientele while at the same time charging sufficient fees to sustain his own family.[54] In those cases, a low level of professional income created great difficulties in sustaining the professional life style that was required for the post. Hence every specialist group had their own success stories and their own tales of relatively impoverished practitioners, with skills but without capital reserves. Unvarnished knowledge might confer cultural power but it did not automatically ensure great wealth. A profession was thus not an automatic passport to great affluence or security.

For that reason, prudent practitioners often supported charities and benefit schemes that provided assistance in hard times. Many funds were highly localised. For example, from 1746 until at least the early 1840s a special charity paid funeral fees and pensions to impoverished widows and orphans of Anglican clergymen in Suffolk.[55] Numerous doctors, professionally aware of the precarious nature of good health, also joined charitable associations. In 1786, two local groups founded the earliest benevolent medical societies to provide mutual help – one in Essex and Hertfordshire, the other the Norfolk and Norwich Benevolent Medical

Society (which is still in existence). Under the initial rules of this latter body, a member subscribed a minimum of one guinea a year in order to ensure *post-mortem* benefits for his widow and children.[56]

Later, too, national organisations were created, alongside these local funds. In 1836 the British Medical Association began its own scheme, which was hived off in 1870 as an independent charity (now the Royal Medical Benevolent Fund).[57] Of course, not all aid was devised exclusively for members of the professions.[58] In 1764, for example, Joseph Priestley as a reforming young minister had launched a 'widows' fund' for all Protestant dissenters living in Lancashire and Cheshire.[59] But the growing participation of the professions in formal financial provision indicated that many had at least some disposable funds and, above all, a willingness to plan ahead against hard times.

Commercial insurers certainly found that an attractive quality. Members of the professions were significant among the early purchasers of life assurance. Indeed, by the 1820s some new companies appealed explicitly to them. The Law Life Assurance Society (1824), founded by a group of London lawyers, was one such. It catered for a wide clientele but also attracted a core of professional investors. Thus a study has shown that, between 1824 and 1842, 30.42 per cent of L.L.A.S. life policy-holders were members of the professions, plus another 6.75 per cent who were government officials. That was a sizeable group. These were minimum figures, moreover, since a number of the 'gentlemen' (here classified with the esquires and nobility) may well have had professional occupations.[60]

Insurance was purchased for a variety of motives. Policies were advertised as a means not only to protect family incomes but also to raise loans and to provide indemnity against unexpected losses. That diversity has been interpreted as an appeal to aristocratic speculation and 'dissipation' rather than to middle-class 'thrift'[61] – assuming that such class stereotypes were in themselves accurate. Yet there is no reason to assume that the use of life-assurance policies, whether to raise money or to insure lives or to provide safeguard against losses, was automatically imprudent or somehow non-bourgeois. On the contrary. It was clear that participation in the money markets had spread well beyond the ranks of the aristocracy, and for motives of much greater complexity than sheer dissipation.

Indeed, naming insurance companies after the professions suggests precisely an attempt to sell insurance by appealing to professional reliability and prudential forethought. Another example of that was the Medical, Clerical and General Life Assurance Society, founded in 1824 by Dr George Pinckard. The name was redolent of respectability, and the first president was the reassuring figure of the Archbishop of York. This Society targeted the medical and clerical professions as prospective insurers (changing its name in 1825 to 'Clerical Medical' as it still remains today).[62] Initially, it provided both whole-life and short-term policies, as well as policies for children, and annuities. Furthermore, it offered also to insure 'impaired' or 'sub-standard' lives, as long as the disability was not immediately life-threatening.

Fluctuations in fortunes were certainly understood to be part of the pattern of professional remuneration. Such diverse levels of earnings were seen as part of a wider pattern of systematic inequalities in British society as a whole. As a result, they were generally accepted as part of the established order of things. The sanguine Archdeacon Paley (1743–1805), who was himself the upwardly mobile son of a clerical schoolmaster, had no doubts. He argued in 1785 that the marked income inequality among the Anglican clergy was positively advantageous. It would provide people at all social levels with a minister of their own 'class and quality', he declared, while at the same time it attracted men of talent into the church to compete for the few great prizes that were also available.[63] Poor curates may have winced at this jovial confidence; but Paley was at least consistent, since he had already preached a resounding sermon on the same theme in September 1782.[64]

Differentials between the different professions were clearly invoked by the calculations of Gregory King in the 1690s. He estimated that a lawyer made £154 per annum; a naval officer £80; an eminent Anglican clergyman £72 (excluding the bishops who drew the prizes at £1,300 on average); an army officer £60; and a lesser clergyman £50. These sums compared poorly with an overseas merchant on £400 per annum; but favourably with the estimated income of an artisan on £38; and very favourably with a labourer on £15. King's figures were, of course, simplifications. They averaged out differentials between town and country, region and region, individual and individual. Nonetheless, his data offer a benchmark for comparisons over time. Later estimates suggest that average professional incomes not only rose but also spread over a broader spectrum. In 1803 Colquhoun suggested that a college Fellow or a headmaster had an income of £600; a superior clergyman (again excluding the episcopate) £500; a lawyer £350; a person in the medical, literary or fine arts £260; an engineer or surveyor £200; a schoolteacher (with some capital) £150; a naval officer £149; an army officer £139; a lesser Anglican cleric and all Dissenting ministers £120. As before, these incomes lagged behind the leading merchant or banker, now with a massive £2,600, or a master manufacturer on £800. But they did very well compared with an artisan on £55 per annum or an agricultural labourer on £31.[65]

Global estimates such as these, of course, need revision and amendment. Modern researchers stress instead the lack of standardisation in professional earnings. There was, for example, a social gulf between the many rank-and-file attorneys making £100 per annum in the early eighteenth century and the few leading barristers making over £10,000 by the end of the century.[66] Modern economists also suggest that cities generate a greater spread of professional earnings than do country settlements, reflecting the greater range of both supply and demand in town.[67] That certainly was the case for doctors in the 1830s and 1840s,[68] and it probably applied to the other skilled services too.

Special factors, moreover, helped to lift or depress the relative performance of the different professions, as the King/Colquhoun figures suggest. Thus the official incomes of army and navy officers rose only slowly. Pay rates were upgraded infrequently – and in the case of the army not at all after 1797. That did not prevent some military heroes from doing well on the strength of prizes and perquisites. But the system was not very generous to those who lived only on their pay. Hence the army was reputed by the mid-nineteenth century as 'a beggarly profession unless a man has a private fortune'.[69] By contrast, the beneficed clergy of the Church of England saw a long-term income inflation between 1700 and 1840, thanks to the work of Queen Anne's Bounty and also to the plural holding of livings.[70] That helped to attract candidates for preferment, even though it left unresolved the problems of poor curates.

Doctors, too, were gradually moving up the hierarchy. An apothecary in 1753 had stressed that 'There is no Profession, no Trade in the Kingdom which we call genteel, that has so few rich Men in it as the different Branches of Physic.'[71] It was penned as a warning to patients, who were misled by a few very wealthy practitioners. Yet over time, the medical profession began to prosper modestly, although with marked discrepancies between the very successful and the rest. By the 1830s, a London G.P. could expect to average some £300–400 per annum, while his country counterpart made some £150–200. And, by the 1850s, leading consultants earned at least £1,500 per annum – some very much more.[72] However, far from all medical practitioners were euphoric about their profession and its remuneration. They complained that they lagged behind the lawyers and the richer clergy. Thus in 1848, for example, the Liverpool physician Joseph Dickinson warned his students not to expect wealth and status as the result of their studies.[73]

Skilled services and professional knowledge thus did not bring automatic or universal benefits to their practitioners. Future research will refine the evidence and, no doubt, also highlight the complexities entailed in generalising about a large occupational group over a prolonged period of time. Nonetheless, the general message of the King/Colquhoun estimates is unlikely to be undermined. That is, most professional incomes were to be found in the 'middling' band; and were generally rising, though not uniformly, between the 1690s and 1803. Moreover, the same pattern continued thereafter, although the scale of the increase in the nineteenth century is still debated.[74]

In consequence, the social destination of most professional families was the loosely defined 'middling' sector of society that came to be termed the 'middle class'.[75] Provided they were successful in the competitive life style that Trollope had identified, theirs was a happy position. With the rest of the middle class, they lacked both the grosser temptations of wealth and the direst problems of poverty, as numerous middle-class propagandists kindly explained.[76] The occupational autonomy of the professions also conferred status and an admired life style. As a result, they clearly ranked above the unpropertied wage-earners, who characteristically (but not universally) worked at the behest of others and who lacked reserves of capital to fall back upon in hard times. At the same time, the working professions equally clearly did not qualify as part of the plutocracy of the very rich and the landed aristocracy.

Exceptions to that rule did, however, occur from time to time, to encourage their fellows to aim high. Thus, in every generation, a handful of professional people soared through into the titled classes; and a much greater number had descendants who did so. That blurred any sharp distinctions between the elite and the middle class. The law, for example, always had the capacity to elevate its leading practitioners, as a tract on *The Grandeur of the Law* noted chirpily in 1684,[77] and that tradition continued in this period. The son of a Staffordshire attorney, Thomas Parker was elevated to become Lord Chancellor, gaining in turn a knighthood, a baronetcy and in 1721 the earldom of Macclesfield.[78] So great was the prestige of the senior judiciary that two of the illegitimate daughters of Lord Chancellor Thurlow and his companion Polly Humphreys (whose own mother ran the famous lawyers' *rendezvous* known as Nando's coffee house) married respectively a baronet and a Scottish peer. However, a third daughter was held to have disgraced the family by rashly eloping with 'an underbred coxcomb'.[79]

Moreover, even lesser lawyers had descendants that rose in the world. A quietly successful Lancashire attorney in the eighteenth century married his daughter to a wealthy brewer's son turned minor politician, Bamber Gascoyne. By that move, Isaac Greene became ancestor to a noble prime minister of the later nineteenth century, Robert Gascoyne Cecil, the 3rd Marquis of Salisbury.[80]

However, it took time before the working professions began to emulate the leading lawyers by themselves receiving the accolade of ennoblement. The first medical peerage did not follow until 1897, when – to the intense chagrin of the physicians, who plumed themselves on their superiority – it was a surgeon who first got the prize.[81] Nonetheless, there had already been numerous medical dignitaries. One such was the physician Sir Hans Sloane (1660–1753), baroneted in the early eighteenth century. Another was the surgeon Sir Astley Cooper (1768–1841). He began life modestly as the fourth son of a cleric and minor poet. But, having progressed to a huge financial and professional success, Cooper was awarded a baronetcy by George IV in 1821.[82]

On the other hand, these professional triumphs were the exceptional pinnacles. And even then, they did not always rest on their laurels but continued in employment, despite gaining honours. For example, when the prudent surgeon Benjamin Brodie was given a baronetcy in 1834, he decided to work harder than ever at his profession. It was necessary, he explained, in order to leave ample means for his son and heir. Otherwise 'an hereditary rank, however small, without some independent fortune, is really an incumbrance.'[83] Here was the voice of prudential planning rather than that of insouciant lordship. Moreover the son, Benjamin junior (1817–80), worked in the parental style and became a research chemist and professor of chemistry at Oxford.[84]

With a few exceptions, therefore, the majority of the working professions remained firmly outside the ranks of the titled nobility. Instead, they collectively advanced into and consolidated their position in the broad embrace of Britain's respectable middle class.[85] These were the circles within which professional men moved easily. There they found many of their friends and business associates as well as – very often – their matrimonial partners.[86] This web of contacts linked the professions together and provided the growing social prestige that helped to underpin the meritocratic ethos. That has been increasingly replicated in many other developed countries too, as the purveyors of skilled services have gathered economic and social strength.[87]

Knowledge therefore did not confer supreme power upon Britain's professions. It did, however, generate a spectrum of social advancement, ranging from the relatively small but encouraging cases of dazzling success, to the solid core of respectable achievement, through to the anxious striving of the long professional 'tail'. All this, moreover, was accomplished despite the mockery of satirists and the doubts of the economists who queried the productive value of 'invisible' services.

Consequently, the professions were key contributors to the growing prestige of the middle class. They were not of course the only members of this important social group.[88] Indeed, the professions shared many social and political assumptions with their commercial and manufacturing peers. However, there were dynamic tensions as well as sympathies within the middle class. The long-term growth of the professions pointed not only to the importance of meritocracy within the wider society but also to 'brain-work' as the basis for merit within the meritocracy.[89] They cultivated an ethos of personal service, which sometimes led them to laugh at the commercial stress upon mere money-making or the landowner's mythical life of empty idleness. For example, one earnest young medical student in the mid-1760s was as disdainful of the 'dull shopkeeper with his thousands' as he was of the 'country booby with his dogs and horses' and the 'mere town rake'.[90] The professions did not monopolise the heterogeneous group loosely defined as Britain's middle class. But their knowledge/power made them a significant and vocal element within it.

NOTES

1 G. Farquhar, *The Stage-Coach: A Comedy* (London, 1705), p. 5.
2 J. Addison, 'Divinity, law and physic overburthened with practitioners', *The Spectator*, 21 (24 March 1710/11), ed. N. Ogle (London, 1827), vol. 1, p. 99.
3 A. Trollope, *The Bertrams* (1859), ed. S. Michell (Sutton, Gloucester, 1986), pp. 1, 5. For the contrasting careers of Trollope's parents, see N.J. Hall, *Trollope: a biography* (Clarendon, Oxford, 1991), pp. 31–5, 38–42, 67–8.
4 Above, pp. 192–3.
5 See *D.N.B.*, *sub*: Charles Edward Trevelyan; D.W. Armstrong, 'Sir Charles Edward Trevelyan, Assistant Secretary to the Treasury, 1840–59' (unpubl. Ph.D. thesis, University of London, 1975), pp. 1–7; M. Moorman, *Poets and Historians: a family inheritance* (Tennyson Soc. Occasional Papers, 1, 1974); and D. Cannadine, *G.M. Trevelyan: a life in history* (HarperCollins, London, 1992), pp. 3–14.
6 D. Duman, *The Judicial Bench in England, 1727–1875: the reshaping of a professional elite* (Royal Historical Society, London, 1983), pp. 50–5; and idem, 'The English bar', in *Lawyers in Early Modern Europe and America*, ed. W. Prest (Croom Helm, London, 1981), esp. pp. 90–5.
7 See P. Virgin, *The Church in an Age of Negligence: ecclesiastical structure and problems of church reform, 1700–1840* (Clarke, Cambridge, 1989), pp. 109–10, 281; and a case study in J.H. Pruett, 'Career patterns among the clergy of Lincoln Cathedral, 1660–1750', *Church History*, 44 (1975), esp. pp. 207–8.
8 The term has been attributed both to Sydney Smith and to Bishop Wilberforce (son of Wilberforce the philanthropist): see *O.E.D.*
9 G. Harries-Jenkins, *The Army in Victorian Society* (Routledge, London, 1977), pp. 39, 42.
10 W. Blackstone, *Commentaries on the Laws of England* (Oxford, 1765–9), vol. 1, p. 33.
11 See P. Lucas, 'A collective biography of students and barristers of Lincoln's Inn, 1680–1804: a study in the "aristocratic resurgence" of the eighteenth century', *Journal of Modern History*, 46 (1974), pp. 227–61, esp. pp. 230–4. But Lucas assumes – problematically – that all sons of 'gentlemen' were offspring of the landed gentry (see p. 228).
12 *D.N.B.*, *sub*: John Hutton.
13 N. Hans, *New Trends in Education in the Eighteenth Century* (Routledge, London, 1951), pp. 109–10, 189–90.
14 Details in *D.N.B.*, *sub*: T.P. Thompson; and Harries-Jenkins, *Army in Victorian Society*, p. 47.
15 See variously P.E. Razzell, 'The social origins of British army officers in the Indian and British Home Army, 1758–1962', *British Journal of Sociology*, 14 (1963), pp. 248–60; J.W. Hayes, 'The social and professional background of the officers of the British army, 1714–63' (unpubl. M.A. thesis, London University, 1956), pp. 64–99; C.B. Otley, 'The social origins of British army officers', *Sociological Review*, 18 (1970), pp. 213–39; and Harries-Jenkins, *Army in Victorian Society*, pp. 12–58.
16 G. Holmes, *Augustan England: professions, state and society, 1680–1730* (Allen &

Unwin, London, 1982), pp. 206–8, 211–12; J.G.L. Burnby, *A Study of the English Apothecary from 1660 to 1760, Medical History,* suppl. 3 (1983), pp. 95–7.

17 M.J. Peterson, *The Medical Profession in Mid-Victorian London* (University of California Press, Berkeley, 1978), pp. 197–9; I. Loudon, *Medical Care and the General Practitioner, 1750–1850* (Clarendon, Oxford, 1986), pp. 31–2.

18 Compare Virgin, *Church in an Age of Negligence,* pp. 110–12, 281, with K.D. Brown, *A Social History of the Nonconformist Ministry in England and Wales, 1800–1930* (Clarendon, Oxford, 1988), pp. 19–49.

19 S.J. Connolly, *Priests and People in Pre-Famine Ireland* (Gill & Macmillan, New York, 1982), pp. 35–43.

20 B. Kaye, *The Development of the Architectural Profession in England: a sociological study* (Allen & Unwin, London, 1960), p. 47. n. 32.

21 Ibid., p. 53.

22 P.J. Corfield, 'Class by name and number in eighteenth-century Britain', in *Language, History and Class,* ed. P.J. Corfield (Blackwell, Oxford, 1991), pp. 114–21.

23 Thus Otley, 'Social origins of British army officers', p. 229, stresses that the gentlemen were not all affluent men of leisure.

24 Virgin, *Church in an Age of Negligence,* p. 281, n. to Table 10.

25 P.J. Corfield, 'The rivals: landed and other gentlemen in eighteenth-century England', in *Land and Society in Modern Britain, 1700–1914,* ed. N.B. Harte and R.E. Quinault (Manchester University Press, Manchester, 1996).

26 M. Miles, '"A haven for the privileged": recruitment into the profession of attorney in England, 1709–92', *Social History,* 11 (1986), pp. 197–210.

27 Lucas, 'Collective biography . . . of Lincoln's Inn', pp. 234–5, n. 3.

28 *D.N.B., sub:* Charles Hutton.

29 See e.g. Otley, 'Social origins of British army officers', p. 233; Virgin, *Church in an Age of Negligence,* p. 110; Barrie-Curien, 'Clergy in the diocese of London', in *The Church of England, c. 1689 – c. 1833: from toleration to tractarianism,* ed. J. Walsh, C. Haydon and S. Taylor (Cambridge University Press, Cambridge, 1993), p. 89; Brown, *Social History of Nonconformist Ministry,* p. 38; Miles, '"Haven for the privileged"', pp. 203, 205; Duman, *Judicial Bench in England,* pp. 165–70; Holmes, *Augustan England,* pp. 145, 164–5, 208–9, 217; Lane, 'Role of apprenticeship' in *William Hunter and the Eighteenth-Century Medical World,* ed. W.F. Bynum and R. Porter (Cambridge University Press, Cambridge, 1985), pp. 96–7; Loudon, *Medical Care and the General Practitioner,* pp. 28–30, 33–4; and Peterson, *Medical Profession,* p. 198, Table 9. Interestingly, both Lucas, 'Collective biography . . . of Lincoln's Inn', pp. 231, 233, and Peterson, *Medical Profession,* pp. 205–6, suggest that the most successful barristers and physicians may have sent their younger sons into the parental profession, reserving the elder sons for some more prestigious destiny. But the data are as yet too scanty to confirm that.

30 Harries-Jenkins, *Army in Victorian Society,* p. 41.

31 See *D.N.B., sub:* John Wesley; and D. Walker (ed.), *A History of the Church in Wales* (Historical Soc. of the Church in Wales, Penarth, Glam., 1976), p. 111.

32 Duman, *Judicial Bench in England,* p. 170.

33 For some English examples, see Loudon, *Medical Care and the General Practitioner,* pp. 34, 201, n. 63.

34 R.E. Wright-St Clair, *Doctors Monro: a medical saga* (Wellcome Historical Medical Library, London, 1964), pp. xi, 27–37, 69–81, 96–117.

35 J. O'Keefe, *The Man-Milliner* (1787), in idem, *The Dramatic Works* (London, 1798), vol. 4, pp. 350, 352.

36 M. Davies, *Athenae Britannicae: or, a critical history of the Oxford and Cambridge [sic] writers and writings* . . . (London, 1716), pt 2, p. xxvi.

37 See Holmes, *Augustan England*, pp. 218–34 for medical fortunes generally; and pp. 221–2 for Radcliffe and Sloane specifically.

38 Holloway's benefaction remains the largest single gift ever presented to London University: N.B. Harte, *The University of London, 1836–1986: an illustrated history* (Athlone, London, 1986), pp. 129–31; and see above, p. 156.

39 See C.C. Trench, *The Great Dan: a biography of Daniel O'Connell* (Cape, London, 1984), pp. 67, 71, 110 (income); 71–2, 102–4, 174, 308 (indebtedness).

40 A building labourer would earn £41/12s. for a 52-week year of completely full employment on a wage rate of 32d. per day or 16s. for a six-day week: data from H. Phelps Brown and S.V. Hopkins, *A Perspective of Wages and Prices* (Methuen, London, 1981), p. 11.

41 *D.N.B., sub*: Thomas Erskine (1750–1823).

42 As related in Brodie's posthumously published memoirs: B.C. Brodie, *Autobiography of the Late Sir Benjamin C. Brodie, Bart.* (London, 1865), pp. 85, 97, 116, 127, 141, 166.

43 M. Reeves and J. Morrison (eds.), *The Diaries of Jeffery Whitaker, Schoolmaster of Bratton, 1739–41* (Wiltshire Record Society, Trowbridge, 1989), pp. xliii–iv, 15–16.

44 I.S.L. Loudon, 'A doctor's cashbook: the economy of general practice in the 1830s', *Medical History*, 27 (1983), p. 265; and for examples, see also A. Digby, *Making a Medical Living: doctors and patients in the English market for medicine, 1720–1911* (Cambridge University Press, Cambridge, 1994), pp. 155–62.

45 G. Eliot, *Middlemarch: a study in provincial life* (London, 1871–2), vol. 3, p. 303.

46 E.B.V. Christian, *A Short History of Solicitors* (London, 1896), pp. 165–6.

47 J. Baker, 'Counsellors and barristers: an historical study', *Cambridge Law Journal*, 27 (1969), pp. 224–9.

48 Medical Registration Act, 21 & 22 Vict., cap. 90 (1858), cl. 31.

49 H. Marland, *Medicine and Society in Wakefield and Huddersfield* (Cambridge University Press, Cambridge, 1987), p. 276, Table 7.4, gives examples.

50 Illuminating information is contained in A.J. Guy, *Oeconomy and Discipline: officership and administration in the British army, 1714–63* (Manchester University Press, Manchester, 1985), pp. 91–110.

51 Marland, *Medicine and Society*, pp. 237, 244–5.

52 For clerical tutoring, see Virgin, *Church in an Age of Negligence*, pp. 87–9. Trollope also depicted such an outcome for a poor but learned clergyman: see A. Trollope, *The Bertrams*, pp. 523, 580.

53 Reeves and Morrison (eds), *Diaries of Jeffery Whitaker*, pp. xxxiii–iv, xl.

54 See e.g. I. Inkster, 'Marginal men: aspects of the social role of the medical community of Sheffield, 1790–1850', in *Health Care and Popular Medicine in Nineteenth-Century England: essays in the social history of medicine*, ed. J. Woodward and D. Richards (Croom Helm, London, 1977), pp. 128–63.

55 The rules of this charity were recodified in 1776: see Anon., *Constitutions by Charter* . . . *of the Charity for the Relief of Poor Widows and Orphans of* . . . *[Church of England] Clergymen* . . . *in the County of Suffolk* (Bury St Edmund's, 1776).

56 A. Batty Shaw, *The Norfolk and Norwich Benevolent Medical Society, 1786–1986* (N.N.B.M.S., Norwich, 1986), pp. 7–8, 16–38.

57 See R.M. Handfield-Jones, *A History of the Royal Medical Benevolent Fund* (private publication, London, 1962), passim.

58 See P.H.J.H. Gosden, *Self-Help: voluntary associations in the nineteenth century* (Batsford, London, 1973), passim, esp. pp. 9–10.

59 This scheme is reported in the *D.N.B.*, *sub*: Joseph Priestley, although it was not mentioned in Priestley's autobiography.

60 R. Pearson, 'Thrift or dissipation? the business of life assurance in the early nineteenth century', *Economic History Review*, 2nd ser., 43 (1990), p. 237; and figures, p. 248.

61 Ibid., pp. 236–54, esp. pp. 238, 242, 252–3.

62 See the Society's 1824 *Prospectus*; and briefing handout on the 'Clerical Medical' by Nigel Wratten, Archivist to the Clerical Medical Investment Group, whose help is acknowledged with thanks.

63 W. Paley, *The Principles of Moral and Political Philosophy* (London, 1785), p. 570.

64 G. Kitson Clark, *Churchmen and the Condition of England, 1832–85: a study in the development of social ideas and practice from the old regime to the modern state* (Methuen, London, 1973), p. 30.

65 Estimates by King and Colquhoun in P. Colquhoun, *Treatise on Indigence* (London, 1806), p. 23.

66 For attorneys' earnings, see H. Kirk, *Portrait of a Profession: a history of the solicitor's profession, 1100 to the present day* (Oyez, London, 1976), pp. 83–91; and especially Miles, '"Eminent practitioners"', in Rubin and Sugarman (eds), *Law, Economy and Society*, pp. 470–502, and pp. i–xii. For barristers/judges, see Holmes, *Augustan England*, pp. 124–35; and Duman, *Judicial Bench*, pp. 105–26.

67 M. Friedman and S. Kuznets, *Income from Independent Professional Practice* (National Bureau of Econ. Research, New York, 1945), pp. 188, 199–212; as quoted in Peterson, *Medical Profession*, p. 222.

68 Loudon, 'A doctor's cashbook', pp. 259–60.

69 Trollope, *The Bertrams*, p. 88. And for details of pay levels, see Harries-Jenkins, *Army in Victorian Society*, pp. 85–8, 100–1.

70 Virgin, *Church in an Age of Negligence*, pp. 70–4.

71 J. Nelson, *An Essay on the Government of Children* (London 1756), p. 143.

72 Full details in Loudon, 'A doctor's cashbook', pp. 249–68; and Peterson, *Medical Profession*, pp. 206–24.

73 J. Dickinson, *On Medical Education: an introductory lecture* ... (London and Liverpool, 1848), pp. 3–5. Thus the mean value of doctors' probates in 1858 was somewhat lower than those of lawyers and clergy in the same year: Digby, *Making a Medical Living*, pp. 164–5.

74 J.G. Williamson, *Did British Capitalism Breed Inequality?* (Allen & Unwin, Boston & London, 1985), pp. 9–13, 36–49, esp. Table 2.4 (p. 12) cites examples of fast-rising professional pay in the early nineteenth century. However, the data have been strongly criticised as too scanty and partial to provide a basis for robust analysis: see R.V. Jackson, 'The structure of pay in nineteenth-century Britain', *Economic History Review*, 2nd ser., 40 (1987), pp. 561–70.

75 See variously P.J. Corfield, 'Concepts of the urban middle class in theory and practice: England, 1750–1850', in *Die Wiederkehr des Stadtbürgers: Stadtereformen im europäischen Vergleich, 1750–1850*, ed. B. Meier and H. Schultz (Arno Spitz, Berlin, 1994), pp. 237–69; J. Seed, 'From "middling sort" to middle class in late eighteenth- and early nineteenth-century England', in *Social Orders and Social Classes in Europe since 1500: studies in social stratification*, ed. M.L. Bush (Longman, London, 1992), pp. 114–35; and comparative survey by R. Koselleck, U. Spree and W. Steinmetz, 'Drei Bürgerliche Welten? Zur vergleichenden Semantik der bürgerlichen Gesellschaft in Deutschland, England und Frank-reich', in *Bürger in der Gesellschaft der Neuzeit: Wirtschaft – Politik – Kultur*, ed. H.J. Puhle (Vandenhoeck & Ruprecht, Göttingen, 1991), pp. 14–58.

76 Corfield, 'Class by name and number', pp. 123–6.

77 H. P. [H. Philipps], *The Grandeur of the Law: or, an exact collection of the nobility*

and gentry of this kingdom, whose honors and estates have . . . been acquired or considerably augmented by the practice of the law . . . (London, 1684).

78 See Holmes, *Augustan England*, p. 133; and *D.N.B.*, *sub*: Thomas Parker (1666?–1732). See also above, p. 93.

79 R. Gore-Browne, *Chancellor Thurlow: the life and times of an eighteenth-century lawyer* (London, 1953), pp. 55–9, 292–4, 346, 360.

80 See R. Stewart-Brown, *Isaac Greene: a Lancashire lawyer of the eighteenth century* (Liverpool, 1921), p. 26; and *D.N.B.*, *sub*: Sir Crisp Gascoyne (1700–61).

81 He was the pioneer of antisepsis Joseph Lister (1827–1912), created Lord Lister on the recommendation of the 3rd Marquis of Salisbury: W.J. Reader, *Professional Men: the rise of the professional classes in nineteenth-century England* (Weidenfeld, London, 1966), p. 150.

82 See Peterson, *Medical Profession*, p. 207; and B.M. Smith, 'Some aspects of the medical profession in eighteenth-century England, considered as a factor in the rise of the professional middle class' (unpub. Ph.D. thesis, London University, 1951), biographical index, p. xiii.

83 Brodie, *Autobiography*, p. 168.

84 *D.N.B.*, *sub*: Sir Benjamin Brodie the younger.

85 Corfield, 'Concepts of the urban middle class', pp. 7–12.

86 Little research has as yet been done into the marriage patterns of the professions; but impressionistic evidence suggests that they tended to find marriage partners not merely from the middle class generally but particularly from other professional families.

87 H.J. Perkin, *The Rise of Professional Society: England since 1880* (Routledge, London, 1989), pp. 1–26.

88 By contrast, Larson implies that the 'professional project' was the main focus of middle-class aspirations, underestimating the occupational and cultural pluralism of the social 'middle': M. Sarfatti Larson, *The Rise of Professionalism: a sociological analysis* (University of California Press, Berkeley, 1977), esp. pp. 90–9, 155–6.

89 Later, there were attempts to align the intelligentsia with the new Labour Party: see P.P. Poirier, *The Advent of the Labour Party* (Allen & Unwin, London, 1958), pp. 82–4. Hence, famously, clause 4 of the Labour Party's constitution in 1918 sought the common ownership of the means of production – in the interests of all 'producers by hand or brain': R. McKibbin, *The Evolution of the Labour Party, 1910–24* (Oxford University Press, Oxford, 1974), pp. 94, 96–7.

90 Letter from John Aikin, c. 1765, quoted in L. Aikin, *Memoirs of John Aikin, M.D.* (London, 1823), vol. 1, p. 9.

10

POWER/KNOWLEDGE?

Thus all knowledge will be subdivided and extended; and *knowledge*, as Lord *Bacon* observes, being power, the human powers will, in fact, be increased; . . .

With these words, Joseph Priestley in 1768 was one of many who referred confidently to Francis Bacon's equation of power and knowledge.[1] That there were linkages seemed obvious. As a result, the reformist Priestley was (at that stage in his life) radiantly optimistic. Since the growth of knowledge was proceeding rapidly, so human capacities would increase simultaneously. And, as that happened, so society would improve:

Thus, whatever was the beginning of this world, the end will be glorious and paradisaical, beyond what our imaginations can now conceive.

This highly positive linkage between knowledge and power could, however, be reversed. As noted already, Michael Foucault has in recent times rejected liberal optimism. For him, power was the generator of knowledge, not its consequence. That was the dark truth that he saw behind the facade. Power did not simply borrow or encourage knowledge as a useful 'front' for authority. The relationship was more complicit and more stark. 'We should admit rather that power produces knowledge (and not simply by encouraging it because it serves power or by applying it because it is useful).'[2] The outward show could be deceptive. Knowledge systems did not simply – or even complexly – constitute mere stocks of information. Instead, Foucault saw a deeper resonance. It was futile to seek 'any knowledge that does not presuppose and constitute at the same time power relations'. And he was not thinking primarily of the state. Power relations could be found anywhere. Thus Foucault analysed micro-institutions, like hospitals, asylums and penitentiaries, rather than formal structures of central government; and he studied discourse rather than guns and battles.[3]

Questions about power/knowledge relationships or knowledge/power potentialities are therefore challenging. And the answers are not self-evident. Such big historical relationships remain difficult to study, since they interlink with so much else. It is possible, however, to built up a response via a more precisely tailored series of questions.

Since this case study has focused upon the professions, an initial query is simply: *Did the professions exercise power and influence in Britain between circa 1700 and 1850?* The answer to that is certainly affirmative – and long before the Victorian reforms systematised the professional institutions and training. Collectively, the expert services wielded direct power over their clients as well as indirect influence. Moreover, the suggestion that they were merely dependents of the aristocracy does not stand close examination. The professions were a meritocratic force in their own right. Yet their emergence is no longer depicted in Whiggish terms of 'progress'. Although very far from all studies of the professions have followed Foucault, his focus upon the strategic power plays that lurk within knowledge systems has encouraged a sceptical 'unmasking' of the cultural production of expertise. The professions, too, remain sensitive to criticisms, against which they have fortified themselves by their own ethics of professional conduct.[4]

These issues were eagerly canvassed in eighteenth- and nineteenth-century Britain. The satires have already been analysed. However, the professions were quick to counter them. Their skills and knowledge were useful to individuals and to society at large. Their ideas did matter. Thus all budding authors were cheered in 1766 by a verse salute to *The Powers of the Pen*. This was written by the minor poet Evan Lloyd. He praised the 'Light toy!' that nonetheless wrought magic – 'in a skilful Hand,/ More potent than a Sorc'rer's Wand!'[5] Such thoughts, which were especially gratifying to Grub Street hacks, serenaded a power that was distinct from that of armies, governments, land or money.

The poet Samuel Taylor Coleridge commented specifically on the new role of the professions. In 1832, for example, he observed that three 'silent revolutions' had already occurred in Britain. One happened 'when the Professions fell off from the Church', by which he meant when the secular professions separated from the clergy.[6] That constituted an upheaval in itself. The second was: 'when Literature fell off from the Professions'; and, thirdly, 'when the Press fell off from Literature'. All these events were undated by Coleridge. The gist, however, was the advent of a diversified society, where the clergy no longer monopolised learning, where the organised professions no longer monopolised literary output, and where the press wrote for mass markets and not for a few wits. These were major changes – for the worse, since by 1832 Coleridge was no Priestleyan optimist – which amounted to a silent revolution.

Power and influence therefore accrued to the professions in increasing measure, as the professions themselves developed and systematised their role. *Did their growing array of specialist knowledge provide the basis for their power?* Was their authority inscribed within their 'modes of discourse'?[7] The answer to that is also affirmative, but with a number of important qualifications. The power of knowledge gained social significance when it related to something of great interest to a given community. It did not, however, invariably have that impact when the subject was recondite. As already noted, the pioneering scholar Elizabeth Elstob in the early eighteenth century found that the public interest in her immense knowledge of Anglo-Saxon was strictly limited.[8] She gained neither social authority nor income from her expertise. Her only reward was a degree of fame in scholarly circles. The social esteem meted out to various forms of knowledge therefore affected its reception.

In some circumstances, it was a question also of belief. Powers could wane if communal validation was withdrawn. For example, the once formidable sanction of excommunication, wielded by the Church of England, fell into disuse when people ceased to fear the consequences of exclusion from the community of believers. That happened in Britain long before the power was formally abolished by Parliament in 1813. As a result, the church lost a sanction against unbelievers. By 1823, a traditionalist, worried by the erosion of social deference, pointed out sadly that: 'The Clergy have undoubtedly lost some importance from the gradual depreciation of the penalty . . . of excommunication.'[9]

By contrast, when medicine was extended as a field of knowledge in the eighteenth century, there was a prolonged rise in the reputation of the doctors. That remained the case, despite the fact that many of their treatments have subsequently been deemed inadequate by the standards of later generations. But applied medicine provided the doctors with a multiplying medical repertoire, which either worked or at least seemed to work sufficiently to convince their patients. The medical profession was therefore able to respond positively to the intense public concern for good health care – a concern that has shown no signs of being sated. The conceptual contents of knowledge systems were therefore relevant to their reception. If they related to matters of great communal interest and/or utility, then their power was augmented. Hence, as the doctors gained credibility, so they were given powers by the state. After legislation in 1828, for example, it took only two qualified medical men to certify an individual as insane – and only one to certify a pauper.[10]

As that indicates, the state intervened from time to time to confirm or underpin professional powers. However, the predominant tradition in Britain was one of self-regulation. The 'free professions' were not an arm of the state, with the exception of the military high command. Thus the gamut of professional knowhow was not a smokescreen for political control. Instead, the authority of experts was enhanced when those who wielded it were self-organised to control its supply and application. The stricter the regulation of entry into a profession, the greater the opportunities for turning the specialist services into income-yielding property[11] – assuming always that there was a sustained social requirement for the expertise in question. In other words, the power of knowledge was increased when it operated within a favourable conjunction of consumer demand and some control of supply. In itself, however, specialist know-how did not always imply a focused system of domination.

Another question then follows. *Was the power conferred by knowledge – even in the most favourable circumstances – absolute?* Here the answer, by contrast, is in the negative. The quest to identify modes of power should not overlook its protean nature. In other words, the existence of professional knowledge-brokers did not end or exclude other sources of authority. The powers of the pen, the pulpit, the wig and the scalpel did not eliminate the powers of the state, the social hierarchy and the purse. Those other sources of power operated their own rival force fields, as the professions were often aware. Recruits to their ranks were not led to expect that expertise would automatically lead to social supremacy. For example, in 1848 an eminent Liverpool physician advised his students that: 'The power of the physician consists not in political influence, but in the ability to relieve the sufferings and miseries of his fellow-creatures – a power, the exercise of which never brings an advantage to ourselves without conferring a corresponding benefit on others.'[12] As that indicated candidly enough, the provision of services could bring some personal reward, though generally not a great fortune. But the exchange was a mutual one. The providers of specialist services gave as well as gained. And the exchange was carried out within a complex social framework, full of competing powers and resistance to power.

Crucially, therefore, it is important to recognise that the recipients of specialist knowledge had their own agendas. The public's understanding might be woefully flawed from the professional point of view. Yet consumer responses were more complex than a mere submission to external power. There was scope for evasion, rival interpretations or outright refusal. That applied to patients who declined the doctor's prescription, litigants who refused to take advice, parishioners who avoided going to church and students who ignored their tutor's best precepts. Other clients, meanwhile, took professional counsel but then neglected to pay for it. There were thus all sorts of permutations that made and marred the relationship between the experts and their public.

Above all, and even more crucially, knowledge itself is not finite and invariate. It can appear cast in stone. Yet it is simultaneously and intrinsically open-ended and always liable to addition and innovation. As the stock of human knowledge has grown, it has become irredeemably diversified. Its power was consequently conferred upon a plurality of power-brokers, as Joseph Priestley had noted in 1768. The expansion of knowledge has provoked the creation of many discrete sub-specialisms, each with its own knowhow, assumptions and technical languages. Once press censorship was lifted – with the lapsing of the Licensing Act in 1695 – there emerged more than one public 'discourse', more than one codified field of expert knowledge. That was apparent in the diversification of the professions. As a result, they constituted a pluralist phalanx within a pluralist society, sharing many cultural assumptions – but not marching as an orderly regiment to a single tune.

It was difficult, as a result, to define the professions in Britain as a unified intelligentsia, who were consciously involved in the dissemination of abstract ideas. Some did fit into this mould. David Hume was a leading figure in the scintillating circle of writers, philosophers and *literati* who gathered in mid-eighteenth-century Edinburgh. An English resident there was impressed: 'Here I stand at what is called the *Cross of Edinburgh*, and can, in a few minutes, take fifty men of genius and learning by the hand.'[13] Even if not literally true, that was a neat tribute to the distinctive contribution of the Scottish capital to British cultural life.[14] Subsequently, too, nineteenth- and early twentieth-century England spawned its own 'intellectual aristocracy' of writers, scholars, academics, scientists and some administrators, who formed a cohesive social group.[15]

Yet British cultural life also contained a robust empiricism which was often expressed in the form of a half-resentful, half-respectful anti-intellectualism. That tradition was well represented even within the professions. Their meritocracy was not based upon the 'merit' of pure intellect but instead upon applied knowledge and personal skills. That view was especially prevalent in the technocratic professions. Samuel Smiles, the eulogist of the engineers, was one who stressed the value of personal ability over mere book learning. He revised Bacon's dictum. 'That character is power, is true in a much higher sense than that knowledge is power', he wrote firmly.[16] Culturally, therefore, the British professions were not all self-declared intellectuals. Only a section of them formed anything like a conscious intelligentsia.[17] The identification of this group was unclear, as it remains today.[18]

If the professions did not constitute an intelligentsia, still less did they represent the entire social spectrum that was designated under the term 'middle class'. The successful professions were undoubtedly part of Britain's changing social configuration. But they cannot be explained simply as embodying the 'rise of the middle class'. The bourgeoisie was variegated. Indeed, as noted above, the professions posed a challenge to those who defined the middle class as essentially owners of capital. The specialist services were founded upon applied knowledge. Thus there was often tension between a commercial ethos of acquisition and a professional ethic of service – a tension that will doubtless continue at least until both groups manage to give each other due recognition.

Given that social dynamics are intricate processes, with their own internal feedback mechanisms, it often becomes difficult to isolate cause from effect. What does that mean, finally, for the general linkages between power and knowledge? Do authority structures deserve causal priority over patterns of cognition? The stimulating perceptions of Michel Foucault certainly stressed that power took diverse forms. It operated indirectly through cultural production as much as directly through mechanisms of state control. But, for him, power was at the root. It 'cannot but evolve, organise and put into circulation a knowledge, or rather apparatuses of knowledge'.[19] That made it dangerous, since it was at once dominant and subtle. 'Power is everywhere', Foucault concluded.[20] Ultimately, his was a sombre vision. Even resistance was formulated within these strategic fields of power/knowledge relations.

Reversing Bacon's equation therefore prompts a further sequence of questions. *Is power the same as knowledge?* The answer to that is clearly in the negative. Foucault himself never absolutely equated the two. Power takes many forms. Military control is one variant. Political authority another. Economic might a third. The influence of ideology, whether secular or religious, a fourth. And all these elements may intertwine. As a result, power is transacted through different forms, to different degrees, with differing amounts of skill, and its impact varies according to the amount and nature of the resistance it meets. Sometimes it was forged by rude force. At other times, it was based upon law. That was the 'distinction which every body is acquainted with, between *mere power* [= force] and *authority*', as Bishop Butler loftily remarked in 1726. For him, the real test was conscience. Had it power to match its moral claims, then it would rule the world.[21] Yet, as he knew, things were not so easy. A satire in 1705 had offered to reveal instead *The Power and Prerogative of the Inexpressible I Know Not What*. Alas, the contents of the tract did not match its promising title. But it mused on complexities and, incidentally, made the bold prediction – eighty-four years too soon – that there would be an imminent revolution against the monarchy in France.[22]

That shows that knowledge can sometimes be faulty and evanescent, while authority structures by contrast often have marked staying power. However, the question can be reformulated more complexly. *Does power produce knowledge?* Here the answer is: to an extent, yes, but only up to a point. Some mental maps were directly linked to patterns of authority. Power generated its own apologias and theoretical justifications. Some perhaps were written cynically. But many were genuinely impressed by the powers that be. The status quo could seem irrefutable, its cultural influence unavoidable. That attitude was found both among the wielders of authority and among their subjects. 'Power, like the diamond, dazzles the beholder, and also the wearer', wrote one admirous clergyman-turned-wine merchant in 1820.[23] Moreover, it was not just the might and glamour of power that impressed but its apparent ubiquity, both locally and nationally. That added greatly to its claims. Existing structures of authority were presented as so 'natural' and pervasive that they were impossible to challenge. They often had legal support and institutional backing as well. As a result, existing power structures often seemed immanent and unavoidable.

Problems, however, follow if Foucault's perception is taken too absolutely.[24] To assert that power can underpin and generate knowledge is not the same as showing that it is the only source. Both phenomena are more intricate than that. Hence the question can be revised: *does power alone produce knowledge?* And answered simply: no. Knowledge is much more than an epiphenomenon of power structures – or of economic structures, come to that.[25] It is generated from plural sources, including experimentation, resistance and opposition to established ideas. Even powerlessness has its own stock of wisdom. The acquisition of knowledge has always entailed more than submission to power. Moreover, human knowhow has demonstrated over time a capacity for expansion, variety, innovation and improvisation. It may diversify more rapidly than do power structures, creating tensions if the powers that be are neither powerful enough to suppress new ideas nor quick enough to adapt. It is of course observable that changes occur within their historical context of long-continuing cultural traditions. But even deep-rooted customs evolve. Thus those who argue for closed-circuit linkages between power and knowledge leave themselves no room for explaining diachronic change.

Historically, by contrast, both have proved highly adaptable and fissile. For example, the professions were, quietly, an insurgent group within British society in the years 1700–1850. As they gained power, so their own knowledge was systematised and applied. Yet it was also debated and continuously renewed. Knowledge is rarely unitary. It often contains contradictions and disparate, unreconciled viewpoints. The professions themselves did not universally agree about the nature of their own professional knowledge. Instead, they often denounced rival systems as the products of quackery or bad faith. Nor, too, has the increasing power of the professions ended these disputes, or put their own knowledge beyond dispute. On the contrary. Now they face a new critical challenge – not to oust an old plutocracy but to adapt a professional meritocracy to function successfully in a mass democracy.

Relationships between knowledge and power remain teasing ones. The holders of one cannot assume that they will have a monopoly of the other. But if power does not alone produce knowledge, what about the reverse? *Does knowledge conversely confer power?* Many have agreed with Francis Bacon's optimistic dictum. It became something of a liberal cliché. For example, the radical surgeon John Aikin encouraged England's dissenters in 1790 that they would soon gain civil rights, since they were knowledgeable people and 'Knowledge is power'.[26] The preaching enthusiast Professor Shepard advised the clergy in 1852 to have faith in the power of the pulpit on the same grounds.[27] Indeed, the dictum was widely adduced as a form of encouragement. Thus in 1848–9, a radical journal entitled *The Power of the Pence* ran a confident sub-title that offered its readers the hope that 'Knowledge is Power'.[28]

However, this too was over-simplified. Knowledge can confer power but it does not automatically do so. It can lead to many other things, ranging at the extreme to vilification. John Keats, the quondam medical student turned poet, saw alternatives. 'Until we are sick, we understand not'; he wrote in a letter of 1818. 'In fine, as Byron says, "Knowledge is sorrow"; and I go on to say that "Sorrow is wisdom" – and further for aught we can know for certain "Wisdom is folly."'[29] In fact, Keats had subtly misremembered. Byron's *Manfred* (1817) decided that 'Sorrow is knowledge'. The march of intellect was not a triumphal progress. In 1876 George Eliot warned: 'It is a common sentence that Knowledge is power; but who hath duly considered or set forth the power of Ignorance?'[30] Moreover, it was always possible to know rather traditional things. One versifier in 1786 satirised the eighteenth century's claims to be an *Age of Genius*. Instead, he urged: 'Yes – tell each coxcomb – tell him to his face,/ The fool's *best knowledge* is to know his place!'[31]

Nothing was guaranteed. Pluralistic models of power and knowledge point to pluralistic linkages and pluralistic outcomes. As the history of the professions showed, there were appreciable patterns but no monolith of power/knowledge. To know was simply to be human. That was hymned by William Mickle, a Scottish author, translator and adventurer. His ode to knowledge in 1761 was a conventional enough tribute to divine wisdom. On the way, however, he lauded his species' capacity for understanding:[32]

> 'Hail Knowledge! gift of Heaven!', I cried,
> 'E'en all the gifts of Heaven beside,
> Compared to thee how low!
> The blessings of the earth, and all
> The beasts of fold and forest share,
> But godlike beings KNOW.'

NOTES

1 J. Priestley, *An Essay on the First Principles of Government: and on the nature of political, civil, and religious liberty* (London, 1768), pp. 7–8.
2 Foucault as cited above, p. 4.
3 Among a huge literature interpreting Foucault, see J. Goldstein, 'Foucault among the sociologists: the "disciplines" and the history of the professions', *History and Theory*, 23 (1984), pp. 170–92; P. O'Brien, 'Michel Foucault's History of Culture', in *The New Cultural History*, ed. L. Hunt (University of California

Press, Berkeley, 1989), pp. 25–46; and essays in *Reassessing Foucault: power, medicine and the body,* ed. C. Jones and R. Porter (Routledge, London, 1994).

4 For an example of the modern genre, see the deliberations of the Centre for Professional Ethics (1977-) , in R.W. Clarke and R.P. Lawry (eds), *The Power of the Professional Person* (University Press of America, Boston, 1988); and countless studies in applied ethics.

5 [E. Lloyd], *The Powers of the Pen: a poem* (London, 1766), p. 1.

6 C. Woodring (ed.), *The Collected Works of Samuel Taylor Coleridge: table-talk, I* (Bollingen Series 75, Routledge, London; and Princeton University Press, Princeton, N.J., 1990), p. 285: entry for 21 April 1832.

7 Foucault's inaugural lecture at the Collège de France in 1970 spoke of 'Orders of Discourse': B. Smart, *Michel Foucault* (Routledge, London, 1985), pp. 72–3.

8 See above, p. 213.

9 E. Nares, *Heraldic Anomalies: or, rank confusion in our orders of precedence* (2 vols, London, 1823), vol. 2, pp. 103–4. See also above, p. 125.

10 See above, pp. 163, 165.

11 See H.J. Perkin, *The Rise of Professional Society: England since 1880* (Routledge, London, 1989), p. 7.

12 J. Dickinson, *On Medical Education: an introductory lecture . . .* (London, 1848), pp. 3–6, esp. p. 4.

13 Reported by W. Smellie, *Literary and Characteristical Lives of John Gregory M.D., Henry Home, Lord Kames, David Hume Esq. and Adam Smith LL.D.* (Edinburgh, 1800), p. 161. See also E.C. Mossner, *The Life of David Hume* (Nelson, Edinburgh, 1954), pp. 370, 409, 559–603.

14 E.g. for learned societies in Edinburgh, see A. Chitnis, *The Scottish Enlightenment: a social history* (Croom Helm, London, 1976), pp. 197–9, 201–10.

15 See variously N.G. Annan, 'The intellectual aristocracy', in *Studies in Social History: a tribute to G.M. Trevelyan,* ed. J.H. Plumb (Longmans, London, 1955), pp. 241–87; J.A. Hall, 'The curious case of the British intelligentsia', *British Journal of Sociology,* 30 (1979), pp. 291–306; and T.W. Heyck, *The Transformation of Intellectual Life in Victorian England* (Croom Helm, London, 1982), esp. pp. 13–23.

16 S. Smiles, *Self-Help: with illustrations of character and conduct* (London, 1859), p. 316.

17 M.S. Hickox, 'Has there been a British intelligentsia?', *British Journal of Sociology,* 37 (1986), pp. 260–8.

18 E.g. E. Shils (ed.), *The Intellectuals and the Powers: and other essays* (University of Chicago Press, Chicago, 1972); G. Konrad and I. Szelenyi, *The Intellectuals on the Road to Class Power,* transl. A. Arato and R.E. Allen (Harvester, Brighton, 1979); A.W. Gouldner, *The Future of Intellectuals and the Rise of the New Class: a frame of references, theses, conjunctures, arguments, and an historical perspective on the role of intellectuals . . . in the international class contest of the modern era* (Macmillan, London, 1979); and B. Robbins, *Secular Vocations: intellectuals, professionalism, culture* (Verso, London, 1993).

19 See M. Foucault, *Power/Knowledge: selected interviews and other writings,* ed. C. Gordon (Harvester, Brighton, 1980), p. 102; and extended discussion on pp. 78–108, 142.

20 Idem, *The History of Sexuality,* vol. 1: *An introduction,* transl. R. Hurley (Allen Lane, London, 1979), pp. 92–6.

21 J. Butler, *Fifteen Sermons Preached at the Rolls Chapel* (Sermon 2) in idem, *Works* (2 vols, Edinburgh, 1804), vol. 2, p. 116.

22 See Anon., *The Power and Prerogative of the Inexpressible I Know Not What: or, a*

brief essay upon the unknown and unintelligible something ... (London, 1705), p. 19.

23 C.C. Colton, *Lacon: or, many things in few words, addressed to those who think* (London, 1820), vol. 1, p. 24.

24 For a theoretical critique of Foucault's objectification of power/knowledge and underplaying of interpretative/subjective context, see esp. J. Habermas, 'Some questions concerning the theory of power: Foucault again', in idem, *The Philosophical Discourse of Modernity: twelve lectures*, transl. F. Lawrence (MIT Press, Cambridge, Mass., 1985), esp. pp. 269–76. J. Baudrillard's brisk instruction *Oublier Foucault* (Paris, 1977), pp. 54–61, esp. p. 59, has also argued that power is socially exchanged or transacted and not merely asserted. By contrast, however, J. Rouse, 'Power/Knowledge', in *The Cambridge Companion to Foucault*, ed. G. Gutting (Cambridge University Press, Cambridge, 1994), pp. 92–114, tries to reread Foucault, in order to defend his formulation from accusations that it assumes an immobilist nexus of power/knowledge.

25 Debates are introduced in e.g. *The Sociology of Knowledge: a reader*, ed. J. Curtis and J.W. Petras (Duckworth, London, 1970); and F. Machlup, *Knowledge: its creation, distribution and economic significance*; vol. 1: *Knowledge and knowledge production*; vol. 2, *The branches of learning* (Princeton University Press, Princeton, 1980, 1982).

26 J. Aikin, *An Address to the Dissidents of England on their Late Defeat* (London, 1790), p. 18.

27 See above, p. 129.

28 Anon., *The Power of the Pence* (London, 1849–9), vol. 1, nos. 1–23.

29 John Keats to J.H. Reynolds, 3 May 1818, in H.B. Forman (ed.), *Poetical Works and Other Writings of John Keats*, vol. 7: *letters 1818–19* (Scribners, New York, 1939), p. 7. The reference was to Lord Byron's *Manfred: a dramatic poem* (London, 1817), p. 12: 1: i.

30 Epigraph to ch. 21, G. Eliot, *Daniel Deronda* (London, 1876), vol. 2, p. 45.

31 T. Busby, *The Age of Genius: a satire on the times* ... (London, 1786), p. 48.

32 W.J. Mickle, *Poems and a Tragedy* (London, 1794), p. 116. The 1761 ode by Mickle (1734–88), a Scottish clergyman's son, was reprinted posthumously by subscription, to provide a benefit for his family.

SELECT BIBLIOGRAPHY

PRIMARY SOURCES

The primary sources for this study are the voluminous quantity of prose, verse and satirical prints that were produced in eighteenth- and early nineteenth-century Britain – not only by members of the professions and for the professions but also about the professions, both individually and generically. That has entailed reading much earnest and high-minded literature (best of all Bishop Butler's *Fifteen Sermons Preached at the Rolls Chapel* [1726]) as well as enjoying much knock-about jest and satire. All individual items that have been quoted are indicated in the endnotes; and any further enquiries should be addressed to the author.

SECONDARY AUTHORITIES

There is a rich and varied literature on all the themes discussed here. This select list of expert works – including their own bibliographies – provides an introduction to the various overlapping research fields.

Power

B. Barnes *The Nature of Power* (Polity Press, Cambridge, 1988)

M. Foucault *Power/Knowledge: selected interviews and other writings, 1972–7*, ed. C. Gordon (Harvester, Brighton, 1980)

A. Giddens *A Contemporary Critique of Historical Materialism*, vol. 1: *Power, property and the state* (Macmillan, London, 1981)

G. Gutting (ed.) *The Cambridge Companion to Foucault* (Cambridge University Press, Cambridge, 1994)

M. Mann *The Sources of Social Power* (Cambridge University Press, Cambridge, 1986, 1993), vol. 1: *A History of Power from the Beginning to A.D. 1760*, vol. 2: *The Rise of Classes and Nation States, 1760–1914*

R. Martin *The Sociology of Power* (Routledge, London, 1977)

P. Morriss *Power: a philosophical analysis* (Manchester University Press, Manchester, 1987)

D.H. Wrong *Power: its forms, bases and uses* (Blackwell, Oxford, 1979)

Secrecy

S. Bok *Secrets: on the ethics of concealment and revelation* (Oxford University Press, Oxford, 1984)

K. Hudson *The Jargon of the Professions* (Macmillan, London, 1978)

G. Simmel 'The secret and the secret society' (1908), in *The Sociology of Georg Simmel*, ed. K.H. Wolff (Free Press, Glencoe, Ill., 1950), pp. 307–76

Satire

R.C. Elliott *The Power of Satire: magic, ritual, art* (Princeton University Press, Princeton, 1960)

M. Mulkay *On Humour: its nature and its place in modern society* (Polity, Cambridge, 1988)

D. Nokes *Raillery and Rage: a study of eighteenth-century satire* (Harvester, Brighton, 1987)

S.M. Tave *The Amiable Humorist: a study in the comic theory and criticism of the eighteenth and nineteenth centuries* (University of Chicago Press, Chicago, 1960)

Professionalisation

A. Abbott *The System of Professions: an essay on the division of expert labor* (University of Chicago Press, Chicago, 1988)

M. Burrage and R. Torstendahl (eds) *Professions in Theory and History: rethinking the study of the professions* (Sage, London, 1990)

—— and R. Torstendahl (eds) *The Formation of Professions: knowledge, state and strategy* (Sage, London, 1990)

C.M. Cipolla 'The professions: the long view', *Journal of European Economic History*, 2 (1973), pp. 37–51

P. Elliott *The Sociology of the Professions* (Macmillan, London, 1972)

E. Freidson *Professional Powers: a study of the institutionalization of formal knowledge* (University of Chicago Press, Chicago, 1986)

A.W. Gouldner *The Future of Intellectuals and the Rise of the New Class: a frame of references, theses, conjunctures, arguments, and an historical perspective on the role of intellectuals . . . in the international class contest of the modern era* (Macmillan, London, 1979)

T.L. Haskell (ed.) *The Authority of Experts: studies in history and theory* (Indiana University Press, Bloomington, 1984)

E.C. Hughes 'Professions', in idem, *The Sociological Eye: selected essays* (Aldine/ Atherton, Chicago, 1971), pp. 374–86; first published in *Daedalus*, 92 (1965), pp. 655–68

I. Illich and others *Disabling Professions* (Marion Boyars, London, 1977)

J.A. Jackson (ed.) *Professions and Professionalisation* (Cambridge University Press, London, 1970)

T.J. Johnson *Professions and Power* (Macmillan, London, 1972)

M. Sarfatti Larson *The Rise of Professionalism: a sociological analysis* (University of California Press, Berkeley, 1977)

T. Parsons 'Professions', in *International Encyclopaedia of the Social Sciences: Vol 12*, ed. D. Sills (Free Press, New York, 1968), pp. 536–47

History of the modern professions (Britain)

A.M. Carr-Saunders and P.A. Wilson *The Professions* (Oxford University Press, Oxford, 1933)

D. Duman 'The creation and diffusion of a professional ideology in nineteenth-century England', *Sociological Review*, 27 (1979), pp. 113–38

G. Holmes *Augustan England: professions, state and society, 1680–1730* (Allen & Unwin, London, 1982)

—— 'The professions and social change in England, 1680–1730', *Proceedings of the British Academy*, 65 (1979), pp. 313–54

E. Hughes 'The professions in the eighteenth century', *Durham University Journal*, n.s. 13, no. ii (1952), pp. 46–55; also reprinted in *Aristocratic Government and Society in Eighteenth-Century England: the foundations of stability*, ed. D.A. Baugh (New Viewpoints, New York, 1975)

N. McKendrick '"Gentlemen and players" revisited: the gentlemanly ideal, the business ideal and the professional ideal in English literary culture', in *Business Life and Public Policy: essays in honour of D.C. Coleman*, ed. N. McKendrick and B. Outhwaite (Cambridge University Press, Cambridge, 1986), pp. 119–36

G. Millerson *The Qualifying Associations: a study in professionalization* (Routledge, London, 1964)

H.J. Perkin *The Rise of Professional Society: England since 1880* (Routledge, London, 1989)

W. Prest (ed.) *The Professions in Early Modern England* (Croom Helm, London, 1987)

W.J. Reader *Professional Men: the rise of the professional classes in nineteenth-century England* (Weidenfeld, London, 1966)

History of the modern professions (continental Europe and America)

D.H. Calhoun *Professional Lives in America: structure and aspiration, 1750–1850* (Harvard University Press, Cambridge, Mass., 1965)

G.L. Geison (ed.), *Professions and Professional Ideologies in America* (University of North Carolina Press, Chapel Hill, 1983)

—— (ed.) *Professions and the French State, 1700–1900* (University of Pennsylvania Press, Philadelphia, 1984)

G. Haber *The Quest for Authority and Honor in the American Professions, 1750–1900* (University of Chicago Press, Chicago, 1991)

B. Kimball *The 'True Professional Ideal' in America: a history* (Blackwell, Oxford, 1992)

C.E. McClelland *The German Experience of Professionalization: modern learned professions and their organisations from the early nineteenth century to the Hitler era* (Cambridge University Press, Cambridge, 1991)

R.S. Turner 'The *Bildungsbürgertum* and the learned professions in Prussia, 1770–1830: the origins of a class', *Histoire sociale/Social History*, 13 (1980), pp. 105–35

Lawyers

R.L. Abel *The Legal Profession in England and Wales* (Blackwell, Oxford, 1988)

P. Aylett 'A profession in the marketplace: the distribution of attorneys in England and Wales, 1730–1800', *Law and History Review*, 5 (1987), pp. 7–13

J.H. Baker *The Order of Serjeants at Law: a chronicle of creations, with related texts and a historical introduction* (Selden Society suppl. series, 5, 1984)

M. Birks *Gentlemen of the Law* (Stevens, London, 1960)

W.J. Bouwsma 'Lawyers and early modern culture', *American Historical Review*, 78 (1973), pp. 303–27

D. Duman 'A social and occupational analysis of the English judiciary, 1770–90 and 1855–75', *American Journal of Legal History*, 17 (1973), pp. 353–64

—— *The English and Colonial Bars in the Nineteenth Century* (Croom Helm, London, 1983)

—— *The Judicial Bench in England, 1727–1875: the reshaping of a professional elite* (Royal Historical Society, London, 1982)

D. Hogan *The Legal Profession in Ireland, 1789–1922* (Law Society of Ireland, Dublin, 1986)

C. Kenny *King's Inns and the Kingdom of Ireland: the Irish 'Inn of Court', 1541–1800* (Irish Academic Press, Dublin, 1992)

H. Kirk *Portrait of a Profession: a history of the solicitor's profession, 1100 to the present day* (Oyez, London, 1976)

D. Lemmings *Gentlemen and Barristers: the Inns of Court and the English bar, 1680–1730* (Clarendon, Oxford, 1990)

J.R. Lewis *The Victorian Bar* (Hale, London, 1982)

M. Miles '"A haven for the privileged": recruitment into the profession of attorney in England, 1709–92', *Social History*, 11 (1986), pp. 197–210

W. Prest (ed.) *Lawyers in Early Modern Europe and America* (Croom Helm, London, 1981)

R. Robson *The Attorney in Eighteenth-Century England* (Cambridge University Press, Cambridge, 1959)

G.R. Rubin and D. Sugarman (eds) *Law, Economy and Society, 1750–1914: essays in the history of English law* (Professional Books, Abingdon, 1984)

D.M. Walker *The Scottish Jurists* (Green & Sons, Edinburgh, 1985)

Clerics

G.F.A. Best *Temporal Pillars: Queen Anne's Bounty, the Ecclesiastical Commissioners, and the Church of England* (Cambridge University Press, Cambridge, 1964)

J. Bossy *The English Catholic Community, 1570–1850* (Darton, Longman & Todd, London, 1975)

C.G. Brown *The Social History of Religion in Scotland since 1730* (Methuen, London, 1987)

K.D. Brown *A Social History of the Nonconformist Ministry in England and Wales, 1800–1930* (Clarendon, Oxford, 1988)

G. Kitson Clark *Churchmen and the Condition of England, 1832–85: a study in the development of social ideas and practice from the old regime to the modern state* (Methuen, London, 1973)

J.C.D. Clark 'England's ancien regime as a confessional state', *Albion*, 21 (1989), pp. 450–74

S.J. Connolly *Priests and People in Pre-Famine Ireland* (Gill & Macmillan, Dublin, 1982)

R. Currie, A. Gilbert and L. Horsley *Churches and Churchgoers: patterns of church growth in the British Isles since 1700* (Clarendon, Oxford, 1977)

R. Davies and G. Rupp (eds) *A History of the Methodist Church in Great Britain*, vol. 1 (Epworth Press, London, 1965)

C. Dewey *The Passing of Barchester: a real-life version of Trollope* (Hambledon Press, London, 1991)

J. Downey *The Eighteenth-century Pulpit: a study of the sermons of Butler, Berkeley, Secker, Sterne, Whitefield and Wesley* (Clarendon, Oxford, 1969)

A. Haig *The Victorian Clergy* (Croom Helm, London, 1984)

B. Heeney *A Different Kind of Gentleman: parish clergy as professional men in early and mid-Victorian England* (Archon Books, Hamden, Conn., 1976)

E.M. Lyles *Methodism Mocked: the satiric reaction to Methodism in the eighteenth century* (Epworth Press, London, 1960)

H.R. Niebuhr and D.D. Williams (eds) *The Ministry in Historical Perspectives* (Harper, New York, 1956)

K.R.M. Short 'The English *Regium Donum*', *English Historical Review*, 84 (1969), pp. 59–78

P. Virgin *The Church in an Age of Negligence: ecclesiastical structure and problems of church reform, 1700–1840* (Clarke, Cambridge, 1989)

J. Walsh, C. Haydon and S. Taylor (eds) *The Church of England, c.1689–c.1833: from toleration to tractarianism* (Cambridge University Press, Cambridge, 1993)

Doctors

E.M. Bell *Storming the Citadel: the rise of the woman doctor* (Constable, London, 1953)

J.G.L. Burnby *A Study of the English Apothecary from 1660 to 1760*, *Medical History*, suppl. 3 (1983), pp. 1–116

W.F. Bynum and R. Porter (eds) *Medical Fringe and Medical Orthodoxy, 1750–1850* (Croom Helm, London, 1987)

A. Cunningham and R. French (eds) *The Medical Enlightenment of the Eighteenth Century* (Cambridge University Press, Cambridge, 1990)

A. Digby *Making a Medical Living: doctors and patients in the English market for medicine, 1720–1911* (Cambridge University Press, Cambridge, 1994)

J. Donnisson *Midwives and Medical Men: a history of inter-professional rivalries and women's rights* (Heinemann, London, 1977)

M. Foucault *Madness and Civilisation: a history of insanity in the age of reason* (1961), transl. R. Howard (Tavistock, London, 1971)

—— *The Birth of the Clinic: an archaeology of medical perception* (1963), transl. A.M. Sheridan (Tavistock, London, 1973)

E. French and A. Wear (eds) *British Medicine in an Age of Reform* (Routledge, London, 1991)

L. Granshaw and R. Porter (eds) *The Hospital in History* (Routledge, London, 1989)

A.W. Hill *John Wesley among the Physicians: a study of eighteenth-century medicine* (Epworth Press, London, 1958)

J. Lane 'The medical practitioners of provincial England in 1783', *Medical History*, 28 (1984), pp. 353–71

I. Loudon *Medical Care and the General Practitioner, 1750–1850* (Clarendon, Oxford, 1986)

W.L. Parry-Jones *The Trade in Lunacy: a study of private madhouses in England in the eighteenth and nineteenth centuries* (Routledge, London, 1971)

M.J. Peterson *The Medical Profession in Mid-Victorian London* (University of California Press, Berkeley, 1978)

R. Porter *Health for Sale: quackery in England, 1660–1850* (Manchester University Press, Manchester, 1989)

—— *Mind-Forg'd Manacles: a history of madness in England from the Restoration to the Regency* (Athlone, London, 1987; and Penguin, Harmondsworth, 1990)

—— and D. Porter *The Patient's Progress: doctors and doctoring in eighteenth-century England* (Polity, Cambridge, 1989)

F.N.L. Poynter (ed.) *The Evolution of Medical Education in Britain* (Pitman, London, 1966)

I. Waddington *The Medical Profession in the Industrial Revolution* (Gill & Macmillan, Dublin, 1984)

P.J. and R.V. Wallis *Eighteenth-Century Medics: subscriptions, licenses, apprentice-ships* (Project for Historical Biobibliography, Newcastle upon Tyne, 1988)
A. Wear (ed.) *Medicine in Society: historical essays* (Cambridge University Press, Cambridge, 1992)

Others

Architects

B. Kaye *The Development of the Architectural Profession in England: a sociological study* (Allen & Unwin, London, 1960)
J. Wilton-Ely 'The rise of the professional architect in England', in *The Architect: chapters in the history of the profession*, ed. S. Kostof (Oxford University Press, New York, 1977), pp. 180–208

Army/navy officers

A.J. Guy *Oeconomy and Discipline: officership and administration in the British army, 1714–63* (Manchester University Press, Manchester, 1985)
J.W. Hackett *The Profession of Arms* (Times Publishing, London, 1963)
G. Harries-Jenkins *The Army in Victorian Society* (Routledge, London, 1977)
J.A. Houlding *Fit for Service: the training of the British army, 1715–95* (Clarendon, Oxford, 1981)
M. Lewis *England's Sea-Officers: the story of the naval profession* (Allen & Unwin, London, 1939)

Authors

V. Bonham Carter, *Authors by Profession*, vol. 1: *From the introduction of printing until the Copyright Act of 1911* (Society of Authors, London, 1978)
J.W. Saunders *The Profession of English Letters* (Routledge, London, 1964)
J. Todd *The Sign of Angellica: women, writing and fiction, 1660–1800* (Virago, London, 1989)

Bureaucrats

J. Hart 'The genesis of the Northcote-Trevelyan report', in *Studies in the Growth of Nineteenth-Century Government*, ed. G. Sutherland (Routledge, London, 1972)
H. Parris *Constitutional Bureaucracy: the development of British central administration since the eighteenth century* (Allen & Unwin, London, 1969)
J. Hart 'The genesis of the Northcote-Trevelyan report', in *Studies in the Growth of Nineteenth-Century Government*, ed. G. Sutherland (Routledge, London, 1972)

Engineers

R.A. Buchanan *The Engineers: a history of the engineering profession in Britain, 1750–1914* (Kingsley, London, 1989)
G. Watson *The Smeatonians: the Society of Civil Engineers* (Telford, London, 1989)

Musicians

C. Ehrlich *The Music Profession in Britain since the Eighteenth Century: a social history* (Clarendon, Oxford, 1985)

Surveyors

F.M.L. Thompson *Chartered Surveyors: the growth of a profession* (Routledge, London, 1968)

Teachers

H.C. Dent *The Training of Teachers in England and Wales, 1800–1975* (Hodder & Stoughton, London, 1977)

A. Engel *From Clergyman to Don: the rise of the academic profession in nineteenth-century Oxford* (Clarendon, Oxford, 1983)

A. Etzioni (ed.) *The Semi-Professions and Their Organisation: teachers, nurses, social workers* (Free Press, New York, 1969)

K. Hughes *The Victorian Governess* (Hambledon, London, 1993)

A. Tropp *The School Teachers: the growth of the teaching profession in England and Wales from 1800 to the present day* (Heinemann, London, 1957)

Professional ethics

E. Durkheim *Professional Ethics and Civic Morals*, transl. C. Brookfield (Free Press, Glencoe, Ill., 1960)

A.H. Goldman *The Moral Foundations of Professional Ethics* (Rowman & Littlefield, Totowa, N.J., 1980)

W.H.S. Jones *The Doctor's Oath: an essay in the history of medicine* (Cambridge University Press, Cambridge, 1924)

I. Waddington 'The development of medical ethics: a sociological analysis', *Medical History,* 19 (1975), pp. 36–51

British state and society

J. Brewer *The Sinews of Power: money, war and the English state, 1688–1783* (Cambridge University Press, Cambridge, 1989)

J.C.D. Clark *English Society, 1688–1832: ideology, social structure and political practice during the ancien regime* (Cambridge University Press, Cambridge, 1985)

P.J. Corfield 'Class by name and number in eighteenth-century Britain', in idem (ed.), *Language, History and Class* (Blackwell, Oxford, 1991), pp. 101–30.

E.J. Evans *The Forging of the Modern State: early industrial Britain, 1783–1870* (Longman, London, 1983)

P. Langford *A Polite and Commercial People: England, 1727–83* (Clarendon, Oxford, 1989)

H. Perkin *The Origins of Modern English Society, 1780–1880* (Routledge, London, 1969)

INDEX